Jung & Film II:

Since *Jung & Film* was first published in 2001, Jungian writing on the moving image in film and television has accelerated. *Jung & Film II: The Return* provides new contributions from authors across the globe willing to tackle the broader issues of film production and consumption, the audience and the place of film culture in our lives.

As well as chapters dealing with particular film-makers, such as Maya Deren, and films such as *Birth, The Piano, The Wrestler* and *Breaking the Waves*, there is also a unique chapter co-written by documentary film-maker Tom Hurwitz and New York Jungian analyst Margaret Klenck. Other areas of discussion include:

- the way in which psychological issues come under scrutiny in many movies
- the various themes that concern Jungian writers on film
- the psychological meaning of images in contemporary culture.

The book also includes a glossary to help readers with Jungian words and concepts. *Jung & Film II* is not only a welcome companion to the first volume, it is an important stand-alone work essential for all academics and students of analytical psychology as well as film, media and cultural studies.

Christopher Hauke is an IAAP Jungian analyst in London, a writer, a film-maker, and a Senior Lecturer at Goldsmiths, University of London.

Luke Hockley, PhD is Professor of Media Analysis in the Research Centre for Art and Design (RIMAD) at the University of Bedfordshire, UK. He also works as an integrative psychotherapist in private practice in London and Bedfordshire.

Contributors: Christopher Hauke, Luke Hockley, John Beebe, Helena Bassil-Morozow, Mary Dougherty, Joanna Dovalis, Don Fredericksen, David Hewison, Tom Hurwitz, John Izod, Michael Jacobs, Margaret Klenck, Lydia Lennihan, Catriona Miller, Michelangelo Paganopoulos, James Palmer, Susan Rowland, Greg Singh, Terrie Waddell and Andre Zanardo.

Jung & Film II: The Return

Further post-Jungian takes on the moving image

Edited by
Christopher Hauke &
Luke Hockley

LONDON AND NEW YORK

First published 2011
by Routledge
27 Church Road, Hove, East Sussex, BN3 2FA

Simultaneously published in the USA and Canada
by Routledge
711 Third Avenue, New York, NY 10017

Routledge is an imprint of the Taylor & Francis Group, an Informa business

© 2011 selection and editorial matter Christopher Hauke and Luke Hockley; individual chapters, the contributors.

Typeset in Times by
RefineCatch Limited, Bungay, Suffolk
Printed and bound in Great Britain by
TJ International Ltd., Padstow, Cornwall

All rights reserved. No part of this book may be reprinted or reproduced or utilised in any form or by any electronic, mechanical, or other means, now known or hereafter invented, including photocopying and recording, or in any information storage or retrieval system, without permission in writing from the publishers.

British Library Cataloguing in Publication Data
A catalogue record for this book is available from the British Library

Library of Congress Cataloging in Publication Data
Hauke, Christopher, 1953–
  Jung & film II. The Return Christopher Hauke and
  Luke Hockley
    p. cm.
  Includes bibliographical references and index.
  ISBN 978–0–415–48896–9—ISBN 978–0–415–48897–6 (pbk.)
  1. Motion pictures—Psychological aspects. 2. Jung,
C. G. (Carl Gustav), 1875–1961. I. Title: Jung and film.
II. Hockley, Luke, 1962 III. Title.
PN1995.H394 2001
791.43'01'9—dc21
                                          2001025532

ISBN: 978–0–415–48896–9 (hbk)
ISBN: 978–0–415–48897–6 (pbk)

For Elizabeth and Mary

Contents

List of films	x
List of figures	xii
Notes on contributors	xiii
Acknowledgments	xix

Introduction   1
CHRISTOPHER HAUKE AND LUKE HOCKLEY

PART I
Image and psychotherapy   15

1. **The decisive image: In documentary film, in Jungian analysis**   17
   TOM HURWITZ AND MARGARET KLENCK

2. **'I thought he might be better now': A clinician's reading of individuation in von Trier's *Breaking The Waves***   35
   DAVID HEWISON

3. **Love, loss, imagination and the 'other' in Soderbergh's *Solaris***   49
   ANDRE ZANARDO

4. ***Birth*: Eternal grieving of the spotless mind**   66
   JOHN IZOD AND JOANNA DOVALIS

5 Soul and space in the Coen brothers' *No Country for Old Men* 92
CHRISTOPHER HAUKE

PART II
Image and theory 97

6 Jungian film studies: The corruption of consciousness and the nurturing of psychological life 99
DON FREDERICKSEN

7 'Much begins amusingly and leads into the dark': Jung's popular cinema and the Other 109
CHRISTOPHER HAUKE

8 Contrasting interpretations of film: Freudian and Jungian 119
MICHAEL JACOBS

9 Individual interpretations: A response to Michael Jacobs 128
JOHN IZOD

10 The third image: Depth psychology and the cinematic experience 132
LUKE HOCKLEY

11 The nature of adaptation: Myth and the feminine gaze in Ang Lee's *Sense and Sensibility* 148
SUSAN ROWLAND

12 Cinephilia: Or, looking for meaningfulness in encounters with cinema 163
GREG SINGH

13 *Twilight*: Discourse theory and Jung 185
CATRIONA MILLER

14 Individual and society in the films of Tim Burton 206
HELENA BASSIL-MOROZOW

PART III
Image, type and archetype 225

15 The shadow: Constriction, transformation and individuation in Campion's *The Piano* 227
MARY DOUGHERTY

16 The dark feminine in Aronofsky's *The Wrestler* 243
LYDIA LENNIHAN

17 The archetype of transformation in Maya Deren's film rituals 253
MICHELANGELO PAGANOPOULOS

18 Coppola's *The Conversation*: Typology and a caul to the soul 266
JAMES PALMER

19 Navel gazing: Introversion/extraversion and Australian cinema 285
TERRIE WADDELL

20 *The Wizard of Oz*: A vision of development in the American political psyche 302
JOHN BEEBE

Glossary 328
Index 332

List of films

The Adventures of Priscilla Queen of the Desert (Elliot, 1994)
Aguirre (Herzog, 1972)
Alice in Wonderland (Burton, 2010)
American Beauty (Mendes, 1999)
Apocalypse Now (Coppola, 1979)
As Good As It Gets (Brooks, 1998)
At Land (Deren, 1944)
Australia (Luhrmann, 2008)
Avatar (Cameron, 2009)

Barry Lynden (Kubrick, 1975)
Batman (Burton, 1989)
Batman Returns (Burton, 1989)
Big Fish (Burton, 2003)
Birth (Glazer, 2004)
Blade Runner (Scott, 1982)
Blue Velvet (Lynch, 1986)
Bram Stoker's Dracula (Coppola, 1992)
Breaking Dawn (Condon, 2011)
Breaking the Waves (Von Trier, 1996)

The Cabinet of Dr. Caligari (Wiene, 1920)
Casablanca (Curtiz, 1942)
Casino (Scorsese, 1995)
Charlie and the Chocolate Factory (Burton, 2005)
Close Encounters of the Third Kind (Spielberg, 1977)
The Conversation (Coppola, 1974)
Corpse Bride (Burton, 2005)

Crocodile Dundee (Faiman, 1986)
A Cry in the Dark (Schepisi, 1988)

Dancemaker (Diamond, 1998)
Dark City (Proyas, 1998)
The Dark Mirror (Siodmak, 1946)
Das Boot (Petersen, 1981)
Daybreakers (Spierig and Spierig, 2009)
The Departed (Scorsese, 2006)
Divine Horsemen: The Living Gods of Haiti (Deren, 1985)
Donnie Darko (Kelly, 2001)
Dr. Mabuse, der Spieler (Lang, 1922)
Dracula (Fisher, 1958)
Dracula (Browing, 1931)

Eclipse (Slade, 2010)
Ed Wood (Burton, 1994)
Edward Scissorhands (Burton, 1990)
8½ (Fellini, 1963)
Evil Angels (Schepisi, 1988)
Eyes Wide Shut (Kubrick, 1999)

Ferris Bueller's Day Off (Hughes, 1986)
Fitzcarraldo (Herzog, 1982)
Forrest Gump (Zemeckis, 1994)
Frankenweenie (Burton, 1984)

The Godfather (Coppola, 1972)
The Godfather, Part II (Coppola, 1974)
Golem (Wegener, 1915)

Goodfellas (Scorsese, 1990)
Gorillas in the Mist (Apted, 1988)
Groundhog Day (Ramis, 1993)

Happy Feet (Miller, 2006)

JFK (Stone, 1991)
Justice League: Mortal (Miller, 2011)

Kundun (Scorsese, 1997)

Let The Right One In (Alfredson, 2008)

Mad Max (Miller, 1979)
Mad Max: Beyond Thunderdome (Miller, 1985)
Mao's Last Dancer (Beresford, 2009)
Mars Attacks (Burton, 1996)
The Matrix (Wachowski Brothers, 1999)
Meshes of the Afternoon (Deren, 1943)
Metropolis (Lang, 1927)
Moulin Rouge (Luhrmann, 2001)
Muriel's Wedding (Hogan, 1994)

Natural Born Killers (Stone, 1999)
New Moon (Weitz, 2009)
The Nightmare Before Christmas (Burton, 1993)
Nixon (Stone, 1995)
No Country for Old Men (Coen brothers, 2008)
North by Northwest (Hitchcock, 1959)
Nosferatu (Murnau, 1922)

Orphée (Cocteau, 1950)

The Passion of Joan of Arc (Dreyer, 1928)
The Passion of the Christ (Gibson, 2004)

Pee Wee's Big Adventure (Burton, 1985)
The Piano (Campion, 1993)
Pinocchio (Luske and Sharpsteen, 1940)
Planet of the Apes (Burton, 2001)
Pulp Fiction (Tarantino, 1994)

Raiders of the Lost Ark (Spielberg, 1981)
Ritual in Transfigured Time (Deren, 1946)

Samson and Delilah (Thornton, 2009)
Scarface (De Palma, 1983)
The Searchers (Ford, 1956)
The Secret Passion (Huston, 1962)
Sense and Sensibility (Lee, 1995)
Shine (Hicks, 1996)
The Shining (Kubrick, 1980)
Sleepy Hollow (Burton, 1999)
Solaris (Tarkovsky, 1972)
Solaris (Soderbergh, 2002)
Stalker (Tarkovsky, 1979)
Star Wars (Lucas, 1977)
A Stolen Life (Bernhardt, 1946)
Sweeney Todd: The Demon Barber of Fleet Street (Burton, 2007)

Taxi Driver (Scorsese, 1976)
The Terminator (Cameron, 1984)
Twilight (Hardwicke, 2008)
The Twilight Saga
2001: A Space Odyssey (Kubrick, 1968)

Vertigo (Hitchcock, 1952)
Vincent (Burton, 1984)
Volver (Almodóvar, 2006)

Walkabout (Roeg, 1971)
Wild Strawberries (Bergman, 1957)
The Wizard of Oz (Fleming, 1939)

The Wrestler (Aronofsky, 2009)

Figures

1.1	Henri Cartier-Bresson, *Young and Old*, Bali Indonesia, 1949 (Magnum Photos/Michael Shulman)	20
1.2	Dorothea Lange, *Funeral Cortege*, 1938 (courtesy of George Eastman House, International Museum of Photography and Film)	21
1.3	Dancer lifted high, Paul Taylor, *Dancemaker*, 1998 (Four Oaks Foundation)	23
1.4	The face of envy, Paul Taylor, *Dancemaker*, 1998 (Four Oaks Foundation)	24
3.1	Kris arriving on *Solaris* (20th Century Fox/The Kobal Collection/Bob Marshak)	51
3.2	Rheya and Kris, with Rheya examining her hand (20th Century Fox/The Kobal Collection/Bob Marshak)	60
15.1	Ada McGrath (Holly Hunter) and her daughter Flora (Anna Paquin)	227
20.1	The relationship between Dorothy and the Scarecrow	308
20.2	The political relationship between Dorothy and the Scarecrow (1)	308
20.3	The political relationship between Dorothy and the Scarecrow (2)	309
20.4	An auxiliary character axis	310
20.5	The pattern of consciousness emanating from the story	310
20.6	Consciousnesses and their political designations	311
20.7	Dorothy and the Scarecrow in relation to their antagonists	314
20.8	The interplay of auxiliary consciousnesses	317
20.9	Stations in Dorothy's political development	321
20.10	Archetypal complexes carrying the eight functions of consciousness as seen in *The Wizard of Oz*	324

Notes on contributors

Christopher Hauke is a Senior Lecturer at Goldsmiths, University of London, an IAAP Jungian analyst in London, a writer, and a film-maker. He is the author of *Human Being Human: Culture and the Soul* (2005) and *Jung and the Postmodern: The Interpretation of Realities* (2000). He co-edited the first *Jung and Film: Post-Jungian Takes on the Moving Image* (2001) and *Contemporary Jungian Analysis: Post-Jungian Perspectives from the Society of Analytical Psychology* (1998). His films include the documentary *One Colour Red*, the short film *Again*, premiered in Montreal, and *Red Or White*, premiered in London. See www.christopherhauke.com

Luke Hockley is Professor of Media Analysis in the Research Centre for Art and Design (RIMAD) at the University of Bedfordshire, UK. He is co-editor of *House the Wounded Healer on Television* (2010), *Cinematic Projections* (2001) and *Frames of Mind* (2008). Luke is an Associate Editor of the *International Journal of Jungian Studies (IJJS)*. In addition to his academic role Luke works as an integrative psychotherapist in private practice in London and Bedfordshire. See www.lukehockley.com

John Beebe, born in 1939, is a physician. After graduating from Harvard University, he attended the University of Chicago Medical School and then went on to a residency in psychiatry at Stanford University's Medical Center, where he served as Chief Resident in the Adult Psychiatry Clinic. Subsequently, he completed his training as a Jungian analyst at the C. G. Jung Institute of San Francisco. He first started writing film reviews in the 1980s in a journal he founded, the *San Francisco Jung Institute Library Journal* (now published by the University of California Press as *Jung Journal: Culture and Psyche*). He later became the first American co-editor of the London-based *Journal of Analytical Psychology*. In his writings and lectures throughout the world, he has often examined paintings, fiction, and movies, drawing upon the insights of Jung's analytical psychology. He is the editor of C. G. Jung's *Aspects of the Masculine* (1989), the author of *Integrity in Depth* (1992), and the co-author (with Virginia Apperson) of *The Presence of the Feminine in Film* (2008). Email: johnbeebe@msn.com

Dr Helena Bassil-Morozow is an honorary research fellow of the Research Institute for Media Art and Design, University of Bedfordshire. She is the author of *Tim Burton: The Monster and the Crowd* (2010) and is currently working on another monograph for Routledge, *The Trickster in Contemporary Film*.

Mary Dougherty is a Jungian psychoanalyst and art psychotherapist in private practice in Chicago. She is the current President of the C. G. Jung Institute of Chicago, a former Director of Training of the Jung Institute of Chicago, a former President of the Chicago Society of Jungian Analysts, and served for eight years on the Executive Committee of the Council of North American Societies of Jungian Analysts. She is a contributing editor to the *Journal of Jungian Theory and Practice* and the *Journal of Analytical Psychology* and has published numerous articles on analytical psychology. She lectures on the clinical uses of film as active imagination, the clinical implications of gender and on the impact of Jung's thought upon creative development and artistic production. As a printmaker and performance artist she exhibited nationally and internationally, with venues including George Eastman House and Franklin Furnace in New York; the University of Chicago; and the Museo Contemporaneo, São Paulo. In 2001, she was awarded the Lifetime Achievement in the Arts award by the Chicago Women's Caucus for the Arts.

Joanna Dovalis is a practising psychotherapist, co-wrote Million Dollar Baby: Boxing Grief for the journal *Kinema* (2005); Grieving, therapy, cinema and Kieslowski's *Trois Couleurs: Bleu* for the *San Francisco Jung Institute Library Journal* (2006); Grieving, therapy, cinema and Kieslowski's *Trois Couleurs:Blanc* for *Jung Journal* (2008); and Grieving, therapy, cinema and Kieslowski's *Trois Couleurs: Rouge* for *Jung Journal* (2008). Her PhD thesis *Cinema and Psyche: Individuation and the Postmodern Hero's Journey* was accepted by Pacifica Graduate Institute in 2003.

Don Fredericksen is a professor of film and faculty affiliate in the religious studies and visual studies programs at Cornell University. He is the author of *The Aesthetic of Isolation in Film Theory: Hugo Munsterberg* (1977) and *Bergman's Persona* (2005), and co-author of *Wajda's Kanal* (2007). He has published a long series of essays on Jungian film and cultural studies in English and Polish translation, including several recent cautionary ones. These include: *Jung/Sign/Symbol/Film* (2001), *Living Symbolically in a Liminal Condition* (2007), *Post-Communist Polish Liminal Documentaries* (2003), *Why Should We Take Jungian Film Studies Seriously?* (2005), *Stripping Bare the Images* (2007), and *Arguments in Favor of a Jungian Hermeneutics of Suspicion* (2008). He lectures frequently in Poland on film and Jungian studies. He practices part-time as a Jung-oriented psychotherapist. An early member of the International Association for Jungian Studies, he currently serves as chairman of its executive committee. He also serves on the board of the Jungian Society for Scholarly Studies.

David Hewison is a Jungian analyst practising in London. He trained simultaneously at the Society of Analytical Psychology and as a Couple Psychoanalytic Psychotherapist at the Tavistock Centre for Couple Relationships (TCCR), where he is a senior clinician and Head of Research and Academic Links. He holds a Doctorate in Couple Psychoanalytic Psychotherapy and is Head of Programme for TCCR's MA in Attachment, Psychoanalysis and the Couple Relationship. He has taught and lectured extensively on Jungian and psychoanalytic themes relating to film, poetry, creativity, love and its vicissitudes, as well as on individual and couple development, and on analytic theory and technique.

Tom Hurwitz is one of America's most honoured documentary cinematographers. Winner of two Emmy Awards, and a Sundance Award for Best Cinematography, Hurwitz has photographed films that have won four academy awards and several more shortlistings and nominations (most recently for *Valentino: The Last Emperor*). Most recently, the PBS series *Franklin* won the 2009 Emmy Award for Best Documentary Special. *Jerome Robbins* won the 2010 Dupont Gold Baton. Other award-winning films and programmes that he has photographed include: *Harlan County USA*, *Wild Man Blues*, *My Generation*, *Down and Out in America*, *The Turandot Project*, *Liberty, Faith and Doubt at Ground Zero* for PBS; *I Have a Dream* for ABC; and *Questioning Faith* for HBO. In addition, films that he has directed have won the

Cine Golden Eagle (*Bombs will Make the Rainbow Break*) and have been shown in festivals around the world. Tom is a founding faculty member of the New York School of Visual Arts' Masters Program in the Social Documentary, was previously on the faculty of The New York University Undergraduate Film Department, and has lectured at National Film and Television School in the UK, and at other institutions around the world. He is the first documentarian to have been asked to join the American Society of Cinematographers.

John Izod is Professor of Screen Analysis in Film, Media and Journalism at the University of Stirling, Scotland, where he has taught since 1978. He has been Head of Department and Dean of the Faculty of Arts. A Fellow of the Royal Society for Arts he is also a Founding Fellow of the Institute of Contemporary Scotland. As principal investigator funded by an Arts and Humanities Research Council grant, he has been leading a three-year project on the cinema authorship of Lindsay Anderson. He has published several books: *Reading the Screen* (1984), *Hollywood and the Box Office, 1895–1986* (1988), *The Films of Nicolas Roeg* (1992), *An Introduction to Television Documentary* (with Richard Kilborn) (1997), *Myth, Mind and the Screen: Understanding the Heroes of our Time* (2001) and *Screen, Culture, Psyche: A Post-Jungian Approach to Working with the Audience* (2006).

Michael Jacobs is a psychodynamic psychotherapist, mainly of the independent tradition, who retired in 2000 as Director of the counselling and psychotherapy programme at the University of Leicester. He is the author of a number of standard texts such as *Psychodynamic Counselling in Action* (2010) and *The Presenting Past* (2006). Retirement gave him the opportunity to apply himself to the arts and psychoanalysis, resulting in *Shakespeare on the Couch* (2008) and teaching a local group an annual course on Film on the Couch.

Margaret Klenck is a Jungian analyst in private practice in New York City. She is a graduate from the C. G. Jung Institute of New York and holds a Masters of Divinity from Union Theological Seminary, where she concentrated on Psychology and Religion. Margaret is currently the President of the Jungian Psychoanalytic Association in New York, where she also teaches and supervises. She is also a member and on the faculty of the Philadelphia Association of Jungian Analysts. Margaret has lectured nationally and internationally and participated in the PBS two-part series *The Question of God: Sigmund Freud and C. S. Lewis* (2004).

Lydia Lennihan is a psychotherapist in private practice in Albuquerque, New Mexico. She is also a painter and a mythologist, and enjoys writing and teaching about dream interpretation, psychology and film, and popular culture. She lives with her husband, Steven H. Wong, and several four-legged friends.

Catriona Miller was awarded her PhD by Stirling University for her thesis *Bloodspirits: A Jungian Approach to the Vampire Myth*. She also has an MA in History from Glasgow University and an MA from the Northern Film School in Leeds, where she specialised in Art Direction. She has published *Angels, Aliens & Amazons: Cult TV Heroines* (2008) and contributed to the *Encyclopaedia of Science Fiction Film Adaptation* (2008) as part of the editorial team. She wrote Dracula was a Woman in *Halloween*, edited by Hugh O'Donnell and Malcolm Foley (2007), I Just Want to be Normal Again in *Investigating Charmed*, edited by Karin and Stan Beeler (2007), and Apocalypse Now, Or Then? in *British Science Fiction Television*, edited by John Cook and Peter Wright (2005).

Michelangelo Paganopoulos graduated from the University of Glasgow with an Honours Degree in Film and TV Studies combined with Music. In 1999 he moved to London to study social anthropology at Goldsmiths College, University of London. Since 2004, he has been a visiting tutor on the Symbolic Systems and Religion course at the Department of Anthropology, Goldsmiths. He has published articles on film and cultural studies, literature and anthropology, and on the monastic life of Mount Athos, which was the focus of his PhD fieldwork.

James Palmer is the senior professor in Film Studies and a President's Teaching Scholar at the University of Colorado. He has an undergraduate degree in English from Dartmouth College and a PhD in Film and Literature from Claremont Graduate School. He is the co-author of *The Films of Joseph Losey* (1993) and has published numerous articles in journals such as *Literature/Film Quarterly*, *The Journal of Film and Popular Culture*, and *Psychological Perspectives*. Recent articles in *Spring: A Journal of Archetype and Culture* have addressed the shadow archetype in Hitchcock and Leconte and individuation in von Donnersmarck's film *The Lives of Others*. Currently the Director of the Conference on World Affairs, he also teaches several interdisciplinary courses, including Jung, Film, and Literature.

Susan Rowland was Professor of English and Jungian Studies at the University of Greenwich, UK and writes on literature and myth, gender, Jung and literary theory. Among her books are *Jung: A Feminist Revision* (2002) and *Jung as a Writer* (2005). Her most recent book, *C. G. Jung and the Humanities*, was published in 2010 and her new project, *The Ecocritical Psyche*, is due for publication in 2011.

Greg Singh was formerly Senior Lecturer in Media Studies at Buckinghamshire New University. He is currently completing a PhD thesis on cinephilia and the encounters with popular film narrative across different media forms at the Department of Film, Theatre and Television, University of Reading. He has published on several film-related subjects, including CGI and contemporary Hollywood, Japanese science-fiction film and neo-noir, and is a contributor to *The Directory of World Cinema: American Independent*. Greg is author of *Film After Jung: Post-Jungian Approaches to Film Theory* (2009), an overview of the connections between film theory and analytical psychology.

Terrie Waddell is a senior lecturer in Media and Cinema Studies at La Trobe University, Australia. She has taught and written widely on contemporary media, gender and Jungian approaches to screen texts. Previous publications include: *Wild/lives – Trickster, Place and Liminality on Screen* (2010); *Mis/takes – Archetype, Myth and Identity in Screen Fiction* (2006); *Lounge Critic – The Couch Theorist's Companion* (co-editor, 2004) produced in conjunction with The Australian Centre for the Moving Image (ACMI) and the former Australian Film Commission; and *Cultural Expressions of Evil and Wickedness – Wrath, Sex, Crime* (2003).

Andre Zanardo is an IAAP Jungian analyst in private practice in Perth, Western Australia. He trained with the Australian and New Zealand Society of Jungian Analysts, and holds a degree in Economics and Industrial Relations. He has a particular interest in the imaginal space and the way psyche manifests artistically and his paper, *Creative use of Aesthetic and Artistic sensibility in Jungian Analysis*, was presented at the Art and Psyche conference in San Francisco in 2008. Andre is a qualified Iyengar Yoga teacher and has led many yoga and self-development residential workshops for individuals and businesses. Andre 'goes bush' into the stunning West Australian coastline and interior whenever possible to indulge his abiding love of the outdoors.

Acknowledgments

We would like to extend our gratitude to all our colleagues in the field of applied Jungian studies and especially those fascinated by film and the moving image. Several people have been generous in their time, interest and activity on behalf of this book and we extend a special thanks to Professor Andrew Samuels, who initiated the Confederation of Analytical Psychology's Conference on Jung and Film in April 2010. Professor John Izod chaired this conference and has contributed to the book and advised in many helpful ways all through. Across the Atlantic, Dr John Beebe has been of invaluable help and our grateful thanks is extended to both of these senior colleagues.

We wish to thank Kate Hawes, our editor at Routledge, for her ongoing enthusiasm for Jungian film studies, our copy editor Sally Mesner Lyons for her diligent attention to the details and our indexer Michael Solomons for the film lists which are always a great guide to the content of any film book.

Last but not least we wish to thanks everyone who read or bought the first *Jung & Film* collection over the last ten years and made this 'sequel' as needed and, we trust, as popular as its predecessor.

Christopher Hauke
Luke Hockley

Introduction

Christopher Hauke and Luke Hockley

This new collection of Jungian writing on film is even more varied than the first. While several chapters deal in fascinating detail with particular movies – such as *Birth*, *The Piano*, *The Wrestler* and *Breaking The Waves* – we have also sought out writers willing to tackle the broader issues of movie production and consumption, the audience and the place of film culture in our lives. Equally, while popular and commercial films (not always the same thing) are well represented, we have also found writers to introduce us to the work of an ethnographic film-maker, Maya Deren, and include a unique chapter co-written by Tom Hurwitz (who is the first documentary film-maker to be admitted into the prized American Society of Cinematographers) and New York Jungian analyst Margaret Klenck.

As a result of this diversity you will find a number of conversational strands that run throughout this collection. While there is broad agreement about the value of the Jungian approach, there is quite a divergence of opinion about how analytical psychology should be used and also what the object of study ought to be. This healthy state of affairs represents the growing maturity of the field. While this may seem contradictory, it is also important to remember that Jungian film theory is still a nascent discipline. The theoretical debates which are endemic in more established disciplines are just beginning to emerge in this field and this makes it an exciting time for both academics and clinicians who are engaged in this work. Collectively we are struggling to agree what binds us and acknowledge where we hold separate and sometimes conflicting interests and points of view. To use a more psychological language, we are letting our individual and collective concerns emerge into consciousness where we can explore and hold the tensions that inevitably emerge.

This happens through the work of writing, our engagement with each other at conferences and online, for example in the Jung Forum hosted by

Routledge (see www.routledgementalhealth.com/blog/jung-and-film). As Alberto Manguel puts it in the opening of *The City of Words*, 'Language is our common denominator' (2008, p. 5) and for us this is the language of analytical psychology as it allows a range of debates to take place. Jungians talk about the individuation process as the lifelong engagement with becoming fully who a person is – not what society or their family would like them to be. So too as a discipline we are beginning to question who we are, what views we hold and how we understand ourselves, particularly in relation to our clinical and academic communities where psychoanalysis has historically held a certain degree of orthodoxy. As such this field is in a process of becoming as it brings the historical and contemporary debates which have structured our understanding of cinema ever more fully into the Jungian arena.

We have organised the book into three parts. *Image and Psychotherapy* discusses the way in which we can see psychological issues under scrutiny in several movies and how movies achieve they emotional effect they do. *Image and Theory* addresses various themes that concern Jungian writers on film. The value of popular movies or their alternative, the difference between a Jungian and a Freudian interpretation, and mixing discourses from other subjects are topics to be found in this section. The last part of the book, titled *Image, Type and Archetype*, is where you will find film analysis which takes Jungian ideas on psychological personality types and applies them in fresh ways that are as different as characters in *The Wizard of Oz* on the one hand, and the culture of Australian film production on the other. There are also four chapters here which address specific movies and film-makers using the archetypal perspective – the unique tool of Jungian cultural and psychological analysis. At the end we have once again included a glossary of Jungian words and concepts to help the newly initiated get orientated. For further reading we suggest the excellent *A Critical Dictionary of Jungian Analysis* (Samuels, Shorter and Plaut, 1986). Of the twenty-two authors and co-authors, nine are working mainly as Jungian psychotherapists with lecturing responsibilities in universities and training establishments. The rest have their homes in universities across the world from Cornell to Stirling, Latrobe, Australia to Strathclyde and Colorado to London. In addition, a number of academics, such as Luke Hockley and Don Fredericksen, have also trained as psychotherapists themselves in the last ten years. Others, such as Christopher Hauke, now also make films themselves. All these influences are present in the chapters which follow – the practical insights of the Jungian psychotherapist, the skilled analysis of experienced thinkers on film and the wide knowledge of the world of film-making and its audience.

Image and psychotherapy

The decisive image: *In documentary film, in Jungian analysis* by Margaret Klenck and Tom Hurwitz opens the book with a closely observed comparison between the ways in which a cinematographer and a Jungian analyst discover images that are vital to their work. Although their fields seem far apart in terms of intention and cultural and professional location, the analyst and the photographer share a human sensibility that seeks meaning in the image, and recognises it when it's found. As they write, 'A decisive image, in analysis and in a documentary, resounds in the lives of the viewers. It clarifies their shared humanity and, one hopes, prompts action that builds upon it' (pp. 58–59).

Another Jungian analyst, David Hewison from London, also approaches film from the point of view of its application to understanding and healing. The title ' '*I thought he might be better now*': *A clinician's reading of individuation in Breaking The Waves* (von Trier, 1996)' takes us to the heart of a film Hewison calls 'an extraordinary study of what it means to be human . . . the results of trauma, and the terrible process of recovery from it' (p. 73). He takes us on a journey of analysis where not only the main characters (Bess and Jan) are tracked for what they show us of the human condition, but the film *itself* is taken as its own unit of analysis.

> *Breaking The Waves* is a description of a personality – more specifically it is about what can happen to a personality during the process of individuation . . . a film that uses a particular set of relationships to explore the movements to and fro between a state of unconsciousness and one of consciousness, and the terrible forces that are involved in this.
>
> (p. 71)

Andre Zanardo, from Perth, Western Australia, writes about Soderbergh's 2002 remake of Tarkovsky's *Solaris*. As a Jungian analyst he finds the intricacies of the inter-personal and intra-personal relationships in the film – often played out as the fantasy of one main character, Kris (George Clooney) – full of material. The tension between the love and the loss, the reality and the imagined, in the relationship between Kris and Rheya highlights for Zanardo 'contemporary post-Jungian themes of "otherness" and becoming "undone"' (p. 76). His focus is on 'psychic self-emergence' and he finds the movie powerful in the way it shows that unless 'we . . . are prepared to truly open ourselves to another, to mourn our losses and lacks, we forestall individuation and cannot break out of a predominantly narcissistic way of living nor genuinely engage relationally with others' (p. 76).

These two chapters show Jungian analysts using movie characters and narrative to address the central human issues of authentic relating – familiar to all psychotherapists – and individuation, fulfilling your potential to be the most authentic version of yourself, which is a more specifically Jungian goal and theme.

The fourth chapter is co-written by John Izod, from Glasgow, Scotland and Joanna Dovalis, from California, USA. Such a transatlantic partnership heralds a chapter that draws upon many commentaries from other writers and the internet who have all been stirred and inspired by a film whose reception was luke-warm at the time of release. *Birth: Eternal grieving of the spotless mind* takes us through the richness of nuance in Jonathan Glazer's film where a widow, Anna (Nicole Kidman), is confronted by a ten-year-old boy, Sean (Cameron Bright), who claims to be the re-incarnation of her dead husband (who was also a Sean). The authors treat the story of *Birth*, which is less to do with Eastern beliefs than grieving and loss, as a many layered essay in individuation, uncovering meaning from the Wagner used in one scene to references to Kubrick's work. Taking seriously the psychological meaning of rebirth, the chapter also focuses on Jungian concepts such as the *coniunctio* and the archetype of the Child. Along the way, this excellent piece of writing also manages to draw the conflicts of class and gender into both a cultural and a Jungian analysis. As the writers conclude of *Birth* – and as we might of this chapter:

> To judge by blog reviews posted by its audience members, the resultant conflict between opposed worldviews (to which the filmmakers cannily offer no resolution) is one of its distinctive attractions. . . . *Birth* challenges the audience no less than its protagonists to think – better, to feel – their way through issues relating to the development of the psyche and rebirth.
>
> (pp. 137–138)

The first of his two pieces in this volume, *Soul and Space* is a delicate vignette in which Christopher Hauke explores how soul and psyche exist in the seemingly barren wilderness of the Coen brothers film *No Country for Old Men* (2008). Supported through a sensitive close textual reading, his suggestion is that no matter what appearances might suggest the world is full of spirit, even if the human psyche might not recognise it. Hauke's is a quintessentially Jungian approach – so much so that it calls to mind the inscription that Jung carved over the door of his house in Kusnacht and which he also had on his tombstone: *vocatus atque non vocatus deus aderit* (called or uncalled, god is present).

Image and theory

The second section opens with an impassioned piece, *Jungian Film Studies: The corruption of consciousness and the nurturing of psychological life*, in which Don Fredericksen puts the case for Jungian film studies to resist the siren call of popular culture and instead get down to the serious business of art house, documentary, animation and personal voice films. Don forcibly argues that in not tackling these types of filmmaking Jungian scholars are doing themselves, their students and the field itself a disservice. Further, he argues that Jungian film theory needs to show a greater awareness of the role that films play as part of cultural system. In so doing, he claims, it would offer penetrating insights into the complexity of the relationship which cinema has with society at large and, in and out of the classroom, would come to accept its ethical, moral and political dimensions.

In *Much begins amusingly and leads into the dark*, the second of his two pieces in this volume, Christopher Hauke explores the shadow, cinema, popular culture and Jung's *Red Book* (2009). In many ways this piece suggests an alternative position to that adopted by Don Fredericksen. Hauke argues that the descent into the underworld of the human psyche offers the opportunity for a meaningful encounter with the unconscious. Focusing on gangster and vampire films he shows how death and life are intertwined and carry the shadow of civilised society. While Jung may have been frightened of 'being bewitched by the banal' (2009, p. 262), as he puts it in his *Red Book*, Hauke shows that beneath the patina of popular culture lies a rich seam of psychological material which is ready to be mined.

Michael Jacobs is not a Jungian but as a senior psychotherapist on the UK scene has long used dramatic illustrations from Shakespeare and the movies in his books and his teaching. In writing about *Contrasting interpretations of film: Freudian and Jungian* Jacobs goes back to a chapter of the original *Jung & Film* (2001) in which Jane Ryan wrote about the movie *Dark City* (Proyas, 1998). He offers a Freudian approach to the film which contrasts with Ryan's (and Fredericksen's) views along the way. Jacobs suggests the film may be interpreted as less about individuation and the hero's recovery of the persona and of identity; rather more about recovering the repressed memories of a childhood trauma . . . Shell Beach, a constant image throughout the film, is a sign that points to those memories; the doctor [Keifer Sutherland] is engaged in trying to hold those memories for him, in much the same way as a therapist holds hints of what the patient may have experienced but appears as yet not to know.

(p. 186)

We thought this was an interesting approach from Michael Jacobs and it struck us that a response from a similarly senior Jungian would offer a creative way to take the discussion forward. John Izod kindly agreed and his chapter *Individual interpretations: A response to Michael Jacobs* follows on. Izod picks up on Jacobs' citing of the original Freudian Schreber case and brings in the idea of the 'third image' which Hockley and Hauke have developed. As Izod notes, 'Keeping faith with the film on screen generally entails abandoning some of the third images that it stimulated when they are tested against the source text. Nevertheless, that refining process usually leaves the critic's responses enriched by the surviving elements of those fantasies.' (p. 196). Finally, Izod pins an *in memoriam* for the original author, Jane Ryan, who has since died tragically too young.

Luke Hockley, who is Professor of Media Analysis at the University of Bedfordshire, has brought together his current ideas on the third image with new illustrative material derived from his practice as a psychotherapist. In this chapter he goes into more detail than ever before in explaining what he means by the third image, comparing the ideas of Barthes with his unravelling of what Jung meant when he referred to 'image'. Hockley describes the third image as arising from the meeting of the first (the image on the screen) and the second (arsing from the act of conscious interpretation):

> It is not the composite of the two, nor something that arises from their juxtaposition. Rather the third image is something new. In some ways it is reminiscent of the manner in which Jung wrote about symbols. In particular, his insight that the symbol (symbolic image) contains a third meaning (*tertium non datur*) that is not logically given. . . . The third image . . . exists neither on the screen, nor just in the mind of the viewer, but somehow enters the space between the two.

(pp. 210–211)

Hockley finishes by offering compelling illustrations of this with two vignettes from his own psychotherapy practice.

Susan Rowland uses her analysis of director Ang Lee's 1995 adaptation of Jane Austen's *Sense and Sensibility* to fashion a critique of Laura Mulvey's seminal article *Visual Pleasure and Narrative Cinema* in her chapter *The nature of adaptation: Myth and the feminine gaze in Ang Lee's Sense and Sensibility*. In doing so Rowland identifies limitations in the Lacanian-derived approach which Mulvey deploys. In its place Rowland proposes a Jungian-based theory of the gaze in which psychic energy is essentially neutral and where the sustaining mythos of the approach allows for feminine and masculine qualities. Her detailed reading of the film draws a variety of mythological parallels (particularly with Persephone) as a means through which to identify how the feminine is inscribed and suggested by the film, and indeed the original novel. While acknowledging this film was directed by a man, Rowland nonetheless mounts a persuasive case for the film being structured around and through the feminine gaze.

In *Cinephilia: Or, looking for meaningfulness in encounters with cinema* Greg Singh provides a compelling account of cinephilia (the love of cinema) as he explores how this idea resonates with analytical psychology. His range of sources are as diverse as they are scholarly. Yet the focus of his chapter remains the cinephile and their special and detailed knowledge of the films which they have fallen in love with – so to speak. Singh suggest that cinephilia provides a way of 'looking into' films that captures our everyday experiences. In this respect his approach is somewhat psychotherapeutic, as he seeks to find meaning by exploring the detail of the commonplace, and viewers' relationship to it. As his reflections on *Star Wars* (1977) demonstrate, Singh's project is a personal one with strong phenomenological and hermeneutic elements. He concludes with an erudite survey of interpretative approaches to the cinematic image noting the power of cinema to recast old myths and in so doing he notes how cinema can provide an opportunity for personal understanding and meaning-making which is as radical as it is progressive.

Continuing the process of seeking to find points of intersection between a Jungian approach and other modes of cultural analysis, Catriona Miller explores the relationship between analytical psychology and discourse theory in her chapter *Twilight: Discourse theory and Jung*. The core of her argument is concern with the way the meaning of any film must be negotiated in terms of personal and social contexts. After first surveying Jungian approaches to the collective, Miller moves on to examine discourse theory before weighing up the relative merits of each approach. She concludes with a case study of *The Twilight Saga* in which she convincingly demonstrates how the different theoretical approaches can be deployed to provide a lucid and compelling interpretation of this multi-media cultural phenomena.

In *Individual and society in the films of Tim Burton* Helena Bassil-Morozow explores what life means for the characters in the movies of Tim Burton, how the central figures in Burton's films struggle to be themselves and how society frames their aspirations – as Bassil-Morozow points out, in this regard Burton's characters are reminiscent of the director himself. To aid her analysis she has recourse to a wide range of mythological motifs which amplify her analysis and provide a better understand the struggle of Burton's individuating heroes. Her approach goes to one of the key aspects of Jungian analytical psychology, namely the struggle that those engaged in the work of individuation undertake in becoming fully themselves and not just the accumulation of life's experiences.

Image, type and archetype

Mary Dougherty, a senior Jungian analyst in Chicago, writes her chapter about *The shadow: Constriction, transformation and individuation in Jane Campion's The Piano*. Dougherty traces the shadow qualities of the four main characters of the film – Ada (Holly Hunter), Flora (Anna Paquin), Stewart (Sam Neill) and Baines (Harvey Keitel) – not only to 'consider how the shadow qualities embedded in each of these characters impact their ego function as well as their relational dynamics with others' (p. 339) but also to (as Zanardo does with *Solaris* and Hewison does with *Breaking The Waves*) 'consider how the relational dynamics between them eventually force each character to confront the unconscious as they make their choices that may or may not foster their psychological development' (ibid.). Readers of the first *Jung & Film* will remember how Dougherty places herself as a practical clinical analyst, keen to use movie material to help insight and healing in her clients – especially those who are women. While analysing film, Dougherty always has her eye on the usefulness for her clients, but here she hopes that exploration of the shadow qualities of these characters in *The Piano* will also offer 'us the opportunity to deepen our understanding of shadow elements not only in our clients but also in ourselves' (p. 339).

Lydia Lennihan, a licensed counsellor from Albuquerque, New Mexico, is also returning in this book. Ten years ago she wrote the highly original chapter The Alchemy of *Pulp Fiction* and this time she is concerned with

The dark feminine in The Wrestler (Aronofsky, 2009). For Lennihan, '*The Wrestler* illustrates the price we pay when we develop the ego in such a way that it becomes identified with the persona' (p. 363) which is the path of the film's protagonist, over-the-hill Randy 'The Ram' Robinson (Mickey Rourke). Lennihan grabs the alchemical symbolic elements in the movie as clearly as she did with *Pulp Fiction* in *Jung & Film*. In *The Wrestler* she compares Randy to the Fisher King – coined by Jung in *Mysterium Coniunctionis* – 'being asked to renew in order to create meaning and wisdom in his second half of life' (p. 365). This leads Lennihan to find imaginative links between the king's connections with water and 'inward drowning, namely dropsy' (ibid.) and the oedema Randy suffers from due to his use of anabolic steroids. The symbolism of salt, of the Ram, Sol and Luna and even the geese (heard when Randy leaves hospital after a heart attack and 'associated with Ares and other warrior gods ... the Great Mother, the descent into the underworld' (p. 368)) are all brought to bear on a fascinating Jungian analysis of the film.

Michelangelo Paganopoulos, who is studying for a PhD in Anthropology at Goldsmiths, had read the first *Jung & Film* and invited Christopher Hauke to a talk he was giving on the Christ image in the figure of Billy The Kid as he appears in several movies since the 1940s. We were interested in the work of this new academic and gladly accepted his chapter on *The archetype of transformation in Maya Deren's film rituals*. Paganopoulos, originally from Thessalonika, Greece, is the only anthropologist in the book, but his use of Jungian ideas not only informs his own field of research but also provides an original angle on this esoteric film ethnographer, showing how Jungian ideas have many unexpected applications. Paganopoulos takes up Hauke's idea in *Jung & Film* that cinema can offer a *temenos* or sacred space, and he finds than Deren's ritual cinema was her way of creating this. Paganopoulos notes how 'For both Jung and Durkheim ritual was a matter of *experience*; the personal way to connect to the wider collective through the luminous experiential concept of the "numinous".' (p. 379) Tracking elements in Deren's films arising from character, lighting, editing and imagery, Paganopoulos offers a complex chapter quite unlike any other, concluding that

> Deren developed her search towards a 'metaphysical' form of cinema, highlighting the importance of cultural understanding based on the 'equivalent character' and 'parallel function' of art and ritual, as the film becomes a cross-cultural counterpoint analogous to the musical structure of a fugue.
>
> (p. 388)

By exploring a film-maker of collective phenomena, the use of Jungian ideas that relate to the individual and the social equally has seldom been more apt or politically valid.

James Palmer's fascinating piece, *Coppola's The Conversation: Typology and a caul to the soul*, focuses on the character of Harry Caul (Gene Hackman) in Coppola's film *The Conversation* (1974). The analysis is a subtle one that blends Jung's psychological theories about personality with the unconscious motifs and themes which Palmer finds in the film. This he sets against the cultural backdrop of 1970s America. Palmer finds considerable significance in the image of the caul and conducts and amplifies this motif to explore its mythological and psychological significance. This leads him to see the film in the light of alchemical imagery and enables the blurring of boundaries between conscious and unconscious material to be seen more clearly. Giving the analysis a grounded quality, numerous references are made to decisions taken during the production process of the film and the serendipitous results that find their way into the final cut.

Navel gazing: Introversion/extraversion and Australian cinema by Terrie Waddell is the penultimate chapter in this collection. She uses Jung's notions of introversion and extraversion to consider the national cinema of her native Australia. As someone who used to work in the Australian film and television industries, she presents highly sensitive and nuanced understanding of the debates. Australia is a country which from the outside is sometimes caricatured as being overly outgoing, yet Waddell persuasively argues for the introverted nature of Australian film-making. As she gradually introduces the full complexity of Jung's typological theory she also develops her argument to show how images, arguments and motifs of Australian cinema are largely framed in terms of its internal domestic context. Waddell also explores the function of Screen Australia (the federal government's direct funding body) and the institutional role it plays in the development and maintenance of this position.

The eminent Jungian analyst and scholar John Beebe closes this book with his chapter *The Wizard of Oz: A vision of development in the American political psyche*, which takes the opportunity this classic film offers to further exploit the insights proffered by the Post-Jungian typological approach. Beebe's account of the film is subtle, complex and presented in the context of contemporary American society and its film culture. The result is a sophisticated interpretation of the film in which Beebe uses his detailed and comprehensive understanding of Jungian typology to deconstruct the characters of the film in relation to social and political developments in America. The film's central characters are variously seen in relation to each other's conscious and unconscious aspects and also to broader issues of authority and power. Beebe concludes with a number of filmic vignettes before noting that contemporary American politics seems to be more about conformity than Dorothy's joyful acceptance of difference.

The growing field

Since the first *Jung & Film* collection was published ten years ago, Jungian writing on the moving image in film and television has accelerated. Luke Hockley's *Cinematic Projections* (2001) was coterminous with *Jung & Film*, as was John Izod's *Myth, Mind and Screen* (2001) which he followed up with *Screen, Culture, Psyche: A Post-Jungian Approach to Working with the Audience* (2006). Hockley published *Frames of Mind* (2007) and began to include more reflections on television which also inspired him to co-edit *House: The Wounded Healer on TV* (2010) with many of the same contributors as this volume you are holding. In the US, John Beebe, a seminal presence in the field, co-wrote with Virginia Apperson a rich monograph featuring many classic movies in *The Presence of the Feminine in Film* (2008). In Australia, Terrie Waddell published her work on the trickster titled *Wild/Lives: Trickster, Place and Liminality on Screen* (2010). She continued her investigation of Jungian ideas on unconscious processes with *Mis/takes: Archetype. Myth and Identity in Screen Fiction* (2006). In the UK and coming from a background in literature, Susan Rowland published *Psyche and the Arts: Jungian Approaches to Music, Architecture, Literature, Painting and Film* (2008), while Greg Singh surveyed academic film thinking with his analysis of how Jungian psychology can expand and inform current film theory in his *Film After Jung: Post-Jungian Approaches To Film Theory* (2009). Helena Bassil-Morozow has also produced a fine book analysing the work of one film-maker from a post-Jungian perspective – *Tim Burton: The Monster and the Crowd* (2010).

In New Orleans, the influential Jungian journal, *Spring: A Journal of Archetype and Culture* devoted its Spring 2005 issue to *Cinema and Psyche*, again with contributions from many of our present writers, including James Palmer and Don Fredericksen. In fact, it has been striking how Jungian writers, academics and analysts alike, are including reflections on movies in their work and in their journals. David Hewison, among others, has contributed film material to the *Journal of Analytical Psychology*, and Christopher Hauke wrote on Cocteau's *Orphée* (1950) for a *Spring* special devoted to Orpheus (2004) and used many movie references and illustrations in his last book *Human Being Human: Culture and the Soul* (2005).

Conferences and film festivals have accepted and included contributions from the Jungian field over the last ten years, with Hauke and Hockley speaking at Art and Psyche in San Francisco in 2008. Singh, Izod, Hauke and Hockley were accepted to present at the long established Screen conference in Glasgow in 2009, an entry into the traditional world of screen criticism begun back in 2003 when Izod, Fredericksen, Hauke and Dovalis spoke at the International Society of Cinema Studies conference in Minneapolis. Hauke and Hockley have lectured regularly to Jungian candidates in training in Zurich, as well as including Jungian film material in masters programmes at Goldsmiths, the University of London and the University of Bedfordshire. Together with Singh, Izod and Bassil-Morozow, Hauke and Hockley held a conference for The Confederation of Analytical Psychology (CAP) in central London in April 2010, where their latest work was aired and discussed.

References

Apperson, V. & Beebe, J. (2008) *The Presence of the Feminine in Film*. Newcastle: Cambridge Scholars Publishing.
Bassil-Morozow, H. (2010) *Tim Burton: The Monster and the Crowd*. London & New York: Routledge.
Hauke, C. (2004) 'Orpheus, Dionysos and Popular Culture. Jean Cocteau's *Orphée* (1950) – then and now.' In *Spring. A Journal of Archetype and Culture, Orpheus, 71*, 127–141.
Hauke, C. (2005) *Human Being Human: Culture and the Soul*. London & New York: Routledge.
Hauke, C. & Alister, I. (eds.) (2001) *Jung & Film. Post-Jungian Takes on the Moving Image*. London & New York: Routledge.
Hockley, L. (2001) Cinematic Projections: The Analytical Psychology of C. G. Jung and Film Theory. Luton: University of Luton Press.
Hockley, L. (2007) Frames of Mind: A Post-Jungian Look at Cinema, Television and Technology. Bristol: Intellect.
Hockley, L. & Gardner, L. (eds.) (2010) House: The Wounded Healer on Television: Jungian and Post-Jungian Reflections. London & New York: Routledge.
Izod, J. (2001) *Myth, Mind and the Screen*. Cambridge: University of Cambridge Press.
Izod, J. (2006) Screen, Culture, Psyche: A Post-Jungian Approach to Working with the Audience. Hove: Routledge.
Jung, C. G. (2009) (S. Shamdasani, ed.) *The Red Book*. New York & London: Norton & Co.

Manguel, A. (2008) *The City of Words*. London: Continuum.
Rowland, S. (2008) Psyche and the Arts: Jungian Approaches to Music, Architecture, Literature, Painting and Film. Hove: Routledge.
Samuels, A., Shorter, B. & Plaut, F. (1986) *A Critical Dictionary of Jungian Analysis*. London & New York: Routledge.
Singh, G. (2009) Film After Jung: Post-Jungian Approaches to Film Theory. London & New York: Routledge.
Waddell, T. (2006) Mis/takes: Archetype, Myth and Identity in Screen Fiction. Hove: Routledge.
Waddell, T. (2010) Wild/Lives: Trickster, Place and Liminality on Screen. Hove: Routledge.

Part I

Image and psychotherapy

Chapter 1

The decisive image
In documentary film, in Jungian analysis

Tom Hurwitz and Margaret Klenck

> True symbolism occurs where the particular represents the more general . . . as living, momentary revelation of the unfathomable.
> (Goethe, 1949: no. 314)

Documentary cinematography and Jungian analysis share a deep respect for the power of images to affect, inform and transform the viewer. Each discipline prepares for the spontaneous arrival of images, each follows sequences of images and each trusts that by engaging with images, meaning emerges. In this essay, we will explore this shared pursuit, with the hope of illuminating what makes an image, in documentary film and in Jungian analysis, a *decisive image*.

Henri Cartier-Bresson, one of the greatest of the mid-twentieth-century documentary photographers, says in his essay *The Decisive Moment*: 'To me, photography is the simultaneous recognition, in a fraction of a second, of the significance of an event as well as of a precise organization of forms which give that event its proper expression' (1952). From another discipline, C. G. Jung wrote: 'The image is a condensed expression of the psychic condition as a whole' (1971: para. 745). These two quotes can orient our exploration of the role of images, both psychic and cinematographic.

A scene unfolds in the desert, at the foot of a high mountain. The photographer/cameraman is filming as he walks, following an old man with a robe around his shoulders who moves unsteadily under the weight of the flat pieces of clay that he carries. As Moses slows his pace, the cameraman moves around him to see a bit of his face. It shows a growing fury. Moses has come to the edge of a small wadi. In the dry riverbed just below him, the members of his clan are dancing around an idol of a cow god.

The cameraman needs a shot that shows both Moses and what he is reacting to. He has already panned from one to the other, showing the two elements of the scene sequentially. He knows that the editor, later, could even remove the pan, placing one image next to the other in a visual sentence. But the weakness implicit in that solution is clear. It tells a story but it is not decisive. Perhaps he could move behind the old man to see the dancing with Moses in soft focus. In his heart, however, the cameraman knows that this would be the cheap solution.

Moses' anger is forming slowly inside him. The cameraman needs to capture this reaction. It is the decisive image of the scene, the one that tells the whole story, not simply the narrative. Jumping into the soft dirt of the wadi bank, the cameraman runs down the steep slope and into the crowd of dancers. He moves around the revelers to the far side of the cow statue. Crouching, steadying his camera near the ground, the cameraman has it now – in the dusk, in the heat of the flames, through the legs of the cow, the dancing Hebrews behind it, the firelight making the nearest figures glow gold, and past them, silhouetted against the deepening blue sky, is Moses. Body shaking, mouth wide, with the firelight flickering in his now raging eyes, he raises the tablets. At once, it is all in a single image: Moses, roaring in rage, dashing his laws against the rocks; the dancers in the foreground stopping in shock; all framed by the gleaming legs of the rude idol, the cause of it all.

The anachronism of the previous vignette is not only the presence of a documentary cinematographer in a biblical scene. Mankind's ability to conceive of recording an event in real time was two millennia away. Photography, unlike the older arts, allows us to actually record a decisive image.

Cartier-Bresson coined the term 'the decisive moment' to describe what his work sought to capture. We are adapting this phrase for our assertions about the nature of image and symbol in both documentary cinematography and Jungian analysis. Documentary still photographers freeze one discrete moment of the real world. Documentary cinematographers work in groups of moments adding movement and rhythm to the resources of the still photographer. Jungian analysts are also attentive to the movement of images in time within the analytic field. *Decisive moment* seems to describe only an event. Because our inquiry concerns the power of imagery itself, we call the subject of our essay *the decisive image*.

One might ask whether the idea of a decisive image can be applied to other, earlier, forms of artistic creation. Works of graphic art lack the immediacy of the photographic record. In a figurative painting, for example, of a battle, we are asked to identify with the event through the feelings and imagination of the artist. We then undergo a process of cognition in which we match our experience of reality to his rendering. By seeing his work, we imagine the reality that he represents. Thus we experience it one step removed.

Modern photography shows us images that are contiguous with what we see in life and brings the very moment of taking the picture, of the event itself, *the actuality* – not its recounting – to the centre of the work of art. It uses the material of reality to create an image. The shock of recognition, experienced in viewing photography, is the source of its special power.

> Of all the means of expression, photography is the only one that fixes forever the precise, transitory instant. We photographers deal in things which are continually vanishing, and when they have vanished there is no contrivance on earth which can make them come back again.
>
> (Cartier-Bresson 1952: p. 4)

We know intuitively that there is something unique in a photograph. With the other visual arts, it shares artifice, organization, and point of view, but uniquely, it works with the very material of seeing. The innovation of photography and film in the history of human art is their ability to imitate perception. Rather than asking the viewer to see as I feel, the photographer asks the viewer to see as I see. In that quality of primary experience lies the power to create an explosion of meaning. Singularly, the photographic image subsumes the interpretation of the artist inside the language of reality, and of the perceived world.

The following two documentary photographs demand that we see as the photographer saw, glimpsing the fierce inevitability of aging. In Cartier-Bresson's *Young and Old*, an old woman regards youth. The young girl passes her, turning casually in her direction, as if dancing, innocently flirting with age and mortality. In Dorthea Lange's *Funeral Cortege*, an old woman stares out at her proscribed future. Both images may have been stalked carefully, but both were perceived and captured in an instant. Each uses circular forms in its composition. The circle is a symbol of infinity, evoking both the limits of life and also life's endless cycles.

Notice how in both photographs there is an accumulation of meaning, from the specific to the archetypal, or as Goethe said: 'True symbolism occurs where the particular represents the more general' (Goethe 1949: no. 314).

20 Image and psychotherapy

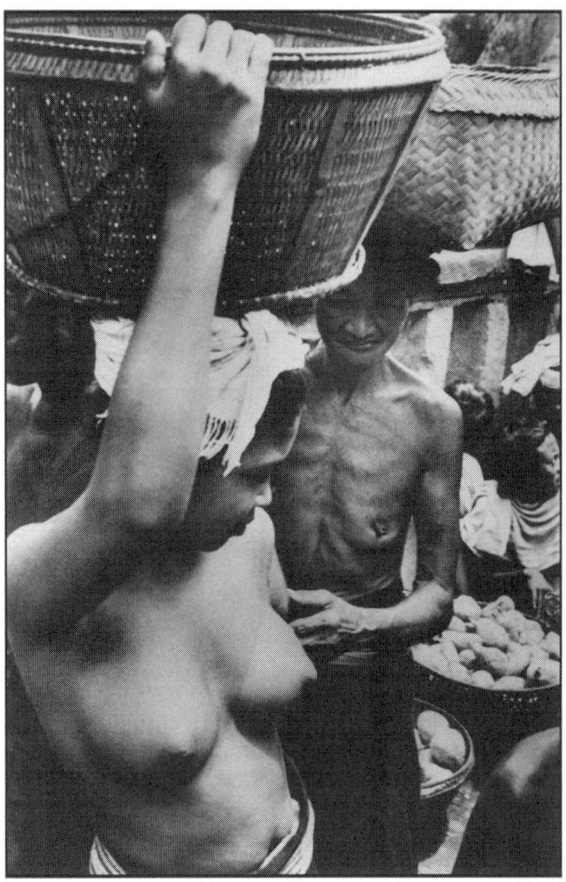

Figure 1.1 Henri Cartier-Bresson, *Young and Old*, Bali Indonesia, 1949 (Magnum Photos/Michael Shulman).

A decisive image is articulate in that it clarifies the revelatory moment, thereby elevating it to symbol. By symbol, we mean the best expression of the inexpressible. As Jung writes, 'the symbolic process is an experience *in images and of images*' (Jung 1969: para. 82). In the instant, the camera captures the image, reveals it, and sculpts it out of the raw material of time and action. A decisive image makes universal that which could just pass by us as merely dramatic, or even mundane. Without the contribution of the artist, photography, and even more so

Figure 1.2 Dorthea Lange, *Funeral Cortege*, 1938 (courtesy of George Eastman House, International Museum of Photography and Film).

cinematography, can be an empty recording of events, simply making snapshots, or fly-on-the-wall records. Examples are everywhere of photos and films that record events, even dramatic moments, but do not come near the goal that we are discussing. The photographer/cinematographer's task is to set a trap in which to snare the random revelation – to reveal its importance, to pull it forward from the transitory into meaning.

It is no accident that documentary photography and analytic psychology arrived in the world within a decade of each other. One of the projects of the twentieth century was to perceive the truth of the inside by seeing the truth of the outside. In another sense, it was to see the way the timeless is perceived in the moment of time. Working in the same landscape of great human progress and great human slaughter, Jung was following the implications of the association experiments – attending to spontaneous word images – and developing his complex theory just a few years before true documentary photography was born. The photographic document, the aims of which Cartier-Bresson described so well, arrived bit by bit as photographers explored the potential of the new medium and its new equipment. First came newspaper men, then Soviet photographers, then the French – Atget and Brassai – and the American social documentarians – Evans, Lang and the FSA photographers. Soon, Cartier-Bresson and the other Magnum photographers followed.

Motion picture technology arrived late in the nineteenth century, and with it the documentary film. However, for two generations, cameras were unwieldy and sound equipment was even more cumbersome. In the mid twentieth century, some pioneers prodded engineers to create a lightweight portable film camera, and the capacity to synchronize sound. Once a system was perfected in the early 1960s, the technology cascaded along with the advance of the form. *Cinéma vérité* or *direct cinema* – the technique of filming what is seen, as it happens, with synchronous sound – was born.

The development of the technique began with a few documentary segments of the *Omnibus* television programme in the early 1950s. Standing on the shoulders of documentary still photographers like Cartier-Bresson, Robert Frank and Gary Winogrand, filmmakers in the United States – Robert Drew, D A Pennebaker, Richard Leacock, Albert and David Maysles – and in France – Chris Marker and Jean Rouche – redefined the documentary film. They followed human stories as they happened.

With this new form, a new role for the cinematographer was also born. Films were now not only about reality, they were made up of reality. It was the cinematographer's job to build art out of the raw material of real life.

The raw material: We are in the rehearsal room of one of America's great choreographers, Paul Taylor. The cinematographer follows the dancers. Dressed in leotards and tights, they rehearse a ballet for a new performance season. Previously in the film, Taylor has spoken about taking care of the feelings of the dancers, and about the need to make use of them all in performance. At the same time, he says, there is no way to be fair.

The camera captures a dancer as she is lifted high on the shoulders of several men (Figure 1.3). At the bottom of his frame, the cinematographer sees a woman company member, watching on the sidelines. She is the understudy, learning the part, marking the movements of the lifted woman with her arms and mimicking the exalted dancer. Rather than following the dramatic lift, the cinematographer gently zooms toward the imitator. In the moment, she drops her arms, her face defeated and

Figure 1.3 Dancer lifted high, Paul Taylor, *Dancemaker*, 1998 (Four Oaks Foundation).

hopeless. Without being privy to her thoughts, we still see a decisive image, the face of envy (Figure 1.4).

The decisive image is that central confluence of subject, action, and meaning that brings the documentary to life by making it memorable and resonant with its audience. That is the prize of the cinematographer's struggle.

To capture the *decisive image*, the cinematographer must improvise, engaging the dramatic events of the real scene as it unfolds. His preparation for this moment has included immersion in the story, practice of his physical skills, sensitivity to the emotions and needs of his subjects, and intuitive awareness of the symbolic implications of the scene as it evolves.

24 Image and psychotherapy

Figure 1.4 The face of envy, Paul Taylor, *Dancemaker*, 1998 (Four Oaks Foundation).

The task of the documentary cinematographer varies from that of the documentary still photographer in that for him, the decisive image must refer not only to the one discrete moment, but also the moments sliding away on either side of it. The still photographer has been able to reject these subordinate moments; the cinematographer must embrace them. Because films are stories, he must capture what happens before and after the key event. He must show how Moses came to the dancing Hebrews, and also show what happens after the people see what their lapse has caused.

What did the cameraman achieve when he 'got his shot' at the foot of Mt. Sinai? If he had simply stood aside and framed the action in a *wide shot* – Moses, a small figure on the right, dancing figures below him on the left – he would have shown us a dramatic scene. However, with his composition – the cow idol framing the blurred revelers, behind them the violence of Moses' act – he has constellated a powerful image. He has used his tools, composition, light, colour and movement, to build a tension of opposing forces – law vs. transgression, monotheism vs. polytheism, civilizing vs. anarchic, Yahweh versus Hathor. In that tension, a symbol is revealed.

For the audience, decisive images are the key images. They are the ones, among the thousands of edited shots, which are held in the memory of the audience and played again and again, as they are re-viewed in mind. 'I'll never forget the shot of Moses when he throws the laws down,' they might say, or, 'remember that scene of the envious dancer?' These are the filmic moments that interact deeply with thought and psyche. They stay in mind and in the culture; they change lives. In fact the memory of the viewer is the final component of *the decisive image:* essential action, artistic vision, resounding memory.

We have looked at the idea of a *decisive image* in still photography and film, and made distinctions between them. We have also described the unique relationship that the cinematographer has to the discovery of the image. Crucial to any art is its craft.

The most important aspect of the cinematographer's craft within the documentary environment is improvisation. He acts with spontaneity to keep revealing the action that is taking place. Every scene has an action, a central dramatic intention. Moses reacts to the revelry of the Hebrews. The understudy longs for and yet hates the dance. The work of the documentary cinematographer is to parse this central truth out of the other distracting elements of the scene – the Hebrews around the Golden Calf talking to each other, for example, or the other rehearsing dancers. The action is continually developing and changing as the emotions of the subjects change. Within the actuality, the documentary cinematographer must improvise, continually visualizing and filming the action until luck, and his own preparation, lead him to the *decisive image*.

The foundation for the improvisation of documentary work is laid in the preparation of the artist. The decisive image is either taken or missed due to the quality of that preparation, which for the documentary cinematographer takes several forms.

- *Story preparation.* In consultation with the director or producer, the cinematographer must be aware of every aspect of the story, and of the subjects that may enter the film. Every aim of storytelling – the themes of the film, the back-stories of the characters – helps determine how any given event is recorded.
- *Relatedness.* The documentarian needs to develop the trust of his subject. There is an ephemeral, active/passive, distant/connected relationship that yields a fertile environment in which the crew

becomes both witness and confessor, while at the same time remaining as invisible as possible. This allows life to proceed and the story to evolve before the lens.
- *Knowledge of editing.* A film is a structured series of shots. Fulfilling the needs of the editor in order to shape a scene – the right shots that deliver the right options for editing, close-ups, wide shots, details – is a key part of the cinematographer's work.

The decisive image is the product of preparation and then of improvisational creation in the moment of the actuality. It takes its place in the larger work of the film and becomes yet more than itself. As it vibrates between picture and viewer, it becomes symbolic, and once it exists in the consciousness of the viewer, it interacts with the viewer's memory, bridging into the future. For it is in the mind of the viewer that the symbol plays its role, like a rock dropped into a clear pool, radiating waves of meaning, backwards and forwards in time, engaging the archetypal. Memory is the synthetic form of the decisive image, the fulfillment of its purpose.

Jungian analysts also seek decisive moments and images. The documentary project and the Jungian analytic one are similar in this way: they both look to the material that is emerging with an eye to the latent, profound meaning-making function of image and symbol.

Both disciplines rely on the human inclination to unconsciously create narrative out of images, and both trust that the experience of engaging with the image itself not only provokes but also transforms the viewer. Further, both disciplines hold that meaning can never be imposed or constructed. It can only emerge from a spontaneous engagement, both unconscious and conscious, with the image.

What Jungians mean by 'image' may be somewhat different to what a photographer means. An image is the expression of something that communicates a resonance beyond the 'thing itself'. Images and symbols are the language of the psyche – the way in which psyche communicates. Jungians insist that engagement with an image activates the movement of libido, the life force, in ways that are both unexpected and healing. As the Jungian analyst Sherry Salman says,

> Symbols are living, emerging images, reflecting active psychological process and pregnant with meaning. They are capable of acting like transformers of psychic energy . . . a symbolic image evokes the totality of the archetype it reflects. Images evoke the aim and

motivation of instincts, creating links to affective experience which heals splits.

(Salman 2008: p. 70)

For example, an image of a dog connotes more than simply one's pet, although that is there as well. An image of a dog contains all that is true for dogs in general – warm-blooded, keen sense of smell, innately trusting and inclined to be faithful, defending the humans who care for them. In addition, an image of a dog carries all that dogs have meant in human imagination – all the myths and tales of guardian dogs, from Cerberus to Lassie. How such an image might move libido would depend on the surrounding images and resonances from a person's life.

Images take many forms – pictures, language, physical manifestations, etc. For example, an analyst might see an analysand's rash as an image of some kind of reaction between the physiology and psyche of the patient. The rash might be both a specific medical condition and a symbol of some fiery, itchy psychic content that is too much for the analysand's system to process. Or, an empty analytic chair, when the analysand is late, is an image that indicates more than a mere absence. It is an image signifying a particular way in which this analysand needs to be 'seen'. As Salman puts it, 'Images give form to emotion and emotions give a living body to imagination; the expression of archetypal possibility is both poetic and dramatic' (Salman 2008: p. 70)

With a photographic image, such resonances and amplifications pertain as well; one does not initially need to be conscious of them in order to be affected. This is also true in much of analysis. 'For the important thing is not to interpret and understand the fantasies, but primarily to experience them' (Jung 1967: para. 342). While Jung goes on to extol the process of analysis that brings the unconscious into consciousness, he is clear in his theoretical and clinical avowal that experience is primary. Without experience, nothing can become conscious.

Engaging and interpreting decisive images in analysis begins with the analyst preparing a space into which the material is welcomed, what Winnicott termed 'the holding environment' and what Jung imagined as the alchemical *vas bene clausum*. The space is prepared in literal ways; by furnishing an office, by setting a fee, by starting and ending on time, etc. But more importantly, analysts prepare to see and listen by opening themselves to the psychic communications that flow between them and their analysands, and within each of them.

Analysts are always seeing with multiple eyes and listening with multiple ears. They listen to the manifest content of what happened to the analysand that day. They listen to the historic narrative of what happened in the past and hear both the literal, reductive story and the underlying interpretation that the analysand holds and cherishes. They listen for the sequence of what comes into the room: the narrative flow, the skips and diversions, the tellings and retellings. They track the images: how, for instance, an analysand might begin by talking about an encounter with a dog on the street, then his childhood dog, then a story about loyalty gone sour, then a reference to his anger being 'unleashed,' and so on. The analyst hears/sees an accumulating field in which the archetypal potential of 'dog' as loyal guardian, fierce protector, is in some important relationship to the personal experience of that instinct gone awry.

Analysis is improvisation, in that the two people truly do not know what will happen in a session; they must be willing to follow psyche's lead. As with any good improvisation, there is an agreed upon project – the idea for a comedy sketch, the idea for a documentary film, the idea of healing – and then openness to discovering what is within.

Through all the seeing and listening, analysts, like cinematographers, are curious. That curiosity takes many forms. But the two that are similar between the analyst and the documentary cameraman are worth exploring here. One is a simple wondering and waiting in a kind of 'advent' attitude for an image to emerge that will usher in something new: the Transcendent Function. The other is an active dialogue with the images as they appear, what Jung called 'active imagination' and its attendant process of amplification.

First, let us look at the transcendent function: it is the moment when, out of the tensions of all the layers of communications, and out of the pressure from opposing gradients within the psyche of the analysand, a new image becomes a symbol. As Jung says:

> If we can successfully develop that function which I have called transcendent ... disharmony ceases and we can then enjoy the favorable side of the unconscious. The unconscious then gives us all the encouragement and help that a bountiful nature can shower upon man. Its holds possibilities which are locked away from the conscious mind, for it has at its disposal all subliminal psychic contents, all those things which have been forgotten or overlooked, as well as the wisdom and experience of uncounted centuries which are laid down in its archetypal organs.
>
> (1967: para. 196)

The birth of a symbol is not willed; it is spontaneous and unpredictable. Analysts prepare for the transcendent function but cannot control it. Yet, like any midwife (or cinematographer), analysts have to be ready to recognize what is happening. They trust what is born will be a unique and proper movement in the individuation of the analysand.

'The transcendent function . . . is synonymous with progressive development towards a new attitude,' says Jung (Jung 1967: para. 159). The transcendent function always marks a moment of new consciousness. It is a decisive moment in that way. Jung's idea of the transcendent function recalls Henri Cartier-Bresson's words:

> To me, photography is the simultaneous recognition, in a fraction of a second, of the significance of an event as well as of a precise organization of forms which give that event its proper expression.
> (Cartier-Bresson 1952: p. 15)

Like documentary cameramen, the analyst is scrambling down the wadi, searching through the images, seeing the patterns, offering points of view, and holding opposites in a frame for the analysand to see things differently. Analysts/cinematographers sift and sort through all the images that arrive in a session – all the symptoms, the stories, the complexes and sufferings – in order to lift up various potentially significant ones for engagement.

But from another point of view, psyche itself is the cameraman, and we are merely the viewers. Psyche is the totality of the personality, which contains consciousness, the personal unconscious and the collective unconscious. Jung saw the whole psychic system as an energetic dynamic, always working to rebalance itself and to integrate its dissociated aspects and complexes.

From this energetic perspective, psyche as cameraman is creating images; psyche as editor is arranging and rearranging them. It is juxtaposing them in old and new ways so as to challenge the ego complex's attitude, selecting just the right sequence and contrast of images to illustrate the condition of the analysand's being at any given moment. Psyche is creating images so that we experience revelation and transformation. A dialogue forms between consciousness and unconsciousness through images, whether those images are expressed in language, drawing, or physical or neurotic symptoms. And just as the cameraman above finds the right composition of Moses, the reveling Israelites, and the Golden Calf to communicate the meaning of the event, so too psyche will call on personal iconography and archetypal story when constellating images. If there is any wisdom in the psyche, it is the wisdom of selecting images that, when taken together, become decisive.

Just as the events that are unfolding before the camera are not of the cameraman's making, so the psychic images are uncontrolled emergent phenomena. It is Jung's position that those images are both communications about the present psychic situation and teleologically purposive, pointing the way to a solution or resolution of the tension depicted in the imaginal event.

The second approach that analysts and documentary cinematographers share is a willingness to let the images themselves build the story. This is an improvisational attitude, which is deeply open to being surprised and confounded. It assumes that there is synergy and spontaneous transformation, and that the world, both inner and outer, is dynamic within its own reference.

One essential tool in this approach is active imagination, a cornerstone of Jungian analysis. This is a process in which one interacts with, but does not willfully control, inner figures and situations. In an active imagination, one moves from symbol to symbol, from image to image, surprised, confused, lost and found, never in charge of anything except the willingness to continue.

For example, an analysand dreams of a woman who is sitting crying in a corner. Upon waking, he starts an active imagination – talking with the woman. The analysand does not consciously imagine what the woman will say; rather he sees what the psyche will say through the woman's voice. If the woman says, 'Oh, I feel like I am a jewel of great worth but no one can see it' then the question is, 'what does this jewel look like?' or, 'what kind of jewel is it?' The analysand's imagination will start to layer in both associative and amplificatory images. If it turns out to be a ruby, then the psyche is heading in one direction; if it is a diamond, then it is another direction. Off the analytic couple goes, following the trail of images, associations and amplifications, which *might* lead eventually to a *decisive image*.

As Jung says, 'The unconscious is continually active, combining its material in ways which serve the future' (Jung 1967: para 197). Images for Jung and Jungians are not static; they are living expressions of psychic energy. The images themselves, with their personal and archetypal dramatic tensions, move libido. They change the direction of the psychic energy, making something new happen in the being of the analysand. Only after the experience can the analyst and analysand together gather the illuminating images. They bring them into consciousness in such a way that meaning is clarified. This organizing process can be said to correspond to the act of composition for the cinematographer.

It is important to remember that not all images are decisive. In order for an image to be decisive, either in photography or in analysis, it must gather energy in a particular way. We suggest that a decisive image must have four elements: a specific contextual relevance, an archetypal resonance, and two opposing elements with their accompanying tension. These four elements form a *quaternio* of energies that produce the symbol, which then becomes the vector for transformation.

For example, in the previously mentioned image of the understudy, the context is the rehearsal. The principal dancer, lifted by the group of men, is almost flying in an exalted pose. Visually and emotionally opposed to them is the understudy. She watches and copies the movement, until her feelings become almost unbearable. The tension between the beauty before her and her own spoiling longings reveals in our decisive image the archetype of envy.

If this sequence were a dream, the same four elements would be applicable. The dream narrative might be something like*: I am at a dance rehearsal. The principal dancers are dancing; a group of men is lifting the lead woman high in the air; she is beautiful. Suddenly I see the understudy far across the room, looking on, quietly learning the movements; she is filled with envy and despair.*

Psyche has chosen a dance rehearsal as the setting. A rehearsal is where one learns a new dance. Dance itself is wordless expression through fully embodied movement in time and space. This dance in particular involves a woman lifted high by a group of men. It is both intimate and exciting. Psyche juxtaposes this related, sensual, elevated dancer with the lonely understudy, marginalized and hopeless.

This image is the dramatic turning point of the dream, which exposes a large rift in the dreamer's being. In her waking life, there would probably be some seemingly unbridgeable gap between the 'dance of her life' or her creative expression, or her sensual related femininity, and her capacity to participate in those aspects of herself. Since an understudy is an assigned position in a dance company, the dream set-up implies some fateful positioning vis-à-vis the dance. She is expected to learn the dance but may never actually dance it.

A 'suddenly' moment in a dream signals a decisive image. In this case, the dreamer's experience of the sensual, powerful choreography that lifts the woman into the air is abruptly interrupted by another aspect of the dreamer's personality – a disempowered, hopeless and envying part. This part appears doomed to learn the dance but not to dance it. In this example, one would assume that there is some immediate personal experience, either inner or outer, which has prompted this dream – some situation which pulls on and exacerbates the inner gap. This element will include the dreamer's personal complexed reaction to the situation. At the core of that personal complex will be an archetype – in this case, envy – which roots the dreamer's emotions into the deep earth of the collective unconscious and the psychoid realm.

By placing the dancing woman in the arms of the men, sailing high in the air in the foreground, and then revealing the little, lonely understudy in the background, psyche counterbalances the elevated female with the undervalued one. This depicts a split in the psyche of the dreamer herself, a field in which she both overvalues and undervalues herself. It also indicates that the split, at the time of this particular dream at least, is very far from being integrated, since the only way for the understudy to 'get in the dance' is for the principal woman, the elevated one, to be injured. There is no inherent reconciliation in this image. The tension of the opposites does not move towards transformation. Envy spoils.

The first element of the *quaternio*, then, is the personal situation in which one part of the dreamer is feeling consigned to the margins – either by an actual waking-life situation or an inner complexed reaction. The archetypal field of envy is the second element. The tension between the positions and experiences of the two women are the third and fourth elements in our decisive image. The four elements combine in such a way that a precise image of the dreamer's psychic situation can be seen. Once it can be seen, it can be engaged; once an image is engaged, it can lead to consciousness, and the possibility of transformation and meaning.

The documentary cinematographer and the Jungian analyst are both attending to the emergence of the symbol. As we have said, they both share a clear-eyed curiosity about what is happening. Because it is clear-eyed, it can also be detached. The cameraman, while discovering the decisive image, cannot be taking sides with either understudy or dancer. His job is to find the image that will illuminate the situation. Likewise, the analyst is essentially impartial. She truly doesn't know what will happen to the analysand, or what *should* happen. The analyst's task, like the cameraman's, is to lift up what is actually happening in the inner and outer reality, and then to trust that the individuating instinct will use this truth for consciousness, healing and growth.

Perhaps the last similarity between the two projects is a grand goal: to add to the common good by affecting something new. Jung was clear that the individuation process must include a return to the community. In *Memories, Dreams, Reflections*, he speaks to this idea:

It is . . . a grave mistake to think that it is enough to gain some understanding of the images and that knowledge can here make a halt. Insight into them must be converted into an ethical obligation . . . The images of the unconscious place a great responsibility upon a man. Failure to understand them, or a shirking of ethical responsibility, deprives him of his wholeness and imposes a painful fragmentariness on his life.

(Jung 1961: pp. 192–193)

Cartier-Bresson put it this way:

I believe that through the act of living, the discovery of oneself is made concurrently with the discovery of the world around us which can mold us, but which can also be affected by us. A balance must be established between these two worlds – the one inside us and the one outside us. As the result of a constant reciprocal process, both of the worlds come to form a single one. And it is this world that we must communicate.

(Cartier-Bresson 1952: p. 15)

There is a moral imperative at the heart of the Jungian project, not merely a personal one. The outcome of an encounter with one's self should not be personal growth alone. It should also compel one to live in the world with clarity, compassion and integrity. A profound encounter with the psyche includes the obligation to act from one's emergent self-knowledge. Likewise, an encounter with strong documentary film images ought to add something new and compelling to a viewer's psyche, moving him or her toward a greater engagement with the world. A decisive image, in analysis and in a documentary, resounds in the lives of the viewers. It clarifies their shared humanity and, one hopes, prompts action that builds upon it.

References

Cartier-Bresson, H. (1952) *The Decisive Moment*. New York: Simon and Schuster.

Goethe, Johann Wolfgang von (1949) *Maximen und Reflexionem*, Gedenkausgabe Vol. 9. Zurich (no. 314).

Jung, C. G. (1961) *Memories, Dreams, Reflections*. New York: Random House (Vintage Books Edition – 1989).

Jung, C. G. (1967) *Collected Works Vol. 7*. Princeton, NJ: Princeton University Press.

Jung, C. G. (1969) *Collected Works Vol. 9*. Princeton, NJ: Princeton University Press.
Jung, C. G. (1971) *Collected Works Vol. 6*. Princeton, NJ: Princeton University Press.
Salman, S. (2008) The creative psyche: Jung's major contributions. In P. Young-Eisendrath and T. Dawson (eds), *The Cambridge Companion to Jung*: New York: Cambridge University Press.

Chapter 2

'I thought he might be better now'

A clinician's reading of individuation in von Trier's *Breaking The Waves*

David Hewison

Writing this chapter has led me to wonder (and not for the first time) whether I actually like Lars von Trier's *Breaking The Waves* (1996). It has also led me to ponder what kind of reading of any film is final? How do we get to understanding a point of view or reading that can seem obvious to another, or even to oneself in retrospect, yet is quite tangential to our initial position on a movie? In this chapter, I shall tackle a number of themes: Lars von Trier's own description of the film; Jungian film criticism; and the Jungian concept of individuation in the context of damaged and damaging masculinity. I end with a particular reading of the film *as personality* that comes from my clinical perspective as a Jungian analyst and couple therapist rather than as a film analyst.

Breaking The Waves is not an easy film. It is, however, very powerful and its viewers fall into two extremes: those who find it extraordinarily moving and thought-provoking and those who find it repulsive and thoughtless. The film won the Grand Jury Prize at Cannes and has been described as one of the truly great works of European cinema of its decade. Made back in 1996, it preceded the series of films made according to the Dogma 95 manifesto that is associated with von Trier's name. We can see in it some of the elements of the Dogma style of film-making, particularly the hand-held camera. But there are other elements that are very much non-Dogma: the use of music, the computer-enhanced chapter titles, and especially the use of time slips where an action is indicated and the film then cuts to it having happened. For example, we see a helicopter in flight and then we see that it has landed; we see characters beginning to go upstairs and then we see them already in the bedroom. The cutting also moves us backwards and forwards in time and in perspective within the same scene. Von Trier does this to lead the viewer forcibly from one moment of emotional intensity to the next. The editing is done not by the demands of the narrative, but by the demands of the emotional weight of the scene. The feeling in the film is not watered-down by linking or atmospheric shots – with the exception of the highly stylised chapter headings – and so there is no real respite for us as viewers, and sometimes no other information about what is going on or why. It also puts great pressure on the actors, who live up to the demand superbly – particularly Emily Watson in her first film role. The original script written by von Trier existed as a kind of framework onto which the actors put their own interpretations and words – the film captures these deliberate and accidental incidents and builds up an emotional weight and truth as a result.

The film narrative brings up several questions. Just what drives Bess to do what she does – is she mad? Why does Jan make her have sex with other men – is he cruel? What is the film saying about the role of men, women, faith and industrialisation in a small society? Is it a film about the power of love, faith and redemption, or the power of fundamentalism, cruelty and perversion? These questions are given weight not just by the film but by the curious statement by von Trier that the film is, in fact, an investigation into the nature of goodness. In the brief essay that accompanies the published version of the script he has this to say:

> In the film there should only be "good" but since the "good" is misunderstood or confused with something else, because it is such a rare thing for us to meet, tensions arise.
>
> The character of Bess is "good" in a spiritual sense ... living mostly in the world of her imagination, never really accepting that things apart from "good" might exist. She is a strong person taking full responsibility of her own life, even though others might think that she is not capable of doing so. Bess is made strong by her belief and by her love. So strong that she masters even rebellion against the strict suppressing rules of the little community and the church that was once so dear to her.
>
> Jan is "good" in a much more difficult way – because he consciously aims to do "good". He inhabits the real world, where doing "good" is of course much harder.
>
> (von Trier 1996: p. 20)

Von Trier goes on to explain something of this difficulty in the real world: that in order to do good by Bess, to help her survive his disablement, Jan has to fool her that he wants her to take lovers and tell him about it. However, this willingness to do good is overtaken by something deadly and destructive as Jan's condition worsens, and as Bess is unable to tell the difference between the sane Jan who loves her and the Jan locked in a nightmare. Von Trier describes Jan as a character who wakes up to realise what he has been doing – behind his own back, as it were – in these terms:

> When he is most affected by his brain damage and medication, he is unable to control himself, and in his stupor will say things that Bess, simple-minded as she is, will believe are coming from the other Jan . . . the sane Jan that she loves, not the confused mixture of subconscious fragments, fear and "drunkenness" from the mind of an hallucinating, dying man.
>
> (ibid: p. 22)

As a result the only option Jan has is to push her away – and yet this is a rejection that is unbearable to her, and so she tries to save him to bring them both together; feeling that she has failed – hearing that he is dying – she sacrifices herself to save him, in a mirror of the way that Jan has tried to sacrifice himself to save her (either actually in trying to overdose, or emotionally in having her committed to a psychiatric hospital to get her away from him, despite his attachment to her).

In the film, Bess is either simple, damaged or someone who is dangerously open to a powerful internal experience. We know that she has been hospitalised and we think it is after her brother died (we don't know what happened to her before that). From the opening moments of the film, when she is angry and agitated at Jan for being late as she waits for the helicopter bringing him for their wedding to land, we know that Bess cannot bear separation. We also know that she is able to be soothed by Jan, is capable of love and can prioritise another person's needs over her own. We know that she finds sex with Jan fulfilling and is grateful that she experiences it as linking her to the sacred. Von Trier suggests that Bess is a very strong character, transformed by her love and her faith, and so we can imagine that she has something good enough inside her, but we also know that she has had to bear more than she can manage in her life. We can see that had she lived anywhere else, things might have been easier for her. Despite its understanding and tolerance of her direct experience of God, the harsh fundamentalism of her community has given her so much else to cope with.

We know that Bess needs to be looked after – and that she tries to solicit help from others – but also that she is not so damaged that she refuses help. Even after the death of her own husband, her sister-in-law

Dodo stays on in order to help Bess. Her psychiatrist, Dr Richardson, is pulled towards her and wishes to save her. Jan, whilst sane, tries to look after her. But Bess has also had experiences of rejection mixed with care. Her mother, despite having rejected Bess's hysterical self-expression during her breakdown, and rejecting her again when she is cast out by the Elders, comes to her in defiance of the rules of their community as she is dying in the hospital. The scenes in which Bess's feelings are turned away from, or clamped down on, by her mother are terribly painful, I think, but they also tell us a lot about life in the community and the price everyone pays to live there. Bess's grandfather, who was able to convey her request to be married to the Elders, is nevertheless unable to put her first, before them, once they have laid down the law. He is even party to her being cast into hell at the funeral, not knowing that Jan has already rescued her body from this further act of cruelty.

What I have recounted is a particular way of reading the film – one that treats the relationship between Jan and Bess as the centre of the piece, and treats the film as a depiction of real life events. Bess's line 'I thought he might be better now' captures her struggle to maintain hope, and to remain faithful to her version of herself, Jan and the world in which she lives. She says the sentence when she is admitted to hospital dying of her wounds and asks to see Jan, expecting his recovery to be the miraculous result as the converse of her damage. What she sees, however, is Jan unconscious, on a ventilator; and then she dies. What we know, and Bess does not, is that against all the odds, Jan survives and recovers to live on but without her. We are invited to believe that Jan's recovery is due to the clarity and strength of Bess's faith, but we don't have to believe it. Indeed, the film allows us to question whether there has been a miracle, whilst simultaneously asserting the act of sacrifice on Bess's part – of this there is no doubt: she gives her life to save Jan. We can wonder, though, of her state of mind when she does so. Is she deluded and manipulated by a perverse sadist or is she acting from an inner certainty that shows her the way God wishes her to go in what would otherwise be a dead end of hopelessness and despair?

I want to question the either/or nature of certain categories. Can one be both perverse and redeemed? Is it possible that redemption might use perversion as its agent or does perversion always kill off redemption? I am also interested in how we understand Bess's statement: 'I thought he might be better now.' These questions invite us to explore some of the ideas we hold about psychological development, health, and the place of faith.

On cinema

What is the advantage of exploring this film from a Jungian psychological standpoint? In the 1920s Jung wrote a paper on 'The spiritual problem of modern man' addressing what he saw as an inevitable psychological/cultural response to an over-emphasis on the spirit or psyche as opposed to the body at that time. Feeling that the cinema was very much a part of this cultural response – a symptom of the imbalance, in a way – he wrote:

> The cinema, like the detective story, enables us to experience without danger to ourselves all the excitements, passions, and fantasies which have to be repressed in a humanistic age. It is not difficult to see how these symptoms link up with our psychological situation. The fascination of our psyche brings about a new self-appraisal, a reassessment of our fundamental human nature. We can hardly be surprised if this leads to a rediscovery of the body after its long subjection to the spirit – we are even tempted to say that the flesh is getting its own back.
> (Jung 1928/1964: para. 195)

What Jung is suggesting in this comment about the psychological state of society is that for every movement in the psyche that goes too far, there is a compensatory process that kicks in. He held to the idea that the psyche is a self-regulating system, which is not under the control of the ego, but which involves the relationship between the ego and what he called the Self. The ego is our conscious sense of ourselves – our identity – and the Self is both the centre of our total personality, conscious and unconscious, and is the term given to this total personality. This is a paradoxical formulation, but one that I hope will become a little clearer as I go on. The regulation of the psyche means that the ego is sometimes at the mercy of the Self, as the Self acts to bring about change in a way that the ego can struggle to integrate and make sense of. This idea of a self-regulating total personality is something that I feel we can use to understand a bit more about the meaning of *Breaking The Waves*. First, though, I need to say something about contemporary Jungian approaches to film criticism, and their relation to a clinical approach. Jungian screen and film criticism is a growing area of interpretation that stakes out a different position to the more familiar psychoanalytic approaches to film and television in that there is a greater emphasis on the image and its links with a collective store of imagery, and the process of amplification that gives rise to the meaning of the film. In her book on Jungian analysis of screen fiction – *Mis/takes: Archetype, Myth and Identity in Screen Fiction* – the Australian academic Terrie Waddell says that it is based on three main assumptions:

> First, images common in dreams, myths and creative art are often projections of unconscious archetypal patterns; second, there is a "collective unconscious" where these patterns are constellated; and third, the gradual conscious unravelling of these structures promotes the development of a more aware sense of self.
> (Waddell 2006: p. 1)

We could say that this leads to a sequence: *Film* ↔ *Image* ↔ *Collective and mythological amplification* ↔ *Meaning of film* ↔ *Meaning of self*.

This links with the work of John Izod, who has looked at how film and televised documentary affects and emotionally engages the viewer. His body of work has explored the view that it is the repetition of mythical themes that is the key to the meaning of film, but in his book, *Screen, Culture, Psyche* (2006), Izod is particularly interested in how these things make an impact on us – pointing out that most cinema isn't particularly meaningful to the audience. He suggests that there are two main types of screenings that do impact upon the audience – and upon the culture of which they are a part. The first is the generic mainstream film that works deliberately with compellingly emotional storylines – these stir up our emotions and engage us in a kind of folk tale type of way: we know the basic plot already and are available for the impact of the latest version of this. Not only this, but we know that millions of others are also watching the film, responding to it, and discussing it later, making it a collective event. The second is the highly personal and intimate documentary (most often only screened on television), with a narrator talking to us directly, taking us into their emotional world. Izod suggests that both types of screening make use of a kind of ritualised repetition, allowing the viewer to identify in some way with what is being portrayed and re-work it inside them. I suggest that *Breaking The Waves* is a kind of mix of the two.

I have a cautionary take on this view of Izod's, which I have written about in a response to an earlier paper by him about active imagination and film analysis in the *Journal of Analytical Psychology* (Hewison 2000; Izod 2000). In this response I suggested that academic Jungian film and screen critics may be in danger of assuming that the process of moving from emotionally charged images, through amplification, to a new sense of self ballasted by its links to mythological material, is possible for everyone. From my clinical experience, I suggested that some people in fact misread films as though it is actually themselves on the screen: they identify with the characters in a way that prevents further development, rather than enabling it. We could say that such people cannot allow sufficient ego flexibility to allow the sequence of *Film* ↔ *Image* ↔ *Collective and mythological amplification* ↔ *Meaning of film* ↔ *Meaning of self* to occur, but instead use the sequence *Film* ↔ *Image* ↔ *Meaning of ego*. Izod refers to my concerns in both the introduction and the conclusion to his 2006 book, 'bookending' what he has to say. This suggests to me that he is acknowledging the validity of a clinical reading of film as well as an academic one, which gives me heart in terms of my reading of *Breaking The Waves*.

A clinician's view of the film

I've indicated that there is a contrast between a clinician's view of film and that of a film or screen critic's. Perhaps the critic working from a broadly Jungian conception of film can find a particular kind of distance from the film itself in order to pick out motifs, themes, and mythological elements. The clinician can also do this – probably – but they may not. It is certainly the case that clinicians will be guided by something other than the film as 'text'; I think it is most likely that they will bring an interest in the film as 'personality'. And they'll do this in a number of ways – one is looking at the personalities of the characters in the film: what do we learn of Jan's way of relating or of the development of Bess as a person?; another is looking at the personality or qualities of the setting, how the scenes relate to each other, what techniques are used to convey atmosphere and so on; and the last is to look at the *film itself* as though it were a person made up of different parts of themselves. In this last version – interestingly associated both with classical Jungian ideas that have their origins in the study of dissociative states, and with contemporary psychoanalytic ideas (most notably of the Kleinian school) that focus on what happens to lost parts of our mind – the various characters are taken not as separate individuals in a narrative, but as depictions of an overall mental and emotional state. Taking the film itself as a person means that we can't just talk of what Jan and Bess are doing, or doing to each other; we also need to wonder what it means that we are given a description of someone called Bess who has a characteristic way of dealing with the world that is given shape in the form of someone called Jan. In this view, Jan and Bess are not treated as a separate people as such, but are considered as a kind of personification of a psyche or state of mind. Another way of putting it is that in a way, the film can be treated as though it were a dream – who knows who all the characters represent and which is the 'real' person of the dreamer? In this present interpretation of the film, I'm taking the real person to be centred around the character called Bess, because she is so clearly the centre of the film.

The film begins with Bess's wish to get married – we can see that the marriage is to an outsider and that Bess has to seek permission not just because of this, but because she is in some ways 'simple' or damaged. We get told that she cannot have children, but we do not know why. One reading of the film, then, is that it is all about Bess's relationship to men, to the masculine, to logos. We can begin to imagine that Bess has not been able to hold onto or to integrate an inner relationship to men – or rather, Bess's innate capacities for relating to and symbolising the masculine elements in her have been either unrealised, or more likely, damaged. We can see it in the array of male characters portrayed in the film – including the absent ones such as her brother and her father. We can see conflict expressed not only through the gang of Elders, including the 'duel' at the wedding between the Chairman of the Elders and Jan's clownish friend Terry, but also through the viciously triumphant casting into hell by the Elders of people who are not like them. In Jan we see a possible salvation: a redeemer who, literally, comes down from the sky to gather Bess up. But his fate is to be damaged and be useless in one way to Bess, yet very powerful in another. From this we might get a sense of her history – a stern, distant father, who at some point dies, and a brother who is close and warm, who is able to make links outside of the community, whom Bess loves terribly, and who is snatched away from her, leading her into a breakdown. Following this, we see that she develops a relationship with a god that is intimate and personal, but unreliable – a kind of mix of the father and brother experiences that she has had. Dr Richardson stands, in this reading of the film, for the brother. We can see in the confessional move towards Bess that Dr Richardson makes the dangers of attachment and intimacy and so wonder also about the erotic and incestuous undercurrents between her and her brother. The men Bess has sex with use her, and yet she goes back – most horribly, to the perverse pair in the boat, who damage her again, and end up causing her death. She does this, so she says, to save Jan – in effect to save the healthy relationship she had been developing to the masculine.

In a reading like this of the film, the funeral at the oil rig, followed by the sound of the bells, and the view from heaven, suggests that it is through a sacrifice of her developing self that Bess is redeemed. Yet, the argument would go, Bess is dead: what kind of redemption is this? If, however, we take the film to represent an internal process led by the Self rather than a realistic representation of external relationships, we can see that there is immense longing, loss, pain and violence associated with Bess's relationship to an experience of maleness that is multi-faceted and unintegrated. The god that goes away and then comes back during the last trip to the big ship has changed in quality. Bess no longer speaks in two different voices during this conversation with god, suggesting that he is no longer separate from her. Either she has now integrated this element of her personality, or she has become possessed by it – become more psychotic. Bess had been able to give witness in the church to the nature of love, so we might feel that she is more able to relate and is less split. When Bess returned to the church – for solace and support in a place she finds deeply helpful to her – she was cruelly rejected. She hears a man in the congregation declaiming on love and perfection: 'Because there is only one thing for us, sinners that we are, to achieve perfection in the eyes of god. Through unconditional love for the word that is written; though unconditional love for the Law.'

Bess's cry in the church, just before the community casts her out, that she cannot understand their meaning of the word love, gives a piercing insight as to the conflicts between the different ways of relating shown in the film. Challengingly, she says: 'I don't understand what you're saying. How can you love a word?' Everyone turns to her. Her grandfather looks down, and seems beaten and ashamed. She continues, fuelled by what she now knows to be true in her very depths: 'You cannot love words. You cannot be in love with a word,' before concluding joyously: 'You can love another human being – that's perfection.' Dressed in her hot pants and revealing top, Bess is the disruptive female trickster to the sterile, asexual masculine community. She brings an affirmation of life that overturns their adherence to a rote text to be preserved rather than something to be lived. She is inviting them to an enlivening and transformational intercourse, and the film asks us whether it is possible to reconcile this view of Bess as full of life and potential with its portrayal of her abuse, betrayal and murder.

Again, if we treat the film as a reflection of real life, then we can't reconcile them – simple. The story of Bess is a tragedy and a waste. The picture of relationships the film gives us is that they are perverse encounters set up to hurt, humiliate and abuse; that love is either absent, unwanted or ineffectual; that reliance on an inner emotional life is both mistaken and omnipotent; and finally, that the director is not only making us watch all this, but also pretending that somehow it is all not like this at all. The director is himself being perverse and inviting us to be likewise.

What if we don't treat this as a reflection of real life, though? Although we are invited to see the film as a kind of documentary because of the bleached-out cinematography, the shaky hand-held camera effects, and the jump-cut editing, there are other elements that are entirely different. In the chapter headings, there is an unreal quality to the film. Colours are over-bright or a particular colour tone is emphasised; there is some animation rather than film. The use of music from the early 1970s seems to pin the time of the action down, in a way that is not really followed up in the film itself (there are some indications of year given by the kinds of clothes worn, cars driven, and the oil industry itself, but on the whole the action is timeless – we don't feel we're watching a dated film, for example). Von Trier has suggested that these scenes represent god's view of what is going on. The final scene of the film, where we return to god's view – this time placed above the swinging, chiming, bells and looking down on to the sea and the isolated oil rig – has to be seen as throwing into doubt not just the integrity of what we have seen, as some people have suggested, but its whole intention as a kind of factual account. I think if we try to read the scene with the heavenly bells as though it was of the same order as the rest of the narrative of the film, we are making a mistake; if we try to read it as a symbol of the fate of Bess – that she has gone to heaven, or that she has been spiritually redeemed – we are making another mistake. I think the purpose of the scene is to remind us of something we will have forgotten, despite the numerous intrusive and disruptive chapter headings, and this is that what we have just seen isn't real. It is a kind of fairy tale, in the same way that Almodóvar's film *Volver* (2006) is also a fairy tale. It shares lineage with the stories from the Brothers Grimm rather than Hans Anderson, and with old myths that deal with sex and death. It is about something other than the story it tells. What might this be?

On individuation

Breaking The Waves is a description of a personality – more specifically it is about what can happen to a personality during the process of individuation. This Jungian concept refers to a particular kind of development of the individual both in relation to themselves – their full internal psychological life – and in relation to others. Often it is taken as a purely internal process, one of coming to some kind of accommodation of the collective unconscious – a shifting of the place of the ego towards the

Self, the centre and circumference of the personality, away from any collective demands. However, it cannot take place in isolation as it is not just driven by deep archetypal potentialities in the person, but is also dependent on the presence of particular kinds of external personal relationships. The most important of these are intimate relationships in which there is the opportunity for a process of immersion, withdrawal and re-immersion in a shared meaningful psychological life. Adult couple relationships are therefore one of the key areas of emotional life for the individuation process and are one of the areas that can best show up false starts, successes, or even retreats in psychological development. *Breaking The Waves* is a film that uses a particular set of relationships to explore the movements to and fro between a state of unconsciousness and one of consciousness, and the terrible forces that are involved in this.

Jung's initial thinking about the individuation process is found in his work on *Psychological Types*, published in 1921 – only a few years after his break from Freud and his own deep psychological turmoil and recovery brought about by his self-analysis of the images and fantasies which came to him as he allowed himself to sink into the unconscious. His comments then about individuation are about the need to find one's own way, against the pressures of general society to conform. As his thought developed, Jung came to see the individuation process as an unfolding of the potential pattern of wholeness within the individual, 'the supreme realization of the innate idiosyncrasy of a living being' (Jung 1934: para. 289), as he put it.

With 'mature' individuation processes, the ego itself is both relied upon and has to relate to a sense of another centre in oneself: the Self which in a sense 'guides' the individuation process. As the individuation process continues, so the person can rely less on infantile defences such as splitting, projection, denial and so on and can instead be more flexible in the way they relate to themselves, to important others around them, and to the world in general.

In an earlier paper (Hewison 2003) about couple relationships in *American Beauty* (Mendes 1999), I argued that there could exist the negative of this process: an anti-individuation. I suggest that the process of anti-individuation is concerned not with the opening up to a developmental experience but with defending against it at all costs. Rigid states of ego consciousness are attained and clung to in order not to have an experience. Somatic sensations take the place of mental images as things cannot be held in the mind. The ego is swept to one side and unreflective action occurs in order to discharge a painful feeling state. Archetypal contents are not 'mediated' or worked through, but are realised in their strong impact on the individual who can then become tangled up in them, without being able to muster sufficient resistance to the emotional maelstrom that then ensues. The world becomes viewed as a simple black and white place where things are only ever 'good' or 'bad' with a total lack of tolerance for ambiguity and ambivalence. Gratitude, concern and mourning cannot occur. Anti-individuation in this sense may be the result of many early developmental factors: the innate physical and emotional constitution of the baby – how much experience they can bear; the 'fit' between them and the mother/environment – how much they have to bear, followed by the later opportunities for reworking their past in new relationships and settings, and whether these can be made use of in a new way.

The question for us is whether Bess's tragedy demonstrates a positive or a negative individuation process: is she becoming more herself, more flexible in her capacities to relate, or is she collapsing in on herself, destroyed by overwhelmingly terrible experiences. On the one hand, the answer is obvious: Bess is destroyed, after having been deluded and abused. How can anyone think otherwise? But on the other hand I propose an alternative reading of the film as a kind of fairy tale or dream, in which the characters in it, including the central character of Bess, are all elements of one personality shown in raw relationship with each other.

From the realist or naturalistic point of view this is hard to imagine; the power of this film lies in how it stirs up our sympathy for Bess whilst showing her ruin and destruction. How can such an emotional attachment not feel 'real'? I have previously taken such a realist view of the film and discussed what it showed of sadomasochistic couple relationships in general, and that of Bess and Jan specifically, as though they were real people, not fictional characters portrayed by actors through the artifice of film (Hewison 2009). Here I want to make the case that the Bess we see on the screen is only part of a larger personality. This 'Little Bess' on the screen is what is left of the personality of what we might call 'Big Bess' after having been traumatised in her childhood and having this trauma repeated in her relationships with those around her, most latterly her brother. Little Bess is what remains intact after Big Bess's personality has been severely damaged and attacked. The film shows us what we would see if we could somehow look inside Big Bess's mind and it shows us a process of repair and death. I am suggesting that the overall process described is redemptive of Big Bess, but that this requires the suffering and death of Little Bess, who has been a kind of part-self, a limited and retarded shadow of what the real personality could be. Not for nothing is Little Bess shown to be a caretaker in the church of a higher power and to challenge the authority of the male Elders who try to control access to god, but who are really only potent in their relationship to hell. *Breaking The Waves* shows us what this internal hell is like for Big Bess, and the path of the film shows us the elements of her personality that need to be gathered together in the process of individuation: a relationship to the body – particularly the sexual body; a highly problematic but promising relationship to the masculine which has been split into loving and hating parts; a forcing through at the very end of a relationship to the good caring maternal function acting in its own right rather than imprisoned and silenced by abusive masculine power; and a terrible ripping apart and letting go of the caretaker self at the end.

In *Breaking The Waves* von Trier delivers an extraordinary study of what it means to be human and to have to relate to oneself and to others. It shows the results of trauma, and the terrible process of recovery from it. With Bess's comment 'I thought he might be better now' we are confronted with the impotence of our conscious will when faced with such damage. The recovery of Jan is a metaphor for the recovery of Big Bess – we don't know how she'll get on and what kind of further recovery she will have; but we do know that she has suffered extremely, and in a heartbreaking way. I really don't know if I like this film. 'Like' seems the entirely wrong word. It moves me deeply every time I watch it, and I treat it with respect, like I might treat a dangerous implement – it's a kind of chainsaw of a film. My reading of it in this chapter as an account of a single personality is only one view; there are others, such as a focus on the feminine, the position of being a woman, and my anti-realism perspective is at a tangent to what von Trier said he was trying to do. The greatness of *Breaking The Waves*, however, is that it can survive different readings and will go on to stimulate many more.

References

Almodóvar, P. (2006). *Volver*. Spain: Canal+ España.
Hewison, D. (2000). Loving the alien? A response to John Izod's Active imagination and the analysis of film. *Journal of Analytical Psychology*, 45(2), 287–293.
Hewison, D. (2003). 'Oh rose thou art sick!' Anti-individuation forces in the film *American Beauty*. *Journal of Analytical Psychology*, 48, 683–704.
Hewison, D. (2009). Power vs. love in sadomasochistic couple relationships. In C. Clulow (ed.), *Sex, Attachment and Couple Psychotherapy* (pp. 165–184). London: Karnac.

Izod, J. (2000). Active imagination and the analysis of film. *Journal of Analytical Psychology*, *45*(2), 267–285.

Izod, J. (2006). *Screen, Culture, Psyche: A Post-Jungian Approach to Working with the Audience*. Hove: Routledge.

Jung, C. G. (1928/1964). The spiritual problem of modern man. In *CW10, Civilisation in Transition*. London: Routledge & Kegan Paul.

Jung, C. G. (1934). *The Development of Personality*, London: Routledge & Kegan Paul.

Mendes, S. (1999). *American Beauty*. USA: DreamWorks SKG.

von Trier, L. (1996). *Breaking the Waves*. London: Faber & Faber.

Waddell, T. (2006). *Mis/takes: Archetypes, Myth and Identity in Screen Fiction*. Hove: Routledge.

Chapter 3

Love, loss, imagination and the 'other' in Soderbergh's *Solaris*

Andre Zanardo

Solaris is a sophisticated, multilayered art piece which – like other great psychologically orientated science fiction films (*2001*, *Blade Runner*, *Dark City*, *Stalker*) – deconstructs our notions of reality, knowing, desire and control. Andrei Tarkovsky's original 1972 film placed considerable emphasis on the complex philosophical, scientific and conceptual ideas contained within the book by Stanislav Lem. Steven Soderbergh's 2002 adaptation, however, principally elaborates a story of love, unrequited loss and the attempts made to redeem or transform ourselves through relationship. It is this contemporary version I will be examining throughout this chapter.

In what follows, I aim to highlight contemporary post-Jungian themes of 'otherness' and becoming 'undone'. I also focus on ongoing psychic self-emergence through encountering loss, lack and absence in relation to another, and the difference between true and false imagination. I argue that unless we embrace these themes and are prepared to truly open ourselves to another, to mourn our losses and lacks, we forestall individuation and cannot break out of a predominantly narcissistic way of living nor genuinely engage relationally with others.

Having outlined the story of *Solaris*, I will elaborate these theoretical positions using the nuanced images, dialogue and relational dynamics of the two main characters, Kris and Rheya, in order to highlight what can happen to us as individuals should we fail to embrace these themes.

Solaris, the film

Gibarian is the mission leader and chief scientist on a space station orbiting the planet Solaris. He has travelled there to study the planet in greater detail as it appeared from observations made from earth that Solaris somehow knew it was being studied. One day, a colleague and friend to Gibarian, Kris Kelvin (George Clooney), receives a confusing and disturbing message from Gibarian, asking him to come to the station. Kris, a psychologist, has been unable to genuinely mourn the suicide of his wife some two years earlier. Gibarian's message is precisely directed to Kris, as if hinting that he knows Kris needs to experience what is happening on the station. Perhaps it could provide answers for Kris as to his deep melancholy, and offer a possible way forward psychologically. Gibarian implores Kris to come to Solaris to 'see for himself' thus inviting Kris to experience what is occurring on the station. Gibarian's comments refer to inexplicable phenomena on the space station orbiting Solaris where his perception and construction of reality and self have been disturbingly questioned. Solaris has been affecting the crew by revealing their deep unconscious desires and memories in apparent hallucinations, later called 'visitations'. These have caused the death of some crew members and left others with many inexplicable experiences.

The distorted and pixilated image of Gibarian after completion of his message to Kris expresses graphically Gibarian's confusion and fractured sense of self, and offers the viewer an impending sense of what is to come for Kris as he embarks on this disturbing mission. Kris, who has existed in a state of despair, imprisoned in the agony and incomprehensibility of his loneliness since his wife Rheya's death, accepts the invitation. He knows he needs to change the psychologically numbing routine of his daily existence which amounts to a depressed withdrawal from a world in which he feels no joy or meaning. He is aware that he has been defending himself from the intensity of his grief and genuine emotion over not only the loss of Rheya but also confusion and guilt over his part in their relationship breakdown.

As the spacecraft carrying Kris approaches the station, we are privy to the majesty of the planet. It is shrouded in what appears to be mist, a mist that imbues the viewer with a sense of its mystery and power. Long, synaptic or vein-like lines parry their way across the surface of the planet. Upon setting foot inside the station, Kris's anxiety is heightened when he sees blood on the landing, discovers Gibarian is dead and sees Gibarian's young son running away. Unable to explain what he sees, Kris is now even more alone and anxious as he begins to experience the inexplicable. He encounters Snow (Jeremy Davies), one of only two remaining crew members, sitting in his room. With an authoritarian tone in his voice, Kris asks: 'Can you tell me what is happening here?' to which Snow answers: 'Well, I could tell you what is happening here but I don't know if that would tell you what is happening.' Kris also meets Gordon (Viola Davis) who begins to cut across Kris's authoritarian tone by insisting she

Solaris: Love, loss, imagination, the 'other' 51

Figure 3.1 Kris arriving on Solaris (20th Century Fox/The Kobal Collection/Bob Marshak).

won't talk about what is happening until it starts to happen to him. Only then may he engage with the crew emotionally and empathetically, rather than just intellectually as if he was still in a position of control.

Initially, Kris is deeply sceptical and the egocentric 'expert' in his character interprets the phenomena reductively as 'merely psychological', and thus explainable – that is, until they begin to manifest for him personally. Gibarian's intuition that Kris needed to go to Solaris was correct, for as soon as Kris falls asleep – that is, a state of mind where his conscious ego cannot control events – he begins to experience visitations from Rheya, and with these, his deep desire for her return. Initially, it is not clear whether Rheya appears to Kris in a dream or in waking reality. The viewer, along with Kris, is therefore faced with having to determine what is real and what is delusional or wishful thinking. Kris is forced to encounter the power of his own desire for a return to a past that is different, and how – in this current intermediate space – he is constructing that past as if it was the present.

The film then takes us on a journey into the relationship between Kris and Rheya before her suicide, shifting seamlessly between past, present and future. It explores the psychodynamics of each character's state of mind leading up to this devastating event, and the 'present' relationship as both come to grips with the realities of their imagination, and the new possibilities between them. We are privy to the shifts in power between them as each suffers their own desperations and desires. The film especially highlights the intensity of Kris's trauma as we see him desperately trying to return to and reconstruct the past, realising, eventually, he cannot undo what has been done or redeem what has been lost.

Jung, relationality, 'otherness' and becoming undone

Carl Jung was at the forefront of developing analysis as a relational dynamic between patient and analyst. Jung stated that analysis is 'dialectical' and demanded the analyst as a person 'participates just as much as the patient' (Jung 1966: para. 239). Jung famously stated that:

> For two personalities to meet is like mixing two different chemical substances: if there is any combination at all, both are transformed. In any effective psychological treatment the doctor is bound to influence the patient; but this influence can only take place if the patient has a reciprocal influence on the doctor. You can exert no influence if you are not susceptible to influence.
>
> (Jung 1966: para. 163)

Jung also saw the opposite of relationship as power: 'Where love [relationship] stops, power begins' (Jung 1990: para. 580). Jung's attitude toward the importance of the relational aspects of an encounter with an Other, along with its unique interdependent, mutually influential and emergent qualities, placed him as a forerunner to more contemporary theories on love, relationship, 'otherness', loss and the power of the imagination.

Without the conscious experience and integration of one's losses, lacks, terrifying abandonments and defensive projections of demand and desire, we are not in a position to know the profound transformative effects of love (and potentially hate), loving and being loved. We are also unable to operate at 'a fully symbolic level of mental functioning [where] a rich network of thoughts, desires, beliefs, fears can be explored and related to for their own sakes not primarily to evoke an action or emotional response in the other' (Knox 2007: p. 554). Without more consciously experiencing our losses and developing a symbolic mental functioning, we are essentially locked into a defensive and or aggressive need for power and control, out of which we continuously use others as objects in order to narcissistically achieve our own ends and self gratification. Thus, essential aspects of self – as an ongoing emergent psychic and relational experience – are disavowed. Central to contemporary Jungian theory is the experience of self as a relational, emergent and constantly evolving multilayered phenomenon, much as Knox, a contemporary developmental Jungian analyst, describes above. If we fail, we become caught in a limited egocentric view of self and remain, as it were, alien to ourselves. In the film *Solaris*, it is from this (through his relationship with Rheya), that Kris is attempting to redeem himself, but it is in this that he catastrophically fails.

The term 'intersubjectivity' is used to describe the way different people's subjective realities are relationally engaged. Psychoanalytically, it has been defined by Benjamin as 'the specific matter of recognizing the other as an equivalent centre of being' (1999: p. 201). Butler (2003), as a cultural theorist who has addressed the relational identity of self, challenges us to think and experience ourselves and 'other' in even more expansive terms. Soderbergh's version of *Solaris* helps us to highlight Butler's themes of the potential transformative effects of being in relationship with, and loss of, an-other. In love, relationship and loss, she states how 'one mourns when one accepts that by the loss one undergoes one will be changed, possibly forever. Perhaps mourning has to do with agreeing to undergo a transformation (perhaps one should say *submitting* to a transformation) the full result of which one cannot know in advance' (Butler 2003: p. 11). She goes on to say that 'when one loses, one is also faced with something enigmatic: something is hiding in the loss, something is lost within the recesses of loss' (ibid.: p. 12). 'Let's face it,' she continues, 'we're undone by each other. And if we're not, we're missing something' (ibid.: p. 13).

Similarities exist between Butler's ideas of mourning, loss, submission and transformation and classical Jungian ideas of how the ego must submit to and be in relation with the unconscious. The result of this relational dynamic cannot be known in advance but is expressed in a new creation, that of the symbolic image, via the transcendent function. The personality is then potentially changed and individuation progressed. Thus progression is as a result of 'undoing' any rigidities of the ego structure as we have known it, allowing an expansion of consciousness as the more enigmatic aspects of our unconscious manifest.

Kris's narcissistic position

The poet Rilke, metaphorically and disturbingly, describes a similar 'undoing-ness' as Butler but uses the term 'beauty' as its mechanism. He writes: 'Beauty is nothing/but the beginning of terror we can just barely endure and we admire it so because it calmly disdains to destroy us. Every angel is terrible' (cited in Cobb 1982: p. 132). We can see some of Rilke's notions of beauty portrayed in the character of Rheya as seen through the eyes of Kris. It seems to me that the loss of the 'beautiful' Rheya, as 'other', has destroyed Kris psychologically. He has been dramatically affected by what he perceives as 'his' loss of Rheya yet has not been able to comprehend anything of the enigmatic which may lay hidden in the loss. He has also been unable to bring himself to understand and experience the greater transformative process of being 'undone' in and through his relationship with her. Kris has conducted 'his' relationship – consciously or not – from a position of narcissistic power through a refusal to be undone and is thus not truly open to the other or available to be influenced by them in any substantial way. For Kris, Rheya has been an object to mirror his own cool, self-confident image. Kris has unconsciously used Rheya as an object of self-gratification with no appreciation of Rheya as a separate being who by being in relationship with him may 'undo' him. The actual relationship has been rooted in the process and dynamics of maintaining an illusion of self-control. In essence, therefore, there was no actual relationship, merely power relations and the maintenance of an already known egocentric identity. We are, in fact, told this in another context early in the film when Gibarian states: 'Our enthusiasm is a sham; we are not interested in other worlds; we want mirrors.'

Warren Coleman, a contemporary developmental and relational Jungian analyst, briefly summarized the Greek myth of Uranos, Chronos and Zeus in his paper on tyrannical omnipotence (Coleman 2000: p. 524). In this myth, Chronos's wife was called Rheya but spelt as Rhea. Chronos, following on from his father Uranos, ate all his children before they could overthrow him. Rhea, however, outwitted Chronos by substituting a stone for her son Zeus who later forces his father to vomit up the other children who later become the Greek pantheon of Gods. Rhea was one of the significant female protagonists, along with Gaia and Hera, who were able to frustrate the omnipotent powers and pretensions of their husbands. During the progression of the film we see how Rheya undoes Kris's omnipotent pretensions – albeit without malice – as the power dynamic shifts in her favour.

In addition to the above, I interpret Rheya as also seeking to transform a wounded, isolated and fragile sense of identity. Despite her initial confidence, she experiences a sense of self that is unrecognized for its own worth. In Kris, Rheya sees the opportunity to try and rectify early significant relationships that have failed to develop or facilitate a more potent sense of interdependent self-agency. Rheya's fragility of self is graphically highlighted in her terror at the felt separation and abandonment by Kris. In this sense, Kris and Rheya are a co-dependent, narcissistic couple, each reflecting the other's needs to get access to a kind of self redemption.

Power relations and the assertion of control

From the beginning, the film highlights, with deft subtlety, the early attraction, curiosity and desire Kris and Rheya have for one another. In one of Kris's reconstructed memories of the past, they are sitting opposite one another on a train, when both have their desires aroused by a short but unbroken gaze without a word being spoken. The attraction is noted as mutual. Rheya gets off the train, leaving a hint of seduction and intrigue in the mind of Kris. The space 'in-between' them and their respective conscious and unconscious minds has been filled with an imaginary fantasy of the other. However, from this point, any psychic self-emergence and transformation through an intersubjective relationship with one another is disavowed through the actions of Kris. How does this happen?

Solaris reveals how Kris and Rheya first meet 'officially' when attending a party hosted by Gibarian. As Kris arrives, both notice and recognize one another. Rheya has a restrained and subtle excitement in her eye at the prospect of meeting Kris and expects to have her desire at least acknowledged. Kris, however, noting the eye contact, walks past Rheya without acknowledging her and with an heir of suave self-confidence and aloofness. One senses he refuses to bring himself to meet her on any terms other than his own because to do so would be to place himself in a position of potential vulnerability and 'subject-to-ness' out of the safe control of his emotions. Rheya immediately feels the sting of Kris's lack of attention and the loss of his previous desire and connection. She feels rejected, and, in a sense, she has been.

Rheya is, nevertheless, prepared to give Kris another chance. Kris, in fact, has sensed the potential for sexual gratification and possible conquest. He goes to approach Rheya near the bar. Rheya knows he's approaching, but again Kris walks straight past to the bar. In that moment, any possibility of a genuine relational exchange – where one can be seen as an equivalent centre of being (a person) – has given way to the dynamics of power and seduction. Kris approaches and they stay silent, looking at each other. Rheya opens with: 'Don't blow it.'

More silence. 'You start,' adds Kris, to which Rheya responds: 'I already did.' An egocentric game of power and control is on! A little later we see, beautifully articulated, just how subtle narcissistic non-intersubjective power dynamics can be. Still early in their relationship – having just made love and being naked in their romanticized desires, expectations and sentimental early exposures to one another – Rheya, in her attempts to be understood and genuinely engaged, speaks to Kris about how her mother, whom we are told was genuinely 'certifiable', would only communicate with Rheya via Rheya's imaginary friend Michachelli. In presenting to Kris intimate, vulnerable and previously unmet parts of herself, Rheya is allowing these wounded, painful and disavowed aspects to be potentially utilized and reconstructed in more expansive, healthy and less defensive relational terms. A potential 'recycling', as Jungian analyst Giles Clark (2006: p. 81) describes it, of these parts of herself for better emotional and relational use may occur through being emotionally met by Kris. However, in Kris's playful response – 'Well, you have come to the right place' – he asserts and inserts the power of his persona as the psychological expert into the creative 'in between' space that both, especially Rheya, are trying to develop. No 'recycling' can take place for either of them.

This dynamic is reinforced again and again. At a dinner with Kris's friends, Rheya's attempts to join them relationally in conversation are silenced. An excessive intellectualism by the friends (Rheya is being spoken at, told and not related to or engaged) is re-experienced as not being heard. This threatens to overwhelm her and she retreats into a silent defensive disengagement. Soderbergh in the editing shows this by having a series of silent frames, from Rheya's perspective, in which we see Kris talking at Rheya with no sound being heard. Rheya has blocked what is perceived to be an attack on her by refusing to hear what is being said, thus creating the very thing she is trying to free herself from – being unheard. Later on, she attacks Kris with the comment: 'I hate those fucking people', after which Kris, equally furious and indignant, walks out. Both Kris's narcissistic power and Rheya's wounded positions are becoming entrenched. A dangerous form of 'shadowy' power is reaffirmed from which Rheya eventually has to take radical action in order to release herself. In Jungian psychology, the shadow equates to, most simply, 'the thing a person has no wish to be' (Jung 1966: para. 470) and often 'forms an unconscious snag, thwarting our most well meant intentions' (Jung 1958: para. 131). In more relational terms, it is vital and vitalizing for us as individuals to form a working relationship with the 'shadow' as an inner 'other' of ourselves in order to try and reduce the degree of projection placed onto a real 'other' that is 'You'. This is one way to develop and expand our personality and consciousness.

In the above situation, the other can only be seen in terms of self as opposed to being genuinely different. What each may seek to transform and/or redeem in themselves as a result of being *in* relationship (as opposed to power) with an-other has now been locked into a form of continuing unconscious 'exile' from self. Eros as the principle of relationship, and of relating, has been sidelined to a process of self-protection, power and control, the opposite of what was initially desired when they first met.

Mourning loss and the possibility of redemption

Bayley provides us with a definition of redemption which is relevant to our themes here:

> The expression "redeemed" has always possessed among mystics a meaning somewhat different from that which popularly obtains. Redemption was believed to be not an act of unconditional mercy or an immediate losing of one's guilty stains . . . but rather a gradual and progressive process, a slow growth and expression of man's spiritual faculties . . . If this said sacrifice is to avail for me, it must be wrought *in* me.
>
> (Bayley 1951: p. 40–41)

The implication of his definition is that one must consciously suffer the losses (the sacrifice must be wrought in me) that 'undo' and disorder our sense of ourselves if we are to try to recover the enigma hidden in the recesses of our losses. Perhaps this enigma is an experience of the ineffable mysterious reality of 'other' which provides the potential for development of one's spiritual faculties. It is not just that we experience these losses; this is a fact of life. It is more what we do with these experiences, how we recycle them or, perhaps more appropriately, what the experiences *do with us*. Paradoxically, it would seem that the more we cling onto this delusion of control and attempt to return back to the metaphoric 'garden of Eden', unaffected by internal and external reality, the less control we actually seem to have. However, the more we consciously suffer the reality of our losses and lacks, the more we redeem ourselves back from an exiled unfamiliarity with ourselves and can participate more fully in the ongoing process of psychic self-emergence.

Naturally, this is dependent on the extent of one's early traumatic experiences of loss, lack and absence. Clark highlights that it is 'psychically unrealistic to expect to transform a position of fundamental fear, disappointment and impotent anger at unmet primary needs into a healthy acquiescence based on trust' (2006: p. 68). However, most of us do not suffer that level of psychic disturbance and can benefit greatly from experiencing what the psychoanalyst Michael Eigen so strikingly describes as the way in which 'we must learn to kill ourselves without end without doing ourselves real injury. We discover ways of killing ourselves that makes us better people' (2001: p. 138).

If we can feel 'the pain of too much tenderness, and to be wounded by your own understanding of love' (Gibran 1980: p. 14), then we can encounter what it means to be undone by an-other, especially those we love. If so, we can engage in a more conscious killing of our egocentric selves, in order to be better people. We do this to not just 'seek mirrors' as Gibarian warns, but to facilitate growth into and encounters with the terror and beauty of an ongoing dialogue with the unknown so as not to forestall individuation. One way to engage in this is to develop, through loss and mourning, an imaginal symbolic capacity.

The imaginary and failing to develop a symbolic experience

While on earth, Kris is in emotional control, or at least he thinks he is. Even in his grief, Kris has refused to give up control in order to genuinely engage with the loss of Rheya. Being anchored in a rational and conscious approach to his grief, expressed metaphorically as still being on earth, Kris does not begin to become genuinely undone until he arrives at the space station, which serves also as a metaphor for an in-between space, a space that is neither fully conscious nor unconscious.

In his paper entitled 'Imagination and the imaginary', Warren Coleman states:

> Real imagination depends on the capacity to acknowledge the absence of what is imagined from the world of material actuality . . . The imaginary is contrasted with this as a defensive misuse of imagination that attempts to deny negation where negation is defined as all those aspects of the world that constitute a check to the omnipotence of fantasy – e.g. absence, loss, difference, otherness, etc.
>
> (Coleman 2006: p. 21)

He goes on to add that:

> Patients in the grip of the imaginary often cling to their fantasies with maniacal force since to give them up would expose them to unbearably painful experiences of absence or loss that may amount to the fear of annihilation. Like Narcissus, their archetypal antecedent, they would often rather die than give up the enchantment of their illusions.
>
> (ibid: p. 23)

Noel Cobb describes

> false imagination as being shot through with fear. It makes no leaps [or too many]. It turns its back on the Unknown and shuts its eyes to the weird creatures of the soul [whereas] True Imagination [is] fearless, is infinitely more mutable and absolutely precise. Its immaculate beauty brings a shiver down to the roots . . . in the end the Imagination places a great responsibility upon us. The image demands a greater morality than that with which we have been content.
>
> (1982: p. 131; see also Corbin 1972, Hillman 1979,
> Kugler 1997, Samuels 1985 and Salman 2006 for
> further in-depth discussion on images and
> the use of imagination)

Clearly by the end of the film we see Kris 'shot through with fear' and 'shivering down to his roots'.

Two questions are now pertinent to the discussion: has Kris constructed an imaginary reality on the station orbiting Solaris, thus defending himself from his losses much as Coleman and Cobb describe, or has a real imaginal symbolic image finally appeared, helping him to facilitate an emergent psychic experience and thus integrate his losses and potentially grasp the implications and transformative effects of the 'immaculate beauty' in the imaginal symbolic experience of Rheya? Perhaps both have occurred.

It seems to me that Kris has been caught in an imaginary experience where his denial of Rheya's loss, his 'negation of negation', and his desperate clinging to 'figuring it out' as a means to prevent the experience of her actual loss, has prevented him from genuinely mourning. It has also prevented him from converting the appearance of an image into a symbolic experience of Rheya. According to Coleman: 'Whereas true imagination has a reality of its own that enhances our being in the world, the imaginary is a misuse of imagination for the purpose of denying everything that opposes the subject's desire' (Coleman 200: p. 23). As the imaginal or true imagination is constructive, real and symbolic, when 'imagination strays and is wasted recklessly, when it ceases to fulfill its function of perceiving and producing the symbols that lead to inner intelligence, the [imaginal world] . . . may be considered to have disappeared' (Corbin 1972: p. 14). Kris has been caught in exactly this.

Gibarian warns Kris of exactly this negation. In a 'visitation', Gibarian (who we know is dead) tells Kris that it is futile to try to resolve what is happening on Solaris. 'If you keep trying to figure it out, you will die here,' says Gibarian, as 'there are no answers, Kris, only choices.' Kris thinks that to figure it out is to fix or solve his problem, that is, he wants to negate his losses and to reassert an egocentric omnipotent sense of control, as he had felt prior to Rheya's death. He desires this, rather than to do what he is really there to do, which is to understand and psychologically transform his own internal trauma through greater insight and integration of the losses he has suffered.

A self-conscious, re-birthed Rheya pleads with Kris to let her go because, she says, 'I'm not Rheya.' She is aware they cannot exist in any place other than in the intermediate place of the station above Solaris – a

Figure 3.2 Rheya and Kris, with Rheya examining her hand (20th Century Fox/The Kobal Collection/Bob Marshak).

metaphor for being inside Kris's tenuous imaginary construction of her. Gordon, who – as discussed earlier – had refused to speak with Kris until he had had 'visitations' himself, also tries to break through Kris's delusion when she angrily highlights to him that on the station, under the affective influence of Solaris, Rheya is 'a mirror that reflects part of your mind; you provide the formula . . . she's a copy, a facsimile . . . and your wife is dead.' But Kris refuses to accept it as he continues trying to reaffirm his delusion that he can comprehend what has transpired and so redeem himself of his loss and his guilt for abandoning her on earth.

So in answer to the questions posed above – that is, are Kris's experiences imaginary or of the imaginal realm – I believe Kris, in letting his imagination stray by reinforcing Rheya as an imaginary reality, lost the opportunity to utilize her appearance as a truly imaginal symbolic experience and thus to further his own psychic self-emergence and his 'inner intelligence', as Corbin states. Kris has enacted exactly what Coleman highlighted above. That is, he has clung to his illusions with maniacal force in order to avoid the actual unbearable pain of Rheya's loss to such an extent that he would rather die than give up his illusion. His imagination was wasted. To put this another way, whether an image is imaginary or of the imagination depends in large measure on our attitude toward it and what we then do with it; how we utilize and relate to it.

The final descent

Approximately two-thirds of the way through the film, Rheya becomes conscious that she is not her original self and is an imaginary construct of Kris's mind. After this point, there is a dramatic quickening of Kris's undoing as he loses power over her. In the early part of the film, it was Rheya seeking a way through Kris's egocentric position to find a mutuality in love. However, by the end of the film, it is now Kris desperately trying to find a way through in order to prevent Rheya from abandoning him. 'But am I really Rheya?' she asks, to which Kris, with a genuinely open and soft vulnerability, replies: 'I don't know any more, all I see is you . . . all I see is you.' And again, toward the end of this scene, Kris, in desperately trying to convince Rheya to stay, says: 'It's what we have . . . it's enough for me.' At this point we can see Kris is, to an extent, undone, as he articulates the very thing Rheya desperately needed to experience in Kris before her suicide, on earth. Rheya needed to feel loved, accepted and related to as an equivalent centre of being redeemed into her own self-agency as a distinct other, separate yet interdependent.

Unfortunately, it is now too late and by the end of the film Kris still chooses to negate his losses by reinforcing an imaginary position.

The viewer is set up and led into the penultimate emotional scene where Kris, in a near psychotic state on the station, is remembering returning home on earth to find Rheya has committed suicide. However, just before this scene, the re-imagined Rheya on the station again offers Kris a point of entry into the symbolic experience of her in her death. Having had herself 'killed' by Gordon on the station (a metaphor expressing her ability to undo herself consciously), she sends Kris a message. In it, she pleads with Kris to let her go:

> It's better this way ... I found the suicide note ... the page torn from the book of poems and I realised I am not her ... I'm not Rheya ... I know you loved me though ... I know that ... I felt that and I love you ... I wish we could just live inside that feeling forever; maybe there is a place where we can but I know it's not on earth and it's not on this ship. That's all I can say right now.

In articulating her love of him in such a way that he feels 'the pain of too much tenderness' and in explaining that he has to let her go, she offers him a pathway to a truly imaginative consciousness by being able to develop a symbolic experience of her through her death. Rheya, as a symbolic image, could now exist in an imaginal world, ever present and real in her actual absence. As a symbolic image she would not fade from memory but continue to inform his memory and creatively develop his future.

Soderbergh reinforces this sentiment when, as Kris weeps and holds Rheya, having returned to discover her dead, we cut to a copy of the Dylan Thomas poem crumpled in Rheya's lifeless hand. We see the final few words: 'Though they go mad they shall be sane, though they sink through the sea they shall rise again, though lovers be lost love shall not, and death shall have no dominion.' In the beginning of the film, Kris played with these words as a tool of seduction and erotic egocentric manipulation without understanding their meaning. Now, however, he is brought face to face with their symbolic power to transform his ongoing relationship with Rheya in her death. Here is the moment of redemption if only he can grasp it. Kris could have chosen to leave the station with Gordon and return to earth; however he doesn't, instead choosing to dwell in the delusion of a life with Rheya. In failing to grasp the moment of redemption, he is then doomed to death, as the actual space station descends into being totally consumed by Solaris. Kris is also overwhelmed by his doubt and unable to answer what has haunted him: 'That somehow he had remembered her wrong and that he had been wrong about everything.'

The closing scene sees Kris reunited with Rheya. He asks Rheya, who is now back with him on an imaginary earth: 'Am I dead or alive?' to which Rheya answers: 'We don't have to think like that anymore, we're together now, everything we've done is forgiven ... everything.' In his delusion, he completes an imaginary self-redemption by having all his 'sins' forgiven, but this can only happen in his actual death, for he has not been able to suffer the losses needed to transform himself in life in order to go on living. 'Otherness' and the radical position it affords us in love was not able to be taken up by Kris. He remains caught in the delusion of his own ego consciousness, trapped in a false imagination, the imaginary thrall of his narcissism, even though towards the end of the film this is drastically diminished. In not offering Rheya recognition for herself as an equivalent 'centre of being', he has forestalled his own self-development and failed to see a bigger picture which could 'solicit a becoming, to instigate a transformation, to petition the future always in relation to the "other" ' (Butler 2003: p. 31). He has also failed to grasp that 'the humanity of consciousness is definitely not in its powers, but in its responsibility: in passivity, in reception, in obligation with regard to the other. It is the other who is first, and there the question of my sovereign consciousness is no longer the first question' (Levinas 1991: p. 112). Any sense of mutual intersubjective psychic emergence into relational being was lost. Had he been able to become consciously 'undone', he might have been able to experience more of what was 'lost within the recesses of loss', or, as Eigen puts it:

> What does not exist is the you I say you are, the me you want me to be. My version of you does not cover the territory. What you say about you does not either [. . .] It is precisely the you I don't know that makes the you I know bearable [. . .] What counts more than knowing is the *Ein Sopf* of you, the unknowable, indefinable You. Always, the inexhaustible Mystery.
>
> (Eigen 1998: p 150)

Conclusion

Soderbergh's *Solaris* is a masterly piece of minimalist science fiction film-making. It does not descend into idealized sentimentality, provide easy solutions or attempt to moralize. Soderbergh has used enormous restraint with dialogue and rhythm, colour and sound. In so doing, he has created a beautifully textural, multilayered 'in-between' space, where the viewer can explore deep questions of reality and the construction of themselves in and through their most intimate relationships and desires.

For me, *Solaris* – via the personal story of love and loss between Kris and Rheya – presents us with a radical contemporary plea for a deeper and more expansive relational engagement with the mystery of the world through the other and through many others. For if 'the shadow of death falls on every separation and in a broad but very real sense growing up is learning how to mourn – of experiencing real loss and of tolerating the pain and disorganization, in which lies the possibility of renewal' (Hobson 1974: p.79), then perhaps Solaris in its most simple form is also a request for more of us to mature beyond our limiting egocentric selves. With greater mourning and integration of loss, lack and absence, we may be able to, as Sue Austin, a Jungian analyst working in the areas of gender and identity, says, 'go back to our own undoings and shatterings, discovering them over and over through the patterns of our desires [and then] . . . see how they arrange us, and how they create us anew in different circumstances, and in different relationships.' (Austin 2009: p. 595). In other words, we may develop a capacity to love others, and therefore ourselves, more expansively, move beyond a limiting narcissism and, through relationship, enter into a deeply imaginative, symbolic and richly lived experience of the world.

References

Austin, S. (2009) Jung's dissociable psyche and the ec-static self. *Journal of Analytical Psychology*, 54, 581–599.

Bayley, H. (1951) *The Lost Language of Symbolism*. New York: Barnes and Noble.

Benjamin, J. (1999) Afterword. In S.R. Mitchell and L. Aron (eds), *Recognition and Destruction* in *Relational Psychoanalysis: The Emergence of a Tradition*. Hillsdale, NJ: The Analytic Press.

Butler, J. (2003) Violence, mourning, politics. *Studies in Gender and Sexuality*, 4(1), 9–37.

Clark, G. (2006) A Spinozan lens onto the confusions of borderline relations. *Journal of Analytical Psychology*, 51, 67–86.

Cobb, N. (1982) Imagination: Image and epiphany. *Harvest: Journal for Jungian Studies*, 28, 130–145.

Coleman, W. (2000) Tyrannical omnipotence in the archetypal father. *Journal of Analytical Psychology*, 45(4), 521–539.

—— (2006) Imagination and the imaginary. *Journal of Analytical Psychology*, *51*, 21–41.
Corbin, H. (1972) *Mundus Imaginalis* or the imaginary and the imaginal. *Spring*, 1–19.
Eigen, M. (1998) *The Psychoanalytic Mystic*. London: Free Association Books.
—— (2001) *Damaged Bonds*. London: Karnac Books.
Gibran, K. (1980) *The Prophet*. London: William Heineman Ltd.
Hillman, J. (1979) Image-Sense. *Spring*, 130–143.
Hobson, R. (1974) Loneliness. *Journal of Analytical Psychology*, *19*(1), 71–89.
Jung, C. G. (1958) *Psychology and Religion: West and East* (Second Edition), *Collected Works 11*. London: Routledge and Kegan Paul Ltd.
—— (1966) *The Practice of Psychotherapy, Collected Works 16*. Princeton, NJ: Princeton University Press.
—— (1990) *The Undiscovered Self with Symbols and the Interpretation of Dreams*. Princeton: Princeton University Press.
Knox, J. (2007) The fear of love: The denial of self in relationship. *Journal of Analytical Psychology*, *52*(5), 543–563.
Kugler, P. (1997) Psychic imaging: A bridge between subject and object. In P. Young-Eisendrath and T. Dawson (eds), *The Cambridge Companion to Jung*. Cambridge: Cambridge University Press.
Levinas, E. (1991) *Entre Nous: On Thinking-of-the-Other* (M. Smith and B. Harshav, Trans.). London: Athlone.
Salman, S. (2006) True Imagination. *Spring 74, Alchemy: A Journal of Archetype and Culture*, 175–187.
Samuels, A. (1985) Countertransference, the mundus imaginalis and a research project. *Journal of Analytical Psychology*, *30*, 47–71.
Soderbergh, S. (2002) *Solaris*. Los Angeles, CA: 20th Century Fox.

Chapter 4

Birth
Eternal grieving of the spotless mind

John Izod and Joanna Dovalis

Most summary plotlines of *Birth* state that Anna, a 35-year-old woman who has been widowed for ten years, is on the point of remarrying when a boy comes to her apartment and announces that he is her former husband. In line with this précis, discussions among writers who have taken Jonathan Glazer's film as seriously as it merits tend to have given primacy of focus to Nicole Kidman's Anna. In privileging this character they are responding to cues latent in the text (some obvious, others less so). To mention the most obvious, the emotionally wracking predicament that afflicts the lissom widow is an inevitable source of narrative interest when a leading film star is playing that protagonist.

David Lowery (2004) remarks of Anna's grieving, 'If you look at this as the story of a woman who comes to believe her husband has been reincarnated, you are only seeing half of the film; you're missing the story of a woman realizing just how much she loved her husband, and how damaged her loss has left her.' We contend, however, that the boy's story has equal thematic weight with Anna's. Not that the mystery surrounding the claims of ten-year-old Sean to be Anna's dead husband has been ignored. On the contrary, it has been considered extensively because the narrative thrust bears on the plausibility or otherwise of his claim. However, the intense experience that the boy undergoes has been insufficiently understood. Questions that have been largely disregarded include why a child should make such a claim in the first place; why (resolutely defying the outrage of his elders) he should stick with it courageously; and why he should then suddenly give it up.

The first words (heard in darkness before light hits the screen) are a lecturer repudiating the idea of reincarnation: 'I'm a man of science. I just don't believe that mumbo-jumbo.' This is Anna's husband Sean (Michael Desautels), who has framed his response in a mock scenario the irony of which echoes through the film. 'Let me say this: If I lost my wife and the next day a little bird landed on my windowsill, looked me right in the eye and in plain English said, 'Sean, it's me, Anna: I'm back.' What can I say? I guess I'd believe her. Or I'd want to . . . I'd be stuck with the bird!'

The opening shot establishes a register at odds with Sean's complacent sarcasm. As he jogs through the wintry gloaming of Manhattan's Central Park, the Steadicam glides after him, not at eye level but about twenty feet above the snow-covered path. The shot continues without a cut for a long minute and a half while the man moves forward resolutely. At the screen's periphery, dim lights, vehicles and apartments bear witness to the city's life, but at such a distance that the runner is isolated by the snowfields around him, the absence of other people in the park and the camera's vicarious eye. That unblinking gaze insists on the actuality of what it shows while simultaneously abstracting it from reality via the gliding overhead view of the runner's back. But the black-clad and hooded man, a shadow figure if ever there was one, is brutishly anchored to the earth as he labours onward. The effect of trailing him is like attempting flight that cannot quite break free from Earth. The aesthetics carry this tension. As Darren Hughes (2006) notes, it is barely colour photography at all, but predominantly blacks, greys and browns. On the soundtrack, Alexandre Desplat's Prelude propels movement. Flutes and bells sparkle sweetly over jabs of brass like metronomes that insist on time's passage, while sombre, spreading strings mark out the symphonic scale of what is to come.

Like other commentators (for example Hughes, 2006; Chaw, 2004, whom the opening shot reminds of the labyrinth sequence in *The Shining*; and Lowery, 2004) we notice resemblances to Kubrick's work. These are particularly marked in the establishment of a register comparable to *Eyes Wide Shut*. As Izod has written elsewhere, both films offer a take on the New York world that they project which embraces both expressionist fantasy and observable reality. Shimmying between the rational and the fantastic, neither film locks into either mode to the exclusion of the other (2006: 52).

Tension between contraries becomes explicit when the title *Birth* is superimposed on the second shot as Sean runs towards an underpass. Reaching it (silhouetted to stress his isolation), he staggers, collapses and dies. The short tunnel has, reasonably enough, been likened to both womb and tomb (Cozzalio, 2006). In evoking the birth canal it provides an image of a transitional space creating movement from one reality to another. However, the final shot of this sequence pulls back to reveal that Sean has fallen beneath a bridge. It makes an obvious emblem for connection; and in retrospect we can see that thematically Sean could not have crossed over since he has given up on maintaining emotional connection. More immediately, the bridge underscores the thematic relevance of the next shot (explicitly connecting contraries) in which a baby is born. Death before birth. Glazer conjoins the opposing termini of life on earth in an order that reverses orthodox secular understanding. The more familiar conventions show the individual as a singular physical being existing from birth to death. The physical birth of the young Sean will be followed ten years later by his psychological birth. Immediately, however, the connection between Sean's death and the birth of a child can be read in two opposing ways – either as mere coincidence or as implying that this birth (like all others?) is rebirth. Throughout the film spectators are drawn to oscillate between sceptical and mystical positions; but the opening set-up brings to mind *2001: A Space Odyssey* which concludes triumphantly with the death of the astronaut Dave and his rebirth as the star child.

The plot proper commences ten years later with a simple sequence that gathers significance as events unfold. Once again we are in a snow-covered landscape, but this time in a cemetery. Anna, isolated in the dreary waste by a long static take, weeps beside Sean's grave. Watching for her return from a car some distance away, Joseph (Danny Huston) is distracted by laughter from a funeral where mourners are amused by a shared recollection of the deceased. Only when we know Anna better can we realise that she would not have countenanced levity at Sean's interment – her unresolved loss the focus of blackest grief.

Anna takes her leave of Sean, trudges back to the car, takes a deep breath, looks at Joseph meaningfully and says 'OK' – nothing else. The reflected branches of winter trees frame the couple through the driver's window – a chill omen. Later we realise she has chosen this moment in the graveyard to accept Joseph's proposal of marriage. It is bizarre, to say the least, that she decides to do this at the very moment she takes final leave of her late husband. Is her grieving incomplete?

The engagement party is thrown in the plush Manhattan apartment where Anna has always lived with her mother Eleanor (Lauren Bacall). Decorously serviced by hired caterers, it is one of those nervy affairs where everyone seems to be tiptoeing on eggshells. Joseph, lit cruelly to make his facial features gross, relates a self-congratulatory account of courting his hesitant fiancée – but she is nowhere in sight. Down in the lobby meanwhile an anxious woman makes her husband go up while she delays. Director of photography Harris Savides first establishes with this character a style of lighting actors' faces that prevails throughout much of the film. Little if any light reflects from the eyes, and what there is steeps the sockets in brown shadows that harmonise dully with the *mise-en-scène*. There's a subtle allusion in this to the living dead of horror films. If the old cliché holds true that in cinema the eyes are windows of the soul, then the psyches of the protagonists in *Birth* are veiled to the point of morbidity.

The anxious woman Clara (Anne Heche) reaches a decision, crosses the street into Central Park and scrabbles among leaves and dirt where she buries her gift. Then she buys an expensive replacement and goes up to the party. In the interim, her husband Clifford (Peter Stormare) has found Anna and affectionately congratulates her while apologising for the length of time since they last saw each other. We are left to wonder why there has been so long a break between people obviously fond of each other. Their ease evaporates as soon as Joseph comes to be introduced. He smoothly rids himself of a guest who belongs to Anna's past by inviting Clifford to 'enjoy the facilities'.

In the lobby ten floors below, a boy of ten has been quietly observing the comings and goings. Next morning, in a less affluent quarter of the city, this same lad, Sean, (Cameron Bright) sits on his bed. His thoughts occupy him so completely that he does not respond when one of his friends calls him out.[1]

The child is barely established before we cut back to more celebrations in the Manhattan apartment – another winter evening, another meticulously organised and stolid event, a family affair in honour of Eleanor's birthday. The matriarch has both her daughters and their men living in the apartment. Not only Anna and Joseph but the heavily pregnant Laura (Alison Elliott) and her husband Bob (Arliss Howard) are at the table. However, the carefully buffed polish of these lives is about to be disturbed by the boy Sean, who arrives uninvited behind late guests – a synchronistic surprise which will deliver them new experience to counterbalance their one-sidedness.

His entry coincides with the lights being doused as Anna walks through the flat carrying a birthday cake crowned by a forest of candles. Unseen in the dark, the boy follows her. Until the electric lights are switched on again, he seems no more material than a ghost, while the candlelit Anna looks like an emanation of his imagining. Are they in the presence of the divine child archetype, the seedling symbol of future hopes and life's potential (Hopcke, 1989: 107)?

The sense that mystery is invading this home of moneyed blandness is further enriched by other factors. Kidman's 'extraordinary stillness' in the role of Anna has been likened to Maria Falconetti's evocation of

Jeanne d'Arc in Carl Dreyer's 1928 film (Chaw, 2004). Cameron Bright invests the same quality in his playing of young Sean. Both actors have razor haircuts that recall Falconetti's role. These striking resemblances and the hypnotic fascination that develops between boy and woman entice us to wonder how deep the connections run. Are both characters, like Jeanne, immolated by passions that they cannot evade?

When the lights come on, Sean disrupts the party by asking to speak in private to Anna. She first humours him, as those adults do in whom the presence of children encourages whimsy, but when he announces with certainty that he is her late husband Sean she bundles him out of the apartment. Her reactions first conflate hilarity and unease, but in the following days the unease intensifies when Sean sends her a note telling her not to marry Joseph. Her family resorts to mockery, which fails to conceal disquiet. In part their anxiety is aroused by the intrusion into their polished lives, in part, we guess, by concern for Anna's hard-won emotional recovery. More, Sean has chafed the persona of every member of this regimented family. Behind the polite masks of New York's upper crust, the boy's persistence excites discordant emotions of which they have no understanding.

Joseph shows the strain first when, denting his suave mask, he intervenes absurdly, like an alpha male pricked by jealousy. The boy has incurred his annoyance by personating the dead husband who has long been both his sole and his soul rival. Ignoring Anna's wishes, he obliges the child to take him to his father (Ted Levine) who happens to be in the building giving music tuition to a client.[2] The adults corner the child and insist he stays away from Anna, but over and over again, Sean says he cannot. The adults use no physical force, but the concerted effect is brutal, culminating when Anna bends down, locks eyes with him and tells him not to bother her again. With that the elegant couple, who are late for a formal event, stride off briskly; but as Anna departs she turns and sees the boy collapse (doubly mordant in echoing her husband's death).

Instantly the shuddering buzz of a hundred rasping strings overwhelms Anna's being, while the clomping of murderous goblin hoofs (pizzicato basses) evacuates her sense of time and place. This, the Prelude to Act 1 of Wagner's *Die Walküre*, takes over the soundtrack while Anna, no longer aware of her surroundings, is hauled by her fiancé into the opera house. As they enter the auditorium, the camera zooms from a wide shot of the stalls into a tight close-up on Anna's face. Having clambered into her seat, she sits transfixed for endless shocked minutes. As the shot runs, the framing (from slightly above eye level) combines with the increased flattening created by an extreme telephoto register to broaden the image of Kidman's face. She looks not unlike an agitated child on the precipitous edge of tears. The shock of Sean's collapse has reopened her wound, leaving her helpless before the dawning conviction that the boy is her late husband reborn.

Kidman's extraordinary performance, augmented by Glazer and his crew into a great cinematic moment, leaves no room for doubt that a powerful mystery is being played out. She encounters the numinous in this episode – an experience charged with sacred terror. Although she has yearned and longed for Sean, nothing, understandably, has prepared her for that desire's obscure fulfilment. Although the film will show us other, mundane aspects of Anna's personality, the force of this apperception never wholly leaves her, nor those members of the audience affected by it.

The drama that Wagner's Prelude anticipates is relevant for two reasons appreciated by Robert Cumbow:

> Siegmund's arrival at Hunding's home ends up breaking up the marriage of Hunding and his wife Sieglinde, as the boy Sean almost does with Anna and Joseph's engagement. Second, Siegmund not only steals Sieglinde from Hunding, but beds her, even though she is his long-lost sister – thus consummating a "forbidden" love, like Anna's love for the 10-year-old boy who might be her long-lost husband.
>
> (Cumbow, 2006)

What does Anna's trauma reveal about her state of mind, interpreted in Jungian terms? Based on the premise that the completion of individuation cannot be done alone, but only in relationship, we consider Anna to be in the phase known to alchemists as the lesser *coniunctio*. Edward Edinger describes the greater *coniunctio* as 'produced by a final union of the purified opposites, and, because it combines the opposites, it mitigates and rectifies all one-sidedness' (1985: 215). Marriage has thus traditionally provided an apt symbol of the completion of individuation. However,

> the union of opposites that have been imperfectly separated characterizes the nature of the lesser *coniunctio*. The product is a contaminated mixture that must be subjected to further procedures. The product of the lesser *coniunctio* is pictured as killed, maimed, or fragmented.
>
> (Edinger, 1985: 212)

To illustrate this dangerous aspect of the lesser *coniunctio*, Edinger cites alchemical texts originally collated by Jung that refer to the out-of-kilter marriage of a widowed mother with her son.

> But this marriage, which was begun with the expression of great joyfulness, ended in the bitterness of mourning . . . For when the son sleeps with the mother, she kills him with the stroke of a viper.
>
> (ibid.)

The concept of imperfectly separated opposites that characterises the lesser *coniunctio* fits not only Anna and Sean's marriage, but also Anna's relationship to Joseph and her fractured state of mind after her commitment to remarry. It also assists our understanding of the boy's attraction to her, where we are in the richly ambivalent territory of the Oedipal complex. Edinger again: 'For the alchemist, the mother was the *prima materia* and brought about healing and rejuvenation as well as death . . . The immature son-ego is eclipsed and threatened with destruction when it naively embraces the maternal unconscious' (1985: 212). Just so – Sean collapses. However, Edinger continues, 'such an eclipse can be inseminating and rejuvenating' (ibid.). Thus the image of the *coniunctio* refers to a phase of the transformation process, in which death can precede rebirth (Edinger, 1985: 214). When Sean enters into relationship with Anna, he initiates a synchronistic event which has the potential to result in their mutual healing.

Like all new beginnings, Anna's engagement to Joseph brings with it not only the potential for joy (though it scarcely touches these two) but also vulnerability, which may spur a potential to regress. If the regression is consciously reflected upon, it may provide an opportunity for further growth. However, while Anna and Joseph's future marriage may be the immediate cause for each of their forthcoming regressions, it will not necessarily prove to be the root explanation.

The striking boy's advent may, as hinted earlier, signal activation of the child as a powerful archetypal image. It can either look back at the past of the person to whom it appears or forward to the future. As a retrospective figure, it represents emotions and unconscious drives that have been excluded or repressed as a necessary precondition to growing into adulthood. This occurs when the individual's development is constrained by the drive to enhance and specialise consciousness, a process which Jung (1951: 162–3) found characteristic of Western cultures. Conversely, when the archetypal image of the child looks toward the future, it does so by representing nascent drives forming in the unconscious that are likely in time to enter and alter the individual's conscious. Jung remarks:

> Our experience of the psychology of the individual . . . shows that the "child" paves the way for a future change of personality. In the individuation process, it anticipates the figure that comes from the synthesis of conscious and unconscious elements in the personality. It is therefore a symbol which unites the opposites; a mediator, bringer of healing, that is, one who makes whole.
>
> (1951: 164)

The child can therefore signal a change in personality before it occurs, presenting to the conscious mind as it does the early intimations of rebirth.

This early in *Birth* the spectator lacks sufficient insight into Anna's psyche to adopt with confidence any of these readings. Nor can we tell by focusing on Sean. One consequence of the driven, internalised power with which Kidman endows the crucial scene at the opera is that although the boy's collapse jolts us through his overpowering grief, we cannot yet empathise with his suffering as with Anna because we cut away from him after he falls. The scene that follows the opera gives us a first, barely audible, clue to his state of being. As his father puts him to bed[3], the continuing pianissimo clomp of Wagner's bass line undermines any illusion that he has reached safety. The worried man tells his wife, 'He says that he's somebody else and he believes that he is.' The parents are not alone in failing to understand the boy's state of mind. That remains obscure, the mystery that protagonists and audience alike are drawn to solve.

Nevertheless, it is plain that a radical change has come over Sean. When his mother (Cara Seymour) comes into his bedroom to comfort him with their good night ritual, the boy refuses to be his old self: 'I'm not your stupid son any more.' His behaviour next day confirms that he no longer fits his old world but is experiencing a second birth of the psyche. He ducks out of school and leaves a phone message for Anna to meet him in Central Park – she will know where to go. As Anna enters the park, unsteady on court shoes in the slush, a synthesised pulse like an anxious heartbeat draws a tense wire that dissolves momentarily into Wagner before she nears the fatal underpass. The point of view is identical to the end of her late husband's run; and echoes of Desplat's score for that scene (underlined by the heartbeat) emphasise the significance of the bridge. As Anna and the boy Sean meet, a runner clatters through the underpass – a moment of synchronicity too striking for the spectator to miss, hinting that the boy and his namesake are connected.

Recovered from the shock he suffered the previous evening, the self-assured Sean asks Anna to arrange for her brother-in-law Bob (a doctor) to test him. His certainty shakes Anna and she retreats abruptly with an aggressive-defensive put down: 'You're just a little boy!' She wants to stop him getting any closer for fear not only that he might prove to be what she most desires, but also because (as the unfolding plot eventually confirms) she resists the stirrings of an awareness that his quasi-magical, synchronistic advent signals the coming of almost irresistible changes in the way she sees, thinks and lives.

Although Anna has survived the loss of her husband, it appears she has learned nothing from the experience and thus has undergone no further maturing of the self. Following the truth requires courage: the boy's persistence means that she will find it tough to dodge the truth on which he insists, that the horizontal move in her life to Joseph will not bring her the safety and security she seeks. The truth that will eventually be revealed is at present literally concealed underground. As Stephen Mitchell puts it, 'Our conscious experience is merely the tip of an immense iceberg of unconscious mental processes that really shape, unbeknownst to us, silently, impenetrably, and inexorably, our motives, our values and our actions' (1993: 22). If ignored, rather than serving development of the self, the unconscious holds the potential to destroy. For Anna and the boy, the synchronicity of their meeting leaves neither of them real choice, since they cannot turn away from what has come powerfully from the unconscious.

In her turmoil Anna tells Joseph about the child's persistence. This second challenge from his rival rankles Joseph who escalates hostilities and has Bob put the boy to the test. The interview is recorded and in playback Sean's astonishing knowledge and confidence transfix Anna's family[4]. Nor does the boy baulk at turning the tables, questioning Bob about his married life and recalling that Laura had not been thought able to bear a child.

Sean's answers reveal significant details about Anna's late husband. He and Anna had married thirty times in thirty days at thirty churches. This saturated, fairy-tale quality colours Anna's romantic memories of her husband. But what can such obsessive behaviour mean in terms of their late relationship? Romance had fuelled their marriage, adding a quality of intensity and excitement to being alive and dreams of their future. But romance lives in newness, mystery, even danger, and may disappear with familiarity. Its intensity gives a false sense of a truly intimate connection which this couple had confused with a connection of depth. From this vantage point Sean's death can be seen as an emblem of romantic love that dies because nothing more real anchors it. It may, as with the boy, excite the idealisation of an adolescent. Yet idealisation is, by definition, illusory. Rather, there are signs of addiction in the multiple weddings, an addiction like any other acting either as a counterfeit high or a container for undigested suffering and grief.

Emotionally, the blissful state of desire is what propels couples to bond in order to initiate a secure attachment – but it is not of itself sufficient to maintain and develop that bond. Anna has found a place where she can feel the spiritual high of the union she seeks in marriage without the hard work of becoming a psychological being. Her idealisation (bathed in illusion rather than a real relationship based on a depth of connection where both people are emerging) inhibits the necessary ego-self axis from developing as part of the individuation process. One of the most painful attributes of marriage is the eventual, unavoidable revealing of both partners' shadows. The shadow may give the relationship its spark but often couples avoid it by attempting to manage the negative emotions it generates (in which case the marriage may last, if firmly invested in comfort, but will not thrive). If the shadow is not consciously dealt with, the intensity of connection from the initial spark may die. One outcome can be that, as we eventually discover of Anna's late husband, the partners will look for it elsewhere. As each partner in an individuated marriage attempts over the long haul to understand and relate to their shadow by increasing their capacity to hold the emotional tension it provokes, they further integrate the unrelated parts of themselves, healing each other and their own psychological splits in the process. In Anna and Sean's *idealised* marriage (going to thirty churches in thirty days) they achieved no such understanding. Looking back at Sean's fatal collapse as he lumbered through fields of ice, we find the image that lets us see where the relationship became frozen.

Continuing the interview with Bob, the boy Sean inadvertently alludes to the poisonous undercurrent beneath Anna's heady romance, although he cannot understand the implications of his words. He mentions that, as her husband, he and Anna had lived with Eleanor because he was seldom home. Finally the lad takes control of the interview: 'Look, you can think whatever you want . . . It doesn't matter. I'm Sean. I love Anna and nothing's going to change that. Nothing. That's forever.' The challenge to Anna's family in general and Joseph in particular is now too direct to be ignored. They summon the boy to stay over at Eleanor's apartment so that Anna can disabuse him of his delusion by proving her intent to marry Joseph. On arrival he moves round the apartment like a Pied Piper reversing the old tale, followed every step by the fascinated adults. He promptly lays claim to his old desk and identifies a visitor whose name he does not know as 'the one that told Anna there wasn't a Santa Claus.'

Cross-questioning the boy gets Joseph nowhere but he cannot stop scratching the jealous itch in his ego. Late at night he goes downstairs in the dark to gaze at the boy asleep on the couch and mutters, 'You don't have me fooled.' Plainly Joseph's saturnine anger puts him into identification with the boy as, driven by irresistible emotions, he (no less than the sleeping child) drifts in semi-conscious realms. Although, with the exception of certain horror film cycles, the image of the archetypal child rarely figures as an adult's shadow, Sean does take on this role in relation to Joseph. The man lacks soul, while the boy has it in abundance. This is a key relationship not only for what it signals about Joseph but also the family into which he is marrying.

Anna is intending to tie her life to a man with a materialist disposition as bankable as her parental family and her late husband Sean, but lacking the scientist's inquiring mind. Joseph fits well in Eleanor's family because none of them has a curious, self-reflective nature. Sheltered in moneyed security whose realism is so insistently grotesque that it lays bare the fantasies on which it is built, their wealth encourages the delusion that the pragmatic empiricism of their professional and social lives endows them with a complete, all round understanding of life, notwithstanding their total neglect of the internal world. Their concrete minds lack the curiosity and imagination that accompany the inner child, both being qualities which act as guides to individuation. These adults are as emotionally dead as the deceased Sean.

This holds true for Anna as well as the others. She is obsessive but not inquisitive – with an obsession so powerful that the boy/man rapidly becomes the carrier of her animus projections to the extent that he almost (but never wholly) seems her invention. That she projects her animus onto a child (whatever the merit of his claim to be her late husband) may be, as mentioned earlier, the first sign of impending rebirth that connection with the archetype of the divine child often foretells. Alternatively, as now seems increasingly likely, it may imply earlier narcissistic wounds that have yet to be worked through.

Indeed, the disturbance caused by the boy intensifies in Anna a complex of which she had no prior awareness. It erupts when she calls on her late husband's old friend Clifford to open her confused heart. With emotion battling reason, unable to make sense of her conflicted passions, she rambles on about her feelings for the two Seans, her suffering, her fears and her wishes – simultaneously knowing the child is not her dead husband yet aching for him to be – in sum, struggling to discover what is real. Eventually she manages to stammer that she needs help. She wants Clifford to intervene and stop her falling in love with Sean again. That she cannot see the absurdity of this request reveals her narcissistic choice of mate[5].

As further evidence for the activation of a complex, the entire monologue concerns herself except when she describes Joseph as having *not* grown insecure over the boy. Since she could not be more mistaken about this in that only Joseph's suave manners mask his anxiety, it raises the thought that Anna represses painful matters that she cannot fail to notice. In her fiancé's case the truth would force her to recognise that his devotion is not an all-encompassing shelter from the doubts and conflicts that come with all relationships. If this is a repeating pattern, she may have denied herself hurtful reflection on her husband's frequent absences from home by repressing the painful awareness that the marriage was not what she thought it was. The psychic energy needed to sustain that repression would add to her relentless grief for a perfect mate ten years after his death. As in all relationships, a constant calibration between closeness and distance – between what feels so suffocating it may threaten loss of self, and what feels too far away, stimulating a fear of abandonment – is a challenging undertaking. If an early relational trauma has been suffered, the ability to sustain an intact connection may become more complex, ending in disruptions such as excessive arguing or passive withdrawal. Anna's prolonged grieving indicates that something was amiss both during and prior to the marriage.

The next day, as agreed with the boy's mother, Anna meets Sean out of school; but rather than despatch him as planned with cold words, she takes him for ice cream and a carriage ride through Central Park – and discusses their mutual attraction! Following her appeal to Clifford for help, these actions can be seen as another aspect of a deep-rooted psychological pattern. Anna needs the men close to her to take responsibility for what she is unconscious of – her own shadow. She wants Clifford to stop her from falling in love. That only makes sense when we see her projecting her demons onto him. In summoning Clifford for help, she has unconsciously picked the very person who cannot assist because his own blindness (soon to be revealed) makes him as unconscious as her. In her previous life her husband's role was to secure her in a hermetically sealed realm of perfect love (which his early death has sanctified), buttressing her world from the vagaries of human behaviour. Joseph is to replace her husband as a stable, middle-aged version of her former mate, forgiven his want of romance because he is wealthy and dignified enough to fill the absences in Anna's life. The boy's function in replacing Joseph as her reincarnated husband will be to reopen the tomb of impossibly perfect lost young love.

The date with ice cream and the carriage ride in the park are, as Cumbow (2006) mentions, a cliché of romantic movies rendered almost comic by the circumstances except that the familiar anxious pulse fades in again, mixed through the older Sean's music. Afternoon wears into evening and Anna watches her young beau – just a healthy boy in this scene – enjoying climbing frames and swings. Meanwhile, Joseph stands like a jilted lover waiting for her in the window of a suitably grand apartment which Anna should be viewing with him as their future home. We zoom in long and slow with reflections of winter-dead trees once again darkening the glass. His self-absorbed face broadens just as Anna's did at the opera, revealing not the inner child he denies but the worn visage of a middle-aged man pushed near to breakdown. Joseph is caught in the Sol Niger, the darkening and depression of a man in the second half of life. Unable to regenerate himself because of a defect of heart, he projects his anima and thus cannot develop a feeling connection. Overly identified with male ego (which tends to overvalue power and material wealth) he nevertheless appears to feel something deep is missing.

Anna brings Sean back to Eleanor's apartment to hear the wedding music, arguing that it might persuade him to give up his fixation (another projection of her own obsession onto an animus figure). Joseph gets back from the aborted house hunting and is about to enter the bathroom when he hears the voices of Anna and the boy. The latter has stepped as casually as a husband into her tub. This image intricately restates the lesser *coniunctio* and recalls Jung's reading of 'Immersion in the Bath'. Here the alchemical King and Queen start their process of individuation by stepping into the bath (the unconscious) together. But, as brother and sister, the royal pair's symbolically incestuous relationship signifies the as yet imperfect differentiation of conscious and unconscious (Jung, 1946: 241–6).

Had Joseph gone into the bathroom, he would have heard Anna once again asking Sean to leave; but, rather than face his suspicions, he turns away. Evasion racks up his tension with his shadow piquing him horribly.

Soon the entire household is lined up in the drawing room to hear the pretentious nonsense commanded for the wedding.

> It appears to be a chamber music recital, but what they are playing is soon revealed to be a rather silly version of the Bridal March from

Wagner's *Lohengrin* that we know as 'Here Comes the Bride,' and we realize that this is another pre-wedding function. But notice that just as a performance of Wagner's *Die Walküre* became the centerpiece of the film's Act One, so this little mini-concert of another Wagnerian piece becomes the pivotal moment of Act Two.

(Cumbow, 2006)

All the family (except the haunted Anna) are gratified by the music's confirmation of their good taste. Although opera goers, they appear blithely unaware of its ominous associations in marking the moment when the newly wed Elsa violates the sole condition her husband Lohengrin has attached to the marriage. By asking who he is as they enter the bridal chamber, she destroys the marriage, precipitating his return to the kingdom of his father and her own death. The scenario plays (if only Anna were aware of it) like an ironic epitaph on what she had left undone in her first marriage by failing to ask her husband who he was. Had she the feminine psychic energy to initiate the necessary inquiry that she ducked, the death of delusion could have led to her rebirth. As it is, through neurotic repetition she risks replaying the whole self-defeating cycle once again.

Meanwhile, the boy again disrupts the calm and goads Joseph by kicking his chair even after his rival orders him to stop. In a set-up borrowed from Kubrick's *Barry Lyndon* (Hughes, 2006; Cumbow, 2006), Joseph's rage erupts as volcanically as Barry's. He lashes out at the infuriating boy – the only time he does anything from deep-rooted passion. As when Barry runs amuck and his peers restrain him from slaughtering young Bullingdon, some of the men present hold Joseph back. He denounces the boy: 'He has no clue how to make something happen!' Yet his very outrage proves him wrong and what really exercises him is maintaining his dignity: 'I'm the one that should be respected, but obviously not.' Then he goes after the boy again and spanks him hard before the adults can haul him off. When finally secured, this scion of Manhattan's finest roars like a humiliated baby, 'He kicked my chair!' But it is the shadow child who has succeeded in ripping open his public persona to reveal Joseph's infantile rage. A child must feel possession over his love object to experience a secure attachment, but Joseph, with his repressed id let free, has exposed his latent insecurities. The false self feigns arrogant security.

Anna gazes appalled at her fiancé's ungovernable anger, confronted with the vortex in his personality she had failed to notice. The other adults (a further echo of Kubrick's scene) are at least as shocked by

Joseph's violation of social decorum as by his attacking a child. But when Eleanor watches him moving out of the apartment, far from rebuking him, she promises to bring Anna round. Eleanor knows a good marital prospect when she sees one and has no intention of letting her daughter lose this prosperous bachelor even though his usually impeccable manners have slipped just this once.

At the climax of the brouhaha Sean had grabbed his coat and run out, the cue for a grieving music that recalls the moments of sorrow after battle in war movies. Anna follows the boy to the snowy street where they kiss tenderly – as simultaneously both child with woman, and lovers. The scene returns to the apartment above and time passes. The sombre music continues with bass notes melded through a synthesiser to produce a sound not unlike distant foghorns. Eventually Clifford arrives and searches through empty rooms (the brown gloom and slow editing never more evident) before discovering Anna in the kitchen. He has come, as asked, to save her from Sean. But before they can talk, the boy materialises and embraces him affectionately as a long-lost friend. Although Clifford does his best gently to assure Anna that the lad is not her late husband, she will not be deflected from her conviction (all the more resolute after the kiss) that she has found him reincarnated. Her inflated mood shows that she has been touched by a numinous presence; she has no intention of giving up either the child or the troubled ecstasy he brings her.

Only when Eleanor sternly threatens to inform Sean's mother and the police does Anna reluctantly rouse the boy (whom she had previously installed in her bed at an hour suited to a ten-year-old) and take him back to his parents in a taxicab. During the ride she begins to fantasise how they might be together. Anna is now caught in the grips of her complex, exhibiting the twin intensities of urgency and compulsion. Her perspective has shifted dangerously: for her the boy is no longer *like* her dead mate, he *is* him. A psychic boundary has been crossed between inner reality and external reality. It seems that if young Sean is to reveal himself as a symbol of renewal, that moment cannot be long delayed.

It quickly becomes clear that matters cannot be reduced to a simple issue of whether the boy either is or isn't the dead man. Although the boy obviously loves Anna, something else is competing for his attention: the memory of an episode in Eleanor's apartment. While everyone else was occupied he had let Clara in. She had immediately instructed the boy to help wash her dirty hands (as if washing her shadow). To Sean it had seemed an odd command that he obeyed politely but without enthusiasm. Clara's order does not surprise, however, when we recognise that children are often left holding what adults are unconscious of (Clara is soon revealed as blinded by sexual greed)[6]. Now, some hours later, the boy recalls the engagement party. In flashback he remembers observing Clara's hesitation and following her into Central Park where he watched her bury the parcel. Clara, who has heard Anna rave about the boy's uncanny knowledge, has now revisited the spot to confirm certain suspicions and has silently shown the boy that she knows. We realise that Sean must have dug it up and that Clara is now mutely confronting him. Retrieval of this package can be read as analogous to the discovery of what lies buried in the unconscious – a gift of wisdom that must be laid bare to consciousness. The ego needs the guidance and direction from the unconscious to lead a meaningful life – paving the psychic road between ego and Self.

With his secret uncovered, the boy takes the package to Clara's apartment. It contains Anna's love letters to her husband; but Clara shocks him by disclosing that the dead man had been her lover. He had given his wife's letters unopened to Clara to prove how much he loved her. So brutal a twist to infidelity proves that his subjective experience of the marriage differed greatly from Anna's. It suggests a significant loss of connection between the couple had ended in Sean's emotional withdrawal and his unrealistic hope to find enduring love with yet another idealised mate. He seems in the affair to have attempted to revive the lost spark of which we wrote earlier – an impossible endeavour without psychological growth so that his death signals the dead end he had reached.

The revelation that the boy has read Anna's love letters appears at first thought to implode the intricate web of mystery surrounding him. It seems that almost all his knowledge must have come from the letters, though he may have discovered other details about the family in equally accountable ways. For example, he may have found out where Anna's husband died – something the letters could not have revealed – by chatting to his friend the janitor. Further reflection, however, shows that the boy's conduct cannot be accounted for solely by causal explanations. They do not explain many factors, not least the deep currents of emotion he feels and cannot fully control. First, no one has put him up to making his extraordinary claim. Second, he does not have a scam in mind. Third, the coincidence of his name and the dead man's may have triggered his interest, but the source of his fascination with Anna lies in the letters' expression of love; for, fourth, he certainly loves Anna. How else to explain his much remarked, unblinking solemnity, his collapse and the sacrifice that he will soon make? Fifth, how can we rationally explain that he recognises his forebear's desk? Or, sixth, that he can identify the woman whose name he does not know who told Anna there is no Santa Claus? The answer may lie in his intuition.

Intuition can play a supreme role in individuation. It is experienced as if it delivers something knowable that mysteriously comes from a place beyond our conscious knowing. In that, it differs from instinct, which is a function of the corporeal senses. Intuition has a feminine quality not to be confused with gender. But Anna, caught in her gender role as a result of her one-sidedness, literalises the feminine, whereas the child's symbolic androgyny could serve as her guide toward integration of the masculine and feminine – as when the alchemical King and Queen bathing together in symbolic incest start the process of bringing masculine and feminine, conscious and unconscious, into balance in the greater *coniunctio* (see Jung, 1946: 241–3).

Sooner or later, every avenue of inquiry opens on the boy's soul. The temporal link between his physical birth and the death of Sean the man opens the idea of reincarnation. Having said which, Clara's objection cannot be ignored – that if he had been her lover reincarnated he would have come to her. But in fact the boy is unmoved by her. However, reincarnation can be considered symbolically as ancestry's invisible pull, linking individuals to both the personal and the collective unconscious; and it seems thus that the boy has knowledge of past life[7].

Clara cannot deny (indeed it arouses her jealousy) that Anna's letters have stirred great love in the boy. He has identified with Anna's need for a perfect loving relationship, and that has enriched his confidence to move from boyhood to young adolescence. It has endowed him with the certainty of his soul's connection to an imago of psychic love – the source of all human love that embodies the higher form of the archetype of relatedness. However, what he reads as the intense love between wife and husband at its most sacred and incandescent is knowledge that he can only receive as an innocent. The letters bring about his second birth.

Inevitably the boy and Anna seek different objects, his goal being a variant of what Erich Neumann terms uroboric incest (1954: 17). Her love letters initiate him into the mystical uroboric union of male and female for which his soul yearns. Renouncing his birth mother, he dissolves the primary union he had shared with her as an infant. Nevertheless, the new symbolic union with Anna that his soul embraces cannot be permanent. She becomes the deeply felt archetypal projection necessary to his development – part mother (providing ice cream treats) and part lover (romantic dates and the warmth of an enveloping pre-sexual eroticism). By definition, a symbolic union with what the mother imago represents (even in its variant form of Anna as mother/lover) cannot be a state of the psyche that endures if the child is to mature healthily and differentiate into its own individuated self (see Neumann, ibid.).

Consumed by her own galling wants, Clara sees nothing of this. She admits to Sean that she had intended to vent hatred on her rival by making the evidence of her dead lover's betrayal an engagement present for Anna – but in the event, she could not go through with it. Ironically, if Anna had known the truth it might have shattered her hypnotic grieving and allowed her to move on (Cumbow, 2006). Be that as it may, Clara tells the boy that had he come to her first she would have explored the possibility of rediscovering her lover in him. Ten years after his death, she is no less in thrall to the memory of Sean than Anna, with the difference that Clara has not been touched by the boy's numinous glow. Greedily she struggles with him and grabs the letters back.

Pounding kettledrums that recall the older Sean's fatal collapse accompany the boy as he flees into the park in crisis. He climbs high into a leafless tree and remains there into the winter night. When the police find him dazed and muddy hours later (he must have slipped from his perch) they can neither grasp what he says nor catch hold of him. 'I thought I was Sean but I found out he was in love with another woman. So I can't be him because I'm in love with Anna.' As he runs off into the dark we, unlike the bewildered cops, realise that he has discovered something significant about himself. It is not the latest adult attack that has made him distraught, but discovering Clara's affair.

The boy runs to Anna's apartment where the maid puts him in the bath – a hint here of baptism cleansing the shadow to initiate rebirth. Anna comes home and goes in to him with a 'plan' (both ludicrous and dangerous) that they should run away, wait until the boy reaches 21, and then get married[8]. This adolescent fantasy meets his pre-adolescent heart's desire, but he has to refuse. For although the mud still sticks to him, he now knows what has sullied him. Other children might have gone home to their parents with the police, but Sean speaks with more maturity than a child of his years or indeed Anna: 'I'm not Sean – because I love you.' He protects her by keeping secret both her husband's betrayal and the disparity between the man and her image of him. Securing an adult's delusion is a tough role for a child, but he does this heroically and at no small cost, personifying the wisdom gained on the postmodern hero's journey. Anna brands him a liar, shakes him yet again with the fierce, self-centred emotions that he has found in all the adults outside his own family – and is lost to him as the woman he loves. When her anger gives way to tears ('You certainly had me fooled – I thought you were my dead husband'), self-pity stops her remembering that the boy had believed it too.

Despite the shock of Clara's revelation, it has had a developmental impact on the boy. Having to face 'his own' betrayal of Anna, he has suffered a rude awakening from the uroboric condition in which he had been sheltering. It brings about his third birth, a transformation of the psyche that now becomes further differentiated in a form suited to a ten-year-old. Neumann describes the developmental stage through which the boy is moving: 'Detachment from the uroboros means being born and descending into the lower world of reality, full of dangers and discomforts' (1954: 39). And again:

> Detachment from the uroboros, entry into the world, and the encounter with the universal principle of opposites are the essential tasks of human and individual development. The process of coming to terms with the objects of the outer and inner worlds, of adapting to the collective life of mankind both within and without, governs with varying degrees of intensity the life of every individual.
> (ibid.: 35)

We see the boy only twice more. Cleaned up after his bath, he sits with Eleanor by the front door, waiting for his mother to collect him – Anna presumably being too distraught to sit with them. Out of nowhere Eleanor says, 'I never liked Sean.' What has drawn this declaration? Here is just one of the interwoven currents of life among Eleanor's family and friends that could have been scripted by Henry James. Bacall – once a beauty with a face no less expressive than Kidman – plays Eleanor as a steely matriarch who has always exercised power over her entire family with the exception only of the older Sean. The boy has both reminded her of that and put her command over Anna at risk. So, her power having survived intact, she now finds no further reason to suppress disapproval of both man and boy. Old enough to be Sean's grandmother, Eleanor could have played the role of wise old woman as head of her family, but she does not. Instead she rules, in place of sagacious advice having only sardonic put downs to offer, as when she first sets eyes on Laura's newborn daughter: 'Maybe that's Sean.'

Eleanor's lack of emotional engagement with either Laura or the infant is striking. Her coldness has left her children suffering from a lack of the mother's nurture. Indulgent and dutiful parenting is not nurturing. Anna's neediness and inability to work through her grief for her husband's death originated in her childhood feelings of emotional abandonment. So Eleanor holds for her daughter the archetypal image of the Devouring Mother deriving from negative experience of parental caring. In Anna's later life it explains a power relationship in marriage with parental overtones in which she subordinates as the younger partner. Eleanor's merging way of connecting is narcissistic in nature, leaving no room for another mind to safely develop needs and wants different from hers. If separation does not take place, the matriarch, so necessary, cherishing and nurturing during infancy, turns in the dawning light of consciousness to an imagined figure of darkness and destruction as she prevents the emerging ego of the child from differentiating itself from the unconscious and establishing itself in its own right (Neumann, 1954: 39–47).

Jung concluded from his case studies that:

> It is not possible to live too long amid infantile surroundings, or in the bosom of the family, without endangering one's psychic health. Life calls us forth to independence, and anyone who does not heed this call because of childish laziness or timidity is threatened with neurosis. And once this has broken out, it becomes an increasingly valid reason for running away from life and remaining forever in the morally poisonous atmosphere of infancy.
>
> (Jung, 1956: 304)

He also saw that a woman who has remained bound to the mother typically lives through fantasies of a hero figure. A man who enters upon a relationship with such a woman 'will at once be made identical with her animus-hero and relentlessly set up as the ideal figure.' (ibid.: 307).

This has been Anna's fate, still playing itself out in her thirties; and just as her own fate contrasts with young Sean's, so too the suffocating propriety of Eleanor's family differs from the homely kindliness that prevails in the boy's home. His 'good enough' parents remain constant in support of their son and, once they have perceived the authenticity of his experience, never gainsay it. By thus making space for him to follow the demands that his own developing psyche places on him, they hold secure the family base to which he now returns.

As we have discovered, things are different in Anna's circle where repression and betrayal are commonplace. Anna has never admitted to herself the thought that Sean might have had a lover. However, as Hughes (2006) suggests, the religious intensity of her grieving may hint that she senses something unthinkable and represses it. Another instance of repression is glimpsed when Bob, though a medical doctor, is embarrassed when the boy refers to Laura's supposed infertility. What unknown story lies behind that flicker of discomfort? For their part, Clifford and Clara behave awkwardly when in Anna's company. It seems probable that Clifford has found out about his wife's affair with Sean and the knowledge lies injuriously between them. In the negative aspect of her personality Clara is an embittered manipulator: witness first her wangling an invitation to Anna's party to take revenge on her lover's wife, and second her attempt to control a ten-year-old boy. However, when plunged into the dreadful predicament of a mistress whose lover has died, she would have found herself trapped in her secret without the socially acceptable right to mourn. It would be in character if, unable to contain her suffering alone, she had vented her gall on her own husband.

We see repression enacted as soon as the boy is out of the picture, when Anna goes to Joseph in his office (as her mother has counselled). Bristling with the majesty of a man unjustly injured, her fiancé ushers her into his boardroom and hears her out impassively. As Jung wrote of Joseph's type fifty years before the film was made,

> The man finds himself cast in an attractive role: he has the privilege of putting up with the familiar feminine foibles with real superiority, and yet with forbearance, like a true knight. (Fortunately, he remains ignorant of the fact that these deficiencies consist largely of his own projections.)
>
> (Jung, 1954a: 90)

Unable to take responsibility, Anna declares (three times in all and not without tears) that she cannot be held accountable for what happened with the boy: there was no way she could have behaved any differently. Then she says (three times over) that she wants to be with Joseph and adds that she wants to be married, to have a good life, be happy and find peace. Although she does breathe an apology, her words only address her own wants – nothing about how she feels or what she might do, no inquiry about how he feels or what he might want, nothing about what they could share. After a pause to make the point that he is in control, Joseph responds, 'OK' (echoing her acceptance speech in the graveyard). She kneels and kisses his hand in fawning gratitude; and in this dreadful manner the deal (a negotiation ensuring Anna's perpetual subordination) is sealed. Where there is no potential for growth, depression cannot be far away – the kiss of death.

The wedding, a stylish affair, takes place in May and at the family's seaside villa (just as Eleanor wanted). While the guests enjoy champagne in the garden, a photographer puts Anna through the interminable poses required of a bride. As he does so, her mind pulls away from the moment and immerses her in a letter received from Sean. Long quiet chords for violins abstract us sadly from the celebrations while in voiceover the boy apologises courteously for having upset the family and making Anna sad. He tells about his life resuming with help from family and experts and reports that the spell has been lifted. As he speaks, we cut away to him sitting for the school photographer, now indeed a cheerful, ordinary boy. Nevertheless, this moment of synchronicity implies some form of continuing connection between him and Anna – a connection impossible for her to ignore.

The boy is free, but his final words, 'I guess I'll see you in another lifetime,' hold Anna in the spell's grip. The quiet strings surge as the world of this wealthy young woman – accustomed to wanting and getting, or at least getting the illusion of having what she wants – is ripped to shreds. We cut to hand-held shots at the beach where she staggers between sea and sand, rejecting both, crazed, unable to commit to death or life, belonging neither to the oceanic womb of the unconscious nor to the security of consciousness and the land. When Joseph finds her on this brink and embraces her protectively, she pulls back towards the waves, unable to respond to him, her beautiful face distorted into a silent Munchian scream (cf. Chaw, 2004). Finally dragged by her new husband out of what seems an eternity of grief, she reluctantly gives way to him. Joseph gently leads his catatonic bride along the misty margins – their future together well outside the range of prediction. We can say, however, that although Anna may yearn for the beloved spiritual experience, and once again hope to find in marriage a feeling of completion in the greater *coniunctio* for which she sought ten years earlier, she has not made the necessary developmental shift to inhabit its psycho-emotional space.

All that said, this may not be the film's only verdict on Anna, because it has not quite finished – at least not for those who watch the credits roll. The sound of waves slowly fades, replaced (just as the title *Birth* hits the screen) by a trite tune that violates shockingly the register of all that has gone before.

> I know that you belong to somebody new,
> But tonight, you belong to me.
> Although we're apart, you're part of my heart
> And tonight, you belong to me.

This perky ditty was recorded by sisters Patience and Prudence McIntyre aged 11 and 14. Notwithstanding the coy, prepubescent sexuality projected by their rendition, it became a top five North American hit in 1956 ('Ronnie', 2003). Fifty years later, however, changes in society's attitudes towards child sexuality augmented by the tune's location, tucked into an ignored crevice at the end of the film, give it a raw impact. Its sudden intrusion, coupled with the harsh break of register, indicates an irruption from the deep unconscious, that 'chthonic portion of the psyche' (Jung, 1927/1931: 31). As we have seen, the intense, warded focus of Anna's mind (not to mention her family's defensive empiricism) has been so profoundly one-sided as to repress unwanted contents deep into the unconscious. However, the more energetically such contents are repressed, the more vigorously they are apt to erupt back into consciousness. This is equally the case for individuals or collectives. When repressed contents erupt, they exert a force that counters or complements the bias of the conscious position. Therein lies the function of 'Tonight You Belong To Me'. Its sentiments are wholly at odds with the empirical circumstances, with Joseph and Anna now wed, but precisely in tune with what may be presumed to be going on in the unconscious. But whose unconscious – Anna's or Sean's (the boy, the man?)? Or somewhere their souls touch? Since we are dealing with the unconscious, we cannot know.

In the world of the well-socialised people who surround Anna (and who celebrate in Eleanor's hedged garden what they consider to be her return to the shelter of marriage), her fixation on Sean can be classified as neurotic and infantile. We interpreted her mindset in this frame, finding its roots in the impositions of a domineering mother and an absent father. The reading is legitimate but limited to what Jung termed the reductive analytical programmes of Freud and Adler – the former focused on the sources of trauma to be found in childhood, the latter on the ego's urge to power (Jung, 1943: 35–40). Differentiating his approach to psychoanalysis from theirs, Jung argued that neurotic symptoms 'are not simply the effects of long-past causes, whether 'infantile sexuality' or the infantile urge to power,' they may also be goal oriented, being 'attempts at a new synthesis in life' albeit they have, as symptoms of psychological distress, yet to succeed (ibid.: 46).

The difference between grieving and mourning is well illustrated by Anna. In effect, she is stuck. She grieves to the end of the film and beyond, but she does not mourn. That would involve a process, a moving forward, and an accommodation with the imaginal world and memories of her first husband. In actuality, the advent of the boy intensifies her grief to the point where only an impossible union with him could resolve it. She seems therefore to fall into the category of the type of people 'who have the whole meaning of their life, their true significance, in the unconscious, while in the conscious mind is nothing but inveiglement and error' (ibid.: 46–7). We are drawn by Jung's observation to consider the soul once again: whether Anna is not transfixed by her craving for that other union, the soul's perfection. Such a union may be impossible in this life, but the appetite for it is inextinguishable where an individual like Anna is in the grip of an ecstatic passion. Through the recorded ages, the intensity of ardent lovers' feelings for their beloved has seemed to them to have the quality of a sacred passion that can bring them to knowledge of the divine. Contemplation on the beloved person (like Dante's longing for Beatrice) generates a wonder so concentrated that it draws the mind of the lover beyond mere physical attraction to penetrate the confusions of his or her emotional upheaval and attain a sense of being touched by the numinous. 'Sean', the doubled image of a godlike man-boy, who in Anna's mind has taken on the dimensions of the perfect masculine, is so powerful a presence that it ought to lead her to birth in the spiritual realm. Sadly no such release into the light appears likely because her conscious mind (despite the pressures to the contrary that 'Sean' exerts on it) remains powerfully dependent on empirical materialism.

A truly beautiful woman, Anna's soul (notwithstanding her infantile tendencies) is rendered hauntingly lovely in its anguish by Desplat's music. His themes, with their suggestion of otherworldly energy, augment her beauty and make her into an unwitting symbol for what she has the potential to be – in the particular Jungian sense in which symbols are forward-looking and constructive and compensate for one-sided, conscious bias (Fredericksen, 2001: 34–5). Her search for soul almost draws her into fulfilment and knowledge of herself, regardless of the cost – but not quite. She turns back at the sea's margin, unable to commit to total immolation.

Birth offers a radical alternative to the familiar perspective on protagonists in which they are understood each to have a psyche, albeit injured to one degree or another. Obviously the film presents such a point of view, but in parallel it plays with another hypothesis compatible with some Eastern religions, namely that on the contrary the psyche has the characters. This belief is related to the postulate that Jung called the *unus mundus* wherein the physical and psychic worlds are both held within the one cosmos (1954b: 538). In a universe in which psyche overarches the physical, the boy's written farewell to Anna, mentioning that they may meet in another life, would be more than a self-deprecating and courteous closing line. Rather it would invoke with sincerity the wished-for prospect of reincarnation. In such a world Sean's karma would require that during his present life he give up Anna because as an unfaithful husband in his previous incarnation he had not earned the right to reclaim that role. He would also have to work out his earlier denial of reincarnation. For her part, Anna too would have karmic work to do. Before she could meet Sean on equal terms, she would need to find the courage to face her intuitions and follow where they lead her without hiding in repression's bolthole.

In the final analysis, *Birth* (perhaps playing to its presumed liberal-minded audience) commits to neither epistemological perspective but lets them both stand. To judge by blog reviews posted by audience members, the resultant conflict between opposed worldviews (to which the film-makers cannily offer no resolution) is one of its distinctive attractions. Playing with so many linked oppositions, *Birth* challenges the audience no less than its protagonists to think – better, to feel – their way through issues relating to the development of the psyche and rebirth while in its very being reaffirming the value of fantasy in securing the psyche's integration.

Notes

1 Although he is ten, his bedroom is still decorated to suit a six-year-old, possibly inferring some developmental arrest.
2 Which explains why the friendly janitor allows the boy into the lobby.
3 Cumbow (2006) notes that the music tutor cannot afford black tie and opera.
4 Another moment of synchronicity seems to invoke the supernatural and thereby authenticate Young Sean's claims: a black cat runs between him and Bob during their interview.
5 As Anna's chosen love object, her husband had been purely ideal, typical of an interrupted adolescence where the necessary phase of de-idealising the parents has not occurred to make it possible to separate from them and become a fully actualised person (see La Planche and Pontalis, 1973: 258–9).
6 Consciousness of the inner child can help direct emotion to transform relationships.
7 'Our ancestors move along with us, in underground rivers and springs too deep for chaos to reach' (Lamb, 2008).
8 Among many details that link *Birth* with *Eyes Wide Shut* is the way Nicole Kidman makes both Anna and Alice Harford coyly bleat the word 'married' like a spoilt girl.

References

Chaw, Walter (2004). *Birth*. Retrieved from http://www.filmfreakcentral.net/screenreviews/psbirth.htm (accessed 28 May 2007).
Cozzalio, Dennis (2006). The mystery of *Birth*. In *Sergio Leone and the Infield Fly Rule* (10 February). Retrieved from http://sergioleoneifr.blogspot.com/2006/02/mystery-of-birth.html (accessed 31 May 2007).
Cumbow, Robert C. (2006). Why is this film called *Birth*? Investigating Jonathan Glazer's mystery of the heart (23 January). Retrieved from http://

www.24liesasecond.com/site2/index.php?page=2&task=index_onearticle. php&Column_Id=86 (accessed 29 May 2007).

Edinger, Edward F. (1985). *Anatomy of the Psyche: Alchemical Symbolism in Psychotherapy*. Chicago: Open Court.

Fredericksen, Don (2001). Jung/sign/symbol/film. In Christopher Hauke and Ian Alister (eds), *Jung and Film: Post-Jungian Takes on the Moving Image*. London: Brunner-Routledge.

Hopcke, Robert H. (1989). *A Guided Tour of the Collected Works of C. G. Jung*. Boston: Shambhala.

Hughes, Darren (2006). *Birth* (2 June). Retrieved from http://www.longpauses.com/blog/2006/06/birth-2004.html (accessed 24 May 2007).

Izod, John (2006). *Screen, Culture, Psyche: A Post-Jungian Approach to Working with the Audience*. London: Routledge.

Jung, C. G. (1927/1931). Mind and Earth. In *Civilization in Transition, The Collected Works*, *Vol. 10*. London: Routledge and Kegan Paul [1964].

—— (1943). On the Psychology of the Unconscious. In *Two Essays on Analytical Psychology, The Collected Works*, *Vol. 7* (2nd edn.). London: Routledge & Kegan Paul [1966].

—— (1946). The Psychology of the Transference. In *The Practice of Psychotherapy, The Collected Works*, *Vol 16* (2nd edn.). Princeton: Princeton University Press [1985].

—— (1951). The Psychology of the Child Archetype. In *The Archetypes and the Collective Unconscious, The Collected Works*, *Vol. 9(i)* (2nd edn.). London: Routledge & Kegan Paul [1968].

—— (1954a). Psychological Aspects of the Mother Archetype. In *The Archetypes and the Collective Unconscious, The Collected Works*, *Vol. 9(i)* (2nd edn.). London: Routledge & Kegan Paul [1968].

—— (1954b). *Mysterium Coniunctionis, The Collected Works*, *Vol. 14* (2nd edn.). Princeton, NJ: Princeton University Press [1970].

—— (1956). *Symbols of Transformation, The Collected Works*, *Vol. 5*, (2nd edn.). London: Routledge & Kegan Paul.

Lamb, Wally (2008). *The Hour I First Believed*. New York: Harper Collins.

Lowery, David (2004). Reversing the gaze (7 November). Retrieved from http://www.road-dog-productions.com/reviews/archives/2004/11/birth.html (accessed 28 May 2007).

Mitchell, Stephen A. (1993). *Hope and Dread in Psychoanalysis*. New York: Basic Books.

Neumann, Erich (1954). *The Origins and History of Consciousness*. Princeton, NJ: Princeton University Press [1973].

'Ronnie' (2003). Patience & prudence: One hit wonders of 1956 (14 May). Retrieved from http://earcandy_mag.tripod.com/rrcase-patienceprud.htm (accessed 17 July 2007).

Chapter 5

Soul and space in the Coen brothers' *No Country for Old Men*

Christopher Hauke

Jungian psychology is more than a psychology of individual minds. Not only did Jung propose the idea of a collective unconscious, thus adding a universal and historical context to depth psychology, but his idea extended beyond the personal psyche to theorise how what we experience as mind or psyche is also outside our heads and in the world at large. In former times this integration of psyche and world was called *anima mundi* or world-soul.

For the last two thousand years of the Christian era, the idea of soul has been cordoned off and reserved as something to define the unique essence of human beings alone as distinct and separate from other things in the world. By 'other things' I mean not only animate creatures as well as inanimate plants and trees, but also the inorganic rocks and rivers, hills and seas. Once humans gave up animism – that scorn of Enlightenment science, let alone Christianity – and abandoned the cheerful habit of populating the world with gods and spirits, as James Hillman says,

> Stones became only stones – trees, trees; places and animals no longer were this god or that, but became "symbols" or were said to "belong" to one god or another.
> (Hillman, 1991: 97)

By juxtaposing man and the landscape, the first few minutes at the start of the Coen brothers' film *No Country For Old Men* (2007) conveys the present-day contrast between a world still full with *anima mundi* and the psyche or soul of men living unaware of any such connection with their environment.

Hillman notes important consequences of such a de-godding of nature:

> As the human loses personal connection with personified nature and personified instinct, the image of Pan and the image of the devil merge. Pan [. . ..] lives in the repressed which returns, in the psychopathologies of instinct which assert themselves [. . . .] primarily in the nightmare and its associated erotic, demonic and panic qualities.
>
> (ibid.: 97–8)

There is a nightmare at work throughout Cormac McCarthy's novel and the Coen brothers' film *No Country for Old Men*. The nightmare is the modern state of criminal behaviour and the ethical void it exposes. This is reflected upon by the aging sheriff, Ed Tom Bell, who comes from a long line of law men yet, 'can't help but wondering how they would've operated these times. The crime you see now it's hard to take its measure.' His narration describes a poignant lack, a loss of humanity experienced in a landscape still full of soul. At the opening of the film, we listen to Sheriff Bell's (Tommy Lee Jones) narrative reflections while, in stark contrast, we are shown still shots of a striking, undeveloped landscape. This is the visual space that will be the setting of Bell's story. The function of such an environment – especially in the early scenes of the film – is more than mere background. The vast presence of the landscape suggests *anima mundi* at work, persisting still, in spite of the hollow attempts of men's aspirations and desires.

After this we see a police officer murdered by a man escaping his custody, and then we are back in the landscape with our everyman hero Llewelyn Moss (Josh Brolin) who is hunting deer. The vast, wide, arid space looks utterly inhospitable to humans, but, tiny, at the left of the screen Llewelyn marches across armed with a rifle. Although they are of such different orders, the landscape and the man are temporally brought together by his hunting, his will. The landscape, let alone the deer, has no say in this. Llewelyn's only participation in the landscape is to exploit it for what he can take, while for us, watching, the photography reminds us of the soul of the space and returns it to us.

In silence, with no music or narration (underscoring how this is not a place for humans) Llewelyn scans the landscape for the deer he shot. Looking down he sees a trail of blood in the dirt. Then, instead of a wounded deer, he spies a dog – man's companion – limping away into the distance, indicating another human presence in the environment. Sure enough, as he peers over a rise he sees evidence of human occupation of the landscape. Far in the distance in an arrangement reminiscent of the covered wagons of old Westerns are five pick-up trucks, quite stationary. Human activity – but nothing is moving. As still and silent as the rocks and the hills, nothing stirs or makes a sound. It is as if the soul of the space has sucked the life out of its human occupiers and replenished itself once more.

As part of his critique of modern consciousness, Jung never ceases to remind us of the implications of de-souling the world:

> We think we can congratulate ourselves on having already reached such a pinnacle of clarity, imagining that we have left all those phantasmal gods far behind. But what we have left behind are only verbal spectres, not the psychic facts that were responsible for the birth of the gods. We are still as much possessed by autonomous psychic contents [. . .] Today they are called phobias, obsessions, and so forth; [. . .] The gods have become diseases.
> (Jung, 1957: para. 54)

In his understanding of the sufferings of modernity, Jung does not speak as a philosopher or even as a Green activist, of course, but as a psychologist. Moreover, that particular type of psychologist: the psychotherapist who seeks ways to think about and treat individuals suffering from this particular wound of modernity.

Once more like a hunter pursuing an opportunity delivered out of the wildness of the landscape, Llewelyn descends to find the dead bodies of dogs and men – their blood soaking their shirts and the ground where they lay, guns still clutched in dead hands. In conventional post-Christian terms, these are men whose souls have departed. Llewelyn is the 'only soul alive'. But soul endures: in the land, the trees, in the wind and the grass. Soul is there whether we like it or not. It is there in this world as much as in the living man.

Cautiously, he opens the cabs of the trucks to check. He jumps back as a blood-stained face utters 'Agua'. Llewelyn denies the man this life essential with a dismissive 'I ain't got no agua.' They are Mexicans. Going to the back of the truck he discovers the reason for their deaths: hundreds of kilo bricks of brown heroin. In this narrative element and image is the further stark contrast of a crop born of the land, grasped by human desires, transformed by ingenious chemistry and reborn as a cashable commodity. A de-souled crop – or is it re-souled – certainly destined to be re-sold on the street and transformed into money. Money which nowadays becomes like water and like soul itself – which animates everything and, in the belief of Llewellyn's and millions like him, makes everything possible.

This is the start of the story of the man with the rifle, how he seeks to regain and hold onto what feels like a fullness of soul that this landscape has delivered up for him.

He surveys the surrounding hills, muttering as he waits for them to speak back. Instead of a reply, far in the distance they show him the tips of a pair of boots. Immobile as the land itself, Llewelyn waits patiently to see if they move. The boots remain as still as the tree that shades them, so Llewelyn judges it safe to approach. On the move again, he is once more a man in pursuit of his will and the landscape and its soul shrink away from his needs and from his concern. We see Llewelyn from a low angle, with the clear blue sky behind, as he finds the 'last man' dead and opens the blood-stained bag beside him. In close-up, we see what he sees. Gone is the landscape, gone are the grass and stones, gone is the broad sky. The hunter's world, the *anima mundi* of this modern man, has shrunk down to one thing. Thousands of dollars in bundled notes. Enough to sell your soul for. Money for the rest of his life. If only he can hang on to it.

After we de-godded the world, the next thing you know, humans think – and act – as if they are the ones in charge. As Hillman puts it:

> When Pan is dead, then nature can be controlled by the will of the new God, man, modelled in the image of Prometheus or Hercules, creating from it and polluting in it without a troubled conscience.
> (Hillman, 1991: 98)

References

Coen, Joel and Coen, Ethan (2007) *No Country for Old Men*. Los Angeles, CA: Paramount Vantage/New York: Miramax.

Hillman, James (1991) *A Blue Fire* (Thomas Moore, Ed.). New York: Harper Perennial.

Jung, C.G., 1957 *Commentary on the Secret of the Golden Flower*, Coll. Wks.13. Edited by H. Reid *et al.* Trans. R.F.C. Hull. London: Routledge and Kegan Paul. Para. 54.

Part II

Image and theory

Chapter 6

Jungian film studies
The corruption of consciousness and the nurturing of psychological life

Don Fredericksen

In the fall of 1993, in the middle of a Cornell University seminar on Jung, film, and the process of self-knowledge, one of the best students brought our discussion about Jung's history of the symbol *vis-à-vis* film to an agitated silence by exclaiming that his normally intelligent professor was, in his words, 'full of crap.' It was not his usual diction or tonal register, but in casting doubt upon the symbolic qualities of *Star Wars* (1977), I had touched an emotionally charged nerve. Like the rest of the class, I tried to take at that moment a measure of the depth and tone of this outburst before responding. It was the genuine article and was subsequently engaged as such, but to this day it troubles me in the same way that the primary focus of Jungian film studies on popular narrative film and television troubles me. (Readers interested in my student's own report of this discussion may wish to read Conn [1997]. We remain on warm speaking terms; perhaps some day we will screen *Star Wars* together and continue the debate.) Reflection upon this fact seems necessary, perhaps especially now, when the recent past has seen the unprecedented publication of a very significant number of books and anthologies of Jungian film studies, including those by Bassil-Morozow (2010), Apperson and Beebe (2008), Cater (2005), Fredericksen (2005), Fredericksen and Hendrykowski (2007), Hauke and Alister (2001), Hockley (2001, 2007), Izod (2001, 2006), Singh (2009) and Waddell (2006, 2009). Reflection is needed now, just as these books herald increased visibility for Jungian perspectives on film among readers and students who may well be encountering such perspectives for the first time. Those of us who engage in this work are at that point where we need to know better the nature and function of our criticism: we need a theory of Jungian film criticism, nested within a theory of film, its creation, and its exhibition.

Whether we acknowledge it or not, our film criticism carries the authority and legitimacy of expertise, especially so for the reader or student whose knowledge of Jung is rudimentary or just beginning. What we say defines in an inductive and performative way the domain of film open to our Jungian lenses. Here arrives the first troubling aspect of our current emphasis upon popular narrative film. This specific mode of film has been dominant since at least 1910 – so dominant that most people mistakenly confound it with film as a whole. But it is precisely in film's other four modes – art cinema, the documentary, the personal film, and animation – where much of the richest material for Jungian hermeneutics resides. We need to serve our readers by pointing this fact out. The barriers against this move are formidable and not specific to Jungians: few film academics teach art cinema, or documentary history; even fewer teach the personal film or animation. Most, if they are aware of it at all, find the personal film self-indulgent, narcissistic in the common understanding of the word, obscure in meaning, or obscurantist in form, and without social merit – rather like the way many persons treat dreams. The absence of these modes from the film curriculum as a whole leaves them in a limbo: they exist, but, by and large, are neither screened nor discussed by those who define the domain and range of film by what they teach. This is a very substantial handicap against the working out of the full power and range of Jungian film studies. For example, the heyday of the American personal film, running from the 1940s through the 1970s, is a mother lode of opportunity for employing Jung's notions of active imagination, amplification, two types of thinking, alchemy, and that very pregnant term Jungians have borrowed from anthropology: liminality. Murray Stein's *In Midlife* (1985) is a richly suggestive source for working with this latter notion. If Jungians don't demonstrate the utility of these notions, no one will, and the personal film will have lost a set of its potentially most revealing hermeneutic mirrors.

The relative invisibility of art cinema, documentary, personal film, and animation is more than matched by the ubiquitous and aggressive presence of the popular film and its critical commentaries, among them the Jungian ones. The latter's focus upon the popular film duplicates the general swing of film studies into self-tagged cultural studies, but it also correlates with a vector within Jungian thought as a whole, for which we can get the gist from this paragraph in Andrew Samuels' *Jung and the Post-Jungians*:

> There is a general move in analytical psychology away from single, big, decorous, numinous expectations of archetypal imagery. The archetypal may be said to be found in the eye of the beholder and not in that which he beholds . . . The archetypal is a perspective defined

in terms of its impact, depth, consequence and grip. The archetypal is in the emotional experience of perceptions and not in a pre-existing list of symbols.

(Samuels, 1985: 23)

Although the implied turn to the ordinary register of life in these claims cannot be equated with a turn to the popular in art, some such conflation is made by writers on popular film, including Jungians. The bridging notion seems to be that of 'collective'. The perspective signaled by the nominal forefronting of the otherwise adjectival 'archetypal' partially parallels the manner in which Jung defines the symbol in *Psychological Types*, but it is also based on a too sharply drawn distinction between 'the eye of the beholder' and 'that which he beholds'. And it ignores the fact that the symbolic character of some symbols – as Jung states – 'does not depend merely on the attitude of the observing consciousness, but manifests itself spontaneously in the symbolic effect they have on the observer' (Jung, 1976: para. 818). Nor does it address the questions of how perspectives might develop, be evaluated in relationship to one another, or be blind to symbolic riches for which they have no detector or container – or how they might be *seduced* by signs masquerading as symbols. This last possibility, in particular, points to my disquietude with claims to have found the archetypal in popular film, although each of them touches this disquietude in its own way.

I am not so naive as to believe that popular film will soon lose its noisy dominance, or that Jungian film criticism will abandon its fascination with this mode of film. Such cultural activities are like heavy ships that require long distances to stop; in the interim, one can only hope to change their vectors slightly by reflecting on their nature and functions. With regard to Jungian film criticism vis-à-vis popular film, this means two things: 1) asking ourselves as Jungians what we wish to accomplish by such teaching and writing and 2) asking about the nature and function of the larger cultural system of which popular film is an animated part. In this way, *we might well continue the focus on popular film, but within a psychologically meaningful critique of the system we find ourselves and it nested within.* Any journalistic-centered theory of Jungian film criticism is going to be deficient; we are not in the business of hitting daily deadlines with scrappy plot summaries. Our work is, to my farmer's son's mind, rather like the cow chewing on its cud; we employ the mind's teeth and taste buds to analyse and savour images and sounds. And our work shares the myriad sensitivities of the animal nose in its reliance upon intuition, the ability to see in and through the surface, beyond what the senses provide. This does not mean that we ignore the surface; if we did so we would be blind precisely to those aesthetic qualities of the artwork that distinguish expression in one medium from another and one work from another. It does mean we reject literalism.

Unfortunately and ironically, Jungian film criticism can feed a kind of *archetypal literalism* when it abstracts any archetypal register from the concrete particularities of a film. Hillman's argument against the symbol and for the image is very credible on this issue (see Hillman, 1977, 1978). One might argue these thoughts along by noting that no greater wonder attaches to the apparent existence of the archetypes than attaches to their myriad manifestation in the material realm. Wonder is no poorer for considering both.

I would suggest that *Jungian film criticism has two tasks: first, to work against what the philosopher R. G. Collingwood calls the 'corruption of consciousness'* – which is precisely the function he calls upon art itself to perform in the powerful conclusion to his *Principles of Art*:

> To readers who want not amusement or magic, but poetry, and who want to know what poetry can be, if it is to be neither of these things, *The Waste Land* supplies an answer. And by reflecting on it we can perhaps detect one more characteristic which art must have, if it is to forgo both entertainment value and magical value, and draw a subject matter from its audience themselves. It must be prophetic. The artist must prophesy not in the sense that he foretells things to come, but in the sense that he tells his audience, at the risk of their displeasure, the secrets of their own hearts. His business as an artist is to speak out, to make a clean breast. But what he has to utter is not, as the individualistic theory of art would have us think, his own secrets. As spokesman of his community, the secrets he must utter are theirs. The reason why they need him is that no community altogether knows its own heart; and by failing in this knowledge a community deceives itself on the one subject concerning which ignorance means death. For the evils which come from that ignorance the poet as prophet suggests no remedy, because he has already given one. The remedy is the poem itself. *Art is the community's medicine for the worst disease of the mind, the corruption of consciousness.*
>
> (Collingwood, 1958: 336, my emphasis)

Consciousness can be corrupted in many ways, some of them conscious, some of them unconscious, *some of the latter archetypal*. The corrupting of consciousness goes hand in glove with its impoverishment. They are tandem impediments to self-knowledge, which Jung reminds us is an act of culture in the broadest sense. We might also reflect on the corruption of consciousness as a correlative of personal and cultural neurosis, whose imbalance Jung at one point attributes to the giving of wrong answers to the fundamental questions of life (Jung, 1965: 143–5). Collingwood has suggested how art itself addresses these issues; it remains to be seen if Jungian film criticism can somehow match art's prophetic function. This process could begin by asking where the prophetic function happens in films, and, with more relevance to popular film, what conditions *frustrate* that function.

Within the text of the film, this means asking after the nature of the stories popular film favours. For example: are they, in Hillman's phrase, 'healing fictions' (Hillman, 1983)? Are they, as the philosopher of art Abraham Kaplan richly suggests, 'pre-digested' and abstract in the way that stick-figures are abstract and photographs of persons are not (Kaplan, 1966: 351–64)? When they touch upon the apparently archetypal register of life, what stories do they use to describe or explain it – remembering not only Jung's claim that an age can be unbalanced because it tells itself wrong or wrongheaded stories, but also his tandem claim that wrong explanations for experiences in the archetypal register can damage the psyche as severely as wrong attitudes toward the physical body can damage the latter.

When we move to the extra-textual realm, we are seeking to nest the film in several generative contexts: personal, institutional, technological, cultural. Some passing examples of what is needed can be given here: we could well use an archetypal analysis of Hollywood as an institution. Thinking through its dynamics as an ever shifting and dramatic dance between the puer's love of possibility and the senex's concern for order, in an environment of dark Eros, constitutes a move in that direction, giving us one Jungian way of understanding Hollywood's dialectic between creativity and economic rationalization.

On the personal level, we need seriously and comprehensively to consider the influence of drugs – stimulants, psychedelics, and narcotics – in the creation of popular film images. Those who know Hollywood culture know their use is pervasive, but among academics a paranoid or moralistic taboo against its serious analysis operates, *as if analysis were advocacy*. Comparative analyses could be helpful here; for example, between the studied and self-acknowledged use of psychedelics by Jordan Belson, a San Francisco personal filmmaker who has created films of extraordinary archetypal power, and their apparently chaotic use by the cast, crew, and director of Oliver Stone's *Natural Born Killers* (1994). The groundbreaking clinical work of the psychiatrist Stanislav Grof, including *Realms of the Human Unconscious* (1976) and *Beyond the Brain* (1985), among other books, is a rich source for ascertaining the personal and transpersonal roots of imagery generated by psychoactive substances. His work, rarely cited in Jungian studies, complements the latter, and offers insight into the nature of archetypal imagery in popular film and in larger fields of archetypal manifestations. And a study like Marcus Boon's *The Road of Excess: A History of Writers on Drugs* (2002) catalogues the several registers of drugs writers have used, and provides one model for work that should be done in film studies, insofar as the latter considers relevant the quality of the membrane between the conscious and unconscious realms of the creative mind.

The cultural nesting evokes more comments than space allows, but Jung's history of the symbol yields a rich set of complications for the study of film. Explicitly and implicitly put forth in *The Archetypes and the Collective Unconscious* (1968) – for me one of Jung's most movingly imagistic works – this history begins with the *living symbol* and moves through myriad *intellectual elaborations* to the *dogmatic symbol*. The latter's function is to protect the majority of persons from the heat of the original experience while nonetheless bestowing some of the symbol's healing *transcendental function* (Jung, 1968: paras 12–24; 1969: paras 131–93). From here 'cooling off' processes continue to the point where the symbol dies to its symbolic function, remaining of historical interest, but *still capable of gripping us in its afterglow. This last stage is of particular relevance to the presence of archetypal imagery in popular film*. Of additional interest to us here is the rapid and apparently inevitable process of the symbol's metamorphosis into a sign, of its movement from the unknown into the registers of the known. Why is this process inevitable? In part, because the passage of time reveals what is originally unknown. In part, because the conscious mind and the cultural consciousness which are confronted by the symbol rather quickly begin the process of intellectual elaboration, cooling it down. In part, because, as the American writer Flannery O'Connor observes, mystery – true mystery – is an *embarrassment* to contemporary culture.

With regard to these matters, my suggestion for a Jungian theory of the broader nesting of the creation of films is rather simple: *let us test the utility of the notions 1) that individual films, larger modes of film, and historical moments in film's history are situated at differing points along the trajectory of the symbols' move from living to dogmatic to dead symbols, and 2) that these differences are important markers of the differing functions films play.*

If we use the terms Jung employed in his own aesthetics essay on literature and psychology, the films at the hot end of the trajectory would fall within the *visionary* mode, while those at the cool end would fall within the *psychological* mode (Jung, 1966: para. 139). I believe that popular film *as a mode* is clearly at the cool end of the trajectory. Here, finessing Kaplan's notion of pre-digestion along the lines that the putatively symbolic register in popular film is the result of much pre-production schematization could be very helpful, with evidence provided by in-depth case studies. (I have touched on this issue in some greater detail in 'Arguments in Favor of a Jungian Hermeneutic of Suspicion' [2010].) There are exceptions, and they bear close scrutiny for their apparent ability to manoeuvre the living symbolic register through the myriad semiotic elaborations of story material typical of commercial narrative film-making as a system of image-production. I would offer as examples Nicholas Roeg's *Walkabout* (1971) and Hitchcock's *Vertigo* (1958); the exceptions are as important to study in this regard as the majority, which are not exceptions.

On the other hand, the other four modes of film provide a more amenable context for the occurrence of the hotter end of the symbolic register. The reasons vary, but the more intimate relationship between the intrapsychic symbolic material and the completed film plays a major role. Intellectual elaboration remains, but the possibility that it serves the symbol's mysterious life rather than commercial interests increases. *The question of what the conscious elaboration of symbols serves is crucial in thinking about the creation and criticism of films, just as it is in thinking about the process of personal analysis.* The ego in the service of the symbol, i.e. symbolically, works differently from the ego in the service of its own already known interests, i.e. semiotically.

Let me now turn to *Jungian film criticism's suggested second task:* to nurture *'psychological life'* – to which it should call film-makers and film viewers alike. One's psychological life is in part constituted by the turbulence of passages from one stage of development to another. As mentioned earlier, Murray Stein's *In Midlife* (1985) provides an excellent example of how such passages, especially the liminal period, can be written about through the hermeneutic of amplification. It also yields one basis for interpreting and evaluating films portraying such passages. More generally, as Hillman expresses it, *psychological life has to do with turning events into experiences through the activity of the reflective moment* (Hillman, 1975: x). Here we need to celebrate those films in which the reflective moment exercises its soul-making function, either momentarily, or more rarely, throughout the body of the film.

This train of thought moves us to consider the film-viewers' situation. In 'The Work of Art in the Age of Mechanical Reproduction' the Marxist critic Walter Benjamin famously maintained that the film viewer is in a state of distraction (1969: 238). This partial truth carries even greater weight in any description of today's television viewer of moving images, the latter, zapper in hand, is often involved in other activities. *Formal containers for turning the events of a film into an experience do not interact well with the distracted mind.* Indeed, keeping viewers in a distracted state of consciousness seems to be a primary function of popular film. Lacking the formal pre-conditions for turning events into experiences, popular film tends to remain an event about events. As such, it does little or nothing to nurture psychological life. I think we as Jungians need to say this, and, when we can, present descriptions, interpretation, and evaluations – and counter-examples – of those failures of form. The American personal film-maker Maya Deren's notion of a *vertical structure* gives us one counter-example at the theoretical level, insofar as it recommends a film form that reveals the psychic depth of events by dropping plumb-lines into them – this against the typical procedure of 'classic narration' which makes events parts of a causal chain: $A \rightarrow A^1 \rightarrow A^2$ versus $A \rightarrow B \rightarrow C \rightarrow D$ (Deren *et al.*, 1970). Vertical structure's logic is more associative and resonant than causal, and it has the power to slow down the distracted 'monkey-mind' of the viewer. Hillman's 'Stories for the Millennium' comes at this issue from a complementary angle, with its talk of needing stories that set themselves in opposition to the ways we have been 'railroaded down the tracks of linear time', and offering instead to 'break up our clocks' with invitations to sit still with 'densities, long descriptive meanders, sudden bursts of action . . . pauses' (Hillman, 1998: 39–41).

If and when the viewer of popular film encounters archetypal imagery, he does so in a way that costs him almost nothing psychologically. This profoundly alters the encounter's psychological value, cheapening it, and *seducing the viewer into believing that the ego can encounter the archetypal register without real consequences.* In this regard, popular film resembles the recreational use of psychedelics, from which little is taken that might deepen one's psychological life. Moreover, film-viewing takes place within a larger cultural environment in which archetypal imagery has slipped free of its traditional moorings to join the contemporary, archetypal version of Babel. In this situation, the probability of archetypal vertigo is higher than a transformative encounter with a living symbol. The historian of religion Huston Smith has cautioned in relation to spiritual experiences *via* psychedelics that the point is not spiritual experience, but a spiritual life. We could well say the same with regard to the psychological register of our lives, noting as we do that the viewing context of popular film puts a deep strain on its use for either spiritual or psychological life.

Popular film will not disappear, nor will the inclination to write about it by Jungians. That granted, let us nonetheless remember that *we are at the service of something deeper than the popular*, something deeper than the semiotic register of living, something beyond the literal. And let us be mindful too that other modes of film hold much that we should be noting for our readers. Thus do we acknowledge the ethical and therapeutic aspects of our work as teachers and scholars of the moving image in the postmodern world.

References

Apperson, V. and Beebe, J. (2008) *The Presence of the Feminine in Film*. Newcastle: Cambridge Scholars Publishing.

Bassil-Morozow, H. (2010) *Tim Burton: The Monster and the Crowd*. London and New York: Routledge.

Benjamin, W. (1969) 'The Work of Art in the Age of Mechanical Reproduction'. In *Illuminations*. New York: Schocken.

Boon, M. (2002) *The Road of Excess: A History of Writers on Drugs*. Cambridge: Harvard University Press.

Cater, N. (ed.) (2005) *Spring 73: Cinema and Psyche*. New Orleans, LA: Spring Journal.

Collingwood, R. G. (1958) *Principles of Art*. Oxford: Oxford University Press.

Conn, A. (1997) 'Star Wars: Always'. In *Film Comment*, *180*(3), 7–8.

Deren, M., Miller, A., Tyler, P. and Thomas, D. (1970) 'Poetry and Film: A Symposium'. In P.A. Sitney (ed.), *Film Culture Reader*. New York: Praeger.

Fredericksen, D. (2005) *Bergman's Persona*. Poznan: Adam Mickiewicz University Press.

Fredericksen, D. (2010) 'Arguments in Favor of a Jungian Hermeneutic of Suspicion'. In M. Stein and R. Jones (eds), *Cultures and Identities in Transition*. New York: Routledge.

Fredericksen, D. and Hendrykowski, M. (2007) *Wajda's Kanal*. Poznan: Adam Mickiewicz University Press.

Grof, S. (1976) *Realms of the Human Unconscious: Observations from LSD Research*. New York: Dutton.

Grof, S. (1985) *Beyond the Brain: Birth, Death and Transcendence in Psychotherapy*. Albany: State University of New York Press.

Hauke, C. and Alister, I. (eds) (2001) *Jung and Film: Post-Jungian Takes on the Moving Image*. London and New York: Routledge.
Hillman, J. (1975) *Re-Visioning Psychology*. NewYork: Harper and Row.
Hillman, J. (1977) 'An Inquiry into Image'. In *Spring: An Annual of Archetypal Psychology and Jungian Thought*. Dallas: Spring.
Hillman, J. (1978) 'Further Notes on the Image'. In *Spring: An Annual of Archetypal Psychology and Jungian Thought*. Dallas: Spring.
Hillman, J. (1983) *Healing Fictions*. Barrytown, NY: Station Hill.
Hillman, J. (1998) 'Stories for the Millennium'. In *The Salt Journal*, *1*(3), 39–41.
Hockley, L. (2001) *Cinematic Projections: The Analytical Psychology of C. G. Jung and Film Theory*. Luton: Luton University Press.
Hockley, L. (2007) *A Post-Jungian Look at Cinema, Television, and Technology*. Bristol and Chicago: Intellect.
Izod, J. (2001) *Myth, Mind and the Screen*. Cambridge: Cambridge University Press.
Izod, J. (2006) *Screen, Culture, Psyche: A Post-Jungian Approach to Working with the Audience*. New York and London: Routledge.
Jung, C. G. (1965) *Memories, Dreams, Reflections* (A. Jaffé, ed.). New York: Vintage.
Jung, C. G. (1966) 'Psychology and Literature'. In *The Collected Works of C. G. Jung*, *Vol. 15*. Princeton: Princeton University Press.
Jung, C. G. (1968) *The Archetypes and the Collective Unconscious*, *The Collected Works of C. G. Jung*, *Vol. 9(i)* (2nd edn). Princeton: Princeton University Press.
Jung, C. G. (1969) 'The Transcendent Function'. In *The Collected Works of C. G. Jung*, *Vol. 8* (2nd edn). Princeton: Princeton University Press.
Jung, C. G. (1976) *Psychological Types*, *The Collected Works of C. G. Jung*, *Vol. 6* (rev. edn). Princeton: Princeton University Press.
Kaplan, A. (1966) 'The Aesthetics of the Popular Arts'. In *Journal of Aesthetics and Art Criticism*, *24*(3), 351–64.
Samuels, A. (1985) *Jung and the Post-Jungians*. Boston and London: Routledge and Kegan Paul.
Singh, G. (2009) *Film after Jung: Post-Jungian Approaches to Film Theory*. London and New York: Routledge.
Stein, M. (1985) *In Midlife*. Dallas: Spring.
Waddell, T. (2006) *Archetype, Myth and Identity in Screen Fiction*. London and New York: Routledge.
Waddell, T. (2009) *Trickster, Place and Liminality on Screen*. London and New York: Routledge.

Chapter 7

'Much begins amusingly and leads into the dark'
Jung's popular cinema and the Other

Christopher Hauke

Shadow, Other, and Jung's 'Hell has its levels'

The Shadow archetype is the obverse to self-identity – it is the Other to all we think we are. Shadow may be defined as that with which we do not identify, that which is rejected as 'not me'. To struggle with the Shadow and to confront the abject, is one of the tasks of individuation – fulfilling one's potential as a unique human being. Throughout *The Red Book* (Jung, 2009), the record of Jung's self-exploration through fantasies and paintings begun in 1913, Jung reports his struggle with many opposed and rejected parts of his nature such as the feminine in himself, the banal, the irrational and magic – all that Jung consciously rejected but now finds he has to include in his being.

At several moments, we find Jung suggesting there may be a place in Hell for the Shadow aspects of psyche which he detects in himself and may be found in many of us. One Hell is for those who reject an affinity with cinema, another is populated by those who reject any identity with the imprisoned, and a third is for people who so hang on to conscious life that they never consider death. While these levels of Hell seem quite different – some apparently banal, some profound – what they have in common is that they are all about rejection. Such acts of exclusion and rejection initiate the struggle with the Shadow archetype.

Ever since the Lumiere Brothers first screened their films in Paris in 1895, popular cinema has been met with rejection and disdainfully valued lower than theatre and other performance arts. Just as the popular novel cannot compare to 'literature', both are accused of being purely commercial and banal. But as any struggle with what we reject and despise in the end brings us more self-understanding, we propose that a similar struggle with popular film – the rejected shadow of film-as-art – is worthwhile. *The Red Book* is Jung's record of his struggle with the opposing parts of himself and the contemporary psyche in general – which includes encounters with popular cinema and the banal. In this period of his thinking and fantasising, Jung is at the start of an individuation crisis where everything he once believed and valued is getting turned upon its head; an agonising crisis brought on by rifts between Jung and the psychoanalytic community, and his sensitivity to the turmoil of Europe at that time. This struggle lasted several years and was a process which would eventually deliver for Jung his own unique insights which became formulated as analytical psychology.

'Bewitched by the banal'

Jung uses a technique of active imagination by which he lets himself drop into his unconscious to see where it leads him, and in one of the early fantasies in *The Red Book* this involves his struggle with the banal.

Jung encounters a maiden in distress who states she is being held in captivity by her father – not from hatred but out of love, as she is the image of his deceased wife. He first regards the maiden as a cliché – a character from a cheap romantic novel and despairs, 'is this not some hellish banality? Word for word, pulp fiction from the lending library?' (Jung, 2009: 262). He is scathing of his own psyche producing such corny material.

> To what nonsense am I damned? Is it my soul that harbours such novelistic brilliance? [. . .] I am truly in Hell – the worst awakening after death, to be resurrected in a lending library! Have I held the men of my time and their taste in such contempt that I must live in Hell and write out the novels that I have already spat upon long ago?
>
> (ibid.)

Despite wondering what possible value he can find in this trash, Jung pursues a conversation with the maiden:

> I: 'My dear child, I believe you, despite everything, that you are real. What can I do for you?' [. . .]
> She: 'What can you do for me? You have already done much for me. You spoke the redeeming word when you no longer placed the banal between you and me. Know then: I was bewitched by the banal.'
>
> (ibid.)

In pursuing our position on popular cinema, I take up this idea of being 'bewitched by the banal' as referring to how a core engagement with what is rejected and despised challenges us to re-assess what we reject in ourselves. I will use the example of a pair of popular film genres that are closely connected – the vampire and the gangster. I will discuss the new vampire movies shortly, but suffice it to say here that until very recently, the vampire films which were popular throughout the 1960s and 1970s seemed to have disappeared. The fact is, from the mid 1970s onward, their vampiric bloodletting had been surpassed and taken on by the gangster movie. As examples of popular cinema, the vampire film and the gangster film have two levels in common: at the level of consumption and production such populist movies are seen as a banal form of popular entertainment, holding little artistic merit and contributing even less to a knowledge of ourselves. Second, at the level of content and narrative, the vampire and the gangster are both about being rejected – those who appear human, but are outside the human sphere, lacking the very humanity that defines us.

Martin Scorsese's *The Departed* (2006) is an example of a popular gangster film from the last couple of years. In the opening scene we are introduced to Frank Costello, the central criminal protagonist of the story whose face we only see in shadow for several minutes, despite him being a main character and a star (it's Jack Nicholson). As Costello's disembodied narration describes his dark philosophy, the camera shoots from his point of view as it seems to float across the street and into a mundane corner store as if Costello is on wings. If this was not reminiscent enough of the vampire, we see him seductively charming two young people, and challenging the values of the Catholic church – extolling the individualism of, not the life of the vampire, but that of the gangster.

Themes of revenge and violence depicted in the darkest scenes of transgressive, barely human criminal activity in Martin Scorsese's *Casino*, *Taxi Driver*, *The Departed* and *Goodfellas*, or in Coppola's *The Godfather* and Brian de Palma's *Scarface* offered more bloodletting than most vampire flicks up to that time.

These gangster movies function for the collective psyche of cinemagoers in the way that they carry, and reveal, for us the Shadow of civilised society, the life we regard as separate from ourselves. With stories that involve action and characters from a very closed community of hoodlums, it is easy for us in the audience to look on smugly as the gangsters destroy each other in a world that is recognisable yet apparently apart from our own. What is seldom mentioned is how close the connection between criminal and civilised life has become. Although hidden in the shadows, criminal activities like the drug trade, prostitution and extortion are influential in structuring the social and material fabric of urban life. Organised crime drives not only aspects of economic life to a real extent, but also the political and legislative response to it that touches us all. The movies helped convince us the gangsters' life of bloody violence was set apart from our own; it was 'over there' – on the screen, or out of sight in the gangster clubs and enclaves.

The Lowly One and his cinema: Jung's epiphany

In his seminars on Dream Analysis recorded between 1928 and 1930 Jung states: 'The movies are far more efficient than the theatre: they are less restricted, they are able to produce amazing symbols to show the collective unconscious, since their methods of presentation are so unlimited' (Jung, 1984: 12).

Before this, Jung did not always think so positively about cinema. Written back in 1913, a further fantasy in *The Red Book* helps us track Jung as he questions his own impulse to reject popular mass entertainment like cinema, and has an epiphany in realising its human significance and value. In this fantasy or active imagination, which he titled 'The Rogue' or 'One of the Lowly' (Jung, 2009: 265–67), Jung is travelling in a homely, snow-covered country and is joined by a dirty-clothed man with scars on his face and only one eye – a tramp 'who does not look trustworthy' (ibid.: 265). Jung and the man strike up a conversation. The man says he is looking for work but does not want to work for a farmer in the countryside. Apart from the hard work and low wages, he says,

> He: "It's boring in the country, one meets nobody."
> I [Jung]: "Well, but there are also villagers."
> He: "But there is no mental stimulation, the farmers are clods."
> (ibid.)

Jung is surprised and wonders how this working dolt can prioritise his 'mental stimulation' before he has even secured his work. He asks the man what kind of stimulation there is in the city and gets the answer:

> He: "You can go to the cinema in the evenings. That's great and it's cheap. You get to see everything that happens in the world." [. . .]

I: "What interested you most about the cinema?"
He: "One sees all sorts of stunning feats. There was one man who ran up houses. Another carried his head under his arm. Another stood in the middle of a fire and wasn't burnt. Yes, it's really remarkable, the things that people can do."

(ibid.)

At first we find Jung sneering: 'And that's what this fellow calls mental stimulation!' In this, Jung shares an elitist attitude that has prevailed since movies began. But struggling with his disdain towards cinema – this mere entertainment for the masses – Jung reflects on his biased view and on the fate of all the anti-popular cinema snobs.

I have to think of Hell, where there are also cinemas for those who despised this institution on earth and did not go there because everyone else found it to their taste.

(ibid.)

Jung then thinks again about the wonders the indigent man says he looks forward to witnessing in the cinema and finds he appreciates the fellow's views even more. Jung compares the cinematic depictions of wonderful feats to the appeal of tales of the Saints and asks himself,

Isn't it a blasphemous idea to consider the *Acta Sanctorum* as historical cinema? Oh, today's miracles are somewhat less mythical than technical. I regard my companion with feeling – he lives the history of the world – and I?

(ibid.)

This reflection ushers in a new interest in the indigent man which Jung's fantasy explores – not Jung himself. We need to remember this is not conscious wondering but spontaneous fantasising; in 1913, Jung is allowing unconscious material to emerge much like a dream over which he has little conscious control. Consequently, we find him wondering at the narrative development of his fantasy, and his emotional response to it as much as we ourselves do, as we read.

The characters of Jung and the man arrive at an inn where, as a 'gentleman', Jung is offered a better table and meal. Jung makes sure his down-at-heel companion joins him to get as good a dinner as himself. It turns out the man lost his eye in a brawl and was imprisoned for stabbing his assailant and Jung is uncomfortably aware of what others will think of him talking to an ex-convict. Jung's self-consciousness over his social position is challenged by a second image of a Hell, as he asks himself, 'Are there also prisons in Hell for those who never saw the inside of one when they were alive?' (ibid.)

At this point, Jung asks himself an ominous question that predicts the course of his own emotional state. It is a question brought to mind directly through his fantasy encounter with the Lowly One:

> Incidentally – mustn't it be a peculiarly beautiful feeling to hit rock bottom in reality at least once, where there is no going down any further, but only upward beckons at best?
>
> (ibid.: 266)

Sometimes, Jung's fantasy itself reads like a screenplay with dialogue, action and scene descriptions. It ends after both men retire and Jung hears a racking cough coming from the other man's room. Jung rushes in to try and help and dramatically relates the man's last moments,

> I open the door of his room. Moonlight floods in. The man lies still dressed on a sack of straw. A dark stream of blood is flowing from his mouth and forming a puddle on the floor. He moans half choking and coughs out blood. He wants to get up but sinks back again – I hurry to support him but I see that the hand of death lies upon him. He is sullied with blood twice over. My hands are covered with it. A rattling sigh escapes from him. Then every stiffness loosens, a gentle shudder passes over his limbs. And then everything is deathly still.
>
> Where am I? Are there also cases of death in Hell for those who have never thought about death?
>
> (ibid.: 266)

The other on the screen

Death is certainly a key other that gets cast into shadow by our modern consciousness and Jung imagines it may produce a Hell for those who have not taken the fact of death on board. In both the popular cinema genres I have chosen, death is a constant feature. Encounters with the gangster or the vampire deliver us into a world of the other.

The vampire flicks of the 1960s and 1970s distanced themselves from our civilised human life in a very different way to the gangster movies.

They showed their world as apart from our own by being set in the fantasy landscape of a Central European fiefdom unimaginable outside the studio, and dressed in a historical period anywhere between 1780 and 1890. The vampire world constituted an Other doubly removed from us on the screen and in an undefined historical space – or a Hell of its own. Similar to the gangster movies, however, our connection to the vampire screen world has been mainly through the visceral thrill of fear – as we identified with a character's demise – or one of enjoyment as we celebrated their survival. Although vampire movie themes of sexuality and male predation on women were further taboo elements recognisable from our civilised lives which supported some partial identification, the way in which such male sexual aggression was disguised as the bloodlust of the vampire enabled us to keep the vampire on the screen as an abjected other with no connection to ourselves or our own world.

The new vampire films such as *Twilight* and the Swedish-made box office hit *Let The Right One In* (2009) bring the lust for blood and the anti-human transgression of the vampire into a modern urban environment. In these films – and in their popular TV counterparts – the vampires are not only just like us in appearance, moving among us, holding down roles in society, but now they even have our sympathy, often depicted as beautiful young people. In *Let The Right One In* the vampire is a scrawny twelve-year-old girl called Eli. This is a new Other to our sense of what it is to be human.

Like Jung as he struggles in *The Red Book* fantasies with revising everything he believed himself to be, the new vampire movie does not allow us to be so sure any more of what is human and what is its shadow. Equally, I believe, the shadow of what is deemed worthy in cinema is challenged by the new form the vampire genre takes today. As the imprisoned maiden says to Jung in his *Red Book* fantasy, 'Only what is human and what you call banal and hackneyed contains the wisdom that you seek' (2009: 263). After his encounter with her, Jung considers what the fantasy has meant for him, 'Without balance you transgress your limits without noticing what has happened to you. You achieve balance, however, only if you nurture your opposite' (ibid.).

Eli, the new vampire in *Let the Right One In*

In *Let The Right One In* we first encounter the protagonist Oskar, a human boy, also twelve, living in an apartment with his mother on a snow-bound housing estate in the Stockholm suburbs. The first thing we notice is his bright white blond hair which is to contrast sharply with

Eli's long, black hair and dark, almost Middle Eastern looks. The contrast between the two is reinforced in another way when Oskar first meets Eli in the middle of the night outside in the snow. We see Oskar practising with his knife what he would like to do to the school bully, when Eli suddenly appears – standing high above him on a climbing frame. The dynamics of dark-versus-light and high-versus-low reinforce this story of a struggle between sameness and difference that gets played out through the relationship between a vampire and a human child.

Eli has just moved into the flats and Oskar has seen the man Eli lives with putting up cardboard to blind the windows. This is the man who, while posing as a father, in fact serves Eli as the one who sources the human blood she needs to survive. We see him attempt to abduct young men at night, truss them up and let their blood – draining it into a two-gallon plastic container. Blood sucking was never so contemporary – or so banal. He is interrupted however when a large white poodle spots him and begins to bark. It bounds over and he has to abandon his duties. The body is discovered and the neighbourhood is on high alert for a murderer. It is immediately after this scene that we see Oskar and Eli meeting for the first time.

Oskar begins to fall in love with Eli, his girl of the night, while, during the day, he continues to suffer his own particular hell at the hands of the school bullies. This sub-plot has a parallel in the world of the adults on the estate, showing them aimless, drinking and quarrelling. Inevitably, it is one of these locals who falls victim to Eli. Eli, like Oskar, loses her 'Dad' – leaving both kids struggling with the growing pains and the *rites de passage* of a twelve-year-old. For Oskar it just means a long trip to meet up with his divorced Dad, while for Eli it means she has to attack an adult and, for the first time, suck blood for herself.

Oskar finds the will to face the bullies through his own efforts to get physically strong and the emotional confidence that comes from knowing he has a friend in Eli. But when a bigger more vicious kid comes after him, it is Eli who arrives to save the day. In return, Oskar saves her from exposure to the mob and travels away with her hidden in a trunk.

This may be a vampire movie but, apart from sensitivity to sunlight, none of the other tropes and clichés of the genre are present. There is no crucifix or garlic to scare the vampire, no stakes through the heart to kill her, no coffins in which to spend the day until the next bloody night. Eli sleeps on a thin mattress on the floor in a barely furnished flat. The title *Let The Right One In* refers to Eli saying to Oskar more than once, 'You have to invite me in.' On the one occasion he tests what will happen if she crosses the threshold of his flat without him asking her to, Eli begins to crack up and disintegrate, so Oskar rapidly says, 'You can come in, you can come in.' It seems that Evil has to be invited in for it to survive in his human presence.

This vampire movie is a tale of good and evil, but as with Jung's struggle with everything he rejects and casts into his shadow, Eli is seen to have more good in her than many of the humans. The bullies choose their vicious persecution of Oskar, but as a vampire, Eli has no choice but to drink blood to survive. The adults show a slovenly miscommunication with each other, while Eli and Oskar work hard to accept their differences – which are extreme.

Jung struggles with the concept of Evil and regards it as an absolute quality, not simply the absence of good as it is rendered by Christian dogma. Accepting that there is evil always present, side-by-side with good, is as important for Jung as the need to accept our contra-gender side as males or females, as well as our irrational, lowly and banal aspects. As Jung puts it: 'The devil as the adversary is your own other standpoint; he tempts you and sets a stone in your path where you least want it' (Jung, 2009: 261).

Watching Oskar, and even Eli, it crossed my mind that the New Testament tells of how Jesus Christ was about their age when he wondered off from his parents, sat down with the Rabbis in the temple and rapped impressively on spiritual matters apparently beyond his years. Alongside the banal, the popular and common, the nonsense and magical – all that is despised by our rational, scientifically validated modern views – the Child is also left behind and regarded as less than fully valid. In a world where adult maturity is the standard, the Child, by definition, is always incomplete, only ever on its way, never arrived, as someone deserving our attention.

In one poignant scene, Oskar's innocent boyish desire to make a traditional, and human, blood bond between himself and Eli, leads him to realise her otherness, and leads Eli to discover the awful tension between her desire for survival and her love for Oskar, who will always be at risk from her vampiric desires.

By depicting the progress of good and evil, the abject and the honoured, the shadow and the heroism in the boy/girl syzygy of Oskar and Eli, *Let The Right One In* offers a new look at these absolutes. This film, arising from a genre of popular cinema, offers an enjoyable opportunity to revise our perspective in a way that compares with Jung's struggle with such oppositions. As he writes of these in *The Red Book*,

> You cannot at the same time be on the mountain and in the valley, but your way leads you from mountain to valley and from valley to

mountain. Much begins amusingly and leads into the dark. Hell has levels.

(Jung, 2009: 265)

References

Alfredson, T. (2009) *Let the Right One In*. Sweden: EFTI.
Jung, C. G. (1984). Seminar Papers, Vol. 1. In W. McGuire (ed.), *Dream Analysis: Notes of the Seminar given in 1928–1930* London: Routledge.
Jung, C. G. (2009). *The Red Book: Liber Novus* (S. Shamdasani, Ed.; M. Kyburz, J. Peck and S. Shamdasani, Trans.). New York and London: Philemon Series, Norton & Co.
Scorsese, M. (2006). *The Departed*. Burbank, CA: Warner Bros.

Chapter 8

Contrasting interpretations of film
Freudian and Jungian

Michael Jacobs

In the companion to the present volume (Hauke and Alister, 2001: 95–109), Jane Ryan provides a fascinating interpretation of the film *Dark City* (Proyas, 1998). The reader may refer to the chapter in its entirety for the richness of its treatment of symbolism in the film, which I shall only summarize here, as, in Ryan's words, 'the journey of the hero, his goal being that of individuation, of psychic wholeness and healing' (Ryan, 2001: 95). From a Jungian perspective the film is indeed capable of such an interpretation, as Ryan's detailed analysis of the characters and of the themes clearly shows. She regards the film as reflecting some of the myths which provide such a treasure house of pointers to contemporary psychological issues as well as virtually timeless existential concerns.

I teach a short course annually in Swanage, England – the town where I live – to a group of intelligent lay residents who are interested in the interface between psychoanalysis and film. I should say from the outset that I am more a contemporary Freudian than a Jungian, but film can of course be interpreted in many different ways. Given the various methodologies which might be employed to interpret either the individual's images, or those which appear in art forms, I prefer not to ask the question of any film or indeed any symbol, 'What does this mean?', but prefer the more modest, 'What *might* this mean?' In film criticism it is obvious, apart from the socio-cultural approach which is less concerned with individual psychology – Marxist film criticism, for example – that even psychoanalysis is divided between Freudians, Kleinians and Lacanians when it comes to interpreting the arts (see for example Radstone's comments in Bainbridge *et al.*, 2007: 243). Freudians tend to see meaning in one way; Marxist film critics in another; and Jungians, coming late to the discipline, though not to the meaning of other art forms, have their own approach.

Each course I teach takes four films, and before viewing I provide background to the film from reviews. Following the screening, I provide course members with digests of psychoanalytic commentaries, either on the film itself or on the psychological issues raised by the film. These form the basis for discussion the week following the screening. The first course used *The Secret Passion* (Huston, 1962), which introduced the group to Freud's early thinking and analytic methods; *Wild Strawberries* (Bergman, 1957), which provided the opportunity for the group to make their own interpretations of the opening dream, as well as reflect upon memories in old age; *Dark City*, of which more below; and *Blue Velvet* (Lynch, 1986), which took the group into questions of sadomasochism and oedipal themes, very much from a Lacanian perspective.

I chose *Dark City* deliberately, because Ryan's commentary is a stimulating interpretation, and her chapter was a means of introducing the group to Jungian ideas – ideas which are not part of our culture in the same way as the (sometimes distorted) better-known interpretations of Freudian ideas. I inserted an extra week to screen part of the video of myself in conversation with Andrew Samuels (1995) to provide a foundation of Jungian concepts, before screening *Dark City*; and following the film I provided Ryan's chapter to the group.

I introduced the discussion session by sketching in further background to the difference between signs and symbols (Fredericksen, 2001) – a sign standing for what is known, and a symbol, in Jung's words, 'the best possible description of formulation of a relatively unknown fact, which is nevertheless known to exist or is postulated as existing' (cited by Fredericksen, 2001: 18). Fredericksen's examples of how the cross might be a sign or a symbol and his contrasting quotations on Metz's and Conti's interpretations of the circle at the end of Fellini's film *8½* (2001: 23–4) were instructive distinctions which I put to the group before they discussed Ryan's chapter.

However, this contrast set me thinking, what might a Freudian approach to *Dark City* suggest about the symbolic themes of that film? Fredericksen argues that there is a significant difference between Jung and Freud in relation to the unconscious, which according to Fredericksen's description of Freud's view is essentially constituted by the repressions of the conscious mind (2001: 28). I find this a very limited view of the Freudian idea of the unconscious, since it is from the unconscious, if we take a typical Freudian view, that the ego emerges. Freud saw the child as born with the unconscious, out of which, in contact with the world, develops the conscious part of the ego. The unconscious may be the place where repressed material is stored, but there is much more to the unconscious than that. Be that as it may, the Jungian unconscious can be described as involving both a personal unconscious and a collective unconscious; and the collective unconscious is not constituted by personal repressions, but by transpersonal factors that predate ego-consciousness.

Fredericksen's argument is that much of the interpretation of film consists, as in Freudian or Marxist criticism, in treating symbols with suspicion, and needing to interpret them, whereas in Jungian criticism symbols have a positive and healing function, if they are heeded. Archetypes cannot be explained finally – the most we can do is translate them into another metaphorical language. What we should do is not reduce, but amplify the image to a point where it is understandable to us, as Jung writes, 'adding further analogies to the one already provided by the symbol ... This procedure widens and enriches the initial symbol, and the final outcome is an infinitely complex and variegated picture' (cited in Fredericksen, 2001: 36).

I am not convinced that this procedure is much different from Freudian free association, which similarly extends the initial symbol as the person shifts from one association to another, all of which are significant – even though I accept the criticism that there often seems to be a final association in a chain of associations. But is there not always a danger that Jungian interpretations of symbols such as circles, the mandala, or water (to take some of the images upon which Ryan reflects) might lead to similar conclusions? As I read Jungian film criticism, I could easily be misled into thinking that symbols are interpreted, although Fredericksen, following Jung of course, prefers to call this process 'amplification' rather than 'interpretation'. There is certainly a different emphasis, Jungian interpretation preferring generally the spiritual over the physical, the transpersonal over the personal, and the healing power of the symbol rather than it pointing to the psychopathological.

A Freudian interpretation of *Dark City*

Fredericksen cites Jung as summarising the power of symbolic art:

> The impact of an archetype ... stirs us because it summons up a voice ... stronger than our own. ... This is the secret of great art, and its effect upon us. The creative process, so far as we are able to follow it at all, consists in the unconscious activation of an archetypal image, and in elaborating and shaping the image into the finished work.
>
> (2001: 49)

This is a compelling argument and I have little quarrel with it, although the emphasis on the unconscious activation of an archetypal image as leading us towards the spiritual, the transpersonal, and the unknown, is deceptive. There may be extraordinary power in the symbols which appear time and again in myths; but there is also extraordinary power in images which relate to all the key aspects of being human – to birth, to death, to the bond between mother and baby, to the family, to sex, to love, to giving birth, to the relationship of parent to child, to the non-human environment, to physical processes of growing and aging, to death itself. And while it is interesting that Freud claimed never to have had the experience of an oceanic feeling, he certainly devoted his life's work to trying to understand these all too human experiences.

After the publication of Freud's *The Future of an Illusion* (1927), a friend wrote to him, agreeing with Freud's judgement upon religion, but:

> sorry that I had not properly appreciated the true source of religious sentiments. This, he says, consists in a peculiar feeling, which he himself is never without, which he finds confirmed by many others, and which he may suppose is present in millions of people. It is a feeling which he would like to call a sensation of "eternity", a feeling as of something limitless, unbounded – as it were, 'oceanic'. . . . One may, he thinks, rightly call oneself religious on the ground of this oceanic feeling alone, even if one rejects every belief and every illusion.
>
> (Freud, 1930: 251–2)

Freud says that he cannot discover this feeling in himself, but many people would recognise what his friend described. People have experiences of a sublime and spiritual nature, not necessarily related to religion, since they can arise from moments of special contact with the world in which they live. Such sublime experience is often found through a sense of communion with nature, although it can also arise from reading poetry, or listening to music, etc. These are occasions when for a few seconds it feels (in the words of Gerard Manley Hopkins) as if 'the world is charged with the glory of God' (cited in Gardner, 1953: 27). These moments come and are soon gone, and we are often left as much in the dark as before, although at the same time we know we have caught a glimpse of something out of the ordinary.

But do these moments have to do with the transpersonal? May they not equally be reminders of the blissful union of mother and baby? Why should images in films not evoke in us powerful responses because they remind us in a deep way of intense moments in our relationships with others – good experiences as well as bad experiences? Andrew Samuels, in our video, agrees that archetypes can stand for common experiences. Common experience may appear to be more mundane than the spiritual, but nonetheless it may be no less glorious, or awesome, for all that.

Might the viewer be moved by *Dark City* for other reasons than the Jungian archetypal symbols which Ryan so beautifully draws out from the images on the screen? Approaching the film from a Freudian perspective I find myself treading a rather different path. I can see the hero's quest as about a different kind of recovery of memories. Ryan makes no comment at all upon one aspect of the film which surely has significance, and that aspect is the images of a fire in which the hero's parents are killed – brief images, but surprising that they escaped Ryan's notice. Could the film therefore be interpreted in a different way, less about individuation and the hero's recovery of the persona and of identity; but rather about recovering the repressed memories of a childhood trauma? Memories are a constant theme that runs through the film, including frightening memories. The trauma here might be the fire, an event or a series of events which the young orphaned hero has repressed, and which he struggles to get in touch with. Shell Beach, a constant image throughout the film, is a sign that points to those memories; the doctor is engaged in trying to hold those memories for him, in much the same way as a therapist holds hints of what the patient may have experienced but appears as yet not to know. In the film, of course, the doctor has extracted the memories from the hero, yet wishes to assist him by helping the memories return to their rightful place.

And there is another trauma – the adulterous affair that the hero's wife has engaged in, which leads to his struggle to free himself from his murderous wishes towards women, towards women who prostitute themselves as he may have felt his wife has. These murderous wishes may have links to another scene examined below. These are deep and powerful emotions, which do not to my mind need Jungian *transpersonal* amplification to comprehend them, nor to explain their power.

Another striking image is the malevolent child alien – contrasted of course with the hero as a boy. The child is vicious. It is the child who shouts 'kill him'. John's struggle is with this child figure representing the murderous wishes, the biting fantasy (there is a Kleinian image here) as when the child tries to bite at John's hands as he clings to the window sill.

It is possible to interpret particular images from this more Freudian perspective, such as the opening scene where the hero wakes in the bath, without memories. Jungian interpretation tends to go for rebirth, but why not as easily see this as the long repressed memory of birth itself and the angst that may accompany it? The dead woman whom the hero fears he might have murdered might then symbolize the dread of having damaged or even killed the mother; the rescuing of the fish, having smashed its container, and returning it to water, might be seen as an act of reparation for guilt at having caused damage to the mother. It might even express a wish in some way to return to the womb.

The dark city is the unconscious, where it is impossible to let the daylight in; where memories of real events get changed by the censorship of the unconscious, protecting the fragile ego from the full force of the memories. Memories then, like dreams, get distorted, sometimes become 'screen memories', not of actual events, but of wishes and desires.

Another interpretation could be a similar one to a Jungian view of trying to find oneself, since there is the continuous pressure of civilization, represented here by the aliens, which is constantly trying to suppress individuality. There is a theme of heart versus mind; indeed the leader of the aliens is Mr Book, which suggests an emphasis on the cognitive and intellectual rather than on emotions. Yet the soul is not in the mind, and the psyche is the seat of the emotions. Despite Freud's elevation of reason, it is an integral part of his theory that the pressure that comes from the conflict of the emotions with reason causes neurosis, and that there is a constant battle between civilization (even that imposed by the Strangers in the film) and individual desire, discussed below.

Is there some significance in the sleep imposed by the Strangers on the citizens? Changes take place during sleep, as dreams also attempt to promote psychic health. Perhaps there is also something about the significance of fantasy – the two people who wake to find themselves rich and living in palatial circumstances. There are references to illusion – on the psychotic detective's walls, and in the underground. There is even the existential dilemma of whether our waking life is but a dream, or whether our perceptions of our waking life have that dreamlike quality to them. We can see things different ways.

Then, just as Ryan wonders about the significance of the names given to the two detectives, we should not forget to question whether there may be any significance to the name of the doctor – Daniel Schreber. Ryan's spelling is slightly different (Shreber), obscuring that in the film the character's name might point towards the famous study by Freud (1911) of the autobiographical writing of the judge Daniel Schreber, called *The Schreber Case*. Schreber was admitted to mental hospital twice, and wrote extensively about his inner experiences, although the censor did not permit publication of all he recorded. Between the two admissions to hospital Schreber had a dream, or at least a thought which occurred between sleeping and waking, that it must really be a rather nice thing to be a woman undergoing intercourse. This was an idea he would have found outrageous when fully conscious. Before being admitted the second time to hospital he went through a night that brought on total mental collapse. His body was racked by spontaneous orgasms, and his mind disintegrated. He was convinced that he was to be transformed into a woman, and that he was being persecuted. After a long period of crisis, Schreber came to a point of resolution, although it was a strange kind of cure, where he saw himself as the Redeemer of the world, and that in order to be this he was gradually being transformed into a woman. It was God's desire to impregnate Schreber and save the world. Remarkably, this transformation led to Schreber reconstituting his personality entirely, as though he accepted the outrageous delusion once he could turn it into this megalomaniacal fantasy; and he seems to have kept sane in public and social settings, while also enjoying this totally insane self in private, keeping both sides in a delicate balance within himself.

Although there is no way of knowing whether the Schreber case history was known to the film's director, might my association here have links to two aspects of *Dark City*? The film contains episodes, perhaps even amounting to a theme, where we see hints of, or full-blown, paranoia. The aliens are trying to find Murdoch and take over his mind – a common fear in psychotic paranoia. That is one element which links to the Schreber case. The other might be the film's strong motif of the changes that take place when time is halted – when people are given different identities. There is certainly the theme of the hero trying to find his own identity, a view shared by Jungian and Freudian interpretation. Then there is also the image of the hero, like the real Schreber's view of himself, as a type of redeemer figure – it is he who saves the city; and in the scene where he is given back his own memories, he is tied to a wheel, which might either be taken as a form of the cross, or more likely Leonardo da Vinci's Vitruvian man – a humanistic redeemer rather than a religious one. The humanistic element is strengthened by the way in which the hero's struggle is against the collective, not necessarily in terms of the collective unconscious as Jungians might interpret the aliens, but in the way Freud wrote of the problem of *Civilization and Its Discontents* (1930). In order to belong in society we have to repress our desires, so there is a constant conflict between needing to bow to the pressure of culture and society, and the wish for individual expression, a struggle which can so easily lead to neurosis. Freud's essay addresses this whole issue.

Schreber's book was seen at the time of its publication as a detailed description of paranoia. Freud's interpretation of Schreber's illness is that it had its origin in repressed homosexuality, particularly in relation to the doctor who assisted Schreber's cure during the first admission to hospital, and whom Schreber saw in his second illness as wanting to persecute him. Repressed homosexuality would explain the fantasy of being changed into a woman, which would shift Schreber from the need to repress his fear of engaging in homosexual sex, to the more acceptable fantasy, which he believed now to be reality, of being a woman engaged in a heterosexual relationship with God.

This association leads me to wonder whether there is a homoerotic element in the relationship of Mr Hand towards the hero. Mr Hand shares the hero's memories and thoughts by being injected with them (the injection having of course a penetrative association); there is a type of closeness even through to the final scene, although perhaps more from Mr Hand to the hero than the other way round. There is, too, to look back to Fredericksen's reference to birds as also being phallic symbols (Fredericksen, 2001: 44), the flying scene right at the end of the conflict, where the hero and Mr Book confront each other, as they rise up through the air. This could well be a phallic battle, an oedipal struggle indeed, which the hero wins, resolving perhaps for him his guilt over his oedipal desires which might have in fantasy have led the hero when a child (in that curious logic of cause and effect which is not unusual in fantasy) to cause the death of not only his father, but also of his mother, in the fire of his passion. The image of the fire and the trauma of losing parents thus returns.

Such were my thoughts and associations as I read the film from my more Freudian perspective. I do not claim these interpretations to be anything other than my own. Yet what I will claim is that a Freudian perspective, far from being reductionist, leads to personal associations that similarly amplify the images and themes of *Dark City*, in the same way (although with very different outcomes) as Jungian interpretation does. Neither my nor Ryan's are of course anything other than personal reflections upon the film's text – and Jungian and Freudian interpretations, as much as Marxist or Lacanian views, probably in the end appeal to different people. Yet the contrasting ideas cannot but fail to demonstrate just how much film can evoke in us, whatever our principal methodology of interpretation may be.

References

Bainbridge, C., Radstone, S., Rustin, M., and Yates, C. (eds) (2007) *Culture and the Unconscious*. London: Palgrave Macmillan.

Fredericksen, D. (2001) 'Jung/sign/symbol/film'. In C. Hauke and I. Alister (eds), *Jung & Film: Post-Jungian Takes on the Moving Image* (pp. 17–55). London: Routledge.

Freud, S. (1911) *Psycho-Analytic Notes on an Autobiographical Account of a Case of Paranoia. Standard Edition, Volume 12*. London: Virago.

Freud, S. (1927) The Future of an Illusion. Standard Edition, Volume 21. London: Virago.

Freud, S. (1930) *Civilization and Its Discontents. Standard Edition, Volume 21.* London: Virago.

Gardner, W.H. (ed.) (1953) The Penguin Poets: Gerard Manley Hopkins. Harmondsworth: Penguin Books.

Hauke, C. and Alister, I. (2001) *Jung & Film*. Hove: Brunner-Routledge.

Ryan, J. (2001) 'Dark City'. In C. Hauke and I. Alister (eds), *Jung & Film: Post-Jungian Takes on the Moving Image* (pp. 95–109). London: Routledge.

Samuels, A. and Jacobs, M. (1995) *In Conversation: Jung and the Post-Jungians* (Video). Leicester: University of Leicester.

Chapter 9

Individual interpretations
A response to Michael Jacobs

John Izod

I am pleased to have been invited to comment on Michael Jacobs' paper since it allows me to echo the warmth of his response to Jane Ryan's work and add my own tribute. Although I had no part in writing 'Dark City', for a too brief period she and I were co-authors. And responding also gives me the chance to celebrate the fertility of recently published Jungian film theory, some developments in which Jane might have wanted to explore in her own film analysis had she lived.

Deploying a variety of nicely judged observations, Jacobs proves his claim that Freudians have much to contribute to the many ways a film can be interpreted. His association of the film's Daniel Schreber with the identically named subject of Freud's inquiry has tantalisingly rich potential, not diminished by credits that give the fictional character the middle name Poe (which surely licenses fantasy). However, Jacobs' only amplification from the real Schreber case disappoints. He makes an unexplained leap from the case history to speculate that a homoerotic attraction draws Mr Hand to John Murdoch. Interpretations, whether Freudian or Jungian, have the greater impact the more completely, precisely and plausibly they respond to the source text, and Jacobs does not show how the association he has uncovered bears on Proyas's Schreber.

It was the historical Schreber rather than the film's character (let alone Hand or Murdoch) who believed he was God's lover. Rendered in archetypal terms familiar to Jungians, he fantasised himself as the female half of a divine syzygy or unified entity of opposing elements. This noble but doomed psychic inflation has a long history in classical myth where, through their ineffable radiance, deities destroy the humans they take as lovers. Such an archetypal fantasy (with its uneasy anticipation of monstrous new birth) does help illuminate Proyas's Schreber because the Strangers use him to ensure their survival and intend to destroy him when their goal is achieved.

The Hand/Murdoch relationship plays out as an inverted echo of the historical Schreber's fantasy. Accepting that the Stranger does show anaemic lust toward Murdoch (which the latter does not reciprocate), the narrative explicitly frames their connection as doubling. Doubling and death-dealing – as witness the monstrous, black-clad Strangers' child (inverting the joyful symbolism of new life that usually attaches to children) who calls for Murdoch to be killed.

The foregoing seems to me to signal the potential for better elaborating Jacobs' Schreber amplification. Right or wrong, it might be worth explaining how I reached this position, not least because it follows an investigative hermeneutic that Jane Ryan might have used.

Jungian film critics attempting interpretation face a paradox that appears to distinguish their endeavours from Freudian practice. Jung advised, and Hillman re-emphasised that, in the context of the consulting room, interpretation of dream material should be delayed as long as possible. This allows the client's imagination to weave more dreams and fantasies, further elaborating the original material and producing a sequence of images the continuities and disjunctions of which assist its eventual interpretation. Readily comprehensible as a protocol for use in the consulting room, the advice has not until recently (and since Jane's death) been obviously available where a critic faces a movie. For the film itself never changes unless passing years degrade its recorded pictures and sounds.

Here Chris Hauke and Luke Hockley's work in developing a hermeneutic circle configuring the place of what they call the third image is valuable. It takes into account first the spectator's bodily presence before the screen. This would have appealed to Jane whose engagement with movies was sensually enriched by the exquisite delight of being present in the cinema facing the material life of the film. So the second point on this new hermeneutic circle is, self evidently, the film itself. And the third, which exists in the 'hard to discern space between the two', is the crux, 'the third image' (Hockley, 2009: 10).

The third image is not a phenomenon of which the spectator is automatically aware, but depends on 'consciously making the choice to look into the film and in so doing to look into ourselves' (ibid.).

> It is in the act of 'looking into' that we find the third image – a sense of how psyche makes meaning through relationship, in this case with the cinema, and this type of introspection may well entail 'losing the plot' of both the movie and of a consensual approach to life.
>
> (ibid.)

Hockley has in mind here the client bringing new meanings to consciousness as a tool to assist the processes of individuation in analysis. But unlike clients (who can make of the third image whatever their emerging consciousness demands), Jungian critics cannot lose the plot. They must honour the connection to *both* the objective, unvarying text *and* to third images, the consequence of subjective exposure to the text. It is a commitment which (albeit lacking the benefit of Hauke and Hockley's theoretical insights) Jane and I had in mind in our parallel readings of *2001: A Space Odyssey* (Izod and Ryan, 2000).

Keeping faith with the film on screen generally entails abandoning some of the third images that it stimulated when they are tested against the source text. Nevertheless, that refining process usually leaves the critic's responses enriched by the surviving elements of those fantasies. My experience suggests that those elements that endure tend to resonate with images founded in myth and archetype, a phenomenon, when experienced, that reassures the Jungian critic that the residue of intense personal fantasy generated by the film text has cultural commonality – that it may have arisen from and in turn touched the transpersonal unconscious (see Izod, 2001: 15–32). Indeed, it was Jane Ryan's commitment to this post-Jungian project of interpreting films while holding passionately in the frame both the personal and the transpersonal that made her such a special colleague and friend.

In memoriam

Jane Ryan was diagnosed with primary pulmonary hypertension – a wasting heart-lung condition – after prolonged and heavy high-altitude work as a flight attendant. PPH immediately robbed her of vitality, killed off any prolonged focus on the writing she had planned, and sucked her into a truly dark place. Prostacyclin, injected directly into the heart every 45 seconds, kept her alive but not immune from physical and mental suffering. She faced early death with the consuming rage that afflicts some victims of heart-lung conditions (including, allegedly, D H Lawrence). Yet through suffocating haze and almost to the last, her emails recorded the search for her truth – with fellow Jungians in New Mexico, through the ancient cultures of that state, and in a late passion to embrace Judaism.

References

Hockley, Luke (2010) 'Losing the Plot: A Story of Individuation and the Movies'. *Quadrant*, *40*(1).

Izod, John (2001) *Myth, Mind and the Screen: Understanding the Heroes of our Time*. Cambridge: Cambridge University Press.

Izod, John and Ryan, Jane (2000) 'Classics Revisited: Accounting for Difference in Two Jungian readings: *2001: A Space Odyssey*'. *The San Francisco Jung Institute Library Journal*, *18*(4), 7–56.

Chapter 10

The third image
Depth psychology and the cinematic experience

Luke Hockley

This chapter aims to offer a fresh way through which to conceptualise the cinematic experience in a Jungian manner. In doing so it draws on clinical theory derived from Jung's writing about 'image', although in terms of both practice and its application to the cinema this takes the discussion some distance from his original formulation. The chapter starts by considering viewers' knowing – or, to use a more psychological term, conscious engagement with – films, and it reflects on the need to interpret and find meaning in what unfolds on the screen. Here Jung's theorisation about 'image' offers a productive way through which to conceptualise this process. It proceeds by suggesting that actually there are three images that need to be considered, namely: the image on the screen; the image that arises from the act of interpretation; and the third image that comes about as the result of an individual's largely unconscious relationship with a film.

This tripartite division is somewhat reminiscent of the distinction that semiotics makes between the signifier, signified and referent. Roland Barthes sets out definitions for the first two of these terms in *Mythologies* (1973) where he presents a taxonomy in which the term 'signifier' refers to the representational aspect of the image. By distinction, he suggests the 'signified' refers to the concepts or meanings that arises from the signifier: these are the 'referents' of the image. Coming back full circle, in *Camera Lucida* (1981) he uses the term 'referent' differently, noting that it is impossible to separate out the image (actually in his case the photographic image) from its referent – the actual object of the image. Barthes then sets out in this later work to create ontology of the photography in which meanings are both frozen and also somewhat animated. The photograph captures the present moment but the interplay of signifieds and their inseparability from various shifting modes of interpretations and their associated meanings ensures that the photograph resists any reductive approach to the creation of meaning.

Similarly, this chapter sets out an approach to exploring the psychological significance of films in which meaning exists somewhere in the interplay between the representational aspects of cinema and what is signified in more conceptual terms. Where it parts company with a more semiotic and Barthian approach is in the way it privileges the individual, arguably with rather too much enthusiasm. The idea of a 'third image' is used to reflect how people talk about films in therapy and the personal meanings they have found in individual films. Often this involves clients in a type of 'misreading' of the film, where the plot and representational aspects of the film take a back row seat to more personal and emotional responses.

This chapter will offer some working definitions of the first, second and third 'images' before considering in more detail what the third image might be. It will draw on the clinical theory of transference and countertransference. In brief, transference is the psychodynamic mechanism whereby a client treats the therapist as though they were another person from their life. Of course, a client's feelings are not always easy to distinguish from the therapist's feelings and the unconscious material that enters the therapeutic space from the therapist's personal life is termed 'countertransference' material. The situation is rather more complicated than this suggests and there is an extensive literature on this subject (cf. Alister and Hauke, 1998; Christopher and Soloman, 2003; Mathers, 2009; Withers, 2003). But for the purposes of this piece it is enough to note that in psychotherapy meaning is co-created between therapist and client and is the result of conscious and unconscious processes. How this works with film will be illustrated with some examples from my clinical work.

What is an image? A Jungian view

When Jung writes about images and their psychological importance, what is he referring to? In different ways he states quite clearly throughout his writings that the psyche is made of images, that image alone is the immediate object of knowledge and that, 'the image is a condensed expression of the psychic situation as a whole and not merely, or even predominately, of unconscious contents pure and simple' (1921, para. 745).

It might at first appear in these pronouncements about the image that Jung has visual images in mind. If this were the case then it would certainly provide a solid basis on which to erect a Jungian psychology of the cinema. But it is a rare event for therapists, other than art therapists, to find themselves working with actual images in a therapeutic session. To do so would be to work with image as 'text', to borrow a term from the humanities. This is not to say that it does not happen, just that it is not a typical part of a regular session. Of course Jung did paint, sculpt, build and write in a therapeutic manner. He also encouraged at least some of his patients to do the same, as can be seen in *A Study in the Process of Individuation* (1934/1950). Jung approached the creative process with a psychological attitude leading to an orientation in which psychology opens the way to a particular understanding of the image.

That said, the psychological focus cannot completely ignore the nature and construction of its object of study – even if Jung occasionally made similar claims (cf. Jung, 1922/1931: para. 121). While literature, music, sculpture, and in our case cinema, may not need Jungian psychology, a Jungian approach to the arts does need the arts; there needs to be an object of analysis, so to speak. So the suggestion is that when considering actual images as 'texts', psychology provides the viewpoint from which the texts are analysed. This is analogous to the clinical situation where a painting produced by a patient is not interpreted within its own terms, but is reframed from a psychological perspective. Later I am going to suggest that there are difficulties in this approach and that if we look elsewhere in Jung's writing about images we can develop a rather different and more radical understanding of the psychological nature of the cinematic.

Sometimes Jung did write about actual images. He analysed (psychoanalysed) artists and their paintings, most notably Picasso (Jung, 1932). But this is not at the heart of what he understood by 'image'. If I am correct about this and Jung does not have in mind actual concrete visual imagery, perhaps he meant dream images. Here we get closer to the spirit of his meaning. But images in dreams are specific types of image and exist only in their recall. The materiality of the dream image comes in our recollection of the dream. Yet it is the fact that dream images provide a bridge between inner and outer worlds that points us in the right direction and takes us closer to what the relationship between psychology and the image is about.

For Jung, dreams embody life's situations, its complexities and difficulties. The dream depicts these sometimes in a slightly transformed way. However, if this was all the dream did that would be the end of the story, as dreams would just be a copy of reality. The dream would be solely mimetic in function. But Jung also suggested that dreams exist in a compensatory manner. As well as encapsulating the current situation as experienced by consciousness, the dream also expresses the situation in the unconscious as it is. In so doing, the psyche attempts to balance and maintain itself. The sleeping consciousness can have a sense of the dream while it is happening which to a greater degree on waking is reified by its telling and retelling. In this respect films are somewhat like dreams for as we will see, cinema, too, belongs partly to the physical world and partly to the unconscious.

Just as is the case for dreams, cinema's psychological significance becomes apparent when the opportunity is taken to reflect on particular films and their meanings. (Izod [2001] makes this point with clarity and conviction.) This is not meant to suggest that 'just' watching a film has no psychological impact. Again, the situation is somewhat analogous to dreaming; while we may not remember our dreams, the act of dreaming is in and of itself beneficial. This still allows for the impact of a dream to be enhanced by interpreting it when we are fully awake. So, too, the act of watching a film may have a beneficial effect and any such qualities are enhanced on further reflection. It is worth noting that here I have in mind the particular effects (and affects) of individual films on individual viewers. The suggestion is that the depth psychological significance of images in general, and cinema in particular, exists in the way they provide a personal and unique bridge between inner and outer worlds.

This gets closer to what Jung means by image. It is important to keep in mind the two ways that Jung writes about images. He is interested in both actual images ('texts') and the somewhat more diffuse and seemingly abstract notion of 'image' *per se*, although as we have noted the two are not always quite as separate as Jung implies. In the following quote he elaborates on the second of these two interests:

> When I speak of "image" in this book, I do not mean the psychic reflection of an external object, but a concept derived from poetic usage, namely, a figure of fancy or *fantasy-image*, which is related only indirectly to the perception of an external object. This image depends much more on unconscious fantasy activity.
>
> (1921, para. 743)

The idea of a *fantasy-image* which Jung introduces has the effect of creating a distinction between this and 'image' itself. What Jung is driving towards is that the fantasy-image is more like a concept or idea than a physical image. As such it can be thought of as an orientation, or a way of interpreting and understanding the psychological meanings of images. This means that the fantasy-image is best understood as a way of looking at, or perceiving, meanings that are derived from actual images closer to a sense of what something means – a felt-sense as much as a cognitive one. For example the image that comes to mind when listening to a piece of music may be directly related to the intentions of the composer (as in programmatic music) or it may arise as a result of the listener's imaginative relationship to the music, or both. Regardless of which is the case, what is noticeable is the total lack of physical images.

As such, the fantasy-image has both conscious and unconscious qualities. As is the case with dreams, there is a reciprocal relationship between the unconscious and consciousness. Dreams contain elements that are mimetically derived from waking life: people we know, places we have visited and so forth. However, in the dream they become agents of the unconscious.

As we will see, this blurring of the divisions between consciousness and the unconscious will be particularly important in understanding the psychological relationship that viewers have with films. Jung expresses this blending of inner and outer worlds neatly:

> It [the image] undoubtedly does express unconscious contents, but not the whole of them, only those that are momentarily constellated. This constellation is the result of the spontaneous activity of the unconscious on the one hand and of the momentary conscious situation on the other. Accordingly the image is an expression of the unconscious as well as the conscious situation of the moment. The interpretation of its meaning, therefore, can start neither from the conscious alone nor from the unconscious alone, but only from their reciprocal relationship.
>
> (1921, para. 745)

To summarise: Jung writes about actual images ('texts') and their psychological interpretation. He also refers to the idea of fantasy-images. These are different to actual images, having a more conceptual and poetic quality. At times Jung also uses image and fantasy-image as interchangeable terms. For our purposes, what is important is the inference that the psychological meanings which individuals derive from images and films are best conceived as something metaphorical and (or) conceptual. They contain both conscious and unconscious qualities and these two aspects need to be seen together.

This is a psychological way of recasting the distinction between the denotative aspect of an image (what it depicts) and the connotative (what it means, suggests and implies). This shifts the balance from an emphasis on meanings collectively carried by an image or film towards an individual's personal relationship and reaction to an image or film. What we are left with is a tension between what is collective and inscribed in a film and the psychological meaning that an individual derives from it. It is this mingling of the individual and the collective that we will now explore.

The image in the cinema

To help reflect further on the relationship between the personal and the collective when watching a film, I am going to return to the suggestion made in the introduction that the cinematic experience can be understood in terms of three types of image, or modes of perception: the first is the image on the screen; the second concerns viewers' mostly conscious engagement with interpretive activity; the third emerges as a result of a spontaneous and unlooked for emotional response to a film. Presenting these different types of relationship to the cinematic image in this way might seem to suggest that it is a question of either/or. But this would be a mistake as it is quite possible to shift between these different modes of perception and relationship to the screen quickly, almost instantaneously. Of course they also can and do overlap, happening simultaneously.

To recap, it is important to be clear that the idea of the third image should not be taken too literally. Instead it provides an imaginative way through which to understand what happens when we watch a film. The idea of the third image is part of a hypothesis about what happens psychologically when we watch films. It comes from a reflection on the experiences reported in the therapeutic consulting room and from detailed and careful consideration of film texts and the act of 'looking into' them. We will take the three images one at time but rather than seeing them in procession it is helpful to imagine them as one translucent idea sliding on top of another as gradually we come to reframe the screen in a different way.

The first image

Perhaps it is obvious that the image on the screen is the 'first image' because it is the source from which all subsequent reflections on its meaning emerge. It broadly corresponds to Barthes' signifier: it is the base from which the chains of meaning emerge. The first image (or signifier) enables the process of meaning-making to take place. For Barthes this is understood in semiotic terms as chains of signification site the signifieds in the broader culture and ideology more generally. I will argue below that when seen in a psychological light, something else is also happening in which an individual's psychological relationship to an image can result in a highly personalised meaning. As such, the first image needs to be seen reframed by the second and third images, as it is through their interplay and overlap that it becomes possible to see how a personal hermeneutic is created which is at the core of the psychology of the cinematic experience.

The first image, then, is largely concerned with the denotative and the mimetic. The denotative function of realist narrative cinema is to present an image of what purports to be a real situation in such a manner that the machinery of cinematic production is rendered invisible. This is to leave aside those film-makers who deliberately draw attention to the audio and visual structure and mechanisms of film-making. Yet even here, it would be possible to argue that such non-diegetic film-making practices convey meaning in a similar manner, with the cinema screen providing the initial source of meaning.

In a similar manner, the physical components of the projection of the image need to go largely unnoticed by viewers so that the mimetic quality of the cinema can achieve optimal effect. Dirty projection screens, whirring projectors and the like detract from the 'believable' qualities of the image. Of course viewers also know that what they are looking at is not real. Every viewer understands perfectly well that what unfolds on the screen is a constructed edifice, an entertainment that has been created with that purpose in mind. This locates the cinema clearly in a discourse of similar entertainments the origins of which are in the dioramas and phantasmagoria of the late seventeenth and early eighteenth century.

Dioramas were large optical entertainments the first of which was opened by its inventor, Louis Daguerre, in Paris in 1823. They took the form of a sizeable painting of roughly 7.5×6.5m, which was exhibited in specially designed buildings. Audiences of around 350 people would watch as subtle lighting effects changed the mode, tone and atmosphere of each painting. Rainbows after a storm, snow-covered landscapes turning into summer scenes and 'moving' waterfalls were all popular effects. The diegetic conceit was successful, and viewers looked through the proscenium arch into the layers of paintings that blended and merged as natural light was skilfully used to draw their gaze into these naturalistic scenes. The idea was to pass off the constructed and artificial as natural and real and the denotative value of the scenes were supposed to be taken at face value. In much the same way, contemporary cinema audiences do not wish to notice the optical and digital effects that are used to enhance the realism of the cinematic experience.

The filmic diegesis is built up of a number of rules or 'tricks of the trade' which mean that viewers do not readily notice edits, transitions of scenes and camera movements such as tracks and pans. It also encodes the narrative information in such a way that it seems natural to read screen space in a psychological manner. This is directly related to the meaning which most people will take away from the film and which they assume emanates from the film screen. This is a view of the cinematic in which meaning is thought of as inscribed in the film, albeit to greater and lesser degrees. It is the case that for each of the three cinematic images the spectator constructs meaning cued on signs inscribed in the text. However, with the third image in particular, the meaning can involve a highly personal insight that has been in some unexpected way triggered by the film. Such a view of the film can be at odds with its consensual or inscribed meaning. Semioticians might refer to this as 'aberrant decoding' but 'getting the meaning wrong' can be part of getting the personal psychological meaning of the film right.

By and large, focusing on the first image provides a consensual approach to understanding films. It assumes that films have a collective and shared meaning that is broadly intended by the makers of the film. As such, the first image deals with entertainment and has a collective presence. It is both the image on the screen and the collective fantasy it stimulates in many who watch it. While some viewers will have a 'privileged' access to the complexity of the film, they nonetheless share a broad interpretive imperative, namely to work out what the film means. This particular interpretive attitude regards the meaning of a film as relatively fixed. Such interpretive flexibility as there is comes from detailed reading of the film and the synthesis of those details into a coherent and convincing interpretation – or, we might say, understanding – of the film.

The second image

The second image, I want to suggest, can be thought of as arising from the act of conscious interpretation. I am aware that here I am not going to do justice to the complexities of the second image – after all it is the basis on which most academic textual interpretation of films proceeds. There are hundreds of books which deal with this topic with considerable sophistication and intricacy. What I present here is acknowledgment of the second image and where it fits within this particular scheme. It is closely related to the privileged viewer who, by dint of specialist knowledge or perspicacious perception, finds in the film a meaning that may be more convincing, or satisfying, than the one found by the majority of viewers. Such a viewer is not content with just the collective meaning of the film but instead requires a more personal insight. It is precisely because it is personal that it means that any insight necessarily distances itself from the collective meaning and edges slightly closer to the personal and the third image.

The second image may be tinged with affect. In part, this affect derives from the sense of superiority in not being content to be swept along with the collective meaning of the film. But the affect also comes from the interaction of the personal with the collective. The interpretive impulse is fuelled by the desire to find something that others have not in a particular film. It therefore stands that personal concerns will come to the fore as it is from individual preoccupations, insights and concerns that we view and understand the film and indeed the world in general. This is the lens of personal interpretation and like every lens it distorts and emphasises in a particular way.

For example, *Blade Runner* (Scott, 1982) is generally understood as a detective film. The twist is that the detective, Rick Deckard (Harrison Ford), whose job is to track down and 'retire' replicants (androids), turns out to be a replicant himself – probably. The critical and fan literature on this film is extensive. There are detailed considerations of inconsistencies in the plot and much speculation about whether Deckard is human or not. The discussion can take on a philosophical air with questions about what it means to be human and in particular the role of feelings in validating our human nature. My own interpretation (2001) of the film saw it slightly differently. Being Jungian in orientation it looked at the constant rain in the film and its possible symbolic significance. Ranging from lustration symbolism to flood creation myth it explored the need to wash away the old and replace it with something more human and heartfelt. What these interpretations share is a focus on the text as a site of meaning. In my case I brought my own concerns with Jung to the endeavour and found something new in the film which other commentators had not seen. There was, I suggest, a blurring between my own conscious and unconscious interests and the detailed consideration of the film. There is, then, an overlap here between the idea of a collective inscribed meaning and a personal need to find a particular meaning, a personal meaning, in the film.

The implication of this is that personal insights can also provide insights into collective meanings. While such an approach still sees the meaning of a film as relatively fixed, it also allows for some uncertainty, as the text is shown to be malleable and responsive to the interpretive act. This is meaning as it arises from the necessarily distorting lens of interpretation.

The third image

The third image comes into being as a result of the first two images. It is not a composite of the two, nor something that arises from their juxtaposition. Rather, the third image is something new. In some ways it is reminiscent of the manner in which Jung wrote about symbols, in particular, his insight that the symbol (symbolic image) contains a third meaning (*tertium non datur*) that is not logically given. Jung does not explain why this is a *third* meaning but I suspect he had in mind that the symbol is not just what the image represents, nor is it solely the personal associations that someone may bring to the image; it has a third meaning, the exact nature and function of which is not available to consciousness and which is archetypal in quality. It therefore follows that part of the meaning of the symbol will remain unconscious, and making it conscious turns the symbol into a sign whereupon it becomes largely denotative in function.

The situation with regard to the third image is not quite the same, although it is similar. The third image comes into being as a result of an individual's reaction to and relationship with the cinema screen. It exists neither on the screen, nor just in the mind of the viewer but somehow enters the space between the two. Film theorists have tried in the past to understand how the techniques of film production stitch the viewer into the narrative of the film – at least in part, and allowing that such stitching is temporary and fragile. This is the work of the diegesis which was alluded to above. Such arguments are often Lacanian in nature and revolve around the need within the subject (their term for the viewer) to reconstruct in his or her imagination a unified and perfect image of themselves, with which they first mis-identified during the mirror phase. The *stade du miroir* is the point at which the child imagines that there is an idea of a psychologically whole version of themselves reflected either in an actual mirror or in the people who surround them, particularly parents.

The idea of the third image provides another way of understanding this search for self-recognition and the need for wholeness. To understand what might be happening for viewers in the cinema it is helpful to reflect on what happens in the therapeutic dyad. Of particular importance here are the parts of clinical theory that deal specifically with transference and countertransference. Transference is the phenomenon by which the patient 'transfers' onto the therapist feelings that are more normally attached to someone else, often from the past. Thus the therapist may become for the client something of an angry father, a loving mother, a destroying mother, a protecting father and so forth. The therapist, by attuning to this fantasy of the patient, is able to help the patient to bring these unconscious ideas closer and closer into consciousness.

If we pause to consider this workaday therapeutic idea we realise just how strange it is. It assumes that clients somehow shift their feelings into the therapist (how we do not know), that these relate to the client's inner experiences, and that they are unaware of this process. The countertransference concerns the manner in which unconscious material in the therapist can get stirred up and unconsciously acted out in the consulting room. When the therapeutic alliance is working effectively, something comes into being between the client and the therapist which they have co-created. Technically this is sometimes referred to as a third in the intersubjective field. This third is difficult to grasp, tenuous and fleeting and it is as much felt in the body as it is experienced in the space between client and therapist.

There are numerous elements that facilitate the creation of this alliance. Regular times for meetings, agreed frequency and length of sessions and so forth. One which is not written about as much as some others concerns looking. The client is of course free to look wherever they want. But many therapists, and I include myself here, look directly at the client for most of the session. This is not a controlling or oppressive gaze, and I have never had a client object or even comment on it. Rather, it is a type of imagined bridge. It seems to be important to bring one's essence, mind, body, intellect and felt sense to the act of trying to understand the client by being present for them. In other words, I am trying to look into the client and if not to merge with them, to meet them half way, in that space between us, as we struggle to bring something into meaning as a result of our relationship.

Perhaps the parallel with the cinema is already clear. The suggestion is that viewers also form a somewhat complicated and multilayered relationship with films. Sometimes viewers will acknowledge the emotions and psychological experiences of the characters in the film (the first image). Sometimes they will, as they look into the film, find 'deeper' and more complicated meanings which come from the sensory signifiers of the film (the second image). Occasionally something more personal happens which seems close to what happens in therapy where the act of being intensely present to another (in this case a film) facilitates the mechanisms of transference and countertransference. My suggestion is that this partly stems from the act of looking, of intuitively 'looking into' the cinema screen for meaning. By looking into the cinema screen, viewers also look into themselves and in the midway point between their bodies and the screen they experience the third image.

As a result it is quite possible for viewers to suddenly have an intensely personal and quite overwhelming reaction to a film that others in the audience do not have. Quite often it is this which viewers, as they become clients in therapy, will want to talk about, somehow intuitively sensing that something intimate and unknown has been awakened. This gives us one way of understanding how it is that different people watching the same film can have quite different reactions to it, for there is a powerful sense in which they have not seen the same film at all but created or found a new meaning in the film which may be at odds with the collective view of what the film is about. I think of this as losing the plot to find the plot (Hockley, 2010). By way of illustrating the diversity of this, a couple of examples from my work with clients may be helpful.

Rachel, a young woman about twenty-five years old, was trying to articulate the benefits as she saw them that she was getting from our work together. It was a struggle for her as she did not have a large psychological vocabulary. Instead she would normally describe herself in pejorative colloquial terms. In one session she commented, 'You know, I'm like the Terminator.' This really puzzled me as the terminator is an android killing machine that does its best to live up to its name. So I enquired, 'In what way?' She responded, 'You know that scene in *The Terminator* where he fixes himself, that's what I'm trying to do.' This comment struck me as both rich and impoverished at the same time and I found myself rather moved as she spoke.

Whatever the Terminator films might be about, they are not predominately concerned with fixing anything. Terminators hunt, kill and destroy – they terminate whatever crosses their path which impedes their mission. Now, my understanding of the work with Rachel was not that we were fixing anything – although she did believe that she was in some way broken. The scene that Rachel had in mind is the one in which the Terminator is hiding in a motel room. He peels back the human-looking but synthetic skin on his arm to reveal a mechanical armature which he sets about fixing. As we worked with the image it became clear that part of Rachel felt mechanical in the way in which she responded to situations, and particular relationships. Somewhat like the terminator, she would set out to destroy her partner, and herself, with sudden bursts of destructive rage – it was this she wanted to understand, and in her mind fix. Here, then, the third image that comes from a film about destruction is an image of healing. From a consideration of an android that is incapable of feeling comes a sensitivity to what it means to relate in a meaningful way. The way Rachel used the film is analogous to the way in which Jung suggests symbols work. The suggestion is that the third image is akin to the act of forming a personal symbol that nonetheless retains a universal quality. As Jung puts it,

> The more abstract, differentiated, and specific it [the symbol] is, and the more its nature approximates to conscious uniqueness and individuality, the more it sloughs off its universal character. Having finally attained full consciousness, it runs the risk of becoming a mere allegory which nowhere oversteps the bounds of conscious comprehension, and is then exposed to all sorts of attempts at rationalistic and therefore inadequate explanation.
> (Jung, 1940: para. 291)

A somewhat different example: Craig's wife has had an affair and he cannot decide whether to forgive her or not. He is absolutely torn about this as he loves his wife deeply but cannot decide if he will ever be able to trust her again. The situation is particularly difficult for Craig as therapy is not a process that he finds easy. He never thought he would be in therapy and he is having to change a lifelong rule of never talking about himself. There is a clear and strong disconnect between his feelings and the rest of him. He is uncertain if this internal barrier was a factor in his wife's affair or if he had no role to play in the matter.

Roughly midway through his work with me, Craig wanted to talk about an experience he had while watching a film. He had gone with his wife to see a romantic comedy. As is the way with such films, the plot of this one concerned a wife who was secretly involved with someone other than her husband, to great comedic effect. Yet for Craig there was nothing funny about this at all. As he put it to me, 'I just sat there. I was frozen. Suddenly my private life was up there on the screen for everyone to see. I felt a huge and sudden cold distance between me and my wife. I couldn't look at her. It was terrifying.'

In this case, the third image is embodied and felt. Again, the plot of the film is lost and along with it the collective meaning of the film. In its place comes a personal narrative, of which the overwhelming affect is symptomatic. While derived from the subject matter of the film, Craig's reaction is powerful and personal, coming as it does from his desire to wall up his inner world and the paralysis he experienced when it temporarily found a way out. In this case, third and first images are closely associated. It was the work of therapy to explore what it was like for him to realise that something he thought was personal and private was actually a sufficiently common experience for a film to be made about it. Craig came to realise that in reality he was not a separate, isolated individual but someone bound in relationship with ties and responsibilities. This was a relief for him but was also anxiety-provoking as he came to see that life was lived in and through him – he was in relationship not just with his wife but with everyone around him. This insight came as he started to comprehend the complexities of his inner world, and the film was one of many prompts through which his unconscious supported this process.

Conclusion

The idea that by bringing two quite separate entities together a third not in either one of them is brought into being may at first appear somewhat strange. Actually it is a fundamental idea that turns out to be at the hermeneutic core of the way in which we make and find meaning in the world. Significantly, this activity fuses imagination, the brain and the body.

Here I want to pursue the metaphor of depth as a device through which to invoke the notion of a depth of meaning. This has resonances with depth psychology and its concern with a 'depth' of self-understanding. It also evokes the to-be-looked-into qualities which are intrinsic to the cinematic experience. The apparent depth of the image phenomenologically prompts viewers to look into the screen, much as we look into our lives and into our dreams for meaning. Here are a couple of other metaphors that tie together perception, the body and depth. In the reproduction of music, separate left and right channels of sound heard at the same time give a striking sense of a wide and deep sound stage. Sounds no longer come from individual left and right speakers but seamlessly fill the space in between with an acoustic image that is not only wide and high but also deep. The same idea holds good for vision. Early stereoscopic images had individual images for each eye which when seen through a special viewer came together to provide a three-dimensional image which provided the illusion of depth. A similar though more sophisticated technology lies behind 3D films. In both these examples the combining of two separate pieces of information produces a third which produces a sense of depth.

It is this sense of bringing two elements together to provide a psychological third which Jung suggests is at the core of how symbols work. As Samuels *et al.* comment:

The symbol itself helps here, for though it is not logical, it encapsulates the psychological situation. Its nature is paradoxical and it represents the third factor or position that does not exist in logic but provides a perspective from which a synthesis of the opposing elements can be made. When confronted with this perspective, the ego is freed to exercise reflection and choice.

(1986: 145)

The depth cues of cinema come not just from the image, powerful though that it is, they also arise out of the third image. It is here that it is possible to find ourselves not only on the silver screen but also in the symbolic space between the image and the viewer. In these transitory and fleeting moments we experience and embody a glance into the symbolic. We are both inside and outside ourselves as temporarily psyche and cinema exist side by side; this is the outer space of our inner selves.

Note

I am indebted to John Izod for his comments on an earlier draft of this piece.

References

Alister, I. and Hauke, C. (eds) (1998) *Contemporary Jungian Analysis: Post-Jungian perspectives from the Society of Analytical Psychology*. London: Routledge.
Barthes, R. (1973) *Mythologies*. Saint Albans: Granada.
Barthes, R. (1981) *Camera Lucida*. London: Vintage.
Christopher, E. and Solomon, H. (eds) (2003) *Contemporary Jungian Clinical Practice*. London: Karnac.
Hockley, L. (2001) *Cinematic Projections: The Analytical Psychology of C. G. Jung and Film Theory*. Luton: University of Luton Press.
Hockley, L. (2010) 'Losing the Plot: A Story of Individuation and the Movies'. *Quadrant*, 40(1).
Izod, J. (2001) *Myth, Mind and the Screen: Understanding the Heroes of Our Time*. Cambridge: University of Cambridge Press.
Jung, C. G. (1921) *Definitions*. In CW6.
Jung, C. G. (1922/1931) *On the Relation of Analytical Psychology to Poetry*. In CW15.
Jung, C. G. (1932) *Picasso*. In CW15.
Jung, C. G. (1934/1950) *A Study in the Process of Individuation*. In CW9(i).
Jung, C. G. (1940) *The Psychology of the Child Archetype*. In CW9(i).

Mathers, D. (ed.) (2009) *Vision and Supervision: Jungian and Post-Jungian Perspectives*. Hove: Routledge.
Samuels *et al.* (1986) *A Critical Dictionary of Jungian Analysis*. London: Routledge and Kegan Paul.
Withers, R. (ed.) (2003) *Controversies in Analytical Psychology*. London: Routledge.

Chapter 11

The nature of adaptation
Myth and the feminine gaze in Ang Lee's *Sense and Sensibility*

Susan Rowland

Introduction: The gendered gaze

Ever since Laura Mulvey's seminal essay, 'Visual Pleasure and Narrative Cinema', the notion of 'the male gaze' has galvanised critical attention to Hollywood films (Mulvey 1975). She argues that the feminine in conventional filmic narratives is construed as an object of erotic masculine attention in a perpetuation of patriarchy. Here the feminine is the passive recipient of *scopophilia*, and as such becomes the bearer of meaning, not the maker of meaning. Three inflections of masculine 'looking' are to be found in the narrative images of such films. First, the films are organised to emphasise the principal male character's gaze at the female, so *objectifying* her. Second, the spectator is co-opted into this masculine sexual position through the persistence of the eroticised feminine on the screen. Third, the product of the two masculine gazes enables the spectator to take the male character's position and 'have' the feminine character as a sexual object.

Two comments are relevant here. Mulvey's criticism remains seminal and controversial in the history of film theory. In addition, her essay has done much to legitimate Freudian psychoanalytic criticism as the central political and gender mode of film studies. So what might be the consequence of looking at a mainstream film, Ang Lee's *Sense and Sensibility* (1995), which, although directed by a man, not only stems from a story by a woman (and a screenplay by a woman, Emma Thompson), but more pertinently from a genre that, arguably, disputes patriarchal structures – the novel?

Moreover, by taking a Jungian psychoanalytic stance, the Freudian stress on the gendered, phallic quality of scopophilia is subtly altered. Where a Freudian interpretation reduces visual pleasure to a sexuality organised around the phallus as the significant organ of pleasure and meaning, Jung regarded psychic energy as essentially neutral *and hence not privileging one gender*. Where Freud (and Lacan after him) considers the Oedipus myth to possess an originating role in the structuring of the psyche, Jung makes room for many potential myths of being. Some of them can even emphasise the feminine!

Both Freud and Lacan regard sexual difference as key to subjectivity. It is the child's 'having' or 'not having' the penis that ensures an orientation to the parents in what may be the first gendered perception. Leaving the Oedipus complex, the boy identifies with the masculinity of the father under threat of castration. Desire for the mother is repressed and so the sexual unconscious is generated. To Lacan, the entry into language enacts the split of subjectivity. We become marked by an unconscious desire forever bound to the mother. Moreover gender identity is dominated by *difference* as different ways of not 'having' the phallus.

The little boy does not 'have' the phallus because this transcendental signifier stands for a fullness of being denied to all those pinioned by the symbolic order. Or to put it another way, the male is split off from the (m)Other by language signifying that very lack. The girl is even more bereft since she is denied the fantasy of the phallus. Her destiny, according to Lacan, is to signify the phallus for the masculine. 'She' is what the masculine 'has' in a vain attempt to assuage 'his' lack.

One question that feminist theorists ask concerns the link between these phallus-oriented ideas to the culture of patriarchy. To what extent are Freud, Lacan and those who follow them tracing out a patriarchal figure, one biased towards maintaining the hegemony of the Father, which is more a historical notion than an essentially human notion? Is the Freudian tradition a re-surfacing of so-called norms of masculine privilege? Certainly, Freud and Lacan did position masculinity in a superior or leading role. On the other hand, feminist psychoanalytic critics have argued long and hard that anatomical *difference* is not the same as human superiority.

What too few gender critics have so far considered is Jung's strategy of removing bodily shape as a *crucial* factor in determining being. Where the Oedipus complex is the Freudian first principle, the idea that is *productive* of the whole psychology, Jung's originating principle is that the unconscious is independently creative of the ego and in part unknowable. Such a belief means that the human body cannot fix meaning. Gender becomes a dialogical process between the creative unconscious (that is creative and fluid with gender as with so much else), and the cultural meanings bestowed upon the sexed body.

Patriarchy exists as a long cultural tradition of privileging certain styles of masculinity. It has no intrinsic validation in the signifying powers of the body. Indeed, in that patriarchy is a stiffening of cultural ideas, the Jungian unconscious will tend to loosen or even challenge it. Such a progressive tendency has little to do with Jung, the cultural conservative, and everything to do with his conceptualisation of an unconscious with the function of signifying the *other* to whatever cultural formation the ego is caught up in. Perhaps this might be a way of understanding the multiple possibilities inherent in relatively recent artistic genres, such as the novel, and even film?

Novels, films and adaptations

As the novelist and critic Ursula K. Le Guin has argued, the invention of the novel does something very strange and interesting to the long mythical tradition of the hero. In 'The Carrier Bag theory of Fiction' (Le Guin 1986), she offers a radical revision of the masculine hero myth as defined by Joseph Campbell in *The Hero with a Thousand Faces* (Campbell 1949). Fascinatingly, in the history of film, Campbell's male hero, defined by his singular person, conquest of the 'other' and reward of a princess, has directly influenced the development of mainstream film narrative. As Don Fredericksen has so effectively critiqued, Campbell's very pared down structure of hero myths was re-framed as a 'formula' for the successful adventure film by Christopher Vogler (2007) in *The Writer's Journey* (Fredericksen 2008).

Le Guin's radical suggestion is a development of the human imagination parallel to that of the male hero. 'He' was surely modelled on the prehistoric hunter coming home with his tales of triumph and disaster. Killing the mammoth is the ur-story of the hero myth. If, instead, the mammoth kills a man, a man who has thereby risked too much, then tragedy is born. Yet besides spears and hunting, Le Guin points out, early cultures ate berries, gathered grains and wool, and surely made cups and holding devices. Alongside the culture of the spear (a missile, which one day goes nuclear) is the tradition of the basket, bundle or bag. It is this tradition of *holding things together to make a relation between them* that eventually surfaces as the novel.

Before novels, the male hero myth and tragedy make their mark in epic poetry. Poetry can tell stories and hold many characters together. Yet the epic does tend to centre on a conquering or faltering hero. The novel, by contrast, may well foreground one hero, and yet by the very nature of the genre will weave him into relationships with others. The novel always has more than one voice to set against any tendency for one 'hero' to drown out all that is 'other' in surrounding voices.

Such an argument begins to suggest a polarisation between the media of novel and film. Novels inculcate those values deemed 'feminine' by centuries of patriarchy, those of relating, eros, body, sexuality. On films has been bestowed the inheritance of the single dominating hero, associated with masculinity. On the other hand, while there is considerable evidence that Hollywood has sought to resurrect the hero myth for ideological reasons, I suggest that the nature of film itself indicates a more complicated relationship with hero myth and gender. In particular, films adapted from novels, I argue here, can retain some of the 'feminine' multiplicity of the novel form. They do so in part by drawing on a greater range of mythical narratives. In fact, so artful is Ang Lee's *Sense and Sensibility* in challenging Hollywood's formula for heroes that the film manages to incarnate a feminine eros and even a feminine 'gaze'.

Of course, Ang Lee remains male and an essentialist approach to gender would rely upon the embodiment of the director to orient an argument about the gaze. However, in looking at deep structures of gender in media such as novels and films, this paper's approach to gender is one of contrasting *myths* which have historically been identified with one gender, yet are not limited to male or female (see below). Hence, it is possible to characterise the film *Sense and Sensibility* as offering a 'feminine' perspective from its 'formal' qualities rather than the corporeal identity of its director.

First of all, we need to consider the precise 'nature' of the adaptation; one that I will look at more deeply by considering both the novel's and film's relation to the non-human world.

Adaptation: Novel to film in *Sense and Sensibility*

Some film adaptations of novels are quite reasonably studied for their differences from the former text. Self-evidently, the most overt 'gap' between written text and film text is the substitution of visual image from verbal imagining in the mind of the individual reader. Sue Perrill's 2002 study of film adaptations of Jane Austen draws attention to the way 'nature' becomes a player in the structuring of meaning. Visually the film plays the gorgeous domestication of nature at Norland Park against the wilder and more sparse beauties around Barton cottage. Hence much of the ironies of the treatment of the impoverished sisters by the wealthy brother who inherits everything are conveyed without words.

Here, too, crucial scenes involving Marianne's painful love for faithless Willoughby become dramatised through a nature taking on romantic, even sublime overtones. Where Austen narrates a simple fall, a twisted ankle and assistance by a gentlemen who turns out to be called Mr Willoughby, the film has Marianne unwisely taking out her unwilling younger sister into a darkening sky. The storm breaks, the girls run down the hill in the driving rain. Marianne falls. A man on a huge horse gallops up, swings down and grasps her wounded foot, soon carrying her to the cottage.

This scene is echoed much later when the abandoned, frail Marianne arrives at a grand house nearby to Willoughby's Combe Magna. Through rain and failing light she climbs another hill to face his house and utter the Shakespeare sonnet that they once read together before a warm fire in a picture of domestic happiness. Marianne is next seen in the arms of a staggering Colonel Brandon, in a deliberate re-staging of Willoughby – with a difference. Colonel Brandon loves Marianne yet has always been considered too old by her. His staggering as he brings her unconscious from the wet hillside both indicates his more advanced age, and subtly suggests his greater reliability.

In the cultural imagination, behind these scenes of passion on rough ground in inclement weather is the author most often contrasted with Austen, Emily Brontë. The film is able, by the intense augmentation of the visual senses, to incorporate aspects of the sublime that *Wuthering Heights*, not *Sense and Sensibility*, achieves in the novel. The sublime is a way of representing what is unrepresentable directly. Ang Lee's *Sense and Sensibility* is both novel-like (evoking Brontë) and novel unlike (Austen) in using landscape to evoke what is erotic, 'other' and an imaginative initiation in the characters. As well as landscape, the use of horses as physical presences hard to control is important in suggesting barely concealed desires.

Perrill recalls the last scene on an uncultivated hill very late in the film. Here it is a calm summer's day with the sea in the distance. Elinor and Marianne sit, so no danger of falling! Here Marianne very deliberately switches her allegiance from Willoughby to Elinor, not Brandon, although it is very clear now that they are to marry. She tells Elinor that it is her sister who should have been her guide; her sister whose restrained behaviour in an unhappy relationship is the model she would now choose. Where Perrill describes the use of landscape to suggest the film's mood of resignation and tranquillity, I find the overt shifting from lover to sister here most striking and I will return to this aspect later.

Julia North's study of the Ang Lee adaptation regards the film as potentially more radical than the novel (North 1999). Although much humour is achieved by mocking sensibility's excesses in Marianne, her mother Mrs Dashwood and young sister Margaret, the film actually *prefers* the dramatic possibilities of sensibility, rather than the more restrained qualities represented by sensible Elinor.

North correctly shows that the film sharpens Edward's romantic qualities and heightens the 'sensibility' half of the title. She draws attention to Elinor's greater emotionality. While the novel grants Elinor 'wild sobbing' on hearing that Edward is free at last, the film gives further outbursts to Elinor over the accusation of being unfeeling beside Marianne's sickbed (Austen 1811/1990: 316). North suggests that the film ultimately tames the rebelliousness of sensibility by absorbing it into the sensible conformity of Elinor. I disagree.

To me the *film* (as well as the novel) validates Elinor's story as one of deep feeling directed to authentic relationships and soulful integrity. Both film and novel agree in portraying conventional norms as dominated by subservience to money. Both Elinor and Marianne serve other gods. Unfortunately for Marianne, she begins willing her own blindness to how far her so-called sensibility is tangled up with values that will conflict with her deepest desires.

For Marianne and Willoughby are not dissimilar in their allegiance to the material comforts that money can buy. What is important to Marianne in meeting her heroic lover is that they should gallop off to a life of ease and comfort. Both novel and film are articulate about the cultural eroticisation of material wealth. The film can linger over gorgeous clothes and big houses, in contrast to a small cottage. Jane Austen is the novelist par excellence of the sexuality of material possessions, as well as the arid limitations of a life dominated by them.

Willoughby's motive in leaving Marianne is that by marrying her he would be significantly poorer; a motive shared by thoughtless Marianne. North argues that the film gives Marianne Willoughby after all, in making Brandon more a parallel figure to the virile younger man. Certainly, Brandon is wealthy compared with Edward and does rescue Marianne from another storm. Yet, I would read the added rescue by Brandon as stressing the *difference* to the earlier scooping up of enthralled Marianne by Willoughby. Moreover, the late scene between Brandon and Marianne (before the wedding at the end), is another same/difference articulation.

Brandon reads to convalescent Marianne in the summer sunshine outside the cottage. Of course this scene deliberately recalls Willoughby's passionate readings by firelight. Yet here between male reader and female listener the mood is of healing and reconciliation. Significantly, they are outside in a landscape of fertility and abundance. Suddenly, they, Marianne in particular, are in a *larger* world than that evoked previously. The reading is clearly the act of a lover, yet also blends with the peace of the natural hillside. Indeed, the way nature seems here incorporated with the scene suggests the completion of a myth. Furthermore, it implies a myth more complex and fulfilling than the truncated male hero myth offered to Marianne by her readings for 'sensibility'.

Sense and Sensibility: From male hero myth to feminine myths

I suggest that both novel and film explore feminine sexuality in the face of the dominance of the patriarchal masculine hero myth. While the arts preserve and transmit a psychologically vital mythical heritage to the imagination, patriarchal distortion in cultural forms means that what Campbell called the 'monomyth' dominates. In *Sense and Sensibility*, Edward and Brandon are punished for not fulfilling the monomyth by conquering the 'other' and seizing their rightful feminine prize. Brandon loses his first love when his martial 'heroism' is not rewarded and Edward is unable to crush his opposing 'other' because it is in feminine form. A patriarchal myth that includes the feminine as submissive prize and the masculine as great warrior is not only a problem for women!

More central to both novel and film is the perspective of young women who await their conquering heroes. Both Marianne and Elinor discover the limitations of this underlying structure. Elinor eventually discovers that Edward does not come for her because he is a hero *for* the feminine matriarchy and not victor over it. Marianne discovers that she and Willoughby are caught by the material and political inflections of the myth in her society. In effect, she and Willoughby are voluntarily imprisoned by the aristocratic overtones of the hero myth. What is erotic about the hero to his prize in this society is, in part, the wealth connoted by his conquest of the Other.

Far less recognised in novel and film is the way that this female perspective on the truncated patriarchal hero myth is augmented by two other myths. For both novel and film offer a feminine viewpoint by drawing upon myths that are less visible. In both narratives, Elinor's story resembles that of 'Eros and Psyche'; Marianne suffers the fate and rescue of 'Persephone'. These two myths which focus on feminine characters simultaneously critique and offer an alternative to the patriarchal possibilities of the masculine hero. Moreover, by adding to the (masculine) myth of the hero, they substantiate the plurality of voices inherent in the novel form. As I will argue, as these several myths work in the film, they not only deepen the psychological reach, they also maintain some of the originating novel's plurality. Ang Lee's *Sense and Sensibility* does much more than the Vogler-inspired Hollywood monomyth of the hero.

Elinor's story echoes the myth of Eros and Psyche, in so far as it mediates between feminine roles. Like Psyche, Elinor faces a mother – Mrs Ferrars or Aphrodite – jealous over any beloved of her son – Edward or Eros. An unlikely Aphrodite, Mrs Ferrars nevertheless is the source of a good deal of the sexual energy in the story: money. She also corresponds closely to the jealousy and life-denying properties of Aphrodite in this myth. Mrs Ferrars/Aphrodite provokes a dearth of love and sexual energy when Eros refuses to loose his golden arrows without being allowed to have Psyche. Edward refuses to seek a bride acceptable to his mother. Psyche is then allowed partial union with Eros but it must be unconscious. She is not allowed to see her lover in the light. Unfortunately, her jealous sisters trick her into fearing that she has married a monster. Taking a lamp to see Eros, who turns out to be divinely beautiful, she accidentally wakes him and is banished from his presence. It takes a long journey of dangerous tasks before Psyche is finally reunited with Eros. One of these tasks is to visit Persephone in her role as Queen of the Underworld.

Elinor, too, is tricked by a jealous sister, Lucy Steele, presented in the novel as one of a pair of competitive, man-pursuing, avaricious sisters. In the film, Lucy's blood sister is omitted but the character is shown to resemble Elinor's grasping sister-in-law. Mrs John Dashwood emphatically prefers Lucy to her husband's sisters until she discovers how far Lucy may thwart her mother's matriarchal plans. Indeed both novel and film turn on the notion of sisters. Elinor herself has to consciously suffer the role of 'sister' to Edward in helping him towards marriage with Lucy. Colonel Brandon, misguidedly believing he is aiding Elinor, offers Edward an income large enough to marry on. He insists in both texts that Elinor convey the offer that will enable Edward to marry Lucy. She is therefore forced to *act out* the role of sister in a painful exercise of self-consciousness surely equal to Psyche's longer tasks.

Aphrodite also sends Psyche to visit Persephone in the Underworld. Elinor also visits that darker place, in particular in the film's dark scenes of Marianne's dangerous illness. Here Elinor shifts her role from a woman defined by her eros (in myth and here masculine), to one much more deeply oriented to the feminine. For it is Elinor who takes on the Demeter role of rescuing Persephone/Marianne. *Sense and Sensibility* is a novel and film in which the sister becomes the nurturing mother. Indeed the sum of the mythical interaction in both texts is a more flexible and individuated formation of the pre-patriarchal Goddess, as maiden, matron and crone. For example, Elinor tells Marianne how much she needs her; it is unclear if Marianne hears but she does begin to recover.

Let's consider Marianne as Persephone. The early part of the novel and film shows her dangerous absorption in self-indulgence rather than as truly inducted into the imagination. Her dreams of a romantic hero allow her to remain partly unconscious of her own worldly attitudes. Lying injured on a sodden hillside, she thinks she sees a hero gallop up on his fine horse to rescue her. What really happens is that Willoughby is Hades who takes her down to the underworld.

It is perhaps significant that in the film the early scenes of Marianne and Willoughby falling in love are dominated by darkness and flickering firelight. We see Willoughby reading Shakespeare's sonnets to his lady. Later, of course, the film does take them outside. An inexplicable moment occurs outside Colonel Brandon's house in which a large party is gathered at his invitation. Willoughby and Marianne are happily engrossed with each other when a messenger rides up to the host. Brandon reads the letter and immediately cancels his party, galloping off with hardly an apology. Willoughby makes unkind remarks about Brandon. Mrs Jennings, a kind-hearted yet insensitive gossip, speculates that the crisis concerns Brandon's illegitimate daughter. Much later in both novel and film it is revealed that the sexual transgression is Willoughby's, not Brandon's. In succouring the orphaned daughter of his first love, Brandon has suffered seeing her fall victim to Willoughby's seduction and abandonment.

So the scene outside Brandon's fine house is a complex negotiation of sexuality masked by strict social codes. Superficially, Willoughby and Marianne are almost unaffected. They lose only a social outing with friends; they drive off together in carefree abandon. A retrospective reading from later in the film/novel shows the event to be an ominous repetition of Willoughby as Hades seizing Marianne. Colonel Brandon's pregnant foster daughter never appears directly in either text. Yet she is more and more cited until she is implicitly compared to Marianne. Brandon later tells Elinor that his first love resembles Marianne. She was cruelly denied to Brandon, married to his brother for reasons of money and ill used until she ran away with a man who betrayed her.

Brandon is here a means for the novel/film to suggest that such risks are run by someone with Marianne's passionate unregulated fantasies. There is more than one portrayal of the underworld in both versions of *Sense and Sensibility*. Marianne falls into an underworld of depression and sickness when Willoughby leaves without hope of return. Her fate is also echoed and preceded by double shadow counterparts in Brandon's first love and her daughter whom Willoughby seduces in a pre-staging of

Persephone's fate. Both these women are consigned to an underworld of prostitution and poverty, until rescued by Brandon.

Yet it is not Brandon who is the primary rescuer of Marianne; it is Elinor.

> Her breath, her skin, her lips, all flattered Elinor with signs of amendment, and Marianne fixed her eyes on her with a rational, though languid, gaze. Anxiety and hope now oppressed her in equal degrees, and left her no moment of tranquillity till the arrival of [the doctor] . . . gave her confidence, comfort and tears of joy.
> (Austen, 1811/1900: 275)

In the novel, Marianne is in danger of dying and her chief nurse is Elinor, who is entirely bound up with her beloved sister's progress. However, the sickbed scene is relatively brief and the real risks not lingered over. It is only the moment quoted above when Elinor fixes upon her sister's body for signs of strengthening health. It is Elinor who is constantly at the sickbed. Mrs Jennings and the doctor aid the process; Colonel Brandon offers to fetch their mother and does so. Yet by the time Mrs Dashwood arrives, Elinor is ready to give the news that Marianne is recovering.

So in the novel, Elinor is the focus upon which Marianne's peril is registered. She is also the carer and nurturer of her sister's recovery. When Marianne suggestively looks at Elinor with a 'rational' gaze, more than physical recovery is indicated. It is rather the sign that Marianne's individuation in a fevered underworld is virtually complete. She looks at her stronger sister as to one who will be the main future model of her-self. In Jung's idea of the self archetype, it is frequently imaged by a wise old man or woman. Such figures portray the centring archetype of the psyche or its ultimately unimaginable wholeness. While Jung's descriptions of self images as a wise old man or even Jesus are easily linked to his lifelong preoccupation with Christianity, he has less to say about the wise old woman.

One place where *The Collected Works* does attempt to explore images of the feminine in women is the essay on the Kore (Jung 1941/1959: paras 306–82). Unsurprisingly, it hinges on the role of the Persephone myth for the modern woman. This story may represent an individuation path for women. Its goal is a retained connection with the unconscious in Persephone's continued residence in the underworld for part of the year. The other key image is, of course, nurturing Demeter, the mother who rescues and who stands for the self symbol of the wise old woman in the woman's individuating psyche.

Another way of looking at Persephone's story and one not directly addressed by Jung is as an articulation of the myth of the Earth Mother Goddess. Frequently, the Earth Goddess sponsors an animistic religion with the sacred earth being addressed through spirits in field, mountain, stream and winds. Another frequent form is the figuring of a triple goddess as maiden, matron and crone, or even a fourth in the addition of a goddess of war, strife and death.

Returning to the novel of *Sense and Sensibility*, Elinor takes on the role of Mother Demeter in shepherding Marianne out of the underworld. Yet this is not to suggest that she is always a mother figure. Rather than any character allegorically bearing the persona of a single mythical figure, the novel is surprisingly fluid. By linking Eros and Psyche to Persephone and by the actual mother behaving more like a sister and vice versa, the novel embodies and critically explores what it is to be a maiden, matron and crone. In Marianne it also explores what it is to be attached through eros to the Goddess of Death.

Elinor's function as a proto-self for her younger sister is made explicit in a later scene, also occurring in the film.

Now, I want to argue that these two scenes, the sickbed and the feminine coniunctio, work differently in the film in a way that enhances the myth. First, let me recap and clarify. Novels may be animated by a deep structuring of myth. In addition, the novel form itself is a mythical structure in that it inherits the ancient organising of experience in a bundle or a web or a network (of relationships), according to Ursula Le Guin (1986). We need here to notice that the mythical web that is the novel is also a mode of the Earth Goddess whose identity as the sacredness of nature is frequently substantiated in *the web of life*. Since plurality is thereby innate to the novel, it is unsurprising if it is the repository of myths marginalised by the dominant patriarchal and monotheistic culture.

The novel is also about *matter* in another aspect of its link to the Goddess. 'She' is matter infused with spirit and so sacred, not divorced from the divine and unredeemable. The novel is about matter because it is about the text-ure of lives in relationships and material social settings. Novels are about our encounters with body and matter in everyday living. In Jane Austen, *matter* is primarily portrayed through its social transformation into *things of cultural meaning* such as houses (especially), clothes, horses, carriages, dining and even nature as *cultivated* rather than left to itself. In the novel of *Sense and Sensibility* 'nature' is indicative of social and psychic meaning.

> "[Elinor] ... The woods and walks thickly covered with dead leaves."
> "Oh!" cried Marianne, "with what transporting sensations have I formerly seen them fall! ..."
> "It is not everyone," said Elinor, "who has your passion for dead leaves."
>
> (Austen, 1811/1990: 76)

Here Elinor's repetition of *dead* leaves draws attention to the dark side of Marianne's dangerous romanticism. Still hopeful of Willoughby, despite his mysterious departure, she is already registering her presence in the underworld taking her ever closer from maiden to goddess of death. Marianne's 'transporting sensations' have formerly been delight in autumnal glamour at Norland. Now she is transported to another place.

Jung (1932/1950) has a powerful evocation of how the novel mobilises matter for the psyche in his description of *Ulysses* by James Joyce. Here what is finally offered to the reader is a material world signifying the higher potentials of the self.

> Try to imagine a being who ... consists also of houses, street-processions, churches, the Liffey, several brothels, and a crumpled note on its way to the sea – and yet possesses a perceiving and registering consciousness!
>
> (CW15: para. 198)

Although Jung constantly treats the self as masculine and infers Christian monotheism, he is, in the spiritualisation of matter here, far closer to the Earth Mother, who is fundamentally prior to division into genders. Moreover, *Sense and Sensibility* in written form is concerned to remind us how much reading used to be a social, bodily and erotic activity. Lacking proper heating, the early nineteenth century household practised reading aloud as a principal form of evening entertainment. Here Willoughby reading to Marianne is an important stage in their courtship.

Reading is thus also a bodily and even perilous occupation. It is emphasised that Marianne's injudicious reading as well as Willoughby's fascinating performances constitute much of her initiation into the underworld. In the novel, myths are presented in a far from cerebral manner so reminding the reader that matter and body are also part of the reading experience.

Of course, film evokes the senses differently. Self-evidently *moving images* with a soundtrack, the form is designed to be watched in cinemas where darkness and physical proximity make the experience paradoxically both social and isolating. There is a sense in which myth and film work together in Jungian terms since both consist of symbolic images plus narrative. Indeed, film demonstrates the mutuality of Jung's notions of symbol and myth. He argued that symbols are images that point to what is only partly known, not yet known, or unknowable (Jung, 1922/1950). They denote aspects of the unconscious. Myths are narratives that best represent and also shape the relations between ego and Other (Jung, 1930/1950).

Consequently, I suggest that myths must contain symbols in order to capture some of the numinous quality of the unconscious. Moreover, symbols should encompass nascent myths for only by active imagination becoming a narrative are their inexhaustible possibilities preserved. Film has images. Whether these constitute symbols is a matter of debate, particularly in the important work of Don Fredericksen (2001). My argument is that in the adaptation of *Sense and Sensibility* both the skills of the film-makers and the mobility of the myth complex in the underlying novel prevent the exhaustion of the mythic material. In particular, the two scenes of Elinor re-solving Marianne, the rescue in the underworld and the stablisation of the self image, demonstrate the re-vivifying of myth.

Marianne lies ill in bed at Mr Palmer's fine house. Colonel Brandon, desirous to be a rescuer, has staggered in with her soaked, unconscious body. Now almost overcome with grief and fear he looks to Elinor to tell him what to do. No sooner has she mentioned their mother than we see Brandon on horseback *galloping away*. Yes, he wants to be the saviour of Marianne, but it is Elinor who is left to bear the crisis. The doctor sleeps and only Elinor is conscious beside her failing sister. Elinor breaks down and weeps, crying that she cannot bear to live without Marianne, frantically kissing her hand. At last Marianne stirs as if in response to the passion. The doctor wakes and pronounces her out of danger. We have previously noted the doctor's role in treating Marianne through bloodletting. Here are connotations of the dying Christ, not to mention feminine references to the menstrual cycle. Marianne has been relieved of 'blood', signifying too much passion, or the unfertilised womb as her body, perhaps, starts to accept the loss of Willoughby.

Elinor's passion over her apparently dying sister in the film is heightened by the underworld qualities of the scene in darkness and sleep. The moment marks the restoration of Eros for both sisters in their mythical archetypes of Psyche and Persephone. Both myths ultimately tell of a woman's need to connect to a deep feminine, one that connotes both the daylight fertility of Demeter and Aphrodite and the deathly Persephone as Queen of the Underworld. Elinor does not say that she cannot live without Edward, but Marianne. Her sister may even be regarded as a shadow figure for her representing the perils of the passion she habitually represses.

Elinor's words over the deathbed are the words of a lover; words that Marianne wants from Willoughby. She has for months been rejecting the sustaining eros of her sister. Here the novel explores just why Elinor is allowed to become her sister's healer in a revived eros. Just before Marianne recovers, Willoughby arrives and tells a horrified Elinor that his feelings for her sister were genuine. The film omits this episode. The visual spectacle of white-faced Marianne and weeping Elinor allows the transition *in the film* from relating to the masculine to a strengthening bond with the feminine. So identified with restraint is Elinor that her abandoned grief almost turns her into Marianne. She unites with her shadow of uncontained emotion, while Marianne permits Elinor as her feminine Other/Self to raise her from the depths.

So finally, when the sisters sit upon a green hill with the sea in the background and Marianne says that she no longer compares her behaviour with Willoughby's but with Elinor's, the moment is one of deep mythical completion. For both sisters, Psyche has completed her mission to the Queen of the Underworld. Indeed, I suggest that this moment is the core of a feminine gaze embedded in the film *for the audience as well*.

Mulvey (1975) structured a masculine gaze from the sum of the male actor and the implied male spectator. Through the way cameras were positioned, the woman is made into an object to be looked at. This then affects meaning and narrative. I am arguing a reverse movement here: the evocation of feminine myth affects the structuring of gaze in the film. In the 1995 *Sense and Sensibility*, each sister embodies a myth that by its symbolic properties draws the viewer's psyche into an individuation with the film text. The combined mythic resonance of both sisters builds a feminine perspective into the animation of matter that is the nature of film. True, we see a male gaze in Brandon looking with desire at Marianne early in the film. Yet it is the narrative and symbolic tensions surrounding the sisters in their mythic descents that mobilises the eros of the text.

If the deepest relationship on screen is that of sisters, its final scene with the boundless wilderness of the sea in the background gives it an impenetrable mystery. Like Jung on *Ulysses*, I suggest the film is finally a self image. It is one that we are invited *to relate to as sisters* in a feminine gaze.

References

Austen, Jane (1811/1990) *Sense and Sensibility*. Oxford: World Classics.
Campbell, Joseph (1949) *The Hero with a Thousand Faces*. Princeton, NJ: Bollingen Series XVII.
Fredericksen, Don (2001) 'Jung/sign/symbol/film'. In Christopher Hauke and Ian Alister (eds), *Jung and Film: Post-Jungian takes on the Moving Image* (pp. 17–55). London and New York: Routledge.
Fredericksen, Don (2008) 'Stripping Bare the Images'. In Susan Rowland (ed.), *Psyche and the Arts: Jungian Approaches to Music, Architecture, Literature, Painting and Film*. London and New York: Routledge.
Jung, C. G. (1922/1950) 'On the Relation of Analytical Psychology to Poetry'. In *The Spirit in Man, Art and Literature, The Collected Works of C. G. Jung, Vol. 15* (R. F. C. Hull, trans.). Princeton, NJ: Princeton University Press.
Jung, C. G. (1930/1950) 'Psychology and Literature'. In *The Spirit in Man, Art and Literature, The Collected Works of C. G. Jung, Vol. 15* (R. F. C. Hull, trans.). Princeton, NJ: Princeton University Press.
Jung, C. G. (1932/1950) '*Ulysses*': A Monologue'. In *The Spirit in Man, Art and Literature, The Collected Works of C. G. Jung, Vol. 15* (R. F. C. Hull, trans.). Princeton, NJ: Princeton University Press.
Jung, C. G. (1941/1959) 'The Psychological Aspects of the Kore'. In *The Archetypes and the Collective Unconscious, The Collected Works of C. G. Jung, Vol. 9(i)* (R. F. C. Hull, trans.). Princeton, NJ: Princeton University Press.
Lee, Ang (1995) *Sense and Sensibility*. Culver City, CA: Columbia Pictures.
Le Guin, U. (1986) 'The Carrier Bag Theory of Fiction'. In C. Glotfelty and H. Fromm (eds), *The Ecocriticism Reader* (pp. 149–54). Athens, GA: The University of Georgia Press.
Mulvey, Laura (1975) 'Visual Pleasure and Narrative Cinema'. *Screen 16*(3), 6–18.
North, Julia (1999) 'Conservative Austen, Radical Austen: *Sense and Sensibility* From Text to Screen'. In Deborah Cartmell and Imelda Whelan (eds), *Adaptations: From Text to Screen, Screen to Text* (pp. 38–50). London and New York: Routledge.
Perrill, Sue (2002) *Jane Austen on Film and Television: A Critical Study of Adaptations*. North Carolina and London: McFarland & Co. Inc.
Vogler, Christopher (2007) *The Writer's Journey: Mythic Structure for Writers*. Studio City, CA: Michael Wiese Productions.

Chapter 12
Cinephilia
Or, looking for meaningfulness in encounters with cinema

Greg Singh

> Every story involves one or more archetypes. To make a good story a single archetype is usually enough. But *Casablanca* is not satisfied with that. It uses them all.
> (Umberto Eco, 1998: 202)

> The increased use of digital technologies in motion picture production has had an important psychological effect on many viewers (cinephiles especially, perhaps) [. . .] Changes in film consumption are not separate from technological developments; they are enabled by them.
> (Christian Keathley, 2009: 2)

A note on cinephilia

The term 'cinephilia' has gained currency in film studies recently. Indeed, a glance at reading lists and specialist publishers' recommendations reveals that there are a number of edited collections and monographs dedicated to the subject (Balcerzak and Sperb, 2009 – a second volume forthcoming; de Valck and Hagener, 2005; Doane, 2002; Keathley, 2006; and Rosenbaum and Martin, 2003 to name a few). Cinephilia has also been the chosen arena for a number of PhD theses in recent years (my own included). The term implies a 'love of cinema', or a love of film-viewing perhaps: doubly significant not only for the fact that the academy usually avoids such emotive and highly subjective terms as 'love' (deemed unscholarly and counterproductive in film analysis, and tragically avoided in the lecture hall), but also because the term has been somewhat demonised in film theory during the past three decades or so as a catch-all label for apolitical film criticism. Additionally, when the word is spoken or read off the page, it sounds and reads like it could be the moniker for a psychological condition or perhaps a disorder;

something to be viewed with suspicion or at the very least, kept at arm's length from humanities disciplines.

It is therefore a minor miracle that cinephilia has been reappropriated by film scholars who have given it its theoretical due: a more thoroughgoing consideration and an open, interdisciplinary debate. I would argue that, as a phenomenon now recognised within film studies as fairly common to encounters with film, cinephilia may actually be thought of more positively as a psychological condition; or, more properly, a reflection of the psychological reality of film-viewing and the creative co-production of meaning that takes place in the dialogue between viewer and viewed. It is, therefore, an arena that should be of great interest to post-Jungian studies, where the object of investigation is the interplay between culture and its consumption, and the fascination that representations in contemporary media of themes such as shame and dignity (to give just two examples that seem to have particular currency in contemporary analytical thinking, among other sensibilities) seem to present.

Whilst certainly not a universal experience, the 'cinephiliac moment' as Christian Keathley has put it on many occasions, is a phenomenon open to all. If one thinks about the practice of relaying one's own film experiences in everyday life, certain patterns start to emerge. As Gibbs and Pye (2005), for example, suggest, when we leave a movie theatre with a group of friends, we tend to recall events that happened in the film in a highly narrativised way. Often, this recollection is accompanied by heightened emotional responses, and the recollections of how the film made us feel as we watched. This recollection, this retelling, adds to the 'making sense' of the film, is one of the many pleasures associated with shared film experiences, and gives the experience of watching film meaning.

Not so much a disorder then, I would argue that cinephilia is a useful term for thinking through a normal pathology of film-viewing that captures something of what people experience through their everyday encounters with film. Here, I am not just talking about shared viewing in a movie theatre, but other encounters with film that have entered the public domain as ordinary viewing practices, challenging our very definitions of what cinema is and can be. Online archiving, tube sites and DVD multi-regional players (as well as the production companies that cater for multi-region, international markets) all became commonplace in the noughties, and continue to play a significant role in film connoisseurship in the twenty-first century. As Keathley puts it in the epigraph to this chapter, technological changes, whilst not determining our love of film in the first place, certainly enable it. These are, I realise, rather general statements, and so I would like to provide an outline of some of the more specific nuances of the term 'cinephilia' in order to elaborate.

Traditionally, the term has been used in film scholarship to describe a variety of phenomena in the encounter with film. Most obviously, perhaps, the term has come to mean the kind of enthusiasm film 'buffs', who attend art house screenings of obscure or hard-to-find films, bring to their descriptions of both the films they watch and their experiences whilst watching them. These 'buffs' are enthusiasts who may be thought to possess detailed knowledge of and an excessive interest in the film stars they watch avidly, the production techniques of a particularly favourite film or, perhaps, the values and meanings mobilised by the contents of films themselves.

It is this detailed level of knowledge, as well as the excessive interest in a particular element of the production, that gives cinephilia its implication for out-of-the-ordinary film-viewing. Indeed, it has often been noted, for example, that the cinephile looks for and delights in the smallest details of a film: the colour of Cary Grant's socks in the crop-dusting sequence of *North by Northwest* (Hitchcock, 1959) provides, 'in dialectical relation to flesh, an elemental lure' for James Naremore (1988: 215); Bela Balasz's 'lyrical charm of the close-up' in some of his favourite silent films (1999: 305–11); the 'admirable face-object' of Greta Garbo, as famously described by Roland Barthes, 'still partakes of the same rule of Courtly Love, where the flesh gives rise to mystical feelings of perdition' (1993: 56).

In reading all of these scholarly examples, such subjective accounts may be said to either dull the objective edge of sharp observation or soften the blow of what can often be considered an emotionally detached analytical style in film theory and criticism. It depends on one's perspective, on how much one is convinced of the benefits of incorporating (or at least, acknowledging) one's own tastes or preferences in scholarship. In my critical opinion, the latter, more affirmative, interpretation of such accounts – fully acknowledging the emotional power of encounters with film – is both appropriate and useful for the purposes of film analysis, and need not detract from the theoretical and critical vigour of film study. I find myself in agreement with John Izod, when he writes that we film academics 'are not good at analysing the pleasures of the text or understanding what those pleasures might mean' (2001: 2). At least, we weren't very good at it – until the renewed interest in cinephilia appeared.

There has been much recent debate in academic circles as to the validity of cinephilia as an adequate way to describe the film-viewing experience, precisely because of its somewhat subjective approach.

Current attitudes in the academy towards cinephilia have redefined how the term is used and what it says about the act of viewing film, and its potential for investigating viewing pleasure has indeed opened up new vistas upon screen analysis. In my own work, I outline this shift of interest in cinephilia by engaging the term as a conceptual framework (the phenomenon of intensity and level of knowledge of material encountered), as an object of study in itself (fans, cults and casual viewing audiences), and as a method for analysing film and our encounters with it (thinking about what film is, what it does, and why it is loved). In this pluralist approach, the policing of borders often associated with academic discipline is done away with in favour of a more affirmative incorporation of critical and subjective encounters with the object of analysis itself.

This has immediate relevance for post-Jungian approaches to film, because cinephilia is used most often to indicate an intensity of engagement with films that involves emotional attachments with cultural objects that, no matter how juvenile they are considered in some circles, how obvious or culturally derivative (e.g. popular fiction film as mass entertainment, the value of which is viewed with suspicion by some), often have the power to strike the viewer as meaningful or perhaps 'speaking' to them in a highly personal and affective way. This reflects a psychological reality in film-viewing that goes beyond mere appearances, something that has been noted by both Luke Hockley (2009) and Christopher Hauke (2009) in their formulations of 'the third image', and a phenomenon that I touched upon in my previous work on post-Jungian film theory (Singh, 2009). Where some traditional Jungian film criticism has tended to fix the meaning of films, privileging some films as pregnant with meaning and others as being barren or bereft of deeper psychological resonance, more recent work in the this particular area tells us, from recollection and descriptions of personal encounters with film (as well as the recollections of clients in the therapy session of their own experiences with films), that this is not really the case. Is cinephilia, then, a way of 'looking into' film that reflects the everyday meaningful encounters that we often experience and share?

In what follows, I use examples from two popular films from the New Hollywood period – *Star Wars* (Lucas, 1977) and *Close Encounters of the Third Kind* (Spielberg, 1977) – to discuss this way of 'looking into' films as an affirmative and meaningful encounter, to help uncover the 'looked-for' in film and how this is expressed in everyday language. I will do this in two ways. First, by reflecting upon a personal 'cinephiliac moment', I will re-examine the similarities and differences between the

Jungian concept of archetypal structure and what the semiotician and novelist Umberto Eco has described as 'archetypical' in popular film characters. This will demonstrate the complexities of negotiating the conceptual categories of audience in film criticism when dealing with processes of meaning-making in the encounter with film. Second, I will deal with the difficulties of analysing such cinephiliac moments in the contemporary media landscape, with its minefields of converging media platforms, technology/interactivity, repeated viewing, and paratextual materials that enhance encounters with film. In taking such an approach, I hope to further the understanding of how we rediscover (time and again) what it was about watching and talking about film that we loved so much in the first place.

Archetypal? Archetypical? Cinephilia and cult encounters with the symbol in popular cinema

Eco's meditation on *Casablanca* (Curtiz, 1942) in his essay *Casablanca: Cult Movies and Intertextual Collage* (1998), is interesting for a number of reasons. Not only does he illuminate one of Hollywood's most popular and best-loved classic texts, but he also explains how that film can be considered a 'cult' text. Along the way, Eco manages to redefine our ideas of what a cult film is, and how some films become cult viewing, whereas others do not. He writes:

> What are the requirements for transforming a book or a movie into a cult object? The work must be loved, obviously, but this is not enough. It must provide a completely furnished world so that its fans can quote characters and episodes as if they were aspects of the fan's private sectarian world, a world about which one can make up quizzes and play trivia games so that the adepts of the sect recognize through each other a shared expertise. Naturally all these elements (characters and episodes) must have some archetypical appeal, as we shall see.
>
> (1998: 197–8)

One might argue that nowhere is this more relevant in contemporary popular cinema than in the Star Wars universe, with not only its blockbuster films and sequels, but also a bewildering array of merchandise, novels, secondary media output, and fan fiction. The Star Wars universe, as a story-world, means an awful lot to an awful lot of people, but as

Will Brooker (2002) points out in his book *Using the Force*, this is not just down to George Lucas's authorial intention, his skill with story-telling, or his preoccupation with reiterating the Saturday movie serials and popular TV Westerns of his childhood in a science fiction setting:

> On one level, *Star Wars* does not belong solely to Lucas anymore; its characters and stories have escaped the original text and grown up with the fans, who have developed their own very firm ideas of what *Star Wars* is and is not about.
>
> (2002: 77)

Brooker's work in this area on fandom and fan-responses to the ownership and meaning of the films they love spans a number of book-length studies and articles, and sits comfortably within a vibrant and growing interdisciplinary body of work in media and cultural studies in the UK (e.g. Barker and Brooks, 1998; Hills 2002). His overall approach to *Star Wars* in particular (but also a number of other popular and cult texts) suggests that fan knowledge and intensity of engagement with their story-worlds (and fans, as anyone who is one will know, defend their ownership status passionately) enriches and enhances the experience of film at multiple, extra-textual levels. This is vital for the contemporary encounter with films, as well as the notion of cinephilia, for a number of reasons related to the sheer accessibility of textual material, and I shall return to this shortly.

There are, obviously, a number of differences between a classic Hollywood text such as *Casablanca* and the Star Wars movies that make comparisons difficult. Indeed, Eco himself points out that the patchwork approach to genre in *Casablanca*, as well as the dazzling array of typology condensed into very few characters, arrived at almost by accident in the film's production process, comes to be invoked consciously as 'intertextual reference' in later films. Eco gives the well-known (yet not entirely correct, perhaps) anecdote that Ingrid Bergman did not know the ending of the film, nor the character her own would end up with as a romantic interest. Therefore, she had to look longingly at both Henreid and Bogart. This performance, for Eco, brings out the ambiguous pleasures of the characters in the film: it rounds them and gives them depth, but also leaves them somewhat less tempered, uneven and heterogenous – in other words, more *human*. It allows the characters to reach out and intertextually quote characters in other films without realising it. Victor Laszlo (Paul Henreid), for example, orders drinks four times during the film's duration, each time choosing a different drink. Eco's guess at this indecision is that 'Curtiz was simply quoting, unconsciously, similar situations in other movies and trying to provide a reasonably complete repetition of them' (1998: 201). To paraphrase, *Casablanca* explains *Raiders of the Lost Ark* (Spielberg, 1981), but *Raiders* does not explain *Casablanca*. *Raiders*' intertextuality is piecemeal compared with *Casablanca*'s, according to this model, and is pre-empted by *Casablanca*'s array of intertextual, energetic archetypicality: as suggested in the epigraph to this chapter, *Casablanca* seems to embody archetypicality *par excellence*.

However, the usefulness of Eco's semiotic approach comes into focus when thinking about the use of the term 'archetype' and the actual appearance of archetypes in the world of the film:

> The term "archetype" does not claim to have any particular psychoanalytic or mythic connotation, but serves only to indicate a pre-established and frequently reappearing narrative situation, cited or in some way recycled by innumerable other texts and provoking in the addressee a sort of intense emotion accompanied by the vague feeling of a déjà vu, that everybody yearns to see again.
>
> (1998: 200)

Clearly here, in the first part of the statement, Eco is referring to archetype in the Jungian sense, but, although he acknowledges that the term has both psychoanalytic and mythic uses elsewhere, he chooses not to make such a claim for his own formulation. His approach is, after all, *semiotic*, and this kind of analysis has proved to be something of a bugbear for post-Jungian scholarship, from Fredericksen (2001) to Hauke (2000), Izod (2001, 2006) and beyond. I have already discussed the eminently reversible aspects of Symbol and semiotic sign in postmodern media texts elsewhere (Singh, 2009) and so will not dwell on it here, except in relation to Eco's statement. If one reads Eco carefully, one may discern acknowledgement of the importance of the term's psychological and cultural potentiality. Where Eco's 'archetype' may be dislocated from the Jungian conceptual framework, nevertheless I think that this does not negate the potential relationship between the two formulations of archetype. Consider what Eco implies here:

> I would not say that an intertextual archetype is necessarily "universal". It can belong to a rather recent textual tradition. . . . It is sufficient to consider it as a topos or standard situation that manages to be particularly appealing to a given cultural area or a historical period.
>
> (1998: 200–1)

Eco is reworking classical Jungian formulations of the difference between Cultural Symbols, which develop over a period of time and come to gain cultural resonance and shared meaning within a cultural practice, and Natural Symbols, which represent underlying and inexpressible archetypal structures in psychic life. The Lone Gunman of Western films, for example, is an enduring Cultural Symbol that takes on particular resonance as a metonym for the taming of the West, embodying rugged individualism and invoking a nostalgia for the closed Frontier. This symbol has taken on a particularly important status in visual terms, as the embodiment of personal elements that are prized in modern Western societies: enterprise, individualism and self-reliance, rugged masculinity and so forth.

This is a very powerful emotional repository for aspirations that are, if suspect to the analytical eye, nonetheless potent and lasting in popular terms. However, Cultural Symbols such as this are kinds of semiotic signs or 'intertextual archetypes'. Whilst perhaps not carrying the numinous weight of an Adam Kadmon, or 'original man' of classical Jungian Archetypal formulation, such signs are, to give them another name, 'archetypical'. They can occasionally take on a patina of meaning beyond their temporality, becoming meaningful through individual and collective encounters over time. Indeed, this has happened to the genre of the Western itself, particularly in its classical Hollywood manifestation, as archetypical of the history of the US, with its tropes of manifest destiny and progressive, civilising trajectory. Elsewhere, Eco writes of Jungian Symbolism that it is:

> characterized by an analogy between expression and content and by a fundamental *vagueness* of the expressed content. . . . If the archetypes are indescribable and infinitely interpretable, their experience cannot be but amorphous, undetermined and unarticulated. Symbols are empty and full of meaning at the same time.
> (1984: 144–5, italics in original)

The Image (or 'third image') brought to the film by the viewer during the act of viewing, as well as the practice of retelling this meaningful encounter, often long afterwards, is clearly a manifestation in micro of this larger and ongoing macro process. The 'sort of intense emotion accompanied by the vague feeling of a déjà vu' that Eco mentions (1998: 200), is thus a part of the cultural life of the film beyond the film text, and an expression of the indeterminate psychological space that exists in that way that is so difficult to articulate verbally, that intensity of experience that can accompany the encounter with film. One could argue that potent archetypical figures such as the Lone Gunman endure in much more recent films than classic Westerns, and for very obvious reasons, precisely due to this indeterminacy. This archetypical figure partakes of symbolism in a psychological, ongoing macro process that is as much a part of our personal encounters with film as it is a collective and shared one. It designates, for Eco (1994: 18), a different idea of symbol: 'Something that sends one back to a mysterious and self-contradictory reality that cannot be conceptually expressed' and yet remains meaningful, and looked for.

My own 'cinephiliac moments' bear this out. The figure of Han Solo, as played by Harrison Ford, provided a focus for my childhood *Star Wars* viewing that I can hardly put into words now. Solo was, for me, everything that I wanted to be (and thought I should be), from the quirkiness of Ford's on-set jokes that were kept in the films, to his way with women ('I'm nice men') and even the way he could get away with wearing a waistcoat and still look cool. Of course, to universalise my own experiences and emotional responses to the Star Wars films would not only be naive, but would also detract from the productive elements of what such recollections can afford the analyst in thinking through such emotional attachments. These moments go far beyond personal experiences, however, and to dismiss them would be like declaring that each individual reading of a film's meaning is utterly unique, and that shared fascinations should be dismissed as coincidence. Recent scholarship on fandom suggests that to get to the meaningful in our film encounters, we need to re-examine what we do when talking or writing about the films we love.

Tom Shone, for example, has written at length on fan reaction to the 1996 *Star Wars* reissues. In his book *Blockbuster: How Hollywood Learned to Stop Worrying and Love the Summer*, he states that:

> They [ILM and Lucasfilm] would end up redoing five hundred shots in the first three movies, inserting wholly new scenes, new characters, changing the motivations of existing ones: in the 1977 *Star Wars* Han Solo was seen to shoot an alien down in cold blood; an added sound effect now made it clear that he was returning fire. A quick clean up had shaded, imperceptibly, into revisionism.
>
> (2004: 280)

What Shone is demonstrating here is very much in line with Janet Wasko's observation that media industries, including Hollywood, distribute 'important ideological and cultural products, with significance for the representation and reproduction of social norms and values' (1994: 3). Not only were these films being regenerated for entertainment purposes on a stylistic-thematic level: they were also engaged in a task to revise earlier cultural and ideological statements, adjusting the values and cultural associations of the characters themselves in order to participate in the ideological life of the 1990s. That is, Han Solo went from being the Lone Gunman with questionable morals – much like, say, Ethan Edwards in John Ford's *The Searchers* (1956) – and a talent for black market operations, to becoming a modern action hero/romantic lead (in line with Harrison Ford's other heroic lead, Indiana Jones) with an obsession to pay back his debts, join the rebellion, and reform his ways; in other words, to become an embodiment of 1990s reconstructed masculinity. This is not an isolated example in the New Hollywood period either: Hauke, in the preceding volume to this present collection (2001), details the changing modes of masculinity reflected in the films of Steven Spielberg from the early 1970s to the late 1990s, marking conscious authorial statements on shifting attitudes towards gender in popular culture. I will return to Spielberg's own revisionist tactics shortly.

This is not, however, to say that Lucas and his team consciously set out to realign the film's ideological axis, but that, in order to seek out the new target demographic to which the reissues were to be marketed, the films would benefit from some narrative shading and alteration. This would have been easily achievable, given the new technology and opportunity. Anne Friedberg has stated that: 'Recent films which have digitally 'revised' film footage from the 1960s – *Nixon*, *JFK*, *Forrest Gump* – illustrate the compelling urge to reprogram popular memory' (2004: 923). In revisionist Hollywood, it seems that the past as a real referent disappears and rematerialises in the form of the cinematic image; an aspect of postmodern experience that sits comfortably within Eco's framework of archetypicality.

In revising one of the key characters in the Star Wars universe (not to mention one of the most iconic figures in New Hollywood) Lucas had fundamentally changed the values embodied in both the films and the universe that they represented. To borrow the postmodern critic Fredric Jameson's phrase, this was an ideological containment strategy that was both a visible and (if purely going by box-office receipts) a highly lucrative move. It shifted emphasis away from a more adult-oriented nostalgia for the Western genre and its binaries of civilisation versus frontier, and established a newer mythology that embodied a neoliberal idealism centred on technology and innovation (in the digital revision) and individual destiny (Solo was always clear-cut, morally speaking, rather than free to choose as his conscience took him). In this one, tiny detail of alteration, a butterfly effect is set in motion regarding the resonance of the Cultural Symbol of the Lone Gunman. Solo's mercenary aspect, his darker side, is a highly seductive one, and the sharp redemption that comes for his character through his reformation is dulled in the revised versions.

In *Star Wars* fan circles, the example of Han Solo's shoot out with the alien bounty hunter Greedo and the added sound effect is infamous. This has potential consequences for the links between the fanish obsession with detail and the debates that form from the discovery of such anomalies, and the cinephile's ways of looking-into film: spotting changes in comparative examples that have the potential to alter the meaning of a scene or character relationship as well as the overall narrative trajectory. For example, one fan, cited by Brooker, stated of the revision that

> This causes the evolution of Han's character throughout the trilogy to carry much less impact. No longer is it a huge struggle for Han to change to someone capable of love for another being and a belief in fighting a good cause.
>
> (cited in Brooker, 2002: 76)

That this change in particular seemed to attract almost universal hatred from fans of the 1977 version of the film is an interesting phenomenon for a number of reasons. Most notable here is the fan perception that Han Solo, as a kind of archetypical space cowboy, had questionable morals that provided the cornerstone of his development as a character throughout the trilogy. To borrow a clinical metaphor, and a Jungian concept note, in narrative terms the Shadow is a particular characteristic of Solo's personality (juvenile, vindictive, selfish and self-serving, boastful) that is confronted and transformed far more effectively than anything Luke or Anakin Skywalker could muster in the narrative arc. The significance of this is that fan commentaries on online discussion forums seemed to save their most vitriolic criticism of the changes for George Lucas and his proprietary and unnecessary alteration of 'their' text. It is the tension between authorial propriety (and presence) and fan anticipation (and production) that Brooker's observations identify so well.

Thus, fanish appropriation of objects and their ownership of them exists beyond authorial propriety, and what audiences do with texts beyond watching and reading them is to express that sense of ownership in a meaningful, shared way. Indeed, if Eco is to be allowed it, this expressive cultural phenomenon has, to an extent, become the norm in postmodern film culture. In cases of intertextual archetypicality, 'we witness an instance of metacult, or of cult about cult – a Cult Culture. [. . . A] way to cope with the burden of our filmic encyclopedic expertise' (1998: 209–10).

Michele Pierson's work on audience and spectacle is useful here (2002), as she focuses on the specialised knowledge afforded the connoisseur or 'buff', the cinephile. She suggests that the desire of the buff to cultivate technical knowledge about the way cinematic spectacle is produced is a desire to break from the institutional convention of the cinematic spectator as passive consumer, and to engage fully with the acts of viewing, collecting and retelling as living and lived experiences. This helps us rethink rather outdated models of viewing and meaning-making, fixed temporally and spatially in the movie theatre, and during the film screening, to refit cinephilia as an ongoing, psychologically 'warm' process.

This model of the co-creation of meaning is somewhat is tune with Roland Barthes' ideas on the punctum in observing a photograph. He writes in *Camera Lucida* (1981: 55) that the punctum is objectively present, but subjectively provocative, and is 'what I add to the photograph and what is nonetheless already there.' The punctum disrupts the ideological unity of the image, and yet brings to it a meaningfulness that engages the observer in a more rounded, full, or pregnant encounter. Barthes' approach to this kind of subjective, at times spontaneous, eruption of meaningfulness in a film-viewing moment has a precedent in his earlier work *The Pleasure of the Text* (1990), where he stated that representation tends to consist of cultural and ideological formations, whereas the notion of figuration erupts through such representational work and inspires an altogether more creaturely, embodied form of experience: *jouissance* (bliss). To clarify, this use of the term *jouissance* is only loosely related to the Lacanian use of the word as the embodied pleasure of the Real in psychoanalytic terms and can be productively used to distinguish the more Freudian scopophilia (pleasure through looking) and jouissance (pleasure through looking into, interpreting or reading). In fact, it can be more concretely associated with Kracauer's materialist phenomenology of modernity, leisure and visual culture as set out in the collection of his essays, *The Mass Ornament* (1994) and in his writing on boredom in particular. Kracauer writes:

> One harbours only an inner restlessness without a goal, a longing that is pushed aside, and a weariness with that which exists without

really being. If, however, one has the patience, the sort of patience specific to legitimate boredom, then one experiences a kind of bliss that is almost unearthly.

(1994: 334)

Kracauer is addressing the problem of modern alienation here, and specifically, the kind of subsistence that characterises modern urban life, distractive mass (consumer) culture, and psychological disquiet. However, the 'legitimate boredom' of which Kracauer speaks, implies a radicalisation of boredom on one's own terms, a shifting of attention from studium to punctum, through a patience that, in spectatorial terms and following Keathley, may be identified as 'panoramic perception' – that is, 'the tendency to sweep the screen visually in order to register the image in its totality, especially the marginal details and contingencies that are the most common sources of cinephiliac moments' (2006: 8). Perhaps what Keathley is attempting to articulate here is a viewing strategy, peculiar to the cinephile, and a boredom that manifests and legitimates itself as 'panoramic perception'.

Thus, those punctuating moments, often spontaneously occurring outside of expectation, on the periphery of popular film texts, operate simultaneously to the studium – the ideologically contained meaning of the visual and narrative make-up of the film. Thus, to make use of cinephilia as a conceptualisation of commodity-identity and identification, it need not rest on an assumed dichotomy of preferred/oppositional reading, but nevertheless acknowledges the roles of shared meaning and personal meaningfulness in the act of viewing film. To extend the complexion of Barthes' critique of the idea of ideological containment, especially in the light of Kracauer's materialist position on boredom, Barthes clarifies his own position in this statement from *The Pleasure of the Text*, in relation to the practice of authorship:

> Does writing in pleasure guarantee . . . my reader's pleasure? Not at all. I must seek out this reader (must "cruise" him) *without knowing where he is*. A site of bliss is created. It is not the reader's "person" that is necessary to me, it is this site: the possibility of a dialectics of desire, of an *unpredictability* of bliss.
>
> (1990: 4, italics in original)

In this sense, one may see the mechanics of creative choices that are necessarily made from an authorial position: one's authorship may be 'visionary' or 'original', but addressing an audience through the institutional filters of ideology, expectation, convention and the commercial sector renders the status of authorship fluid, and ultimately may be said to amplify the phenomenon of the punctum even further – flying as it does, in the face of institutional convention. Such cinephiliac moments are, for want of a simple phrase, all the more significant for standing out to *you* as a member of the audience (or possibly a member of a specialist or cult audience) and are therefore meaningful connections between text and audience in collective relations of exchange (rather than, say, between private relations of author and reader).

As Eco has observed, 'Many modern theories are unable to recognize that symbols are paradigmatically open to infinite meanings but syntagmatically, that is, textually, open only to the indefinite, but by no means infinite, interpretations allowed by the context' (1994: 21). I would suggest that Barthes' meditations on the dialectics of desire allow for such open, though not infinite, readings of meaning, further implying that the ongoing meaning-making process is driven by a desire akin to cinephiliac desire to keep such symbolic figures (as the Lone Gunman in my own particular case) alive. For, as Eco goes on to write, 'Any act of interpretation is a dialectic between openness and form, initiative on the part of the interpreter and contextual pressure' (1994: 21).

Together-apart: A post-Jungian approach to cinephilia and media technologies

Although enabled through technology, this is by no means an entirely new phenomenon. Indeed, as Eco writes in *Semiotics and the Philosophy of Language*, 'The eschatology of human consciousness is a continual creative repetition of its archaeology. In this way, naturally, nobody can assign to symbols a final truth or a coded meaning' (1984: 147). In the act of film-viewing it is, in a way, the search for expressing how cinema has the power to create such meaningful experiences, engaging our project of consciousness so powerfully and, to paraphrase Eco, this dialectic is related to the human way of reducing the world to a manageable format. (1994: 21)

In his essay Interactive Audiences? (2004) the comparative media analyst Henry Jenkins suggests that a new participatory media culture is taking shape at the intersection of three interrelated phenomena:

1 New technologies have enabled consumers to archive, appropriate and repurpose media content.
2 Contemporary subcultures (such as fan groups, cult audiences, etc.) promote DIY production, utilising technology as platforms for

dissemination of materials and information (e.g. fan fiction, secondary production, commentary and so forth).
3   The flow of images and narratives across multiple, horizontally integrated media channels has enabled (and Jenkins uses the term 'demanded' here) more active modes of spectatorship.

However, Jenkins takes care to point out that this new interactivity, a kind of utopian consumerism, is not autonomous of powerful business interests: he suggests that contemporary audiences are more akin to marketing concepts than 'semiotic democracies' (2004: 158). This is important, because the ideas behind the concept and method of cinephilia laid out in this chapter so far rely on these intersections in order to become fully productive as lived phenomena. It is, in other words, not just the psychology that runs the show here, but more likely, psychology's adeptness at adjusting to contemporary story-telling, its appropriation of technology for more integrated media experiences, as well as the media's appropriation of traditional symbols and narratives in new environments for its effective incorporation of the contemporary psyche, in order to sell goods and services. It is, in other words, a potent mix of the old and the new.

As John Izod writes, this is where Jungian screen theory comes into its own for 'its capability to model the ways in which the subjective and felt experiences of spectators arise from their encounter with the screen text. . . . It can show how a screen text seeks to open a viewing position for audiences' (2001: 8). This occurs through the micro processes of the act of viewing, a dialectic between openness and form as mentioned previously, through the interplay of image on screen and the investment of psychic energy (libido, or emotional intensity, in post-Jungian terms) in the objects encountered: an interplay already described as the 'third image'. The extent of emotional investment is, of course, somewhat dependent upon the nature of the encounter, the taste of the individual (which is a conscious attitude rather than an unconscious desire), and the image's relationship to other images/textual flows familiar to the cultural setting. This cultural setting, to clarify, includes the cultural status of the text, but also incorporates the status of the text in relation to the viewer.

This relation is articulated in cinephilia, and even more so, in fandom. As Izod goes on to say, fans are 'likely to align themselves with their heroes and heroines and partake imaginatively in patterns of life and adventure with little if any connection to the world they inhabit by day' (2001: 17). This approach obviously implies the sense of escapism that, say, *Avatar* (Cameron, 2009) can bring to the experience of the viewer in their encounter with a spectacular, fictional (technological) world. Such results are somewhat collective, shared as they are in cultural commentary (both professional and informal), with points of general agreement and contention as to the meaning of such spectacles. However, it can run to far more personal or idiosyncratic experiences, as in my own cinephiliac moments described here: my identification with Solo, perhaps, or my (mis)understanding of Roy Neary's transformation in *Close Encounters*, as described below.

What is interesting about Izod's perspective is his take on the psychological work of the imagination *after* the actual viewing experience, and this aspect of his work ties in neatly with my own in relation to what happens in the re-telling of the cinematic encounter, discussed earlier. He writes: 'After the film has ended, active imagination takes over and develops the recollected cinematic imagery by fusing it more completely with personal fantasy material. In the process both are liable to change' (2001: 17). It is this aspect of Jungian psychology that proves the most effective in negotiating what actually happens in contemporary cinephilia: in the re-telling of our encounters, active imagination stirs and drives the emotional intensity of the encounter. The power is in the recollection. This may in the event be slight and unimportant – trivial even – in its manifestation, but is a potential site of transformation that compels the theorist to concentrate analysis on meaningfulness and the recollective experience, rather than on the screen and its images as somehow repositories of archetypal material.

This approach is a good fit for contemporary cinephiliac practice, relying as it does on the intersection between technology, DIY secondary production, and narrative flows across multiple platforms. It suggests that recollective experiences, grounded in this intersection (and enabled more *or less* on the technology itself) of contemporary media cultures, fashions and shapes the potential for meaningful cinematic engagement and exchange. What seems a characteristic of some Jungian thinking is that this aspect of cinematic technology and the use of that technology in engaging the film viewer might be viewed with suspicion. Often Jung's work and that of his followers can be interpreted as dismissing technology in favour of a more natural, less technological past. This is, thankfully, the view of a minority of thinkers working with post-Jungian ideas.

Luke Hockley (2007), for example, has written at length on this matter, clarifying some of Jung's more obtuse points on the subject whilst at the same time offering a new insight into the uses of Jungian psychology in his commentary on media technologies. In very brief summary, Hockley suggests that, in tune with Jung's general principle of psychology being two-faced, the psyche is both forward-looking and backward-looking, respectively representing the images of 'intellect' and 'soul'; and that 'the danger inherent in the intellectual project is that it forgets to look back, and instead tries to live solely in the new myth of progress' (2007: 111).

One can see how this kind of statement has been misappropriated to convene a sense of loss for a nostalgic past in Jungian commentary. What Hockley omits here but implies in his argument is that this latter interpretation is every bit a part of the new myth of progress, as is the fascination with and over-investment in progress. This is largely down to the ways late capital has alienated the two aspects of world view. In a unified psyche, the forward- and backward-looking aspects are in dialogue with one another. However, modernity, and in particular, late capital, has severed this connection into an either/or relationship where technological progress is something of a corporate media obsession (and in particular, what one might call a rhetoric of innovation), and is coupled with a nostalgic longing for a lost past that never existed (in populist terms, the 'golden age' defence). In cultural theory, this severing and either/or character of history is associated with the term 'alienation'. Politically speaking, it is a remarkably lucid and seductive form of fascism that is often reproduced in the popular press, but is equally as likely to characterise some traditions of academic historiography. In this interpretation, what Hockley's work does, along with the work of other post-Jungians, is essentially to seek the dialogue between the two aspects that have been drawn into conflict and alienation, in order to overcome the fascist rhetoric that predominates.

If one seeks to embrace the best that technology has to offer, without being enamoured of its progressive possibilities, this can open up a new path for analysing cinematic encounters. This is largely because of the enabling function that contemporary media technology performs in relation to our viewing patterns and practices. One key pattern that has emerged that is of great importance to the phenomenon and practice of cinephilia is the way that films may now be viewed repeatedly, and at leisure. Repeated viewing, essentially, affords not only an indefinite pleasurable encounter with a film text, but also allows the analyst to develop different viewing practices; practices more akin to the cinephile's view, where attention becomes panoramic, and focus falls upon the smallest, most trivial details amongst the competing elements on screen.

My own case in point, a reiteration of a cinephiliac moment from Spielberg's *Close Encounters*, explores a way that post-Jungian ideas can be useful for thinking through domestic media technologies, applying them in the exploration of meaningful connections in film culture. The encounter with cinema in this case is complicated by the fact that one can access extra-textual information in the Ultimate Edition DVD box sets and other ephemeral media. Information is included on techniques used to create various shots and sequences in the 'making of' documentary in the DVD special features, for example, as well as information on authorial intentionality and how such intentionality was at odds with the studio's insistence on revisions to the original theatrical release.

Such additions are species of 'supplementary' text in Derrida's terms: 'The supplement adds itself, it is a surplus, a plenitude enriching another plenitude, *the fullest measure* of presence' – intervening, filling in a figurative void, as if there were something missing in an originary utterance (1992: 83). In this case, there is an institutional anxiety of missing returns, and a need to increase box-office receipts for which the Special Edition (released a year after the original theatrical release, complete with alternative ending) enables a presence of authoritative or otherwise authentic spectacle. Alternatively, such additions may be thought of as 'paratexts', following Gerard Genette (1997): any (literary) text is rarely presented in an unadorned state and is accompanied by productions that enable a text's presence to be felt within a public domain. Book covers, marketing materials, reviews, and so on exist to promote the text's presence, selling it and supplementing the meaning-making process in the act of consumption. The commodity identity of such textual elements has therefore been implied in the contexts of critical philosophy and in literary theory and may be extended here to include contemporary remediated film.

Typically in contemporary film cultures, this is achieved through DVD commentaries, special features, or word of mouth on blogs. The act of viewing and the act of retelling a film (whether from a producer or consumer point of view) are therefore quite separate, though intertwined, elements of cultural experience and help shape an encounter with film in fundamental ways. This aspect of the concept of cinephilia has arguably moved on in the age of DVD but, if anything, is more urgent. In respect of 'reading' the DVD text as an entity, the consumer has been acculturated to certain expectations – for example, DVD 'extras'. The disappointment of the DVD enthusiast who receives a mail-order DVD copy of a favourite film, only to discover that it 'has no extras', is a vivid image, and one which reflects upon the changing contemporary audience dynamic – their reading of the text in terms of monetary *value*.

In an early domestic scene in the original theatrical edition of *Close Encounters*, Roy Neary (Richard Dreyfus) is seen playing with a train set. A music box plays *When You Wish upon a Star*, a song made famous as a Jiminy Cricket number from the Disney feature *Pinocchio* (Luske and Sharpsteen, 1940), while Roy is clearly preoccupied with playing, as well as watching the television with his children. His wife Ronnie (Teri Garr) takes responsibility for sending the children to bed, before taking a phone call from Roy's bosses at work. The emphasis seems to be located, in this scene, upon Roy and his preoccupations rather than his position within the family (which appears to be that of an emotionally neglectful father).

In the Special Edition, the same scene opens with an establishing shot of identical suburban condominiums at night. With the inclusion of this shot, already the meaning of the scene takes on a different nuance. The close-up of the music box, with its intertextual reference to Pinocchio, is replaced with a contextual reference to surburbia: the family home is one of discrete standards (size and shape, but also moral and cultural) and functionality rather than a place of commune or fantasy. Although both the toy and the housing represent kinds of realist context, they are different: the *Pinocchio* reference is familiar, the music box kitsch; by contrast, the housing shot suggests a more socially aware realism, one that, while not at odds with domesticity, nevertheless points towards the social roles of the family, to familial psychological economy, rather than the psychological needs of the individual.

The change in the way the different scenarios, via the manipulation of editing, shot choices and differences in narrative material, engage the viewer is related to the way the availability of problematics changes as a result. This can be additionally demonstrated in changes in verbal material. For example, Roy's phone call differs markedly in the two editions.

In the first edition, the voice on the other end is authoritarian and monotone. Roy hears the following message:

> Neary. Listen to me now. Get over to the Gilmore substation. We've lost power up and down the line. There's a drain on the primary voltage.

In the Special Edition, the voice is rather more incredulous and panicked:

> Neary. The [incoherent] director reports a [frantic mumbling] ... We're losing power across the grid! Has the outage hit you yet? ... Neary? ... Neary?!

Both versions of the conversation end in blackout, with the children cheering in the background. Only repeated viewings, comparative analysis, and a panoramic perception of events and meanings can bring out the full measure of these textual differences, much like the viewing practice of the cinephile. The important point to establish here is the way that such relatively small changes can produce such significant changes in the enunciation of narrative. As a result of the changes to the telephone conversation, other conclusions about Roy's character are enabled and foreclosed. Instead of a boss who is in control of the situation and confident in telling Roy what is happening, he becomes a boss who is out of control, and seems to be pleading with Roy to solve the problem. This switch suggests a characterisation that, because of Roy's subsequent behaviour, may be read as changed from one of wilful insubordinate to a simplified case of misconduct.

Conclusion

As Walter Benjamin observed:

> Only a thoughtless observer would deny that there are correspondences between the world of modern technology and the archaic symbol-world of mythology. Initially, the new technology appears no more than that. But in the next childhood memory, it has already changed its features. . . . Through its interest in technical phenomena, its curiosity about all kinds of discoveries and machinery, every childhood ties technological achievement to the old symbol-worlds.
> (1983: 49)

This startling and prescient observation is notable for two reasons: first, as part of his leviathan Arcades Project this entry performed a role of introducing themes to Benjamin's meditation on modernity and capital informed by the status of image and the importance of technology. Second, it pre-empts a second tract that explicitly connects the over reliance of Jung and his followers upon the causal relationship between art and intuitive teleology with the aestheticisation of politics and the rise of fascism. That is to say, the careless attribution of a deeper meaning to images leads us to read the image in a literal way, forestalling the dialectic of desire apparent in the psychological exchange between viewer and viewed put forward in this chapter. If we are to get beyond this connection between Jung and fascism (with its own historical problems), post-Jungian film scholarship needs to fully account for a cinephilia that is open, negotiable, and non-reactionary. This means, effectively, recognising the affective power of intertextual archetypicality, and the potential these images have in recasting old myths for personal understanding and meaning-making in our encounters with cinema.

References

Balasz, B. (1999) The Close-Up. In Leo Braudy and Marshall Cohen (eds.), *Film Theory and Criticism: Introductory Readings* (5th ed.). Oxford: Oxford University Press.

Balcerzak, S. and Sperb, J. (eds.) (2009) *Cinephilia in the Age of Digital Reproduction*, Vol. 1. London: Wallflower Press.

—— (forthcoming) *Cinephilia in the Age of Digital Reproduction*, Vol. 2. London: Wallflower Press.

Barker, M. and Brooks, K. (1998) *Knowing Audiences: Judge Dredd, Its Fans, Friends and Foes*. Luton: University of Luton Press.

Barthes, R. (1981) *Camera Lucida: Reflections on Photography*. New York: Hill and Wang.

—— (1990) *The Pleasure of the Text* (Richard Miller, Trans.). Oxford: Blackwell.

—— (1993) *Mythologies* (Annette Lavers, Trans.). London: Vintage.

Benjamin, W. (1983) N [Theoretics of Knowledge; Theory of Progress]. In G. Smith (ed.), *Benjamin: Philosophy, Aesthetics, History*. London: University of Chicago Press.

Brooker, W. (2002) *Using the Force: Creativity, Community, and Star Wars Fans*. London: Continuum.

Derrida, J. (1992) *Acts of Literature* (Derek Attridge, Ed.). London: Routledge.

de Valck, M. and Hagener, M. (eds.) (2005) *Cinephilia: Movies, Love and Memory*. Amsterdam: Amsterdam University Press.

Doane, M. A. (2002) *The Emergence of Cinematic Time: Modernity, Contingency, The Archive*. London: Harvard University Press.

Eco, U. (1984) *Semiotics and the Philosophy of Language*. Bloomington, IN: Indiana University Press.

—— (1994) *The Limits of Interpretation*. Bloomington, IN: Indiana University Press.

—— (1998) *Casablanca*: Cult Movies and Intertextual Collage. In *Faith in Fakes: Travels in Hyperreality*. London: Vintage.

Fredericksen, D. (2001) Jung/sign/symbol/film. In C. Hauke and I. Alister (eds.), *Jung & Film: Post-Jungian Takes on the Moving Image*. Hove: Brunner-Routledge.

Friedberg, A. (2004) The End of Cinema: Multimedia and Technological Change. In L. Braudy and M. Cohen (eds.), *Film Theory and Criticism: Introductory Readings* (6th ed.). Oxford: Oxford University Press.

Genette, G. (1997) *Paratexts: Thresholds of Interpretation* Cambridge: Cambridge University Press

Gibbs, J. and Pye, D. (eds.) (2005) *Style and Meaning: Studies in the Detailed Analysis of Film*. Manchester: Manchester University Press.

Hauke, C. (2000) *Jung and the Postmodern: The Interpretation of Realities*. London: Routledge.

—— (2001) "Let's go back to finding out who we are": Men, *Unheimlich* and returning home in the films of Stephen Spielberg. In C. Hauke and I. Alister (eds.), *Jung & Film: Post-Jungian Takes on the Moving Image*. Hove: Routledge.

—— (2009) The Six Thirds: Movies and the Third Image. Conference paper, *Screen*, University of Glasgow, July 3–5.

Hills, M. (2002) *Fan Cultures*. London: Routledge.

Hockley, L. (2007) *Frames of Mind: A Post-Jungian Look at Cinema, Television and Technology*. Bristol: Intellect.

—— (2009) Cinema and the Psychotherapeutic: In-Between the Screen and the Viewer. Conference paper, *Screen*, University of Glasgow, July 3–5.

Izod, J. (2001) *Myth, Mind and the Screen: Understanding the Heroes of our Time*. Cambridge: Cambridge University Press.

—— (2006) *Screen, Culture, Psyche: A Post-Jungian Approach to Working with the Audience*. Hove: Routledge.

Jenkins, H. (2004) Interactive Audiences? In D. Harries (ed.), *The New Media Book* (2nd ed.). London: BFI.

Keathley, C. (2006) *Cinephilia and History, or, The Wind in the Trees*. Bloomington, IN: Indiana University Press.

—— (2009) The Twenty-First Century Cinephile. In S. Balcerzak and J. Sperb (eds.), *Cinephilia in the Age of Digital Reproduction*, Vol. 1. London: Wallflower Press.

Kracauer, S. (1994) *The Mass Ornament: Weimar Essays*. London: Harvard University Press.

Naremore, J. (1988) *Acting in the Cinema*. London: University of California Press.

Pierson, M. (2002) *Still in Search of Wonder*. New York: Columbia University Press.

Rosenbaum, J. and Martin, A. (eds.) (2003) *Movie Mutations: The Changing Face of World Cinephilia*. London: BFI.

Shone, T. (2004) *Blockbuster: How Hollywood Learned to Stop Worrying and Love the Summer*. London: Simon and Schuster.

Singh, G. (2009) *Film After Jung: Post-Jungian Approaches to Film Theory*. London: Routledge.

Wasko, J. (1994) *Hollywood in the Information Age*. Cambridge: Polity Press.

Chapter 13

Twilight
Discourse theory and Jung

Catriona Miller

Introduction

This chapter is a highly speculative attempt to bring together two seemingly opposing theoretical perspectives in order to expand the capabilities of both. Jungian film analysis and discourse analysis are both useful ways of thinking about and describing films, a kind of translation or re-rendering of film imagery into another vocabulary. The suggestion is that there may be a value in bringing together the vocabularies of Jungian theory and discourse analysis.

The two perspectives are 'seemingly opposing' because those following a Jungian model are essentially engaging in a phenomenological project (focusing on the interiority of consciousness), whilst those following a discourse analysis model are essentially engaging in a (post) structuralist project where 'consciousness is always mediated through a prior network of signs, concepts and values which enable us to make sense of our experience' (Bradley, 2008: 30), even if that 'network of signs, concepts and values' is unstable, contingent and transforming.

Film, one of the dominant cultural forms of this era, is itself unstable, contingent and transforming. The Hollywood mode may tend to heighten and thrust a preferred meaning at the audience, demanding that the viewer look or listen at particular elements through the use of close-ups or the manipulation of the soundtrack, but its construction is more intricate than such a mode might seem to suggest and the audience's relationship with the film is another level of intricacy again. The task of trying to capture the multimodal details of moving pictures and their relationship with an audience is daunting to say the least and calls for an approach capable of handling these intricacies.

It seems that Jungian theory and discourse theory both reach the same problem albeit from different directions. They both arrive at the fuzzy boundaries of self and society. Since the meaning of any given film must be negotiated with a personal *and* a social context, the attraction of film may lie in this very point. Film is at the boundary of self and society; its meaning is constructed by both and requires a theoretical model that can address both.

This chapter will explore the hazy terrain of self and society, discussing first some key Jungian concepts and then the idea of discourse, before suggesting areas where both approaches might gain from one another. It will then go on to consider *The Twilight Saga*, comprised of *Twilight* (Catherine Hardwicke, 2008); *New Moon* (Chris Weitz, 2009); *Eclipse* (David Slade, 2010) and *Breaking Dawn* (Bill Condon, 2011), as a case study.

This is a tentative first approach to a complex set of issues which calls for a certain degree of 'theoretical bilingualism' with all the potential for mistranslation that such an undertaking implies.

The Jungian perspective

While both Jung and those writing from a Jungian perspective have demonstrated a great interest in culture they have also tended towards a suspicion of the 'collective', at least in a social sense. As Singer and Kimbles point out, 'Jung was so suspicious of the life of groups and the danger of archetypal possession in collective time that he tended to divorce the development of the individual from the individual's life in groups' (Singer & Kimbles, 2004a: 3–4). They even suggest that the collective life has fallen into the Jungian shadow, 'suspended in the ether somewhere between the much more important and meaningful individual and/or archetypal realms' (Singer & Kimbles, 2004a: 4).

In a way this is surprising because despite the predisposition toward privileging the role of the personal or individual over the collective or societal, a number of Jung's key ideas, such as the collective unconscious and archetypes, acknowledge the importance of culture, and there has been a growing body of work exploring film from a Jungian perspective as a collective expression of culture (cf. Waddell, 2006, 2009; Hockley, 2007; Singh, 2009; Bassil-Morozow, 2010).

The layer that Freud terms the unconscious, Jung suggested was a *personal* unconscious, but he went further. Rather than simply being the repository of repressed personal memories or experiences, Jung perceived through empirical observation of his patients and his own self analysis how the unconscious contained imagery that did not appear to originate from personal memories or conscious experience. Faced with the possibility that these images seemed to reflect universal modes of experience shared by all humanity, Jung concluded that there was a common part of the psyche. He called it the collective unconscious. He theorised that it contained patterns of perception common to all, describing it as a 'common psychic substrate of a suprapersonal nature' (Jung, 1959/1968a: para. 3).

At the same time, however, Jung did allow 'that on an evolutionary level, the environment has left its mark in the patterns of the instincts and archetypes which we see today' (Jung, 1960/1969: para. 328). Whilst wishing to avoid the Lamarckian fallacy (that acquired characteristics can be inherited), nevertheless there is a growing suspicion that culture and society has a much greater impact upon the individual than might have previously been suspected (Lumsden & Wilson, 1981; Stewart & Cohen, 1997), so that on some level 'endless repetition has engraved these experiences into our psychic constitution' (Jung, 1959/1968a: para. 99). The suggestion is that social experience, culture and/or society had an effect on the development of humanity so that within the collective unconscious 'certain features, the archetypes or dominants, have crystallised out in the course of time' (Jung, 1953: para. 151).

Jung initially called these 'dominants' primordial images and he regarded them as forming part of the foundation of the psyche, then in 1919 he introduced the term archetype. He clarified – 'the contents of the collective unconscious have never been in consciousness and therefore have never been individually acquired, but owe their existence exclusively to heredity' (Jung, 1959/1968a: para. 88). To complete an earlier quote: 'Endless repetition has engraved these experiences into our psychic constitution, not in the form of images filled with content, but at first only as *forms without content*, representing merely the possibility of a certain type of perception and action' (Jung, 1959/1968a: para. 99).

So the 'collective unconscious does not develop individually but is inherited. It consists of pre-existent forms, the archetypes, which can only become conscious secondarily and which give definite form to certain psychic contents' (Jung, 1959/1968a: para. 90). The archetype *an sich* remains unknowable. It is 'an invisible, universal component of the collective unconscious' (Waddell, 2006: 13) whereas the archetypal image is the knowable manifestation of the archetype.

The archetypal image is 'essentially an unconscious content that is altered by becoming conscious and by being perceived, and it takes its colour from the individual consciousness in which it happens to appear' (Jung, 1959/1968a: para. 6). It is determined by social and historical influences (Waddell 2006: 13). The way in which an archetypal image becomes conscious at any given time is influenced by the person in which it happens to arise, but also by necessity by the culture in which that individual is immersed.

Thus, two of Jung's key ideas, the collective unconscious and archetypes, both recognise the importance of culture. A third crucial idea of Jung's, that of the complex, also recognises culture in how it functions. The Jungian analyst Jacobi suggests the complex has a composite character:

> Every complex consists primarily of a "nuclear element", a vehicle of meaning, which is beyond the realm of the conscious will, unconscious and uncontrollable; and secondarily, of a number of associations connected with the nuclear element, stemming in part from innate personal disposition and in part from individual experiences conditioned by the environment.
>
> (Jacobi, 1959/1974: 8–9)

Samuels also recognises its mixed nature, indicating that a 'complex is not just the clothing for one particular archetype (that would, more accurately, be an archetypal image) but an agglomerate of the actions of several archetypal patterns, imbued with personal experience and affect' (Samuels 1985/1994: 47).

So the complex is both 'conditioned by the environment' and 'imbued with personal experience', and thus acknowledges the role of culture, although without indicating exactly how the environment might affect the manifestation of a complex. More recent expansions of Jungian theory have attempted to grapple with this problem, with the introduction of the idea of the cultural unconscious and then the cultural complex.

Henderson suggests that the cultural unconscious is

> an area of historical memory that lies between the collective unconscious and the manifest pattern of the culture. It may include both these modalities, conscious and unconscious, but it has some kind of identity arising from the archetypes of the collective unconscious, which assists in the formation of myth and ritual and also promotes the process of development in individuals.
>
> (Henderson, 1990: 102)

This suggests that the role of culture in the formation of individual subjectivity is crucial.

The acceptance of a cultural unconscious opens the door for the suggestion of the cultural complex that has been defined as arising from 'repetitive, historical group experiences which have taken root in the cultural unconscious of the group' and that they can 'seize the imagination, the behaviour and the emotions of the collective psyche and unleash tremendously irrational forces in the name of their "logic" ' (Singer & Kimbles, 2004b: 187). Singer and Kimbles further clarify:

> We define a complex as an emotionally charged group of ideas and images that cluster around an archetypal core. The basic premise . . . is that another level of complexes exists within the psyche of the group (and within the individual at the group level of their psyche). We call these group complexes "cultural complexes" and they, too, can be defined as an emotionally charged aggregate of ideas and images that cluster around an archetypal core.
> (Singer & Kimbles, 2004b: 176)

Once again this suggests that despite the Jungian preference for discussing the personal or the archetypal (or collective unconscious), culture has a mediating role between the two. The concepts of archetype and complex recognise the intricacy of the personal/collective interface, and culture is recognised as having some sort of role, however oblique that might be. However, Jungian theory has been less adept at finding a structured way to take account of cultural influences, or explaining the mechanisms through which culture comes to have influence over individual subjects. Culture is not a static entity, or even a collection of entities, and explaining how a cultural complex might come to be activated, constituted, or constellated requires further examination.

The concept of 'discourse', drawn from cultural theory, can assist in giving a fresh framework through which to consider the workings of culture both around and within the psyche. Discourse analysis, with its attention to specific operations of culture and its awareness of repetitive imagery/concepts/language across discourse planes (of the media for example) helps to bridge the gap between the archetypal and the personal. By describing the mechanism through which culture operates and circulates it is possible to see that the concepts of cultural complex and discourse are attempting to describe, albeit from very different disciplines within the Academy, the same observed phenomenon. Jungian theory, travelling from a phenomenological position, comes to the boundary of culture. Discourse theory, travelling from a (post) structuralist position, comes to the boundary of the subject and the issue of agency, even though agency in this case is understood as the capacity to act, and not as the self-originating, transcendental subject of phenomenology (Barker & Galasinski, 2001: 17).

The discourse perspective

Discourse analysis has many different schools and approaches and a full consideration of these lies beyond the scope of a chapter like this (for overviews, cf. Jaworski & Coupland, 1999; Wetherall *et al.*, 2001; Barker & Galasinski, 2001; Wodak & Meyer, 2009). Briefly, discourse analysis initially arose from a linguistic perspective, the term coming from the French word *discours*, meaning conversation, speech, dialogue, which is in turn derived from the Latin *discursus*, meaning 'to run around'. So, at its simplest, discourse was the study of language in use (Wetherall *et al.*, 2001: 5).

However, in the 1980s, following Foucault, discourse analysts began to look beyond language to include other ways of 'making meaning' and the definition of discourse grew broader and more complex. Discourse was no longer held to be simply descriptive, but to have productive properties. For example: 'Discourse is language use relative to social, political and cultural formations – it is language reflecting social order, but also language shaping social order and shaping individuals' interaction with society' (Jaworski & Coupland, 1999: 3) or: 'Language does not mirror an independent object world but constructs and constitutes it. Culture is said to "work like a language" and identities ... are held to be social and discursive constructions' (Barker & Galasinski, 2001: 1). And so in a broader context, 'the study of discourse is the study of human meaning-making' (Wetherall *et al.*, 2009: 5).

So discourses are able to mould the attitudes, beliefs, behaviours and power relations of the people involved in any given language event. In other words, discourses actively shape the understanding of reality. They help individuals to understand, to make sense of, to construct and to negotiate social reality. They not only spontaneously arise from culture, but they actively determine culture. 'Discourse analysis is therefore not only about the retrospective analysis of allocations of meaning, but also about the analysis of the ongoing production of reality through discourse, conveyed by active subjects' (Wodak & Meyer, 2009: 37).

It is the question of the 'active subject', however, that gives rise to some difficulties within discourse analysis because, at least from a Foucauldian perspective, the subject is entirely constructed by discourse. Foucault insisted that 'subjects are gradually, progressively, really and materially constituted through a multiplicity of organisms, forces, energies, materials, desires, thoughts, etc.' (Foucault, 1980: 97). For Foucault the subject is wholly and only the product of history – there is no inner subject.

While Foucault provides very useful ways of considering how individuals are affected, indeed created, by the discursive formations within which they exist, he is less able to 'provide us with an understanding of how and why particular discourse are "taken up" by some subjects and not by others or how a subject produced through disciplinary discursive practices can resist power' (Barker & Galasinski, 2001: 31). It is the question of agency (the capacity to resist subject positions created by discourse) and choice (the choice to act) that is less clear in Foucault's work.

In some ways, perhaps, this is the biggest obstacle in bringing together a Jungian description with one based on discourse analysis. The ways in which 'identity' is thought to be constituted are in conflict. Discourse analysts tend towards the position that identity is produced by discourse. Jungians tend towards the idea that identity is a universal core arising from archetypes (however that may manifest in an individual). There is a sense in both perspectives, however, that there must be a link between the 'inner' subject and the 'outer' discourse, but how that link might work is unclear.

Some discourse analysts, such as Hall (1996), however, have looked to psychology to forge that link. In particular, they have looked to psychoanalysis to make the connections, which is understandable given the prominence of Freudian and Lacanian perspectives in cultural studies more generally. That said, the cultural and historically specific nature of Freud and Lacan's ideas have proved a stumbling block. Even so, it may be that the Jungian idea of the cultural complex will provide a more satisfying link between the discursive subject and the interior subject; as a concept it may prove to have better descriptive properties than those of classical and Lacanian-informed psychoanalysis.

It is interesting that there has always been some difficulty in describing what discourse is – as one writer put it, the notion of discourse is 'essentially fuzzy' (van Dijik, 1997: 1) – but there has been equal difficulty in creating a hard and fast definition of the archetype. As Jacobi said, it 'is impossible to give an exact definition of the archetype, and the best we can hope to do is to suggest its general implications by "talking around" it' (Jacobi 1959/1974: 31), suggesting perhaps that the archetypes themselves are discursive in nature. But despite the difficulties in articulating these larger, hazier constructs or metaphors, there has conversely been some similarity in language in the attempts to describe cultural moments/artefacts/ideas by both Jungians and discourse analysts, which perhaps can be summed up in three areas: choice of metaphor; recognition of affect; and an acknowledgement of the flow of time and its transformation of culture.

Some provisional observations

There is a tendency when speaking of cultural moments (phenomena, texts, enunciations, happenings) to be aware that a number of elements come together, sometimes quite suddenly, and rise to prominence. These 'moments' are not single or discrete items. Rather, they are the result of an accretion of images and ideas which, along with experiences and emotions, cluster together. Seen from a distance, they take on a discernible shape. There is use of terms and metaphors like *zeitgeist* or 'nodal points' to indicate that a composite of ideas and experiences have come together.

For example, part of the definition of a cultural complex arises from its existence as a 'cluster of ideas' or a 'web of story and emotion' (Singer & Kimbles, 2004a: 7). It is an 'aggregate of ideas and images' (Singer & Kimbles 2004b: 176). In discourse theory, Foucault describes the discursive formation as follows:

> Whenever one can describe, between a number of statements . . . a system of dispersion, whenever, between objects, types of statements, concepts, or thematic choices, one can define a regularity (an order, correlations, positions and functionings, transformations), we will say . . . that we are dealing with a discursive formation.
> (Foucault, 1969/2002: 41)

Jäger & Maier prefer a more fluid metaphor and suggest the idea of discourse is a 'flow of knowledge' and that such flows which 'centre on a common topic are called discourse strands' (2009: 46). Discourse strands can become entangled into discursive knots, as any given collection of texts or enunciations can contain multiple discourses (on race *and* gender, for example); at the same time discourse strands can be traced across many individual texts. For example, one could choose to look at the discourse strand of gender across a genre of film, such as Clover's (1992) examination of the 'final girl' phenomenon in the slasher movie genre. Or one could choose to examine a single film and all the discourse fragments it contains: gender plus race plus capitalism and so on, such as Eco's essay (1985) on *Casablanca* (Michael Curtiz, 1942) or Haslam (2005) on *The Matrix* (Wachowski Brothers, 1999).

What all these ways of conceptualising recognise is that culture is complex in nature. There is also a recognition, however tacit, that there appears to be a steady flow of culture which, from time to time, throws up overlapping and multiform expressions of the *same* idea or image, which is then raised to a collective awareness and appears to take on an energy of its own.

This is the second element that helps to raise such moments to prominence: the affect or emotion that can be invested within such cultural combinations. Around the idea that cultural components clump together to form a more powerful entity is a recognition of the role of emotion in marking out a such a cultural assemblage. As Jungians Singer and Kimbles put it quite succinctly: 'Intense collective emotion is the hallmark of an activated cultural complex' (Singer & Kimbles, 2004a: 6). But discourse theory, too, has noted that emotion is not absent from consideration of culture. Barker & Galasinski note that whilst Foucault has provided useful tools for understanding how individuals are constituted by discourse, he 'does not provide us with an understanding of the emotional investments by which subjects are attached to discourse' (Barker & Galasinski, 2001: 31). It has been suggested in fact that any attempt to modify one's subject position within discourse (necessary if any possibility of resistance or the 'choice to act' is to be conserved) requires an 'emotional shift in being' (Hall, 1996). Emotion, although defined in a performative sense (one *does* emotion, rather than *having* it), is seen as an marker of change.

Discourse strands (cultural complexes) seem to rise to prominence when invested with a certain level of emotional energy, though it seems likely that it is the pre-existing emotional state which causes cultural imagery to be *recognised* as a 'cultural clump' rather than causing it per se. However, exactly how this process occurs requires much more detailed observation of culture generally. It may be possible that individual choices slowly begin to shift the flow of discourse, but how those individual choices come to be possible takes the argument full circle. Both discourse analysis and Jungian analysis seem to reach towards the language of metaphor and symbol in trying to pin down these moments and both, ultimately, are forced to acknowledge the flow of time and its transformation of culture, even if neither is precisely sure how those transformations arise.

Jungian theory has long had a connection to the study of symbols, and much discussion has gone into trying to make clear what is distinctive about a Jungian approach to symbols. Jung himself made clear that a 'view which interprets the symbolic expression as the best possible formulation of a relatively *unknown* thing, which for that reason cannot be more clearly or characteristically represented, is *symbolic*' (Jung, 1971: para. 815). By way of contrast a known thing that stands for another known thing is simply a sign.

When it comes to considering culture in general and films in particular, Jungian approaches have been concerned with uncovering the deeper meaning of symbolism within any particular text or film, which, in Jungian terminology, usually means looking for the archetypal element within the symbol, and largely does so through the methodology of amplification which 'involves use of mythic, historical and cultural parallels in order to clarify and make ample the metaphorical content of dream symbolism' (Samuels *et al.*, 1986: 16). Amplification, at least to some extent, seeks to understand symbols within a cultural framework. However, this is only to some extent because, through association with the timeless archetypal, there has been a tendency to take the symbol out of history. An uncomfortable relationship exists between the acknowledgement that symbols are 'specific to this time and place' manifestation of culture, while at the same time representing a timeless archetypal node of the collective unconscious. However, it is also suggested that it is the role of symbols to have this 'mediating, bridge-building quality' (Jacobi, 1959/1974: 98).

To return to Jäger and Maier's idea of the discourse strand, they note that the strands 'have a history, a present and a future. In order to identify the changes, ruptures, ebbings and recurrences of a discourse strand, it is necessary to analyse longer periods of time' (2009: 51). To analyse only synchronically is of some use to be sure (e.g. analysing one film), but a diachronic approach gives a better sense of the direction of change (e.g. analysing a genre of film over a period of time). A discourse approach is perhaps more inclined to consider context, intertextuality and recontextualisation, recognising that discourses intersect with one another across micro and macro fields of action (ibid.: 90). The tendency of Jungians examining a symbol has often, by way of contrast, been to move straight to mythology as explanation, without much consideration of how that mythological motif is transmitted and resituated within a contemporary framework – see, for example, Slater's (2005: 8) analysis of *Ferris Bueller's Day Off* (John Hughes, 1986), where the central character is referred to as 'a pitch perfect channelling of the god Hermes.' Although context is often acknowledged as important, in practice it is not always given the same degree of attention as the archetypal element of the image. It is this meticulous attention to cultural detail that discourse analysis brings to the theoretical conversation that Jungians engaged in any form of cultural analysis would certainly benefit from participating in.

However, discourse analysts might do well to listen to the Jungian conversation around symbols, for one suggestion of a way to mingle these discursive fragments, strands and knots has been to redeploy the concept of the symbol as in fact more than just symbol, but *collective* symbol. These collective symbols (Drews *et al.*, 1985: 265) provide a repertoire of images from which a picture of reality may be constructed. 'The most important *sociocultural function* of the collective symbolic seems to consist in the *integration of discourses* and thereby also in the integration of practices' (Drews *et al.*, 1985: 270). 'Through collective symbols we interpret reality, and have reality interpreted for us, especially by the media' (Wodak & Meyer, 2009: 48). An intriguing echo of the Jungian symbol's 'mediating, bridge-building quality' (Jacobi, 1959/1974: 98).

It is undoubtedly premature to suggest such a thing, but it may be that what discourse analysts call a discursive knot, or a discursive field, Jungians would be inclined to call a cultural complex or an archetypal image.

So once again, both Jungian theory and discourse theory arrive at the fuzzy boundary between self and society in discussing the question of subjectivity and the thorny issue of how, if we are products of our social context, we achieve agency and the ability to resist or change those discourses. Barker & Galasinkski suggest that 'the best we can do is produce another story about ourselves' (2001: 46), which is, perhaps, what all culture is – another story about ourselves.

This may be what film offers to a greater or lesser degree: a space to explore both society and self; a space to tell these stories about ourselves. I say greater or lesser degree because Hollywood film, with its industrial context and firm emphasis upon profit, is more inclined to simply reproduce and reiterate agreed upon discourse, whilst independent film, with its craft-based context and emphasis upon the individual voice of the film-maker, *could* be argued to demonstrate an interest in those discourses which are contested. If films are other stories about ourselves then film *theory* ought to be able to explicate those stories in all their complexity albeit through translation into yet another vocabulary.

Film is one of the dominant cultural forms of the twenty-first century. There is a constant cascade of multimodal narratives. Film has been able to connect with its audiences in an almost unique way and psychologists have long tried to understand this, suggesting a connection with the unconscious, whether that be from the Freudian idea of fantasy or the Lacanian idea of the Imaginary Order, or the Jungian idea of an archetypal dimension. But film too has its discursive properties. It is a collective effort (the film cast and crew); materially, it arises out of specific industrial contexts; more equivocally it arises out of discursive formations or cultural consciousness and thus embodies any number of discursive fragments or collective symbols.

The Jungian approach to film analysis has had a tendency to focus on one text at a time (which classical film theory itself might be accused of doing), looking for imagery that can be fitted into archetypal categories. This tendency to inductive analysis can also be prone to reification. It is all too easy to slip from using the idea of the archetype as a useful metaphor to treating it as a material entity which provides the 'answer' to a film analysis, rather than opening up a symbol to all its potential meanings. Discourse analysis, insofar as it has been applied to film (often implicitly rather than explicitly), has had a tendency to concentrate upon structure and the reproduction of discourse, rather than perhaps appreciating the role of affect and emotion in audiences' responses to film.

A combination of these approaches might yield a more fruitful description of what film does, because any film is likely to be doing/being any number of things: it might be part of a specific instance of a personal and a cultural complex, it may very well contain imagery with an archetypal core, but how that energy is expressed will depend upon the conscious elaboration that has taken place by all those working on the film and their cultural contexts. A film will contain synchronic discourse fragments *and* be part of diachronic flow of discourse making up a discourse strand. As such it more than a complex, it is a multiplex.

In a effort to explore some of these intricacies, the final section of this chapter will consider a single case study, *The Twilight Saga*, in order to demonstrate how the combination of archetypal and discursive approaches helps to illustrate the complex (multiplex) nature of a film.

Case study: *The Twilight Saga*

The Twilight Saga (Meyer, 2005–8) began as a quartet of books aimed at the juvenile fiction or teenage market in America and became first a global publishing sensation and then a cinematic success story. The narrative of Stephenie Meyer's quartet concerns the teenage heroine Bella Swan (Kristen Stewart), who moves to the small town of Forks to live with her father. There, she falls in love with fellow high school student, the glamorous Edward Cullen (Robert Pattinson). Edward, however, is over a hundred years old and he, and his entire 'family', are vampires. The plot of all four books and films largely revolves around the central question of whether Edward will be able to control his blood lust for Bella and whether Bella will become a vampire.

Meyer has sold 45 million books in the US and another 40 million globally (Grossman, 2009). Two Hollywood movies have been released with at least two more to come. In 2009, cinema box-office performance in the US reached an all time high, thanks in part to five blockbusters, of which *The Twilight Saga*'s second instalment, *New Moon* was one (Young *et al.*, 2010). The UK box office also reached an all-time high, with *New Moon* again being partly credited for this success (Davoudi, 2010).

For such successful books and films, the more usual kind of Jungian reading would seek to illuminate the archetypal dimensions of the narrative and characters, showing where the film's symbolism intersects with archetypal images and gives access to the collective unconscious, through the method of amplification. A discursive approach would require quite a similar method perhaps – a diachronic sampling of the discursive knot of 'vampire', though the conclusions would be different.

The vampire in the 21st century is an extremely well established cultural trope, perhaps loosely defined as a creature that drains the life force of the living, and modern historians and writers (both academic and fiction) have constructed a 'history' or genealogy of the vampire that seems to stretch back into the origins of human consciousness.

For example, although the connection is not uncontested, it may be possible to trace vampire-like creatures back to the second or even third millennium BCE, where in Mesopotamian mythology there are mentions of a demoness, or group of demons called Lilitu or Ardat Lili thought to be the precursor of the 'night hag' mentioned in Isaiah 34: 14. This 'night hag' (or 'strange woman of the night', a more technically accurate translation supplied by Dr S. Nicholson, University of Glasgow) is said to be Lilith, thought in Rabbinical literature to have been Adam's first wife. Her epithet was 'beautiful maiden' but she was described as 'frigid and barren, husbandless, a maid of destruction who roamed the night attacking men as a succubus, or drinking their blood' (Burton Russell, 1977: 92). She was depicted as being winged and taloned, surrounded by owls and jackals: the Queen of the Night relief acquired by the British Museum in 2003 is said to be a depiction of this figure. Dating from the post-Biblical era, Hebrew incantations have been found, designed to keep Lilith away from children, for whom she was said to have a special hatred. Incantations using a divorce formula were sometimes issued to persuade her to leave men to whom she had become attached (Patai, 1964; Lesses, 2001).

Further amplification of the vampire motif might be sought in the many medieval vampires of Eastern Europe, such as the Bulgarian *ubour*, a creature with only one nostril and a barbed tongue which causes all kinds of mischief, but drinks blood only when it cannot get food (or dung) and is created when a person meets a sudden and violent death, when a cat jumps over a corpse, or when a spirit refuses to leave its body by sheer force of will (Bunson, 1993: 259).

However, these kind of vampires, whatever their claims to historical significance, do not appear to be very helpful in exploring the imagery of Meyer's vampires. From the Jungian perspective, this vampire of folklore can be associated with the shadow archetype, yet, Meyer's vampires are not so obviously 'shadowy'. They are cursed, supernatural beings but they are not responsible for epidemics of plague and misfortune as the vampires of folklore so often were. Meyer's vampires are not sub-human, rather they are super-human and thus more properly associated with the vampire of fiction, originating with the Romantics in nineteenth-century Europe.

In the early nineteenth century, the Romantics, building on a number of literary traditions (balladry, gothic literature, stories from Eastern Europe), drew the vampire towards the contrasexual archetype, although the shadow associations were not excised entirely. John Polidori's Lord Ruthven (Bleiler, 1966) was a heartless seducer and murderer of society maidens, whilst Count Dracula cut a destructive swathe through young Victorian womanhood. Later celluloid Counts, such as Bela Lugosi in *Dracula* (Tod Browning, 1931), Christopher Lee in *Dracula* (Terence Fisher, 1958) or Gary Oldman in *Bram Stoker's Dracula* (Francis Ford Coppola, 1992), wooed and charmed their brides with promises of immortal love. This is much closer in feeling tone to the contemporary vampire and Meyer's Edward Cullen.

The more usual kind of Jungian reading of *The Twilight Saga*, therefore, might suggest that Edward should be viewed as being of the night, a monster from the unconscious, born of the shadow archetype though perhaps more specifically an animus-inflected shadow figure. He is the disturber, an erotic, dangerous, potentially destructive, probably murderous, figure but as Annis Pratt puts it in relation to her idea of the greenworld lover, this is the figure who 'leads the hero away from society and towards her own unconscious depths . . . an incorporation into the personality of one's sexual and natural forces' (Pratt, 1981: 140). In this sort of reading, *Twilight* is a Jungian *bildungsroman* building upon a literary and cinematic tradition of the vampire as a kind of 'fatal lover', desirable but calamitous.

Meyer, however, has gone further than any previous version of this story by excising even *more* of the vampire's shadowy characteristics. 'I don't want to be a monster,' says Edward in *Twilight* and Meyer makes the Cullens both potentially deadly yet very moral. Meyer's vampires are not destroyed by sunlight. They avoid sunlight because it makes them glitter and reveals their inhuman nature, but it does not harm them and Edward is rendered even *less* morally ambiguous than previous romantic vampire heroes because he and his family only drink the blood of animals.

Edward is tempting to Bella, but he is not tempting her to her doom. Rather, this vampire lover seems to be tempting Bella towards realising her potential as a powerful vampire in her own right. So Edward could be described as an animus figure, who brings the Self into focus for Bella. He draws her from 'ordinariness' towards 'extra-ordinariness' and assists her in discovering her latent powers. In the end, Bella is made into a vampire, but she loses nothing of her sense of self in the process, and she gains in strength and confidence, able, in the end, to use her vampire powers to prevent bloodshed and all-out war with the 'evil' vampires, the Volturi. The hero's journey retold, perhaps.

The benefit of examining *The Twilight Saga* from a historical/cultural perspective is that it becomes clear that the vampire motif has developed and transformed over the years. If there is a continuum from shadow archetype to contrasexual archetype, this is the farthest away the vampire gets from the shadow. Edward Cullen is the most sympathetic, least morally ambiguous, most heroic vampire to date. In demonstrating a time frame to the vampire myth, it becomes more obvious that it is a cultural motif under (re)construction and that as the role of women in society has changed, so the nature and power of the vampire image has changed. The narrative of *The Twilight Saga* seems to suggest that the vampire as an archetypal image has become less shadowy, perhaps as women have gained a stronger sense of their right to equality with men.

The Jungian approach, with its focus on films as individual entities, sitting apart from the production context which created them, sometimes inadvertently subscribes to the auteur theory which regards the director as the authorial voice and source of meaning. Directors may give specific form to an idea at a given time but they are not responsible for a 'big bang' type of creation, something from nothing. Nor is it sufficient to suggest that the director is giving expression to an archetype, consciously shaping an archetypal image arising from the collective unconscious, as this sidesteps the role of culture (and discourses) in shaping the director in the first place. The Jungian approach thus has a tendency to bypass the cultural, moving straight from the individual to the archetypal.

Thus, whilst a more usual kind of Jungian analysis might be prone to ignoring the production and commercial contexts of a film franchise like *The Twilight Saga*, a more traditional kind of *media* analysis might start by examining the mechanisms and processes by which such a thing was fabricated. A discursive perspective, however, might throw up other possibilities in its translation of the film to another vocabulary. *The Twilight Saga* exists within a flow of discourse where it might be described as a discursive knot marking a shift within the representation of the vampire.

For *The Twilight Saga* is not the only 'new vampire' narrative that has arisen in recent years, though the medium of expression has to some degree shifted from cinema to television. Beginning with *Buffy the Vampire Slayer* (1997 – 2003, 20th Century Fox), but including *Being Human* (2009 – ongoing, BBC), *Vampire Diaries* (2009–ongoing, CBS), and most prominently HBO's *True Blood* (2008–ongoing) based on Charlaine Harris's Southern vampire novels (another series of novels by another female writer), television is proving to be a fertile medium for vampires. The flow of culture tangling around the vampire motif, however, is not limited by medium. Novels, music, fashion and film – *Let the Right One In* (Alfredson, 2008) or *Daybreakers* (Spierig & Spierig, 2009) for example – all contribute to this discursive knot.

In itself this is nothing new, for, as suggested above, the vampire motif has proved fascinating and resilient, but there is a fresh surge of affect surrounding vampires in general and Edward and Bella in particular that suggests that a reforged or new cultural complex has come into being. There is little doubt that for audiences of *The Twilight Saga* there is certainly a great deal of affect tied up in the films. One journalist at a 'meet the stars' event in London described 'the hysteria that . . . quickened into a bacchanalian frenzy' (Laing, 2009). The Facebook fanpage is reputed to have six million members and the posts certainly display a great deal of passion. It should also be noted that this is not limited to a teen phenomenon, as the website twilightmoms.com demonstrates.

Much of the excitement centres around the two stars, Kristen Stewart and Robert Pattinson. In fact, the decision to cast handsome actor Robert Pattinson in the lead role of Edward the vampire in the Hollywood film of *Twilight* may have a great deal to do with the popularity of *The Twilight Saga* brand over and above the attractiveness of the character of Edward within the novels alone, for *The Twilight Saga* has burst the bounds of its text. It exists in multiple forms. It has become multimodal and transmediatised and as such classical film theory itself, with its emphasis on text, struggles to keep up. Discourse theory, with its emphasis on flow is perhaps better placed to offer some observations. The discourse fragments within *The Twilight Saga* range from feminism (changing representations of masculinity as well as femininity), postmodernism, moral politics and religious discourse to Hollywood film.

For example, as suggested earlier, the films might be positioned within their production context, that is the Hollywood system, although Summit Entertainment is technically an independent. However, the Hollywood system of film-making itself exists within a consumer capitalist discourse. The aggressive trans-mediatisation of the narrative as a commodity (book, film, lunchbox, boardgame, jewellery) into a franchise and a brand demands some attention because this large global audience partly exists because of its commodified nature.

The narrative might also be positioned with a number of other discourses, such as an American discourse about 'Old Europe', where the corrupt Volturi (vampires of Old Europe) are contrasted against the 'good' Cullens (vampires of the New World). The issue of the Native American werewolf Jacob Black (Taylor Lautner) opens up a range of other discourses around race and history that might also be explored, not least because Stephenie Meyer is herself a practising Mormon. The Book of Mormon, which purports to be 'a history and religious record of three groups of Middle Easterners who traveled to the Western hemisphere over a 1,500-year period and who played an important role in the establishment of ancient American civilization' (Arrington & Bitton, 1992: 145), puts an interesting perspective on Meyer's decision to make one of her key characters a Native American. Even a cursory search of the internet, however, reveals a concern that Meyer's Mormonism, although not explicit within the narrative, influences her characters. An article in *Time* for example considers the 'erotics of abstinence' (Grossman, 2008) demonstrated in Edward and Bella's relationship. 'Mormon young people live in a world where abstinence of all kinds is the rule, not the exception' (Bushman, 2008: 114) and premarital sex is certainly forbidden. Hence, Edward insists on marrying Bella before they consummate their relationship, though, in the narrative, this is largely attributed to the fact that Edward was a young man in 1918.

So a classical Jungian approach might begin by seeking instances of archetypal images within the narrative, whilst a traditional media studies response might begin with a textual analysis of the films themselves, followed by a deconstruction of the discourses which constitute the text. However, as much as discourse analysis is an extremely useful method of examination, it is rather less good at making meaning from the analysis, and can become stuck in ever more detailed descriptions of the discourses at work in any given text. Both approaches have their limitations.

Ultimately, the huge success of *The Twilight Saga* can hardly be attributed to the narrative of the novels or films alone, as popular as they are, for *The Twilight Saga* exists beyond simply books or movies. There are board games, replica jewellery, bags, lunch boxes, comic books, action figures, as well as other licensing tie-ins, such as an in-restaurant promotion deal with Burger King, confirmed for the third film, *Eclipse*, released in 2010. A spokesman for the Contender Entertainment Group said 'Twilight has the potential not just to be a success in its own right, but to be the starting point of one of the biggest film and licensing phenomena of the early 21st Century' (licencemag.com, 2010). The 'Twihard' fans are so passionate that 6,500 of them queued overnight to see the stars in person at the 2009 Comic Con convention (Pickard, 2009). *The Twilight Saga* is a trans-media phenomenon, a cultural and commercial sensation, and it is no longer enough to explore the archetypal dimension of the vampire motif, with no recourse to consideration of the very contemporary discourses that produced the cultural assemblage that can be labelled *The Twilight Saga*.

A single film might be fractal in nature, i.e. reflecting a wider archetypal dimension, but if a text/film/discourse fragment is being described as archetypal in some way, then it ought to be part of a larger discourse strand or plane, or be a discursive knot. A diachronic reading of multiple discourse fragments in the discourse plane of the media is more convincing as evidence of shifts in archetypal imagery and thus in telling us something about the current state of society than a synchronic reading of arche typal imagery within a single filmic text, however detailed that reading might be, although ultimately 'explanations of any kind can only ever involve the replacement of one way of describing the world with another' (Barker & Galasinski, 2001: 61).

A postmodern understanding of text is that it is a palimpsest and intertextual, referring at all times to other texts, but it can also be suggested that postmodern subjectivity itself is not just complex or multiple, but actually intertextual. Subjectivity is derived and evolved, constituted by the discourses that surround the individual, but the subject can also affect discourse. The subject can have agency, the capacity to resist subject positions created by discourse, and the choice to act. The Jungian perspective, with its formulation of the cultural complex, may be in a good position to help map out the fuzzy boundary between subject and society, where choices are made to resist or comply.

A Jungian reading of film, which simultaneously utilises discourse analysis's close attention to cultural context, offers an interesting and useful way to begin reading the 'fabric of traces' in any film or collection of films that can take account of both the experience of the interior subject and the cultural discourses that help to constitute it.

References

Arrington, L. & Bitton, D. (1992) *The Mormon Experience: A History of the Latter-Day Saints*. Champaign, IL: University of Illinois Press.

Barker, C. & Galasinski, D. (2001) *Cultural Studies and Discourse Analysis*. London: Sage Publications Ltd.

Bassil-Morozow, H. (2010) *Tim Burton: The Monster and the Crowd: A Post-Jungian Perspective*. Hove: Routledge.

Bleiler, E. (ed.) (1966) *Three Gothic Novels*. N. Chemsford, MA: Courier Dover Publications.

Bradley, A. (2008) *Derrida's Of Grammatology*. Edinburgh: Edinburgh University Press Ltd.

Bunson, M. (1993) *Vampire: The Encyclopaedia*. London: Thames & Hudson.

Burton Russell, J. (1977) *The Devil: Perceptions of Evil From Antiquity to Primitive Christianity*. Ithaca, NY: Cornell University Press.

Bushman, R. L. (2008) *Mormonism: A Very Short Introduction*. Oxford: Oxford University Press.

Clover, C. (1992) *Men, Women and Chainsaws: Gender in the Modern Horror Film*. London: BFI.

Davoudi, S. (2010) UK box office sales reach high of £1bn. *Financial Times*. Retrieved from: www.ft.com/cms/s/0/78918aa2-0510-11df-aa2c00144 feabdc0.html?catid=61&SID

Drews, A., Gerhard, U. & Link J. (1985) Moderne Kollektivsymbolik: Eine diskursttheoretisch orientierte Enführung mit Auswahlbibiographie. *Internationales Archiv für Sozialgeschichte der deutschen Literatur* (pp. 256–375). My thanks to Professor Hugh O'Donnell for translating key passages.

Eco, U. (1985) *Casablanca: Cult Movies and Intertextual Collage. SubStance*, Vol. 14, No. 2, Issue 47 (pp. 3–12).

Foucault, M. (1969/2002) *The Archaeology of Knowledge*. New York: Routledge.

Foucault, M. (1980) *Power/Knowledge*. Brighton: Harvester Press Ltd.

Grossman, L. (2008) Stephenie Meyer: A New J. K. Rowling? *Time*. Retrieved from: www.time.com/time/magazine/article/0,9171,1734838,00.html

Grossman, L. (2009) It's Twilight in America: The Vampire Saga. *Time*. Retrieved from: www.time.com/time/magazine/article/0,9171,1938712,00.html

Hall, S. (1996) Who needs identity? In S. Hall & P. du Gay (eds.), *Questions of Cultural Identity*. London: Sage.

Haslam, J. (2005) Coded Discourse: Romancing the Electronic Shadow in *The Matrix*. *College Literature*, Vol. 32, No. 3 (pp. 92–115).

Henderson, J. (1990) *Shadow and Self*. Wilmette, IL: Chiron.

Hockley, L. (2007) *Frames of Mind: A Post-Jungian Look at Cinema, Television and Technology*. Bristol: Intellect.

Jacobi, J. (1959/1974) *Complex/Archetype/Symbol in the Psychology of C. G. Jung*. New York: Princeton University Press.

Jäger, S. & Maier, F. (2009) Theoretical and methodological aspects of Foucauldian critical discourse analysis and dispositive analysis. In R. Wodak & M. Meyer, *Methods of Critical Discourse Analysis*. London: Sage Publications Ltd.
Jaworski, A. & Coupland, N. (eds.) (1999) *The Discourse Reader*. London: Routledge.
Jung, C. (1953) *Two Essays on Analytical Psychology*, CW7. London: Routledge & Kegan Paul.
Jung, C. G. (1959/1968a) *The Archetypes and the Collective Unconscious*, CW9(i). London: Routledge & Kegan Paul.
Jung, C. (1960/1969) *The Structure and Dynamics of the Psyche*, CW8. London: Routledge & Kegan Paul.
Jung, C. (1971) *Psychological Types*, CW6. London: Routledge & Kegan Paul.
Laing, O. (2009) Stephenie Meyer: A squeaky-clean vampire queen. *The Observer*. Retrieved from: www.guardian.co.uk/books/2009/nov/15/profile-stephenie-meyer-vampire-queen
Lesses, R. (2001) Exe(o)rcising Power: Women as Sorceresses, Exorcists and Demonesses in Babylonian Jewish Society of Late Antiquity. *Journal of the American Academy of Religion*, 69(2), 343–75.
licencemag.com (2010) Contender signed for *Twilight* in UK. Retrieved from: http://www.licensemag.com/licensemag/Fashion/Contender-Signed-for-iTwilighti-in-UK/ArticleStandard/Article/detail/576367?searchString=global%20merchandising%20rights,%20twilight (accessed 9.3.10)
Lumsden, C. & Wilson, E. (1981) *Genes, Mind and Culture: The Coevolutionary Process*. Cambridge, MA: Harvard University Press.
Meyer, S. (2005) *Twilight*. New York: Little, Brown and Co.
Meyer, S. (2006) *New Moon*. New York: Little, Brown and Co.
Meyer, S. (2007) *Eclipse*. New York: Little, Brown and Co.
Meyer, S. (2008) *Breaking Dawn*. New York: Little, Brown and Co.
Patai, R. (1964) Lilith. *Journal of American Folklore*, 77(306), 295–314.
Pickard, A. (2009) Comic-Con: Revenge of the Nerds. *The Guardian*. Retrieved from: http://www.guardian.co.uk/culture/2009/jul/29/comic-con-2009-revenge-nerds
Pratt, A. (1981) *Archetypal Patterns in Women's Fiction*. Brighton: The Harvest Press Ltd.
Samuels, A. (1985/1994) *Jung & the Post-Jungians*. London: Routledge.
Samuels, A., Shorter, B. & Plaut, F. (eds.) (1986) *A Critical Dictionary of Jungian Analysis*. London: Routledge.
Singer, T. & Kimbles, S. (eds.) (2004a) *The Cultural Complex*. Hove: Routledge.
Singer, T. & Kimbles, S. (2004b) The emerging theory of cultural complexes. In J. Cambray & L. Carter (eds.) (2004) *Analytical Psychology: Contemporary Perspectives in Jungian Analysis*. Hove: Brunner-Routledge.
Singh, G. (2009) *Film After Jung: Post-Jungian Approaches to Film Theory*. Hove: Routledge.

Slater, G. (2005) Archetypal perspective and American film. *Spring Journal*, 73, 1–19.
Stewart, I. & Cohen, J. (1997) *Figments of Reality: The Evolution of the Curious Mind*: Cambridge: Cambridge University Press
van Dijk, T. (1997) *Discourse as Structure and Process*. London: Sage.
Waddell, T. (2006) *Mis/takes: Archetype, Myth and Identity in Screen Fiction*. Hove: Routledge.
Waddell, T. (2009) *Wild/Lives: Trickster, Place and Liminality on Screen*. Hove: Routledge.
Wetherall, M., Taylor, S. & Yates, S. (eds.) (2001) *Discourse Theory and Practice: A Reader*. London: Sage.
Wodak, R. & Meyer, M. (eds.) (2009) *Methods of Critical Discourse Analysis*. London: Sage Publications Ltd.
Young, S. M., Gong, J. J. & Van der Stede, W. A. (2010, February) The business of making money with movies. *Strategic Finance*, 35–40.

Chapter 14

Individual and society in the films of Tim Burton

Helena Bassil-Morozow

Tim Burton makes deceptively simple films. They are narratively straightforward, uneven, visually rich, and emotionally dense; as a rule, their grotesque characters, encased into massive mythological frames, are borrowed from elsewhere – traditional fairy tales, classics of world literature, contemporary fiction, and popular culture. As far as his visuals are concerned, Burton operates with a multicoloured web of references which include Gothic architecture, German expressionism and sci-fi kitsch. His films' plotlines are roughly sewn together, rather like Edward Scissorhands' costume. The author does not even try to hide their obvious seams, loose threads, hanging buttons, holes and shabby patches. Narratively and visually, Burton's films are pure Gothic *Haute Couture*.

However, these evidently non-academic films full of popular motifs and edited with such impressionistic imprecision express one important psychological idea. Or, rather, they express many psychological ideas but one of them, like an umbrella metaphor, extends to cover a whole range of issues that concern the individual in contemporary society: social independence, the degree and intensity level of interaction with your social group, creative originality, introversion, peer pressure, family influence, and complex relationship between personal freedom and capitalism. In this sense, the seemingly unsophisticated Tim Burton is the champion of the individual. The Western way of life is simultaneously praised and criticised for being too neglectful of community, too pro-choice, too supportive of independent thinking. Burton's approach to these contemporary issues can be termed a 'hidden politics'. He never discusses the issue explicitly, does not have slogans or banners, and is far from organising his own 'pro-individual' party. What he explores in his films, in a deceptively apolitical way, is how modernity and its recent transformations have altered the place of man in society. His works are creative investigations of the limits to human freedom in a world that claims to be constantly pushing the boundaries, to be freer than ever.

For more than twenty years Tim Burton has been making films about lonely introverts at war with their communities; geniuses struggling to achieve artistic independence, or even just to live in solitude; outcasts fighting for the right not to be 'normal', to be as eccentric as they wish; artists advocating decadent rebellion, intellectual self-indulgence – and often harbouring murderous thoughts aimed at the passive, emotionally primitive and intellectually stagnant 'crowd'. The Burtonian heroes' vision of society is simplistic – typically they divide the world into 'me' and 'them', not delving into the terminological and conceptual differences between the family, social circle, peer group, community, society and the crowd. All they know is that the outside world is capable of limiting their freedom.

The result of their stand-off with society is outlandishly melodramatic or spectacularly (and, on some occasions, *bombastically*) dismal. The bedraggled, 'unfinished' Edward (Johnny Depp) from *Edward Scissorhands* (1990), after the initial attempt to be 'like anyone else' and find his place in the bland suburbia, ends up retreating to his Gothic castle, and resigning himself to a life of eternal isolation. In *Sweeney Todd: The Demon Barber of Fleet Street* (2007), Benjamin Barker (Johnny Depp) is so disillusioned with common people, with their baseness, vanity and greed, that he decides that the only way to make real social change is to mince them up and serve them in pies to their equally stupid and lowly fellow creatures. On a lighter note, Pee Wee (*Pee Wee's Big Adventure*, 1985), played by Paul Reubens, is 'a loner and a rebel'; seven-year-old Vincent Malloy (*Vincent*, 1984) fantasises about dying in a dark room, away from his aggressively normal parents; Batman (Michael Keaton), who only loves the crowd from the height of his urban castle, makes the point of appearing in public dressed in a funny suit because this is how he feels amongst 'them'; Alice (Mia Wasikowska) from the recent *Alice in Wonderland* (2010), literally escapes into a hole in the ground (which can be read as a metaphor for the unconscious) when faced with a group of expectant friends, relatives and guests who all want her to marry a ludicrous little lord. Not only are they not prepared to integrate, to listen to the voice of 'the majority', they insist, at times tragically, at times hysterically, that being different is a divine right.

This emphasis on uniqueness and singularity makes Burton's films ideal candidates for Jungian and post-Jungian film analysis. Jung had a special term for the dynamics between the individual and society – he called it individuation. For him, this meant finding your own path, defending your wishes and choices against the opinion of the majority and ultimately balancing the benefits of integration with the perils of mountain-top loneliness. Insisting on being 'yourself' and going against the cultural or ideological mainstream is a rather heroic venture. Jungian analyst Jolande Jacobi describes individuation as the process of self-fulfilment and self-scrutiny (Jacobi, 1973: 106). Putting an emphasis on your personal achievements and rights, however, does not necessarily mean becoming an impenitent self-seeker:

> By individuation [man] does not become "selfish"; he fulfils his individual nature, which is something very different and must not be confused with egoism or individualism. He becomes not only an individual but also a member of a collectivity, and the wholeness he has achieved in contact, through consciousness and the unconscious, with the whole world.
>
> (Jacobi, 1973: para. 106–7)

Burton's individuating heroes are first caught up in the mechanical entrails of Western modernity, and then wounded, cut up, fragmented or even destroyed by the very machine they helped to create. Burton slides up and down the diachronic scale of the modern era, boldly picking narrative elements and bits of contemporary myths to construct a portrait of the fragmented (capitalist) individual. The narratives he chooses do not glorify rationality, progress, ambition, money and other emblematic capitalist values; on the contrary, they emphasise the shadowy, Gothic, counter-progressive side of modernity. Thus, *Corpse Bride* (2005) contains kitschy allusions to Gothic-Revivalist medievality. The fake literary Gothicism of the second part of the eighteenth century was a reflection, 'through a glass darkly', of the newly emerged bourgeois values; it was a distorted reappraisal by the middle-class mentality of the feudal, unenlightened, pre-industrial past. As David Punter writes, the middle class, as the principal audience for Gothic fictions, 'displaces the hidden violence of present social structures, conjures them up again as past, and falls promptly under their spell' (Punter, 1980: 418; Horner, 2002: 204). Burton also skilfully re-examines the principal concerns of the Romantic Explosion: scientific progress, diminishing of religious authority, urbanisation, pollution, loss of communal ties and, especially, optimistic, rational individualism which presupposes that human beings are capable of managing their instincts and forming an enlightened, democratic society consisting of independent, clearly thinking citizens.

Together with Washington Irving, Mary Shelley and Edgar Allan Poe, Burton distorts Enlightenment hopes and capitalist ideals into various abominable monstrosities. His Ichabod Crane (Johnny Depp), loosely based on Irving's character from *The Legend of Sleepy Hollow* (1820), is a forensic scientist trying to 'understand' the unconscious, and prodding with his cold instruments the unexplainable, animalistic headlessness of crime. Burton's Frankensteinesque heroes – Vincent, Edward Scissorhands, Jack Skellington, Dr. Finkelstein, dream about making new creations, joining the pieces together, 'creating life out of lifeless matter' – but, like the original Victor Frankenstein, end up breaking things apart. Instead of democratic citizens pursuing their own interests while respecting other people's rights, in Burton's films we have Poesque loners: isolated, cornered, mad, misunderstood, steeped in egoistic self-dramatisation, wasting their lives, refusing or failing to occupy their utilitarian function in the machine of society, and having little intent to integrate.

But Burton does not limit himself to Romanticism: his diachronic scale of literary references also includes, refracted through the prism of postmodern garishness, allusions to and creative recyclings of Victorianism (*Sweeney Todd*, 2007; *Alice in Wonderland*, 2010), industrial London (*Sweeney Todd*), narrative and visual elements of popular modernism (German expressionism as exemplified in Gotham city from *Batman*, 1989 and *Batman Returns*, 1992), sci-fi and UFO mania of the 1950s (*Ed Wood*, 1994, *Mars Attacks*, 1996) and the anti-war stance of the 1960s (*Planet of the Apes*, 2001). Burton refuses to follow historical precision, observe textual and terminological accuracy, or be faithful to the spirit of the original text (except in the case of Edgar Allan Poe, of course). Even Roald Dahl's classic, *Charlie and the Chocolate Factory* (1964), metamorphoses in Burton's hands into an industrial-capitalist story involving a creative, lonely weirdo in search of an oxymoronic amalgam of identity and integration. In Burton's films, it is the feeling that matters.

All these loosely mapped and disparate references and subjects are united by the underlying theme of the complex relationship between the individual and society. This is not the mechanistic pre-industrial community, as desribed by Emile Durkheim, in which all members are held together by an inherent solidarity and do not aspire to become 'personalities' (Durkheim, 1964: 131). Burton is interested in the other type of community, termed by Durkheim 'organic', because its members, speaking metaphorically, are a collection of various organs, each with its unique function, working harmoniously for the benefit of the body (ibid.: 182). In such a society a strong emphasis is placed on independence, uniqueness, indispensability and competition. Its members are essentially free individuals – although their behaviour is controlled and limited by the government, legal systems, workplace regulations, or even by the remains of what used to be the familial structure and familial traditions.

When the dictatorship of the custom, tradition and religion is lifted – the ritual, Victor Turner argues, is specifically created to induce people 'to want to do what they must do' Turner, (1992: 56) – and the freedom of personal choice is introduced, human beings do not automatically become wonderfully and boundlessly emancipated. Throughout his career Burton has been striving to show that, with all the hoopla about personal choice and uniqueness, 'commonness' and 'normalisation' have not disappeared and the threat to the individual remains. Modernity has turned small groups into fragmented, urbanised masses, conglomerations of separated individuals whose minds can be harvested, and then lumped into a gigantic shadow, for political purposes, economic gain, or even out of sheer 'will for power' by a group of unscrupulous persons.

Burton tends to portray society as being prone to bouts of collective madness, as a collection of lost souls incapable of intellectual independence, and hence constantly on the lookout for a loony leader. The aloof experiential perception of society is very similar to Jung's elitist analysis of contemporary politics and social behaviour. Reflecting on the catastrophic events of the twentieth century, Jung postulates that 'masses are breeding grounds for psychic epidemics' (Jung, 1959: para. 227). Without a genuine communal base (or even where such a base *is* present), the survivalist 'herd instinct' can easily turn into its own shadow:

> Society, by automatically stressing all the collective qualities in its individual representatives, puts a premium on mediocrity, in everything that settles down to vegetate in an easy, irresponsible way. Individuality will inevitably be driven to the wall.
> (Jung, 1953: para. 240)

All human control comes to an end when the individual is caught up in a mass movement because

> identification with a group is a simple and easy path to follow, but the group experience goes no deeper than the level of one's own mind in that state. . . . But as soon as you are removed from the crowd, you are a different person again and unable to reproduce the previous state of mind. The mass is swayed by *participation mystique*, which is nothing other than an unconscious identity. Supposing, for example, you go to the theatre: glance meets glance,

everybody observes everybody else, so that all those who are present are caught up in an invisible web of mutual unconscious relationship. If this condition increases, one literally feels borne along by the universal identity with others.

(Jung, 1959: paras. 226–7)

Burton paints disturbing pictures of 'collective madness'. Both the Joker (Jack Nicholson) and the Penguin (Danny De Vito) charm the citizens of Gotham city into becoming a pliable mass with one brain only to massacre them later; the inhabitants of the pastel town in *Edward Scissorhands*, although distinct personalities, all end up chasing hapless Edward into his hilltop castle, in imitation of the classic Whalean monster-crowd stand-off; in *Mars Attacks!* (1996) the green-headed Martians use ray guns to eliminate the brainwashed people of the United States. The Joker sums up the relationship of the crowd with its shadow; before puncturing the gas-filled balloons at the Gotham City Anniversary Parade, he declares from his throne: 'Now comes the part where I relieve you, the little people, of the burden of your failed and useless lives. But, as my plastic surgeon always said: if you gotta go, go with a smile.'

Instead of consistent, responsible, mature, 'harmonious individualism' as envisaged by the paragons of Enlightenment ethics, we witness in Burton's films the tragic split between independent thinking and social obedience. The surface of modern society is torn, the machine is broken, and this is exactly how Burton represents it – metonymised, divided, ragged, full of gaps and holes. It is, according to his aesthetic, in dire need of repair. The heroic modern individual is an orphaned child, who, after God's death, is helplessly looking about for guidance and direction.

The problem with the father

In Burton's films, the issue of the 'absence' of God and the theme of the end of paradisiacal 'order' take the form of the perennial conflict between fathers and sons. The father–son dynamic he depicts starts on a personal level and extends to cover the whole of society, making his hero the archetypal representative of the Western man seeking to restore the lost ontologicity.

Burtonian paternal authority figures, despite being very different, nevertheless have one thing in common: they are the cause of their sons' unhappiness. The father may be a helpful, generous and wise god like the Inventor in *Edward Scissorhands*, the young and irresponsible creator from *Frankenweenie* (1984), the family-neglecting adventurer in pursuit of his selfish needs from *Big Fish* (2003), a stern and demanding patriarch like Willy Wonka's parent, the fondly remembered fathers of Bruce Wayne and Alice, or the Penguin's unsympathetic parent – but he invariably leaves the child on its own in a complex and unfriendly world. Sometimes the father is too young (and careless), sometimes too old (and feeble), often far too authoritarian and stringent – but he is always imperfect in some way. By dying, by leaving home, by being emotionally unavailable or by not being interested in his child's development, the symbolic father makes the young person's life very difficult, and his future uncertain and full of conflict.

In his essay on the child archetype, Jung discusses the importance of the abandonment motif. Translated back into the language of personal development, it symbolises self-reliance, ambition and drive – even when they have been attained through isolation and hardship. Abandonment, Jung writes, is necessary because it kick-starts the personality's development (Jung, 1959: para. 285). The child is a future hero, or a future personality, and therefore has to be prepared for any prospective challenges. Jung postulates that the child

> is all that is abandoned and exposed and at the same time divinely powerful; the insignificant, dubious beginning, and the triumphant end. The "eternal child" in man is an indescribable experience, an incongruity, a handicap, and a divine prerogative; an imponderable that determines the ultimate worth or worthlessness of a personality
> (Jung, 1959: para. 300)

James Hillman notes how in myths and fairy tales young heroes are often wounded, or they have a disability which 'seems to identify the puer spirit with heroic destiny' (Hillman, 1987: 101). As for the origins of the ailment, Hillman points at parents: 'Everyone carries a parental wound and has a wounded parent' (1987: 101). He discusses examples of such parent-inflicted wounds in ancient mythology:

> Pelops is chopped up by his father, Tantalus, who served his son boiled to the gods to eat. . . . The boy Ulysses is wounded while he is with his grandfather, and by a "parental" boar. The soft spot in Achilles (and in Baldur) comes from the Mother. Achilles is held by the heel and dipped into the bath to make him invincible – except for where she held him. His fatal wound is precisely where his mother touched him under the guise of protecting him. One wound of Hercules occurs in a battle with a Father and Son (Hippokon and his

sons). This father–son conflict wounds Hercules in the hollow of his hand; and in another tale Hercules kills his own children.
(1987: 101)

Interestingly enough, in most cases the primary 'carer' in Burton's films is the male parent, while the mother is relegated to the background. It is the father, and not the female parent, who 'gives birth', looks after the child, and then abandons it to its fate. The protagonists' mothers, at best, play secondary roles or serve as a context. At worst, they are altogether not mentioned. In *Vincent*, for instance, the mother represents the 'normalising' patriarchal voice of society; in *Edward Scissorhands* (Peg) and *Big Fish* (Sandra) she is given the role of a guardian angel, a kind of feminine stability to balance out the unreliability of the father figure; in *Sleepy Hollow* she is victimised. Such a 'swap', Erich Neumann explains, is mythologically correct. In fact, it frequently occurs in some world religions with a patriarchal base, for instance, in Christianity and Hasidism (2002: 61–2). The constellation of the primal relationship in these religions is transferred to God, and the role of the mother is taken over by the father (ibid). In this case, any negativity on the part of the 'child' which comes with a dissatisfactory primal relationship will be shifted onto the father figure (on the personal level) or on to God (on the metaphysical plane).

Whether or not such a neglect of femininity by Burton is indicative of a sexist attitude is open to debate. Far from being sexist, it could simply be down to the question of Burton's creative influences. Narratively, he tends to follow the scheme of the Frankenstein myth, in which the feminine (Victor's own mother, his fiancée Elizabeth) is presented as a sexless 'angel' and relegated to the background while her functions – gestation and birth – are performed by a man who plays 'the creator'. In Burton's films, such patriarchisation and usurpation of traditional feminine roles does not change the protagonist's destiny. His problem lies not in the parent's sex, but in the fact that he was rejected or abused by the parent. The father could have been good and attentive, but instead he chose to play 'the terrible mother'.

This initial connection with the mother (or, in the patriarchal tradition, the male parent playing her role) is extremely important for the subsequent psychological development of the individual as it influences the ability to relate and integrate. The positive primal relationship leads to the formation of the *positive-integral ego*, 'an ego that is able to assimilate even the negative or unpleasant qualities of the outer and inner worlds, such as deprivations, pain, etc.' (Newmann, 2002: 58). The child with the *positive-integral ego* can easily deal with the split between automorphism and cultural adaptation, and is able to endure inhibitions imposed on them by the group into which they are born.

A negative constellation of the primal relationship occurs wherever the infant, speaking figuratively, 'loses' its mother; or, to be more precise, loses the emotional connection with her. It can happen due to the parent's inadequacy, death or separation – or may even be dependent on other factors outside the personal mother's conduct (ibid.: 73). Such a loss of emotional connection leads to the dissipation of the baby's faith in the foundation of its existence.

The Burtonian baby, *puer* or hero 'remembers' the paradisiacal state of complete unity with the father (or, in the case of Ichabod Crane, the mother), and seeks, in his creative activities, to bring him back. Many of them – Edward Scissorhands, Will Bloom (*Big Fish*), Ichabod Crane (*The Legend of Sleepy Hollow*), Alice, Willy Wonka (played by Johnny Depp), inherit their parents' ambition or talent – which is a form of preservation of personal traits in the next generation. The *puer* is also – openly or repressedly – angry. Another researcher on attachment and adandonment, John Bowlby, notes that 'anger is an immediate, common and perhaps invariable response to loss' (Bowlby, 2008: 65). Anger, he writes, is an integral part of the grief reaction (ibid.: 65). The pain of rejection (or what Burton's protagonists perceive as rejection), sharp as it is, turns into a blade; the separation gap becomes the wound. The edge and the injury, the tool and its by-product, engage in a mutually dependent destructive-creative relationship, which does not always end badly – but invariably generates a lot of pain in the process.

The edge and the wound

Parental faults (including being human, being fallible and dying) are often narratively presented in Burton's films as flashbacks. Edward remembers his father's exciting laboratory and the uncanny assembly line, the present of rubber hands and lessons on good manners. Willy Wonka, upon hearing the trigger word 'parent', starts reminiscing about his own father – a sadistic-in-his-professional-perfectionism dentist who banned his son from eating sweets and made him wear horrendous dental braces. In *Alice in Wonderland*, the heroine's father also appears exclusively in flashbacks, during which he talks to her about his travels and reminds her about the importance of being different. As he puts it, 'You are mad – but then all the best people are.' In *Big Fish*, Ed Bloom's wild and fabulous youth is shown through the eyes of Will Bloom 'in the present'. In *Batman* Bruce Wayne returns in his reccurring nightmares to the alley between Pearl and Philips – a dark corner of Gotham where as a child he witnessed his parents' murder. These narrative flashbacks, some nostalgic, others terrifying, pinpoint the moment of trauma and locate the instant in time when the protagonist was made different – or even when the hero was *made*. The carer's fault in the past had caused the child to be imperfect, faulty, incomplete.

The idea of 'incompleteness' is a key ingredient in Tim Burton's ontology. He is very keen to show it in all its complexity and multi-leveledness. At the lowest interpretive level – the visual, the physical – Burton expresses incompleteness in the form of metonymy; or, to be terminologically precise, synecdoche. His characters literally fall apart: the inhabitants of the entire town of Halloween are constantly (and happily) disintegrating, and so do Beetlejuice (Michael Keaton), the Red Queen's courtiers, and Sparky the bull terrier. This visual metonymisation also has a metaphorical base. The abandoned child falls apart, the hero is crippled, wounded, bleeding, he is in pain, he is eternally suffering, forever trying to find, and replace, his missing parts. Edward Scissorhands, Emily the Corpse Bride, Catwoman (Michelle Pfeiffer) are all physically disjointed, and internally broken. Speaking about the character of Sally in *The Nightmare before Christmas*, Burton explains his interest in broken, detached and incomplete bodies and souls:

> I remember drawing Jack and really getting into these black holes for eyes and thinking that to be expressive, but not have any eyes, would be really incredible. Sally was a relatively new character; I was into stitching from the Catwoman thing, I was into that whole psychological thing of being pieced together. Again, these are all symbols for the way that you feel. The feeling of not being together and of being loosely stitched together and constantly trying to pull yourself together, so to speak, is just a strong feeling to me.
> (Salisbury, 2006: 123).

Interestingly enough, the Burtonian heroine is as broken as his male protagonists. Catwoman's costume, roughly sewn together, is conceptually similar to Edward's punk attire. Sally and Emily the Corpse Bride are blue-faced, dead, and constantly disintegrating. Even Alice, after being sucked into the Wonderland of the unconscious, undergoes a series of bodily deformations and transformations, which symbolise female obedience and feminine pliability. Being too small or too big for your surroundings, not being able to fit in, being a pawn in someone else's game, being forced to accept the rules without questioning them – this is what Burton, who is sensitive to the issues of identity crisis and oppression, responded to in Carroll's original text. In fact, Burton's fragmented females are often 'made', 'unmade' or asked to squeeze into narrow, deforming stereotypes by men who have power over them. Sally is literally torn between her mad scientist husband, Dr. Finkelstein, and the romantic hero Jack Skellington. Selina Kyle/Catwoman in thrown out of the window by her boss, the mayor of Gotham City. When her broken body is licked back together by urban cats, she stops being a meek executive assistant and becomes a female avenger. 'Not fitting in' leads to falling apart, but Burton's heroines are prepared to take the risks that come with being a fighter and a rebel.

In Burton's cinematic traumatology, the most commonly injured part of the body is the hands. Edward Scissorhands feels that he 'is not finished' because, instead of the specially designated rubber limbs, humanoid and soft, he has cold, sharp and very uncooperative razors. Sally's badly sewn arm keeps falling off, and she has to stitch it back to her body. Ichabod Crane's hands have stigmata which bleed each time he remembers his mother's ghastly death inside the iron coffin with spikes. The wound, therefore, was given to him by his father. The second arch enemy of Batman, the Penguin, does not have human hands at all – he is a bird, he has flippers. Wonka wears gloves – a symbol of sterility, emotional fragility, self-protection. Meanwhile, Sweeney Todd reckons that his arm is only complete when it is gripping a lethal razor.

James Hillman establishes a direct link between the symbol of maimed hands and artistic imagination. Hands are the physical instrument of creativity, and as such are the obvious metaphor for talent. Maimed hands, therefore, would mean defective talent; the impossibility to reach perfection either in oneself or in one's creations. The hands, he writes,

> may be clever and manipulative, but there is difficulty at hanging-in or hanging-on to the *matter at hand* so that it can be resolved. Knots are sliced open with a brilliant stroke, rather than carefully sorted out strand by strand.
>
> (Hillman, 1987: 104)

This is certainly true of Edward and his 'logical extension' Sweeney Todd. Edward is a wounded artistic personality whose detachment from real life means that he cannot perform basic everyday tasks without other people's help. He cuts threads, slices meat and chops cabbage for his adoptive mother Peg, but cannot balance a pea at the tip of his blade finger. Similarly, the demon barber, although his fingers are capable of doing things with amazing precision when working a blade along the client's neckline, chooses to slice, cut, chop, pierce and mince up the vulnerable flesh rather than glide carefully and follow the facial contours. Sweeney Todd transforms his existential anguish into his clients' physical agony.

The unbearable pain, Hillman argues, generates the fantasy of being repaired:

> The inabilities of the hands are sometimes repaired in dreams by surgical operations. A slug-like worm is pulled out of the metacarpus of a woman who feels herself slow at grasping ideas. A surgeon operates painstakingly, seemingly for hours, at the base of a young man's right fingers, as if the careful slowness is the operation itself, giving a base to the patient's deft but fluttery fingers that drop everything too soon. A young potter's hand is cut open down to the bone. He is horrified and fascinated by the sight. The dreamer can now see that his hand which forms is itself formed by deep, hard, ancient structures and that the shapes he makes have a preformed interior pattern. The dream has released an archetypal sense of what he is doing.
>
> (1987: 104)

Edward's surgical operation, as we know, did not happen due to the doctor's untimely departure. Unfinished, he cannot retain the treasure with which he is entrusted; or, as Hillman puts it, 'the talent placed in my hands does not necessarily become mine. To seize the talent may realise it, but it also may make the talent vanish' (1987: 105). With the executive (spiritual) function of the hands wounded, the imaginative function cannot control itself, and eventually fails to attain the desired perfection:

> The man whose lifestyle follows the puer and lives from the spirit shows wounded hands when he cannot handle gifts or manage that spirit which comes and goes of its own accord. His handicap reminds him of his limits, keeping him to the fingers of fantasy rather than the fist of control.
>
> (ibid.: 105).

T S Eliot transformed the Arthurian Waste Land and its wounded proprietor, the Fisher King, into the symbols of broken modernity. Similarly, in Burton's fantasy worlds, the hands become the symbol of impaired potential. Hands come to represent the pain of the creative process, the end goal of which is to carve beauty and symmetry out of chaos, to restore the (idealised, non-existent, paradisiacal) order in the kingdom. The creative process itself becomes the way to God.

Not only does the Burtonian hero wound the people he loves and hates – friends, enemies, community – he also self-harms. As Donald Kalsched rightly points out, 'the traumatized psyche is self-traumatizing' (Kalsched, 1996: 5). The edge of the protagonist, metaphorised in the form of sharp objects – scissors, razors, needles, swords – represents a danger to his integrity, to his own self. 'The edge' is a prominent extended metaphor. It evokes numerous cultural and linguistic moments associated with living 'outside the norm': knives, shadows, punks, edgy teenagers, geeks, and the sharp corners of creativity. The art, Burton is trying to tell his audience, is a two-edged weapon. It is unsafe to be an artist: it is painful; it brings with it a lack of social and psychological stability and takes away the chance of leading 'a normal life'. Burton's imperfect artists often turn the blade, initially aimed at society, onto themselves. Edward's face is covered in scars and cuts. Little Vincent Malloy, rather suicidally, imagines himself dying alone in a dark room, exasperated and exhausted by his Gothic fantasies. Jack Skellington's edgy ambition nearly costs him his life when he dares to become 'Santa Claws' and dispatches tons of ugly presents to the children of the town of Christmas.

Although some of Burton's characters, speaking figuratively, 'commit suicide', others, not without difficulties, achieve painful reparation. But even when the wound heals, in its place always remains a scar or a stitch – the silent reminders of the power of the edge.

The factory and the city

If the modern individual is broken, if his Paradise is lost, there must have been a time when he felt 'whole'. To discuss the idea of 'incompleteness' and 'brokenness' on a larger scale, Burton uses two clusters of metaphors: the city and the factory. The factory, with its assembly line, is a place of both creation and destruction; a place where things are made and where they decay (like Jack Napier's face, for example).

The idea of 'mechanical construction from parts' appears in *Frankenweenie*, *Pee Wee's Big Adventure*, *Edward Scissorhands*, *Batman*, *Charlie and the Chocolate Factory*, and *Sweeney Todd*. Burton keeps using this image because, like its original, the motif of the creation of the Frankenstein monster, it refers to the loss of the idealised pre-modern paradisiacal state. To explore the borderline between pre-modernity and modernity, Burton presents two contrasting 'production methods' of making people and things: true customisation and mass manufacture. 'Early technology', like the Inventor's conveyor belt or the clumsy instruments of Ichabod Crane, symbolises in Burton's aesthetic the nostalgic, utopian unity of orderly God and rational man – or rather, the last moments of the God–man alliance, shortly before it is broken up. For instance, Edward Scissorhands is a unique product, a handmade, lovingly crafted creature made personally by his father. As such, he is talented and otherwise different from the mass-produced inhabitants of the pastel town. Pee Wee's comical 'breakfast production line', although mechanised, still refers to the idea of product originality rather than mass manufacture. The Burtonian God of rational mechanics carefully constructs his children from parts. The problem is, he is imperfect, and his 'products' end up being flawed, damaged and faulty.

In her essay Material Girl: The Effacements of Postmodern Culture, the feminist philosopher Susan Bordo explains the origins of the 'mechanical body' paradigm:

> In a culture in which organ transplants, life-extension machinery, microsurgery and artificial organs have entered everyday medicine, we seem on the verge of practical realization of the seventeenth-century imagination of the body as machine. . . . In the early modern era, machine imagery helped to articulate a totally determined human body whose basic functionings the human being was helpless to alter. The then dominant metaphors for this body – clocks, watches, collections of springs – imagines a system that is set, wound up, whether by nature or God the watchmaker, ticking away in a predictable, orderly manner regulated by laws over which the human being has no control.
>
> (2001: 1099)

According to Burton, the problems begin when the mechanical God is replaced by the entrepreneur, and craftsmanship is substituted by the assembly line. Instead of 'faulty' but unique individuals, as initially dreamt of by the Enlightenment idealists, the factory of modernity started to produce identical, bland, easily governable human beings – perfect cogs for the capitalist machine. These identical creatures are destroyed and dissolved in the entrails of the faceless and unstoppable production apparatus. In *Sweeney Todd* and *Batman*, the industrial image of the assembly line transmutes into a homicidal horror. The opening credits of *The Demon Barber* show a *disassembly* line consisting of various pieces of pie-making equipment, machinery and underground pathways – an unfailing system for the disposal of dead bodies and the resulting litres of blood. Similarly, in *Batman* the Enlightenment technological dream turns into its opposite. The Joker does not cut and mince his victims – he chemically breaks them down. After the death of his former boss, Jack Napier is left in charge of Gotham's industrial empire, and establishes control over the city by chemically modifying cosmetic and hygiene products. With his acid-induced smile, the Joker is chemical industry personified – his industrial might can only be confronted by another entrepreneur, Bruce Wayne. The owner of Wayne Enterprises, Batman is simultaneously fighting with the shadow of technology, the collective shadow and the shadow of his capitalist self.

Coupled with the idea of 'production as destruction' in both *Batman* and *Sweeney Todd* is the image of the urban jungle. Victorian London, with its mighty criminal underworld, run-down housing, diseases, pollution, industrialisation, dull landscape and vulgar entertainments is an archetypal match for the temporally later metropolis that is Gotham city. They are the ultimate breeding grounds for mass infections – be it physical or moral. Moving along the scale of modernity, Burton refuses to discern between the human psychology of its 'earlier' and 'later' phases. The city makes isolated individuals vulnerable; people of contemporary New York (or Gotham City) are as prone to mind control as the inhabitants of Victorian London.

As usual, Burton is always honest about his visual influences:

> So few great cities have been built. *Metropolis* and *Blade Runner* seem to be on the accepted spectrum. We [Burton and the production designer Anton Furst] tried to do something different although people tend to lump things in categories. We conceptualized Gotham City as the reverse of New York in its early days. Zoning and construction was though of in terms of letting light in. So we decided to take that in the opposite direction and darken everything by building up vertically and cramming architecture together. Gotham City is basically New York caricatured with a mix of style squashed together – an island of big, tall cartoon buildings textured with extreme designs.
>
> (Fraga, 2005: 23)

What Burton and Furst built was, in fact, a shadow of New York – the reverse, problematic side of the modern metropolis. In this, his creative aims are not that different from the maestros of expressionistic chiaroscuro. Sandwiched between the two world wars, Robert Wiene (*The Cabinet of Dr. Caligari*, 1920), Fritz Lang (*Dr. Mabuse, der Spieler*, 1922; *Metropolis*, 1927), Paul Wegener (*Golem*, 1915) and Friedrich Murnau (*Nosferatu*, 1922), instead of showing the bright technological future, chose to portray the darkness descending onto urbanised humankind. Closed urban spaces endorse isolation and promote claustrophobia and fear of external control. A typical expressionist antagonist (Dr. Mabuse, Nosferatu, Dr. Caligari, Rotwang) is a maniac (usually unfocalised) who takes or makes an attempt to take control of the minds of unsuspecting citizens. Actually, *Caligari* was originally devised by the writers Carl Mayer and Hans Janowitz as an allegory of political authoritarianism during the First Wold War: 'Caligari stood for the state, while Cesare represented the sleepwalking masses who had been sent by the millions to kill and to be killed' (Skal, 2001: 41). German expressionist films reflect the biggest problem of modernity – the amalgamation of personal shadows into one collective evil.

It is not surprising, then, that Tim Burton, who has always been suspicious of crowds and collectivity, borrows from the Germans both thematically and stylistically. The Gothic cathedral in *Batman* refers to Modernism's indebtedness to architectural Gothic, and symbolises the sublimated collective guilt of the city's inhabitants. The dark angularity and verticality of Gotham's architecture delineates spaces in which people are so cut off from each other, emotionally as well as physically, that their dark sides start to merge.

In *Charlie and the Chocolate Factory*, the city–factory dynamic is also uneasy and grotesque. In spite of the playful and inventive character of the manufacturing process, and the 'sweetness' of the final product, Wonka's factory is an integral part of the town's gloom, sameness and dreariness. Like Pee Wee, who enters Hollywood with eyes wide open, unaware of the perils and intricacies of the film industry, Willy Wonka is an oxymoronic naive capitalist. His faith in humankind is shattered when spies hired by other firms steal secrets of his amazing products. Unlike the 'common people', Wonka prefers to generate his own ideas rather than purloin somebody else's. People who steal intellectual property lack creativity; they are people without imagination. Although eccentric and 'unfinished', wounded by his father, he is still an original personality, whereas the copycats are so dim and lustreless that they seamlessly merge into the dreary industrial landscape.

Naive or not so naive, Wonka the entrepreneur casts a shadow; it is he, the capitalist, who encourages, and then exploits, the grey uniformity of landscape and people. The world of 'commoners' and his factory differ not just in colour, but also in size. The production designer Alex McDowell elucidates the concepts behind the set:

> The very first thing to do was to establish the polar opposites of the environment. One was the town, and one's the factory. The factory looms over it, and in a direct line from that, way down in the bottom of the hill, is a little crumbling house, which is also a unique structure in the town. All the rest of the town in between the Bucket house and the factory is basically identical generic housing.
> (McDowell, 2005)

This visual decision presents the factory as a symbol of nonconformism and creativity, while Charlie's house is a metaphor of humbleness and the very human gesture that is sacrifice.

In continuation of the idea of mass sameness and uniformity, Oompa Loompas, the workers at Wonka's factory, all look identical (played by one actor, Deep Roy). The Oompa Loompas' identical appearance alludes to the replaceability of workforce within the impersonal production apparatus. This, in its turn, brings about the question of alienation in capitalist society; for, in the last instance, it is Willy Wonka who owns the factory and controls the production process. He is the brain behind the enterprise. This exploitation of unambitious sameness, luckily, is redeemed by the little boy Charlie – a boy very common in his uncommonness. In the film, Charlie represents humanity; he becomes Wonka's link with both 'the father' and 'the crowd'. The boy becomes the redeemer of modernity, and, as the new director of the enterprise, becomes the guarantor of 'capitalism with a human face'. Thanks to him, Wonka's gloved hand, the damaged hand, the hand of the imperfect creator, is finally ready to shake the hands of common people.

Conclusion

Via his hidden politics Burton maintains that industrialised modernity, with its emphasis on private success, personal achievement, speed, productivity, capitalist efficiency, and almost heroic uniqueness, has led to the creation of disjointed urban communities. Individuals in such a society are united only by the incorporeal gods of government and media, linked by the conflicting voices 'from above'. Modernity placed the individual in the midst of the dark metropolitan maze, where he is blindly groping towards the exit, in constant danger of stumbling upon an ideological Minotaur or a cultural monstrosity. It does not help that an anonymous voice from the loudspeaker is issuing him with contradictory directions.

Suffering from the illnesses of their age, Burton's rebellious individuals form a complex, dynamic and interdependent triangle with God/the father on one side, and society on the other. The three parts of the triangle are connected by invisible threads through which pain, generated by abandonment, travels from the father to the son, and then from the son to society and back. When the protagonists (and antagonists) choose to channel their undiluted, raw, untransformed existential anxiety into society, the result is similar to the proverbial 'eight corpses' of Hamlet. The frustrated avengers and disillusioned teenagers Edward Scissorhands, Sweeney Todd and the Penguin are literally or figuratively killed off when the edge they point at society is turned back on them.

The hero also has the choice of transforming the destruction and pain into creative achievement. In this sense, the Burtonian individual is closer to the crowd than he may think. Instinctively, he knows exactly what he wants. The attempt to reach out to society may not always be successful, but it counts as a positive achievement. When the hero decides to use his suffering 'for the benefit of the people', creating haircuts and topiaries like Edward, saving lives like Batman, making chocolates like Wonka, he takes a step towards reparation and completion, and seeks to close the parent-inflicted wound, which, on a higher metaphorical level, also happens to be the gap between him and society. When his hand reaches out and touches, the dead God is – even if temporarily – revived.

References

Bordo, Susan (2001) Material Girl: The Effacements of Postmodern Culture. In Julie Rivkin and Michael Ryan (eds.), *Literary Theory: An Anthology*. Oxford: Blackwell (pp. 1099–1115).
Bowlby, John (2008) *The Making and Breaking of Affectionate Bonds*. London: Routledge.
Durkheim, Emile (1964) *The Division of Labour in Society*. London: Collier Macmillan.
Fraga, Kristian (ed.) (2005) *Tim Burton Interviews*. Jackson: University Press of Mississippi.
Hauke, Christopher (2000) *Jung and the Postmodern: The Interpretation of Realities*. London and Philadelphia, PA: Routledge.
Hillman, James (1987) (ed.) *Puer Papers*. Dallas, TX: Spring.
—— (1977) Puer Wounds and Ulysses Scar. In *Puer Papers*. Dallas, TX: Spring (pp. 100–28).

Hockley, Luke (2001) *Cinematic Projections: The Analytical Psychology of C. G. Jung and Film Theory*. London: University of Luton Press.
Hogle, Jerrold E. (2002) The Gothic Crosses the Channel: Abjections and Revelation in *Le Fantôme de l'Opera*. In Avril Horner (ed.), *European Gothic: A Spirited Exchange 1760–1960*. Manchester: Manchester University Press (pp. 204–23).
Horner, Avril (ed.) (2002) *European Gothic: A Spirited Exchange 1760–1960*, Manchester: Manchester University Press.
Irving, W. (1820/2008) *The Legend of Sleepy Hollow*. Charleston, SC: Forgotten Books.
Jacobi, Jolande (ed.) (1953) *Psychological Reflections: An Anthology of the Writings of C. G. Jung*. London: Routledge and Kegan Paul.
—— (1973) *The Psychology of C. G. Jung* (Eighth Edition) (Ralph Manheim, Trans.). New Haven, CT and London: Yale University Press.
Jung, C. G. (1953) The relation between the ego and the unconscious. In *Two Essays on Analytical Psychology*, CW7 (H. Read, M. Fordham, G. Adler, Eds.; R. F. C. Hull, Trans.). London: Routledge & Kegan Paul.
Jung, C. G. (1959) *The Archetypes and the Collective Unconscious*, CW9(i) (H. Read, M. Fordham, G. Adler, Eds.; R. F. C. Hull, Trans.). London: Routledge & Kegan Paul.
Kalsched, Donald (1996) *The Inner World of Trauma: Archetypal Defences of the Personal Spirit*. London: Routledge.
McDowell, A. (2005) Designer Chocolate. Special Features (Disc 2). *Charlie and The Chocolate Factory* (2 Disc Deluxe Edition). New York: Warner Brothers (DVD).
Matthews, Clive J. and Smith, Jim (2007) *Tim Burton*. London: Virgin Books.
Neumann, Erich (1959) *Art and the Creative Unconscious: Four Essays*. Princeton: Princeton University Press.
—— (2002) *The Child: Structure and Dynamics of the Nascent Personality*. London: Karnac.
Punter, David (1980) *The Literature of Terror: A History of Gothic Fictions From 1765 to the Present Day*, Vols. 1 and 2. New York: Longman Group Ltd.
Rivkin, Julie and Ryan, Michael (eds.) (2001) *Literary Theory: An Anthology*. Oxford: Blackwell.
Salisbury, Mark (ed.) (2006) *Burton on Burton*. London: Faber and Faber.
Samuels, Andrew (1985) *Jung and the Post-Jungians*. London: Routledge.
—— (1993) *The Political Psyche*. London: Routledge.
Skal, David J. (2001) *The Monster Show: A Cultural History of Horror*. New York: Faber and Faber.
Turner, Victor (1979) *Process, Performance and Pilgrimage*. New Delhi: Naurang Rai.
—— (1992) *Blazing the Trail: Way Marks in the Exploration of Symbols*. Tucson and London: The University of Arizona Press.

Part III

Image, type and archetype

Chapter 15

The shadow

Constriction, transformation and individuation in Campion's *The Piano*

Mary Dougherty

Figure 15.1 Ada McGrath (Holly Hunter) and her daughter Flora (Anna Paquin).

The opening image in *The Piano* (Campion, 1993) is a blur of moving vertical objects that we can distinguish only in the second shot. It is a woman looking out from between her fingers. The voice of a young girl speaks:

> *The voice you hear is not my speaking voice, but my mind's voice.*
> I have not spoken since I was six years old.
> No one knows why, not even me.

The woman, in a dark Victorian dress – presumably the speaker – walks from under a tree.

> *My father says it is a dark talent and the day I take it into my head to stop breathing will be my last.*

There is a smash cut to a girl roller skating down an interior corridor. Boisterous sound disrupts the internal mood of the first images, then shifts back to the internal mood again. The camera pans a bedroom, a girl is sleeping in bed and a woman is taking off her skates as the voiceover continues:

> *Today he married me to a man I've not yet met.*
> *Soon my daughter and I shall join him in his country.*

The camera tracks the woman, bending to examine a piano in a shipping crate labelled New Zealand. Again the internal monologue continues:

> *My husband said my muteness does not bother him.*
> *He writes and hark this: God loves dumb creatures, so why not her!*
> *'Twere good he had God's patience for silence affects everyone in the end.*
> *The strange thing is I don't think myself silent – that is because of my piano.*
> *I shall miss it on the journey.*

The woman caresses the piano, sits down and begins to play.

She plays the piano as she herself is taken up in its sound. The rhythmic thud of a walking stick can be heard over the music with the camera following the silhouette of a female figure approaching and then appearing at the door. The woman playing the piano looks up and sees this older woman. She abruptly stops playing.

Within this short sequence we are introduced to Ada McGrath (Holly Hunter). It might be more accurate to say that we are located inside her world – an internal world within which her silence forges a barrier against all others except her daughter and her piano. Ada's capacity to reflect on her silence as a 'dark talent' suggests that she has some awareness of its negative impact. However, this awareness does not appear to engender a capacity or perhaps even a willingness to modify her silence. Her response to the older woman's appearance at the door suggests a defence against anyone who might intrude on her solitary relationship with the piano. We can anticipate that both her silence and her attachment to her piano are isolating strategies that make her feel safe. However, we can also assume that these same strategies may constrict her psychic development and leave significant aspects of her personality as undeveloped shadow. The eventual modification of Ada's silence, the attachment to her piano and the undeveloped shadow aspects of her personality are core themes in this film and will be of central importance in our exploration of Jung's concept of the shadow.

In this chapter, we explore Jung's concept of the shadow by tracing the shadow qualities of the four main characters in *The Piano:* Ada, a young mute woman, Flora (Anna Paquin), her daughter, Stewart (Sam Neill), her husband by an arranged marriage, and Baines (Harvey Keitel), Stewart's estate manager. We will consider how the shadow qualities embedded in each of these characters impact their ego function as well as their relational dynamics with others. Further, we will consider how the relational dynamics between them eventually force each character to confront the unconscious as they make choices that may or may not foster their psychological development. It is my hope that our exploration of shadow in relationship to these characters offers us the opportunity to deepen our understanding of shadow elements not only in our clients but also in our selves.

Jung's concept of the shadow has been described in two ways: first, as the entirety of the unconscious, that is everything we fail to recognize about ourselves; and, second, as the 'personification of certain aspects of the unconscious personality, which could be added to the ego complex but which, for various reasons, are not' (von Franz, 1974/1995: 5). As the dark, unlived, and repressed side of the ego complex, the shadow is composed of both unexamined and undeveloped unconscious processes as well as disowned aspects of the personality. Shadow aspects of the personality often contain frightening instinctual forces that can inundate ego consciousness and its adaptive environment. Because these unwanted aspects of the personality have been repressed, the shadow can also manifest itself compulsively (Dawson, 1997: 261).

Jung did not regard his theories as proven entities but rather as 'auxiliary tools' to be used to explore the possible significance of individual experience (ibid.: 256). For this reason we will explore Jung's concept of the shadow as applied to the individual experience of our four characters. We will observe a number of sequences throughout the film in some detail, just as we did above, in order to trace ego and shadow formation as disclosed in the interactions between these characters. We will ponder their attractions and repulsions, their longings and confrontations, their blind spots and projections as well as their turning points and transformations. Finally, we will explore cultural aspects of shadow by observing some of the ways the film portrays the juxtaposition between Western and native peoples, their relationship to the land and each other.

The cut to the underside of the boat slicing through blue-green luminous water propels the film's narrative as well as Ada from the dark interiors of her father's home in Scotland to the land of her husband – a strip of beach wedged between the voracious sea and a seemingly impenetrable wall of vegetation. Ada, her daughter Flora, her possessions and finally the piano are deposited on the beach by sailors. The captain is worried about leaving these two females on 'this dead shore' with no one to greet them. He asks Ada if she would prefer to come with them to Nelson. Ada vehemently signs her response to Flora who speaks her mother's message: 'She says "No" – she says she'd rather be boiled alive by natives than get back in your stinking tub.'

The vehemence of Ada's reaction again suggests her defensiveness in relationship to others. It could be argued that she was reacting out of fear and loss of control having landed on this desolate beach to be the wife of a man she has never met. However, it also appears that Ada had no capacity to consider the captain's suggestion. It was possible that he was right, that weather conditions were too rough for anybody to get through. But Ada's defiant reactions shut down any possibility for her to consider his suggestion. Instead her defensive stance took over and allowed her only a haughty rejection of his offer.

This particular interaction alerts us to a defensive aggression that underlies Ada's silence. In tracing shadow aspects of her personality we could say that her use of aggression functions with other isolating strategies that ward off the normal demands of human interaction and disable her from being able to negotiate interactions with others.

Following von Franz's description of shadow, Ada is unable to access unconscious or shadow aspects of her personality that could be added to the ego complex but which, for various reasons, are not. The film does not reveal the various reasons for Ada's silence or her attachment to her piano. But, as Jung reminds us, 'the symptoms of a neurosis are not simply the effects of long-past causes but also unsuccessful attempts at a new synthesis of life – seeds that fail to sprout owing to the inclement conditions.' (Jung, 1917/1926/1943: para. 67). We could say that Ada's silence and the attachment to her piano contribute to the inclement conditions that prohibit the seeds of her adult development from taking root. Her adult potentials, including her recognition and expression of adult desires, are withdrawn from conscious scrutiny (ibid.: para. 438) and remain repressed in the shadow side of her psyche. The result is that despite Ada's defiant will in relationship to others, she remains psychologically a girl.

Ada's response to the sailor also highlights how she uses her daughter as an extension of herself. Flora does not just speak her mother's words but expresses her mother's emotions. She delivers her mother's message infused with her mother's vengeance.

Throughout the first third of the movie, the symbiotic nature of Ada and Flora's relationship is portrayed with Flora functioning not just as the voice for her mother but also as a part of the defensive structure that sustains her mother's neurotic symptoms.

Although Ada creates a place of rest for her daughter, her longing for her piano dominates her psyche as exemplified in her being unaware of the rising tide. Flora climbs on the piano and Ada attempts to save their possessions against the tide. Later, Ada devises a makeshift shelter from a petticoat. Despite these caring efforts on behalf of her daughter, she nevertheless remains girl-like in her interactions with Flora, remaining in a world of shared fantasies between them.

I believe it is significant that it is Flora who interrupts this fantasy world inside the tent with her own thoughts about the external reality they are about to face: 'Mamma, I was thinking. I am not going to call him Papa; I am not going to call him anything. I'm not even going to look at him.'

It is early in the morning as Maori men and women make their way through the bush. Stewart appears preoccupied – his best suit and hat are smeared with mud. He stares at an image of a woman – the image he has carried these many months. He appears nervous and concerned now that she's here. Baines, his estate manager, asks him: 'Are we stopping?' Stewart does not reply. He takes off his hat and combs his wet hair close to his head using the daguerreotype as a mirror – then refocuses on her image. Baines asks again and then finally tells the Maori that they are stopping for a while. Stewart becomes aware of their having stopped and with some irritation says, 'We must get on,' taking a last look at his wife's image, unaware that he himself caused the delay.

In this brief interaction between Stewart and Baines, we are introduced to the shadow dynamics within and between these two men. Stewart's introversion and Baines' extraversion each embody the shadow qualities of the other – 'the value of one is the negation of value for the other' (Jung, 1917/1926/1943: para. 80). Stewart, the introvert, appears unsure of himself and slow to act while Baines, the extrovert, appears confident and outgoing, able to mediate between Stewart's uncertainty and the resulting confusion among the Maori. While Baines appears comfortable in this somewhat chaotic situation, Stewart emerges from his internal preoccupation irritated that the group is stopping. As we will come to see, Stewart's overly 'good' persona is often overtaken by an intense irritability (ibid.: para 306).

From the point of view of the conscious attitude, the shadow is the inferior function – the component of the personality that is repressed. As the film unfolds, both of these men come up against the shadow of their inferior function as seen in Stewart's attempts to relate to Ada through control and in Baines' own entrapment of Ada with his manipulation. The inferior function must be made conscious in order to produce a tension of opposites, without which no forward movement is possible (ibid.: para. 78). But only one of them will be willing to suffer the experience of becoming conscious of the qualities and intentions of their inferior ego function which leads to a serious consideration of the shadow and its integration (Jung, 1973: 234.)

The group arrives among the scattered boxes along the beach as well as the petticoat tent. Ada and Flora remain inside this tent. Stewart formally introduces himself, taking off his hat: 'You will have to wake yourself – I have men here to carry your things.' Ada and Flora emerge from their petticoat tent amidst the fascinated Maori. Stewart proceeds as the man in charge, at one moment shouting to Ada, 'Can you hear me' and at the next moment speaking about Ada as if she can't hear, 'You're small, I never expected you to be so small.' He appears awkward and nervous, all the while trying to manage his irritation behind a nervous smile. He continues to give orders to the Maoris through Baines to take the boxes, tables and suitcases but there is no mention of the piano. In an aside to Baines, Stewart asks him what he thinks. Baines looks at Ada and is capable of actually seeing her: 'She looks tired.' Stewart, on the other hand, remains internally preoccupied, with no empathy for what Ada has just endured: 'She's stunted, that's one thing.'

Stewart lacks any understanding of the importance of the piano and is indifferent to the demands of Ada and Flora that 'it must come.' He remains aloof and distant, unable to show any empathy for the exhaustion of their journey. Ada is likewise irritated and internally preoccupied. She lacks any understanding of the challenge of transporting all of her possessions over rough terrain. She remains cold and defiant, unable to greet Stewart with even a modicum of politeness, let alone warmth.

This initial interaction between Ada and Stewart has not gone well. We could imagine that Stewart had hoped for a different meeting, one in which he might kiss her hand. Ada has perhaps hoped that her former life could continue – only now under the protection of a husband. Both their longings are subsumed in the power struggle over the piano. Ada is left isolated, longing for the piano, now stranded on the beach at the mercy of the sea. And Stewart is left isolated, longing for he and Ada to begin again, this time with a chance for a better outcome.

An aerial shot tracks the path of Ada and Flora through the dense bush, then cuts to a close-up of their shoes as they struggle through the tangle of roots and mud. In another interaction between Stewart and Baines, we encounter cultural aspects of the shadow. Stewart gets angry when the Maoris refuse to follow the trail because it goes through a sacred burial ground. He is convinced that the Maori just want to go the longer way to make more money. Again Baines steps in and mediates the confrontation, assuring Stewart that the Maori know another trail. Stewart has no empathy for the traditions of the Maori. His judgment of the Maori participates in Western culture's projection of shadow onto native peoples. 'Like the construction of ego, the construction of culture engenders shadow with some beliefs and behaviors being suppressed that make up the unconscious, repressed and denied shadow of the culture' (West, 2007: 14). Although this film is set in Victorian times, as a modern film it knowingly juxtaposes the beliefs and behaviours of Western and native peoples and thus portrays the inevitable projection of the European shadow onto the native Other.

From the initial shots of Stewart's rain-drenched house, surrounded by dead trees, the prospect for Ada's new life seems ominous. The power struggle between Stewart and Ada as described above continues over the wedding photo. Stewart insists on his persona version of how the happy couple should look – if there is not going to be a proper wedding there should at least be a proper photograph. Nothing would stop him, not even the rain. Ada resents being forced to play the role of happy new wife and rips off her wedding gown to show her disgust. Subsequent interactions between them could be characterized as a series of attempts by Stewart to initiate affection between them – 'to begin again' – and a series of refusals by Ada to allow him to penetrate the sealed vessel of her heart. Both characters remain locked in their adaptive ego stance feeling victimized by the other.

Ada and Flora continue to cling to each other in such a way that their relationship denies all others any chance of intimacy with them. It even bars interaction with the other women in the immigrant community. It could be said that the defensive function of their relationship preserves old ways of being for both Ada and Flora and that any potential for corrective emotional experience is trapped in the unconscious shadow (Jung, 1984: 255). Ironically it turns out that the piano itself, once a core element within their defensive relationship, becomes the vehicle that penetrates it. It is Ada's longing for her piano that forces her to seek outside help.

Ada and Flora make their way along wooden planks, attempting to avoid the ubiquitous mud. They arrive at Baines' cabin, which is different to Stewart's. It sits in a brighter, leafier clearing, not separate from the bush but a part of it. Baines, too, is different from the other settlers – living among the Maori as a part of their culture, speaking their language and incorporating their face markings. Ada trusts that he can navigate his way back to the beach and to the piano. Despite his initial refusal, Ada and Flora stubbornly will him, without words, to change his mind.

A wide-angle shot transports us back to the beach. Ada comes alive as she plays the piano – allowed to breathe again. Flora, too, is taken up in the sound of her mother's playing, twirling and tumbling as a part of her mother's happiness. Baines has never heard music like this or seen a woman so passionately absorbed. As he witnesses Ada, we can imagine that something in himself is coming alive.

It is after this experience that Baines offers to trade 80 acres of his land in exchange for the piano. This is a bargain that appeals to Stewart because he is always eager to get more land. And then Baines makes his move: 'I'd have to get lessons – not much use without them.' The deal for the exchange is set between the two men: Baines is to get the piano, Ada is to teach Baines to play and Stewart will see that she does. Ada is livid when she is told of the bargain but has no voice – in any sense – to alter the situation.

The piano is transported to Baines' cabin and a piano tuner is secured from a neighbouring island. When Ada and Flora appear at Baines' cabin, Flora quickly discovers that the piano has been tuned. She is astonished at the tone. Baines insists that he only wants to listen to her play. Ada feels caught between her longing to play and her resentment that he has her piano. But the seductive power of the piano absorbs her resistance and she plays under the gaze of George Baines.

The piano becomes the fulcrum around which the interactions of Ada and Baines revolve. In turn, those interactions generate the life circumstances that are to grind down their ego defences. Jung makes the point that old ways of reacting are preserved in most personal interactions with little chance for their being corrected. Unlived capacities and desires remain repressed in the unconscious shadow. It is not until the right gradient is discovered in opposition to the conscious attitude that the confrontation of the shadow becomes possible. Ada's desire for the piano and Baines' desire for Ada are the necessary gradients that create the life circumstance in which a tension of opposites within each of them is constellated. This tension of opposites eventually allows them to experience feelings that ultimately allow each of them to access and make conscious the projected shadow content that each carries for the other (Jung, 1917/1926/1943: para.76–78).

Baines negotiates his own bargain with Ada. She plays and he listens. He sits behind her – sometimes closing his eyes, sometimes staring at her. Baines is drawn to Ada's self-contained silence. Her playing makes him hear. It opens his mind and fills his heart. One day he finds himself kissing her neck. She suppresses a cry. Conscious that he has made a mistake, a proposition springs fully formed from his mind: 'There's things I'd like to do while you play – if you let me you can earn your piano back.' The arrangement they make is mutually crafted. Both negotiate the agreement to satisfy their own desire, and both keep the power dynamics inherent in their arrangement repressed in the unconscious shadow.

Flora experiences her mother's arrangement with Baines from outside his cabin. She is angry at her mother's insistence that she stay outside just like the dog, Flynn. Left on her own, she enacts her resentments with Flynn. At one moment she pushes a stick at him through the floor of the porch to force him out into the rain. The next moment she becomes the comforting good mother: 'Poor baby, what horrid little person put you in the rain and shoved you with a stick?' Thus Flora acts out the two sides of how she feels. Like the dog, she is kicked out in the rain – and at the same time she is comforted by the person who kicks her out. Esther Harding states that children often live out their shadow sides with this kind of ignorance. But she reminds us that the hidden desires motivating our actions are not limited to childhood (Harding, 1945: 13).

For Baines, the piano is a glorious intrusion in his rough life, like Ada herself. He, too, seems possessed by the piano as this beautiful thing that brings Ada to him. But gradually he finds himself wishing that she would come to him for more than the piano and grows concerned about how she feels about him. For Ada, the piano is hers and it is her determination to win it back that brings her to Baines. Yet even as Ada resists the growing sexual energy between them, she is flattered by his advances as well as shaken by sensations in her body that Baines has awakened.

The growing intensity of their shared passion is reflected in the hurt and suffering they inflict on one another. When she resists his request to lie with him, he shuts the piano against her. When he tries to sit next to her at the community play, she rebuffs him with a vengeful smile. At the same time, their shared intensity also constellates the opposite attitude that is lived by the other: Baines is confronted by the self-contained refinement and capacity for internal reverie as lived by Ada; and Ada is confronted by the embodied magnetism and self-assured sexuality as lived by Baines.

Baines is devastated by Ada's rebuff at the community play. His mood is altered and distant at Ada's next visit. Baines tells her 'play what you like' and then disappears. After some minutes, Ada looks for Baines and finds him standing naked before her. He asks simply: 'I want to lie together without clothes on – how many would that be?' She is torn between wanting to flee and wanting to earn precious keys. She holds up the finger of both hands. 'Yes, ten keys,' says Baines. Flora notices that the piano is silent. She and we look through a crack in the wooden boards of the cabin, watching Ada gradually surrender to Baines' touch, his good and gentle kisses.

The next day, Flora and three Maori children play a game with tree trunks that enacts the tender exchanges she saw. The Maori women nearby are chatting, unconcerned with the game. Stewart on the other hand is horrified by the nature of their game. 'Never behave like that, never, nowhere,' he tells Flora. As Flora is whitewashing the 'shamed trunks' as a punishment, she reports to Stewart about the lessons: 'She never gives him a turn, she just plays what she likes. Sometimes she doesn't play at all.' Stewart asks, 'When's the next lesson' and Flora answers, 'tomorrow.'

The next day, Flora and Ada arrive at Baines' cabin to find the piano being carried away by a group of Maori men. Ada hurries into the cabin distraught. She signs frantically, demanding to know what is happening. Baines is clearly in pain. 'I've had enough. This arrangement is making you a whore and me wretched. I want you to care for me but you can't. It's yours. Leave.' Ada looks dismayed at the action of Baines. She feels a combination of confusion and rejection and, at the same time, a sudden elation that the piano is hers.

Stewart comes upon the Maoris moving the piano and stops them. He goes immediately to Baines. He is concerned that the returned piano means that he will have to pay for the 80 acres. Baines assures him that there is no payment – that he has given the piano to Stewart's wife.

Baines did not want the piano. And Baines did not want to take Ada as part of his bargain with Stewart or his arrangement with Ada. She was no longer just an anima projection; she was now the woman he loved. Baines thus confronts his shadow, embedded within this arrangement, as he becomes conscious that his manipulation of her was for his sexual control. At the same time, their arrangement had created life circumstances that opened his heart. He did not try to escape his depression but suffered it. And in so doing he was able to make use of unlived energy trapped in the unconscious to confront the shadow side of his own actions. 'The encounter with the shadow is invariably experienced as a mortification; humiliating, despicable parts of oneself have to be confronted and integrated; the feelings of guilt and worthlessness have to be suffered, taken on and worked through' (Stevens, 1990: 235).

The piano has been moved into Stewart's house and now he is asking Ada to play. But she stands back from the piano and lets Flora play. She then walks past the piano and wanders out the door, into the bush – into the unconscious. Now that the piano is hers, there is no legitimate reason to visit Baines. Ada is adrift. The psychic energy once absorbed by the piano is now freed from its old loyalties and flows backward into the unconscious, activating all the things in her that were never developed, including her adult sexuality and her capacity to feel (Jung, 1917/1926/1943: paras 90, 105). These energies now engulf Ada, pulling her away from Stewart, from Flora, and from the piano and towards Baines.

Ada arrives at his cabin disoriented, fragile and confused. Baines invites her to sit but she doesn't. 'Ada,' he says, 'I am unhappy because I want you. Because my mind is seized on you and I can think of nothing else. This is how I suffer.' Caught in her own silence she is unable to speak of her feelings for him. He asks her to go. She steps towards him; eyes filled with tears she begins to hit him – shocking them both. They stand face-to-face, speaking words of love without words. Like sleepwalkers they are enfolded in their awkward tenderness, their emotions guiding their instincts.

Stewart has followed Ada and is outside the cabin. He hears the deep sighs of lovemaking from within the rough building. He peers through the cracks in the boards to see Ada with Baines. He is unable to move, transfixed by his wife's beauty and by the bodily enactment of love that he has never known.

George watches as Ada dresses. 'Ada, I need to know, what will you do? Will you come again? Does this mean something to you?' She answers by lifting his shirt and burying her face in his chest. Baines looks her in the face: 'If the answer is yes, come tomorrow.'

The next day arrives. Ada waits until Stewart departs to continue his endless task of fencing the perimeter of his land. She leaves the house without disturbing Flora at play and goes down the path to George's cabin. Stewart materializes before her. He knows where she is going. She tries to walk past him but he seizes her, his split-off passion erupting with compulsive force. His eyes seem more animal than human, enraged, wounded and uncomprehending. He drags her back again and again, finally pressing her under his weight against the earth. From the beginning, Stewart and Ada were in a power struggle – at first for possession of things: a piano, a photograph, a piece of land. But now it is a struggle over the possession of Ada – where Stewart wishes to have her and Ada wishes to resist. 'Where love reigns, there is no will to power; and where the will to power is paramount, love is lacking. The one is but the shadow of the other.' (Jung, 1917/1926/1943: para. 78). It is only Flora's distraught cry for her mother that unwittingly saves Ada from Stewart.

Stewart boards up the house and bars the door from the outside before nightfall. He has to teach her a lesson. Just as we can understand his sexual violence towards Ada as a compulsive expression of his own sexual desire through taking sexual control of her, we can understand his imprisonment of Ada as an expression of the way in which he has always imprisoned his own emotional self (Dawson, 1997: 263). Despite his conscious intention to love Ada, his innate capacity to love and be loved has been split off and boarded up in the unconscious shadow.

Ada appears later that night as if pulled deeper inside herself, playing the piano in her sleep. Still later, she rises again, this time with the impulse to touch her husband. Ada is trapped in the house but her desire had been awakened with a directionless longing for the touch of skin. She lifts the bedclothes and his nightshirt, exposing his chest. His eyes welling with tears, Stewart is caught in conflicting emotions at his wife's touch – both wanting her to continue and, at the same time, being horrified. Finally, he turns from her unable to bear the tension: 'I want to touch you, why can't I touch you? Don't you like me?'

When the unconscious gains ascendancy, it wields a force that can invalidate all conscious contents (Jung, 1917/1926/1943: para. 344). At this point in the film, the ego consciousness and adaptive personas of all four of the characters are disintegrating and the unconscious shadow is in ascendancy. Not knowing that Ada has been locked in her house, Baines assumes her answer is no and prepares to leave his cabin, his livelihood and his life with the Maori. Flora separates from her mother and aligns with Stewart, chastising her mother for trying to see Baines. Stewart is caught between being aroused by his wife's touch and, at the same time, being filled with shame and disappointment at not being allowed to touch her. Ada, too, is in the grip of the unconscious shadow – no longer constricted by her wilful isolation, – she succumbs to the repressed desire rising within her and her longing to be with Baines.

Ada and Flora awake the next morning to find Stewart ripping down the boards that imprison him. Stewart comes in after dismantling his fortification. 'We must get on, I've decided to trust you to stay here. You won't see Baines.' Stewart is once again hoping that things between them can 'begin again', that with a new start, he and they can be in relationship in the way he always imagined. But as soon as Stewart leaves, Ada engraves a love message for Baines on the side of a piano key. She wraps the key and tells Flora to take this package to Baines.

But again, Flora is also caught up in the ascendancy of the unconscious shadow and takes the fork in the road that brings her mother's message to Stewart. Stewart reads the message and races back to the house with axe in hand. He first attacks the piano and then drags his wife to the chopping block, demanding: 'Do you love him? Is it him you love?' Stewart's full rage and fury, so long repressed by his need to maintain his virtuous persona, is now unleashed. Flora screams. Ada stands and then collapses.

Again, Flora is used – this time to transport her mother's severed finger with a message from Stewart to Baines: if Baines sees her again, he will chop off the next and the next.

That night Stewart carries a lamp into Ada's room. She is asleep but he speaks to her as if she were awake. 'You pushed me too hard, you cannot send love to him, you can not do that. Even to think about it makes me very angry.' Some moments later he says, 'I meant to love you, I clipped your wings, that is all.' He notices she is sweating and pulls the covers down to cool her. He begins to stroke the exposed skin of her thigh then buries his face between her legs. But she wakes without speaking and he gently replaces her gown. Stewart watches her as if listening to her speak, so faint and distant that it requires great concentration. As he watches her, his face transforms as he leans closer, still listening.

Stewart moves through the shadows of the dark bush to Baines' cabin. Baines wakes with a start, Stewart's gun in his face. Stewart speaks: 'I look at you, at your face. I have had that face in my head, hating it. But now I am here seeing it . . . It is nothing . . . you have your marks, you look at me through your eyes, yes, you are even afraid of me.'

Stewart appears altered by the catastrophic events of the day and is no longer the closed and contained man. Just as he had been able to listen to Ada's wordless speech, he is able to see through his shadow projection onto Baines to the man himself. Stewart asks Baines: 'Has Ada ever spoken to you? Have you ever heard words?' Stewart lifts his hand to his forehead: 'She has spoken to me. I heard it here. I heard her voice here in my head. I watched her lips. They did not make the words. Yet the harder I listened, the clearer I heard her, as clear as I hear my own voice. She said, "I am afraid of my will, of what it might do. It is so strange and strong." She said, "I have to go . . . Let me go . . . Let Baines take me away . . . Let Baines try and save me . . ." I wish her gone . . . I wish you gone . . . I want to wake and find that this is all a dream . . . That's what I want.'

Stewart was able to listen to, and to hear, Ada's intuitive communication through his own intuitive function. He was also able to respond to who she really was and not who he wanted her to be through his feeling function. Although these functions, these capacities, were available to him at that moment, they will most likely never be integrated, because he 'wants to wake up from them'. He wants to wake up from this dream, from the penetration of split-off potential, and find himself safe once again in his introverted sensate world – a world within which his prescribed duty is to maintain fences around his property and around his psyche. Unless the neglected shadow aspects participate in life, the wholeness of the individuation process cannot be reached (Jacobi, 1967: 43). It appears that Stewart isn't able to suffer the recognition and integration of these events but rather wants to re-establish the rigid divide between conscious and unconscious that has always kept him safe even as it inured his emotional alienation and psychological poverty.

Meeting one's opposite is not a thought-out compromise but rather a result of suffering a conflict. 'We learn by experience, mostly unpleasant, through collisions of all kinds, through disappointments and illnesses that we, as much as other people, have shadow qualities' (ibid.: 39). We can integrate unconscious content only when it is grasped not just intellectually but according to its feeling value. Suffering is an indispensable part of it.

Flora's angel wings are fallen. Ada, too, is altered as she emerges into the morning sun. Ada, Flora, Baines and the piano are gathered on the beach to set sail for Nelson, leaving this life behind. Baines insists that they bring Ada's piano and it is securely mounted on the canoe. But once at sea, Ada insists that it be thrown overboard. Baines tries to assure her that the piano can be fixed but she wants it gone. And yet as Ada watches the ropes snake past her feet, she places her foot in line with the rope. Should she not share the same fate as the piano? Were she and her piano not one? The rope tightens and grips her ankle – pulling her overboard.

As Ada is pulled under by the weight of the piano, something else inside her allows her to make another choice. This is the moment in the film that portrays how the conflict of opposites in Ada's life takes her to the breaking point. Such a peak of tension is necessary for activation of the transcendent function. According to Jung, the transcendent function is the capacity of the psyche to transcend the gulf between such opposites – between the conscious and the unconscious – to which no solution can otherwise be found. Then, 'if all goes well, the solution seemingly of is own accord, appears out of nature. Then and only then is it convincing. It is felt as grace' (Jung, 1961: 335).

Just as she frees herself from the rope and the piano that is dragging her down, Ada is finally able to kick off her former constriction and struggle to the surface to encounter new possibilities.

> *What a death. What a chance. What a surprise.*
> *My will has chosen life.*
> *Still it has had me spooked and many others beside.*

We are told by her young voice that she now teaches piano in Nelson and that she is learning to speak. Having survived the struggle between opposites, it appears that a point of equilibrium has emerged, allowing a new, more solid foundation for Ada's personality. It is this that will allow Ada to live out both her life with Baines as well as her life with the piano (Jung, 1917/1926/1943: para. 365).

But the film does not end here. Unlike Stewart, who wants to wake up from his confrontation with the shadow as if it were a dream, Ada continues to reflect on that shadow part of her life that was not chosen, because it is her dream. Again, the young voice of Ada affirms her active participation with unconscious processes – gaining possession of them by allowing them to possess her (ibid.: para. 368). She reminds us of the ongoing mystery of the unconscious shadow, that the shadow is never emptied, that the shadow is never gone and that the shadow always requires us to relate to it in the depths of psyche.

> *At night I think of my piano in its ocean grave and sometimes of myself floating above it. Down there everything is so still and silent that it lulls me to sleep.*
> *It is a weird lullaby and so it is; it is mine.*

There is a silence where hath been no sound.
There is a silence where no sound may be,
In the cold grave — under the deep, deep sea.

Note

My thanks to Dr. Boris Matthews for his scholarly contribution to the preparation of this paper.

References

Dawson, T. (1997) Jung, literature and literary criticism. In T. Dawson and P. Young-Eisendrath (eds.), *The Cambridge Companion to Jung*. Cambridge: Cambridge University Press.

Harding, E. (1945) *The Shadow*. New York: Spring Publications.

Jacobi, J. (1967) *The Way of Individuation*. New York: Harcourt, Brace and World.

Jung, C. G. (1917/1926/1943) *On the Psychology of the Unconscious, Collected Works 7*. Princeton: Princeton University Press.

Jung, C. G. (1961) *Memories, Dreams, Reflections*. New York: Random House.

Jung, C. G. (1973) *C. G. Jung Letters, Volume 1* (G. Adler, ed.). London: Routledge and Kegan Paul.

Jung, C. G. (1984) *Dream Analysis: Notes on the Seminars given in 1928–1930* (W. McGuire, ed.). Princeton: Princeton University Press.

Stevens, A. (1990) *On Jung*. London: Routledge.

von Franz, M.-L. (1974/1995) *Shadow and Evil in Fairy Tales*. New York: Spring Publications.

West, R. (2007) *Out of the Shadow: Ecopsychology, Story, and Encounters with the Land*. Charlottesville and London: University of Virginia Press.

Chapter 16

The dark feminine in Aronofsky's *The Wrestler*

Lydia Lennihan

>
> *Cassidy:* He was pierced for our transgressions, He was crushed for our iniquities. The punishment that brought us peace was upon Him, and by His wounds we were healed.
> *Randy:* What's that?
> *Cassidy:* It's from *The Passion of Christ*. Never seen it? Dude, you gotta. It's *amazing*.
> *Randy:* Huh. I'll have to check it out.

This is a conversation early on in the film *The Wrestler* (Aronofsky, 2009), when Cassidy (Marisa Tomei), a stripper in her mid thirties, is talking to Randy 'The Ram' Robinson (Mickey Rourke), a professional wrestler in his late forties. The subject of Christ and sacrifice is introduced through the lens of cinema, spectacle, and spectator. This is something Cassidy and Randy are intimately and painfully familiar with, as their professional identities, their personas, are based on their performances and their bodies. Jung describes the persona as 'that which in reality one is not, but which oneself as well as others think one is . . . the temptation to be what one seems to be is great, because the persona is usually rewarded in cash' (Jung, 1990/1950, para. 221). They use their professional names with each other, as they have no idea who the other is outside of their identities of performance.

The baby boomer generation (those Americans born between 1946 and 1964) represents the collective unconscious that this film speaks to, as it progresses into its elder years. Like the character of Randy, we are acutely aware of the aging process as we unexpectedly lose the physical strength and mental acuity that we used to take for granted and friends of our own age die. We don't recognize the older face that stares back at us in the mirror; its unfamiliarity startles us at times. According to a study by Deborah Hasin, we are getting more depressed as we age. She states that there has been a 'shift in highest lifetime risk from young to middle-aged adults in major depressive disorders' (Hasin, 2005). In an interview with Joan Arehart-Treichel, Hasin says she 'suspects that it may reflect depressed baby boomers moving into middle age – the same age cohort reflecting their increased risk as they march through the decades.' (Arehart-Treichel, 2005).

The Wrestler illustrates the price we pay when we develop the ego in such a way that it becomes identified with the persona. This is done at the expense of cultivating relationship and feeling with ourselves, particularly the relationship with the Self. If Randy 'the Ram' is the king who must die in order to live, then perhaps 'he has become the carrier of a myth, that is to say, of the statements of the collective unconscious' (Jung, 1989/1954, para. 349) that we need to pay attention to for our own renewal in our elder years. Jung states that 'the need for renewal [is] self evident, since the magic of the king decreased with age' (Jung, 1989/1954, para. 369).

At the film's opening, we see Randy's heyday illustrated in posters and newspaper clippings from the 1980s, when he was in his prime and performing at Madison Square Garden to large crowds. The movie begins twenty years later, with Randy in an elementary schoolroom, exhausted after his latest small-town match, sitting bent over in a metal folding chair, drinking a miniature bottle of Jack Daniels as he collects himself. The elementary school room prefigures the necessary return and regression to the pre-wrestler identity of 'Robin' that Randy will have to experience if he is to survive, by reclaiming and developing his feeling function. He is now in his late forties, broke, alone, and exhausted, with his options running out. Unknown to him, his heart, the organ of feeling, is in need of a bypass. Randy has dealt with his body's aging process and its vulnerability by denying it what it needs, and he is now literally killing himself with his stock in trade. The main relationships in his life besides his wrestling colleagues are Cassidy, who is also at the end of her performance career, and his estranged daughter Stephanie, a recovering alcoholic. Both women represent the dark feminine; the wounded feeling that Randy needs to engage with to resolve his suffering. He becomes bitter and impoverished as his body continues its disintegration process and takes his once profitable livelihood away. Cassidy plans to remake herself and start a new life with her child, and Stephanie is making amends and is back in college, but Randy has trouble making a break with his old identity. His stage is the wrestling ring, placed above the adoring crowd, at an altitude that cultivates inflation of the warrior/hero, and with it, isolation. The story takes place in northern New Jersey during winter, and we can feel the chill of the frozen snow in the damp grey air.

As Randy drives home after the match, the camera focuses in on a small action figure of 'the Ram' from his World Wrestling Federation days mounted on the dashboard. Later, when Randy is locked out of his trailer because he is behind on the rent, we see a collage he has made inside his van of his glory days. He gazes at the shrine of his past victories in the ring, downing various prescription drugs for his pained body with a cold beer before he falls asleep in his sleeping bag. Randy wears his wounds visibly, and continues to seriously hurt himself in the wrestling matches he participates in to pay his rent. His persona and the past seem to be the only things Randy has left to sustain him. His parka has electrical tape covering a tear in the sleeve, and he now wears a hearing aid and reading glasses. He is an old, scarred warrior now, and his laboured breathing turns into billows of mist in the frozen air, hinting of his heart disease and his 'waterlogged unconscious complexes' that will soon undo him (Edinger, 1985, p. 42).

Much like the king in Jung's *Mysterium Coniunctionis* (1989/1954), Randy is being asked to renew in order to create meaning and wisdom in the second half of his life. In the 'Allegoria Merlini', which Jung discusses in *Mysterium*, 'the king has numerous connections with water. . . . The motif of drowning also takes the form of an inward drowning, namely dropsy' (Jung, 1989/1954, para. 360). Randy suffers from edema, or 'dropsy', produced by the anabolic steroids he injects, which increase blood sodium (salt), causing the retention of water and damage to the ventricles of the heart (George, 2003, p. 168). Like the king in Jung's story, Randy retains water internally that 'already has that decomposing and dissolving property which anticipates the king's dismemberment' (Jung, 1989/1954, para. 361).

Alchemically, 'the outstanding properties of salt are bitterness and wisdom,' they both 'form a pair of opposites with a third thing between. The factor common to both . . . is, psychologically, the function of feeling. Tears, sorrow and disappointment are bitter, but wisdom is the comforter in all psychic suffering' (Jung,1989/1954, para. 330). Salt, as the symbol of bitterness and wisdom, is a process for working through painful, dark feelings, and is 'coordinated with the nature of woman,' also known as *luna sal*, the moist realm of the dark feminine, the soul, and feeling. It is aligned with the moon and the earth; the underworld of the darkness, and compensates for the solar masculine (Jung, 1989/1954, paras. 321, 330). The salt in Randy's blood is a symbol for his challenge to work through his feelings of melancholy, which reside in the realm of the feminine underworld; in other words, through his relationships with these two women, which are grounded in facing his own fears.

The king, like the ram, has to be sacrificed or killed for life to be renewed. He 'represents a dominant of consciousness, such as a generally accepted principle of a collective conviction or a traditional view' (Jung, 1989/1954, para. 424). The collective consciousness that Randy symbolizes is one of inflation, performance, and brute force. The dominant attitude in the US is one that devalues the feeling function, relationship, and the feminine. Like Randy, we collectively need to compensate for the one-sidedness of our own culture.

The domain of the feminine, the elderly, the lunar hero, and the vulnerable, along with their feelings, does not interest our culture. We want to be entertained, and we bore easily due to our inability to hold onto any thought or emotion longer than a sound bite. We grasp the TV remote control, but the images that flash across the screen have become meaningless and without depth. The psyche searches for a new symbol in this desolate landscape, but finds precious little. 'The psyche no longer feels wholly contained in the dominant, whereupon the dominant loses its fascination and no longer grips the psyche so completely as before' (Jung, 1989/1954, para. 505). The fabric of the collective, a delicate material at best, unravels and frays in terms of the relationships that are the substance of society. The individual now comes before the community, and social cohesion decays.

The Wrestler illustrates the need for the integration of these two opposites: light and shadow, bitterness and wisdom, masculine and feminine, creating a third option, the transcendent function, 'the function of *feeling*' (Jung, 1989/1954, para. 330).

Randy and Cassidy are modern versions of Aphrodite (Venus) and Ares (Mars), ancient and powerful gods who had several children together, including the god Eros (feeling) (Chevalier and Gheerbrant, 1996/1994, p. 32, 40). They are archetypes that held the mysteries of life, death, and war. Jung tells us that 'Venus appears as the feminine aspect of the king' (Jung, 1989/1954, para. 416), or his anima. *The Wrestler* illustrates how these archetypes of the masculine and the feminine have been trivialized and split in our culture. Instead of the sacred temple whore or *meretrix*, who represented the 'arcane substance in its initial "chaotic", maternal state' (Jung, 1989/1954, para. 415), the dark feminine is now reduced to a flat persona of sexual object. Ares is now an enfeebled old and angry warrior, not the god who fought at Troy. He lacks the 'dark, chthonic aspect of nature' (Jung, 1989/1954, para. 427) which he needs as a matrix to experience his own suffering and death. The opposite of the solar king 'is his own feminine chthonic aspect which he has forgotten. Sol's reflected light is the feminine Luna, who dissolves the king in her moistness' (Jung,1989/1954, para. 506). But our king Randy is more like Jason, who returned victorious but inflated, clutching the Golden Fleece, having betrayed the feminine and learned nothing from his tragic relationship with Medea. He dies alone and old, crushed beneath the hull of the Argos (Chevalier and Gheerbrant, 1996/1994, p. 443–44). Indeed, when Randy climbs into the ring for the last time, he is wearing the Golden Fleece of the sacrificed Chrysomallos, the beloved ram of Hermes, and has also rejected and been discarded by the dark feminine (Cirlot, 1971/1962, p. 120).

In *Mysterium Coniunctionis*, Jung describes the king as violent and 'morally defective' with an inflated and thirsty ego so that 'when he drinks he is overwhelmed by water, i.e. the unconscious, and medical help becomes necessary' (Jung, 1989/1954, para. 365). The king must dissolve in the unconscious and symbolically die in order to be renewed (Jung, 1989/1954, para. 381). Inevitably, our king Randy has a heart attack after a particularly brutal performance that involves a staple gun piercing and traumatizing his body, reminiscent of the suffering that initiates undergo (Turner, 1972/1967, p. 96). His heart cannot tolerate the pain and immolation of the flesh. Randy literalizes the symbolic death of the king because, as a warrior, he knows no other way to behave, and he is not yet ready to face the changes in his world and his body. He has not confronted the dark feminine, the aging body that is unconsciously bearing his suffering.

After Randy has his heart attack, he wakes up in the hospital, where his doctor tells him he has had a close brush with death, and that he needs to retire from wrestling. Randy's response is that he wants a second opinion; he is in denial – embittered and angry that his body has betrayed him. As he leaves the hospital, we hear geese in the background for the first time. Geese are symbolically associated with Ares and other warrior gods (Green, 1992, p. 126). Geese also symbolize the Great Mother, the descent into the underworld, and are an 'offshoot of the symbol of space-time, representing the dangers and fortunes of existence, prior to the return to the maternal bosom' (Cirlot, 1971/1962, p. 120). The geese foreshadow Randy's necessary pilgrimage to the underworld and the unconscious, his only chance for survival via a renewal through the anima. He must 'transform himself into the *prima materia* in the body of his mother, and return to the dark initial state which the alchemists called the "chaos".' (Jung, 1989/1954, para. 381). When he is called by his birth name 'Robin' in the pharmacy, he cringes at the sound. The name of the person who existed before Randy took on his identity as 'The Ram' is no longer familiar or desired. The affect Randy experiences upon hearing his younger name again suggests regression to the origins of the self and a return to painful childhood feelings, to vulnerability, and to the mother.

Randy's illness makes him realize that, although he has a few adoring fans left, he is alone. He tells Cassidy of his heart attack, and asks if she will start a relationship with him outside of the club. She tells him she cannot 'cross that line' between her professional and personal life, but suggests that he attempt a reconciliation with his daughter. She reluctantly offers to meet him at a used clothing store to help him find a gift for Stephanie, and they kiss, at which point she abruptly leaves. In the day, she is 'Pam,' a single mother who is planning on leaving the strip club and her professional persona to begin a new life.

When Randy tells his daughter of his heart attack, her reaction is not what he expects: 'You are such an asshole. What do you want from me? ... You want me to take care of you. ... Well I'm not going to do that. Where the fuck were you when I needed you to take care of me? ... I don't care if you had a heart attack, fuck you!'

In working through his feelings with Stephanie, Randy admits he has been a neglectful and narcissistic father during his daughter's life. He knows nothing about her, not even what she would like as a gift. He eventually spends time alone with Stephanie, and tells her, 'I just wanna tell you. I'm the one who was supposed to take care of everything. ... and now, I'm an old broken down piece of meat and I'm alone. I just don't want you to hate me.' We again hear the geese in the background as he drops Stephanie off and she hesitates in committing to a dinner date with him. After this hopeful meeting with his daughter, and the promise of a possible relationship in the kiss from Pam, Randy calls his promoter to cancel his scheduled twenty-year-reunion fight with his opponent from Madison Square Garden, 'The Ayatollah.' We feel optimistic that Randy will succeed in this, his most difficult bout of all, the descent into his feelings and the chthonic feminine, instead of acting out the destructive warrior in a bout that will literally, not symbolically, kill him.

We then see Randy at a wrestling match as a mere spectator this time, trying to adjust to not being in the centre of the ring. He has also taken a job in the supermarket deli, accepting the fact that he can no longer wrestle for a living. Regardless of his protesting, his nametag ironically has his 'birth' name of 'Robin' on it, a bird that symbolizes the spiritual link between heaven and earth (Chevalier and Gheerbrant, 1996/1994, p. 87). He is successfully making his descent from his throne and his persona. Happy about the possibility of relationships in his life, he goes to the strip club to thank Cassidy for her part in his successful reunion with Stephanie, but she is now polite and reserved, and tells him that a relationship with her is impossible. Humiliated and angry, Randy shoves money at her for a lap dance, since he is now 'just a stupid customer.' Cassidy refuses his money and is deeply hurt by the exchange. Randy storms out of the club, immersed in disappointment and anger, yet here he has another chance to work through his emotions via the feminine. Jung observes that, 'disappointment . . . is not only the mother of bitterness but the strongest incentive to a differentiation of feeling' (Jung, 1989/1954, para. 334). Randy needs to differentiate his feelings and reflect; instead he goes from victory to defeat in minutes. There is no nuance or any in-between state for him.

Randy reacts by going out with his old friends, and stays out all night drinking and having sex with a 'ring-rat' female admirer. This leads to him missing his dinner date with Stephanie. When Randy tries to apologize, she tells him, 'I don't hate you. I don't love you. I don't even like you. I was stupid to think that you could change.' It is a painful end to their tenuous reunion, and their relationship.

Randy returns to work the next day, and a customer asks him if he is 'Randy the Ram.' The more Randy denies it, the more the guy keeps insisting until Randy is so angry and frustrated that he intentionally slices the end of his thumb off, and, smearing blood on his face like Ares in battle, storms out of the market. In this scene, the salt here 'assumes the appearance of blood.' Jung quotes Dorn the physician as saying 'salt, the natural balsam of the body, is begotten from human blood. It has within it both corruption and preservation against corruption, for in the natural order there is nothing that does not contain as much evil as good' (quoted in Jung, 1989/1954, para. 337). Randy climbs into his van, soothing himself by saying, 'Oh Robin, Robin.' But then he catches himself, and disconnects from his painful feelings once again by answering back, 'It's not Robin! It's *Randy*!' The opposition of thinking and feeling, masculine and feminine, bitterness and wisdom is painfully rendered in this scene, all symbolized by Randy's blood and its inherent salt. It is at this point that Randy drives off to call the promoter to tell him the anniversary fight is back on. He goes home to peroxide his hair, spray on a tan and shave his body hair in preparation for his final match. If Randy cannot descend into the realm of the dark feminine and feelings, he will again attempt to literalize the king's death in the ring in order to stop the existential pain and identify with the divine. It is ironic that to do so he is seen to be preparing his body and himself much as a woman would for a man.

As Randy is loading up his van for his trip to the match, Cassidy arrives. She tells him, 'Look, I know I came off like a bitch the other day and I'm really sorry. You know I didn't mean those things that I said. You're not just another customer.' But Randy has already made up his mind. He hands her a flyer for the Fanfest event, and drives off. He cannot stay with the pain or feel the emotions and vulnerability that a relationship with Cassidy requires. Horrified that he is going to fight again, Cassidy drives all night to attend the match, arriving just as Randy is finishing saying a prayer before he goes on stage. She pleads with him not to fight, but he tells her, 'The world don't give a shit about me.... Hey, you hear them? *This* is where I belong. I gotta go.' Randy climbs into the ring, grabs the microphone and, as he looks back at Pam, he tells the audience how much he appreciates them, especially when 'you can lose everything that you love and everyone that loves you.... You're my family.' Randy wrestles with the Ayatollah, who is surprised at Randy's aggression. He offers to lighten things up, but Randy refuses. Staggering on the mat, with great difficulty Randy climbs the ropes to execute a final 'ram jam,' the move that he is famous for. The last shot we see is of Randy airborne, his arms in the sign of the ram on either side of his head. Unable to deal with the one-sided bitterness of salt in this world, he would rather leave it by flying into the heroic otherworld of the archetypal warrior.

Randy attempts, but fails, to descend and confront the feminine, as expressed in his feelings and vulnerability, and his unconscious. He acts as if his body does not exist in real time, but, like a statue of a god, is immortalized in past victories and glory. James Hillman tells us that 'transformation, to be genuine and thorough, always affects the body' (Hillman, 1993/1965, p. 71). He goes on to say that 'the medical image of health, with its expectations upon life, simply does not allow enough for suffering ... the disease is the suffering not from which the patient must be saved but the condition necessary for salvation' (ibid., p. 158–59). If this idea is transposed onto the collective unconscious of the baby boomer generation, we see that we, like Randy, need to confront not only our suffering and aging bodies, but our souls. To do this, we need to navigate between the opposites of *Logos* and *Eros* and find the third thing, the transcendent function, to find wisdom, not bitterness, in aging.

Collectively, we need the lunar salt, the descent into the darkness and the shadow, but in our culture 'the sun [is] always shining and smiles back. There is no room for any prestige-diminishing weakness, so the *sol niger* [black sun] is never seen. Only in solitary hours is its presence feared' (Jung, 1989/1954, para. 330). In one scene, as Randy is crying, he tells his daughter, 'I am a broken down piece of meat, I'm alone.' He realizes the need to feel, to suffer, to be in relationship in order to attain balance.

Our dominant collective consciousness also needs to face the darkness, the suffering of the body, of life, of our own salt. Otherwise, we will 'suffer a spiritual death in so far as [we] cannot get beyond [our] one-sidedness of the cultural collective,' and worse, deprive ourselves of the profound meaning of life, and with it, our own death (Jung, 1989/1954, para. 257). Jung found that 'at the dissolution of living bodies it [salt] is the "last residue of corruption," but it is [also] the "prime agent in generation." ' Jung notes that salt is identified with the uroboros, the dragon biting its own tail; its end is its beginning (Jung, 1989/1954, para 338). In the rotting flesh is the birth of the emerald tablet, the gold that is the individuation process. Our culture's feelings reside in the collective shadow that we work so tirelessly to avoid, 'for it is a bitter thing to pass through this valley of the shadow. . . . As the alchemists said, it begins with the *nigredo*, or generates it as the indispensable prerequisite for synthesis, for unless opposites are constellated and brought to consciousness they can never be united' (Jung, 1989/1954, para. 346).

References

Arehart-Treichel, J. (2005) Growing Depression Risk Faces Baby Boomers. In *Psychiatric News*, *40*(21), 20.

Aronofsky, D. (dir.) (2009) *The Wrestler* [DVD]. Beverly Hills, CA: Twentieth Century Fox Home Entertainment.

Chevalier, J. and Gheerbrant, A. (1996/1994) *The Penguin Dictionary of Symbols*. (J. Buchanan-Brown, Trans.). London: Penguin Books.

Cirlot, J. E (1971/1962) *A Dictionary of Symbols* (2nd ed) (J. Sage, Trans.) New York: Philosophical Library.

Edinger, E. F. (1985) *Anatomy of the Psyche: Alchemical Symbolism in Psychotherapy*. La Salle, IL: Open Court.

George, A. J. (2003) Androgenic anabolic steroids. In D.R. Mottram (ed.), *Drugs in Sport* (3rd ed.) (pp. 138–83). London: Routledge.

Green, M. (1992) *Animals in Celtic Life and Myth*. London and New York: Routledge.

Hasin, D. (2005) Epidemiology of Major Depressive Disorder Results From the National Epidemiologic Survey on Alcoholism and Related Conditions. *Archive of General Psychiatry*, *62*, 1097–1106.

Hillman, J. (1993/1965) *Suicide and the Soul*. Dallas, TX: Spring.

Jung, C. G. (1989/1954) *Mysterium Coniunctionis: An Inquiry into the Separation and Synthesis of Psychic Opposites in Alchemy*. Bollingen Series XX, Collected Works, Vol. 14 (R.F.C. Hull, Trans.). Princeton: Princeton University Press.

Jung, C. G. (1990/1950) *Concerning Rebirth*. Bollingen Series XX, Collected Works, Vol. 9 (i) (R.F.C. Hull, Trans.). Princeton: Princeton University Press.

Turner, V. (1972/1967) *The Forest of Symbols: Aspects of Ndembu Ritual*. Ithaca and London: Cornell University Press.

Chapter 17

The archetype of transformation in Maya Deren's film rituals

Michelangelo Paganopoulos

Introduction: Deren's 'ritualistic' cinema

A ritual is an action distinguished from all others in that it seeks the realisation of its purpose through exercise of form. In this sense ritual is art; and even historically, all art derives from ritual.

(Notes from *Ritual in Transfigured Time*)

Maya Deren (1917–1961), the dancer, film-maker, and avant-garde artist, made an effort to create a 'ritualistic form' of cinema (Jackson 2002: 131) by developing the avant-garde theatrical concept of 'primitivism' – a return to the archaic 'roots' of ritual as the revitalization of the 'carnival spirit' in ecstatic performances characterized by ambivalence, the 'irrational', the 'subliminal', and the grotesque. It was seen as a 'quasi-mystical therapeutic' way of liberating the unconscious (Innes 1981: 16; 1993: 14), expressed in archaic tongues, and using gestures ('*Gestalt*'), an acting method taken from the Brechtian theatre used to alienate the audience through using puppet-like caricatures instead of characters. Furthermore, the 'Theatre of Cruelty' of Antoine Artaud, the 'Theatre of the Absurd' of Ionesco and Pinter, the 'Poor Theatre' of Jerzy Grotowski, and the 'Holy Theatre' of Peter Brook all produced *liminoid* performances, meaning 'individual products' with 'collective or "mass effects" ' (Turner 1982: 54–55; 1987: 29–30), which were staged as initiation rites. As in rituals, the directors engaged their limited audiences into the performance by demanding their active participation, aiming for the collective transformation of both actors and audiences 'into *an-other*' (Innes 1993: 11). The themes of their plays were also ritualistic, based on archetypal and universal myths. Artaud called this the 'total theatre', a term he coined from his research on Balinese theatre in describing 'an impression of inhumanity, of divinity, of miraculous revelation', and achieving 'the total effect of revelation, whose crests sway rhythmically, responding consciously, it seems, to the slightest movements of their bodies' (Artaud 1988: 220–221).

In three short silent films, *Meshes of the Afternoon* (1943), *At Land* (1944), and *Ritual in Transfigured Time* (1946), Deren incorporated 'ritualistic' elements to technically develop a new form of film-making, in an effort to create a film event in which the audience would actively engage through the movement of the camera, rhythmical editing, and photography enriched with archetypal symbolism:

> Ritual is an act whose very form is so principal . . . that it passes far beyond casual naturalism . . . the main effort has been to create dance out of non-dance elements by filmic manipulation. In this sense, the pattern . . . transcends the intentions and the movements of the individual performers and for this reason I call it Ritual . . . Being a film ritual, it is achieved not only in spatial terms but in terms of a Time created by the camera. Time, here is not an emptiness to be measured by a spatial activity which may fill it. On the contrary, in this film it not only actually creates many of the actions and events, but constitutes the special integrity of the form as a whole.
>
> (Deren, cited in Jackson 2002: 138)

In this context, Deren's film-rituals are manufactured 'total events'. Crucially, she distinguished between performance and form, in terms of the former being 'consciously chosen' while the latter functions from the unconscious (Jackson 2002: 136). The form of her films, the hypnotic rhythm of editing, use of hand-held camera and discontinuity of freeze frames, spatial fragmentation and reversal of movement, use of slow-motion to stretch time and close-ups to exaggerate emotion, all contribute to the manipulation of time and space. By disorienting the viewer, she created an initiatory experience, a 'rite of passage' (Van Gennep [1909], cited in Turner 1967: 93–111), which would actively work on and engage with the unconscious of the audience. The director Deren controls the aesthetical world of the audience's conscious *cosmos*, becoming the charismatic priestess in a film-ritual, which aims to transform each viewer from within.

Hauke and Alister have described cinema as a kind of '*temenos* . . . an active imaginative space . . . which can then engage the unconscious'. Watching a film in a cinema is an experience of 'psyche-in-projection' that is 'set apart' from daily life, 'in a dark place dedicated to this purpose ... where psyche can come alive, be experienced and be commented upon' (Hauke and Alister 2001: 2). From this post-Jungian perspective, cinema is a kind of 'Celluloid Church ... a modern metaphor of Durkheim's sacred "Church" ' (Paganopoulos 2010: par. 1, 3): the separate space in which 'collective representations' (Levy-Bruhl 1926) express a unified system of belief that supports a moral order through 'things apart and forbidden' (Durkheim 1979: 29). For both Jung and Durkheim, ritual was a matter of *experience*; the personal way to connect to the wider collective through the luminous experiential concept of the 'numinous' (Otto 1958: 5–11). This is manifested in both rituals and films, which bring on the surface certain *a priori* forces kept within us: on the one hand, Jung's concept of 'collective unconscious' which assumes the primacy and reality of the psyche, and on the other, Durkheim's concept of 'collective consciousness' which begins with 'society' as the *a priori* external force that influences our everyday being.

Deren's films about rituals illustrate the tensional but also complementary relationship between the collective unconscious (internal) of the director and the collective consciousness (external) of her society. Particularly, *Ritual in Transfigured Time*, which portrays the initiation and descent of a young girl into the dark abyss of her soul, is Deren's personal journey from the surface of the collective consciousness of her bourgeois background into the depths of her unconscious. The film's rich dream symbolism of the metamorphosis of widow to bride invites 'Jung's theory of symbols of transformation [which] provides a language to understand the permutations of desire in cultural psychology' (Williams 2001: 121). By referring to the archetypal themes of transformation in relation to anthropological approaches to phenomena of possession, as filmed in her documentary *Divine Horsemen*, this chapter will highlight Deren's fusion of fiction and reality in making her life the heroine of her films, in order to reflect on the 'dark' Other as the collective libido of Western culture.

The theme of transformation in *Ritual in Transfigured Time* (1946)

This film begins by showing two sides of womanhood: a sophisticated lady of higher society, played by the writer Anaïs Nin, is juxtaposed with the wild and free spirit of the Trinidad dancer Rita Christiani. The opening frame is divided by a dark wall between two doors that lead to a bright room at the background. Anaïs Nin appears standing at the left door, smiling at the camera. She moves behind the wall to the right side of the frame, picks up a thread of wool, and returns to the left of the frame, where she begins to knit, posing at the camera, as if she is in a 1950s television advertisement. Suddenly, Christiani enters the frame from the camera's position in the foreground. In a close-up, she looks ecstatic, slowly moving in trance through the right door. The camera follows her hypnotic movement, taking us into her dream world. As Rita enters the room, Anaïs remains still, like a statue with her arms outstretched, holding the wool, and positioned in such a way as if they are calling for Rita, who approaches with her right hand outstretched. The scene resembles a spiritual séance: Anaïs calling for the spirit, which arrives in the form of Rita. She sits opposite Anaïs, and starts pulling the wool into a ball. This movement initiates a choreographed scene of knitting, which is reversed by technical means, as in a process of deconstruction. Anaïs begins to talk, to smile, and is confident, in contrast to the lost spirit of Rita, who stares silently into space. Suddenly, Maya Deren appears at the back of the room, looking at the two women, but only Rita takes notice of her. Deren is discontented with Anaïs, who continues with her reversed choreographed movement, but this time filmed in slow-motion and accompanied by close-ups of her frozen facial expressions which exaggerate the hypocrisy of her face. She moves like a puppet, as if she is controlled by strings, or the very thread that she thinks she controls. Her puppet-like presence, as in the caricature characters of Brechtian theatre, ironically undermines her bourgeois way of life.

Rita, in between the two women, or two worlds, waits until the thread finishes, and then submissively follows Deren through a third door which leads to a bourgeois party of high society. It is a male-dominated and aggressive world of lustful fake smiles. Rita dances elegantly, floating around the crowd. Her movement reveals her spiritual nature in contrast to the aggressive movement of a crowd of men competing over her. As in the portrayal of Anaïs, freeze frames interrupt the continuity of the film, revealing in close-ups the hypocrisy of those bourgeois smiles; the real faces underneath the masked *personas*. Rita begins to feel increasingly anxious and entrapped by this male-dominated world. As she looks for an escape, she falls out of the sky into the arms of the living statue of the choreographer Frank Westbrook.

The third sequence takes place in a Roman amphitheatre. Westbrook's body postures imitate those of ancient Hellenic statues, the classical 'perfect body'. But despite their playful relationship, he betrays and ignores Rita, continuing with a set of self-indulgent moves, as she disappears alone in the wilderness. But then the film turns into a nightmare, as he runs after her. Freeze frames show him moving from one statue to the next, as he/they approach her. Terrified, she runs with dance-leaps towards the ocean. She then falls into the dark abyss of deep water, wearing a white wedding gown. The symbolism of the final scene, which is shot in negative, is amplified by the sharp contrast of the brightness of the falling bride and the darkness of the abyss of her soul. Inside the ocean, she is transformed and reborn into a bride, as if she is a butterfly. For Jung, water 'is the commonest symbol for the unconscious . . . which lies, as it were, underneath consciousness' (1968a: 18):

> Whoever looks into the mirror of the water will see first of all his own face. Whoever goes to himself risks a confrontation with himself. The mirror does not flatter, it faithfully shows whatever looks into it; namely, the face we never show to the world because we cover it with the *persona*, the mask of the actor. But the mirror lies behind the mask and shows the true face.
>
> (Jung 1968a: 20)

Marcel Mauss (1985) in his essay on 'the notion of the person' and the 'notion of the self', drew an evolutionary chart of the development of the *persona*, beginning with the sacred use of masks in rituals, continuing to the legal constitution of the Roman person, and through the Christian 'moral person' to contemporary concepts of the 'self'. Deren reveals the bourgeois mask that hides the real self/society underneath it, as she reverses the 'mirror of water' towards the world she comes from, reflecting on the hypocrisy of her own life in New York. The still-frames of extreme close-ups of the anonymous crowd show their faces frozen, as if they are wearing a mask, revealing the male aggression underneath the hypocrisy of the bourgeois etiquette of conduct. The instinctive escape of Rita into the ocean expresses Deren's own desire to escape from the constraints of bourgeois life and transform into *an-Other*: 'a long-drawn-out process of inner transformation and rebirth into another being. This "other being" is the other person in ourselves . . . the inner friend of the soul . . . Our attitude towards the inner voice alternates between two extremes; it is regarded as undiluted nonsense or as the voice of God' (Jung 1968a: 131–132).

Jung wrote that the blocking of the psyche can lead 'to an accumulation of instinctuality and in consequence, to excess and aberrations of all kinds . . . among them sexual disturbances' (Jung 1967: 169). In Deren's film, these are portrayed by Rita's terror of the male perfect body, and her instinctive reaction to run towards the ocean, away from bourgeois life, and into absolute darkness: 'The treasure which the hero fetches from the dark cavern is life: it is himself, new-born from the dark maternal cave of the unconscious where he was stranded by the introversion or regression of libido' (Jung 1967: 374). In liberating herself, Rita walks into the ocean as if she commits suicide. In this sense, the last sequence portrays a self-sacrifice, which Jung describes as the precondition of the manifestation of the Archetype of the Transformation of the Libido. The act of letting go 'is really carrying the sacrificial act on itself' and shows 'individuality in the highest sense' that 'can be called transcendent' (Jung 1969: 258). The ambiguity of the transformation is visualized in the final shot of the metamorphosis of Rita, which carries a multiple and dynamic meaning, amplified by its negative association – shot in negative film – to the institution of marriage (on 'amplification' see Fredericksen 2001: 34–40). The negative film ironically reverses the meaning of the Jungian theme of 'sacred marriage', 'the integration of the conscious and unconscious by analogizing it along gender lines as in alchemical symbolism' (Hauke and Alister 2001: 6–7). In this context, *Ritual in Transfigured Time* reverses the 'subjective' and 'natural transformation' of a girl into a bride, to the metamorphosis of a widow to a bride, making the film in itself an ambiguous transcendental experience, which ambitiously aimed to transform the audience participating, as in the process of 'transformation induced by ritual' (Jung 1968a: 119–134).

Hauke and Alister observed that Jung 'saw a good deal of the pathologies of the individual and of society as arising from our failure to attend to a sophisticated, conscious rationality and other aspects of the psyche such as the spiritual, historical, communal, and fantasy' (2001: 7). In the film, these two realms are juxtaposed through the conflict between the two women who call for Rita, representing two extremes: on the one hand, Anaïs, embodying the promise for a bourgeois, secure and sophisticated way of life, but entrapped in a wedding dress; and on the other, Deren, who encourages the promise of, and desire for, absolute freedom, symbolized by the liberation of Rita into the dark abyss. During the party scene, Rita is 'depersonalized', meaning she is alienated from the social environment. This is illustrated by her unique elegant movement which contrasts with the aggressive male crowd. She is structurally 'invisible' – in a *liminal* state of mind, 'betwixt and between' life and death, as if she is 'un-dead' (Turner 1967: 95–96).

> A ritual is characterized by the de-personalization of the individual. In some cases it is even marked by the use of masks and voluminous garments, so that the person of the performer is virtually anonymous;

and it is marked also by the participation of the community . . . as a homogeneous entity in which the inner patterns of relationship between the elements create, together, a large movement of the body as a whole. The intent of such a depersonalization is not the destruction of the individual; on the contrary, it enlarges him beyond the personal dimension . . . the collective is the creative artist.

(Notes from *Ritual in Transfigured Time*)

Rita is in a state of trance, as if she is possessed. The two women inside Rita, Anaïs and Deren, visualize the process of 'dissociation of consciousness that cannot any longer control the unconscious' (Jung 1968a: 40). Jung associated phenomena of possession with 'the same archetypal figures that activate the deliriums of psychotics' (ibid.). The struggle between consciousness and the unconscious makes it 'necessary to integrate the unconscious into consciousness . . . [and] arises the need for a synthesis of the two positions. This amounts to psychotherapy even on the primitive level, where it takes the form of restitution ceremonies' (ibid.). In this context, Levi-Strauss (1963) investigated the efficacy of symbols in shamanistic healing rituals, in a synthetic process of preconscious and conscious structures of the human mind, in order to show the affinity between shamanic curing and psychoanalysis.

In anthropology, possession has been defined as a 'formula of experience and emotion' (Kapferer 1983: 245), expressed through psychogenetic symbols in myths and rituals (Obeyesekere 1981: 14). Possession has 'the potential for individuation' (Corrin 1998: 101), in which the self finds expression 'within a symbolic' and a 'cultural order', through the body, 'the locus of negotiation between the spirits and the initiate and of the redefinition of her [initiated] identity' (ibid.: 85, 89). For Jung, the synthesis of unconscious contents into consciousness results in a 'psychic transformation', a rebirth that 'we recognize as an individuation process' (1968a: 147), 'the process by which a person becomes a psychological "in-dividual", that is, a separate, indivisible unity or "whole" (ibid.: 275). In this context, the film portrays the process of Rita's 'individuation', that is, 'a life in which the individual becomes what he always was' (Jung 1968a: 40).

Possession in *Divine Horsemen: The Living Gods of Haiti* (1953/1985)

At the end of *Ritual*, Rita/Deren escapes into the ocean. Rita's journey continued in Deren's real life, as she satisfied her libido by crossing the ocean towards the 'Oriental'. From 1946 to 1954, she frequently travelled to Haiti, gathering visual material of *Vodoun* dances, which she filmed between 1947 and 1951, and recording in a diary her own experiences of possession. She published her book in 1953, but the film was edited in 1977, several years after Deren's death, by her third husband Teiji Ito and his wife Cherel. It was released in 1985 as a documentary, with an added voiceover, under the title *Divine Horsemen: The Living Gods of Haiti*. During her trips, Deren met the ethnographer Madame Odette Rigaud and the psychologist Miss Ericka who were investigating possession as a healing process. After an incident with a seriously ill child, Deren came to question her own ethics on the field, and particularly her use of modernist poetic aesthetics for recording real situations. While in the beginning she thought of *Vodoun* only as a 'religion', disconnected from the reality of everyday life, during her fieldwork she realized that the practice is of as much importance as structure: 'Deren now realizes that in order for a visual representation of religious rituals to make sense, they need the observer's understanding of the rituals' "metaphysical context" ' (Jackson 2002: 151; Morris 2006: 195). In doing this, she described her personal experiences after being possessed by the *lwa* spirit of *Ezili Freda*, the archetype of 'a white woman, sensual, seductive with love of fine clothes and jewellery' (Morris 2006: 197). One evening when, among a number of *loa* spirits, the *Damballah* (the serpent spirit) and the *Agwe* (lord of the sea) visited the community, Deren suddenly fell possessed by *Ezili Freda*:

> The singing is at my very ear, inside my head. This sound will drown me! "Why don't they stop? Why don't they stop?" . . . It is too much, too bright, too white for me; this is its darkness. "Mercy!" I scream within me. I hear it echoed by the voices, shrill and unearthly: "Ezrulie!" The bright darkness floods up through my body, reaches my head, engulfs me. I am sucked down and exploded upward at once. That is all.
>
> (Deren 1953: 260)

The experience records the moment when the *loa* enters her body, echoing the transformation of Rita in the final sequence of *Ritual*, as both are gradually absorbed in the 'bright darkness' of lost consciousness. As the title of the film suggests, it is thought that the *lwa* enters and 'mounts'/'rides' the head of the possessed who becomes the living embodiment of God: 'To understand that the self must leave if the *loa* is to enter, is to understand that one cannot be man and god at once . . . The serviteur must be induced to surrender his ego, that the archetype become manifest' (Deren, quoted in Jackson 2002: 156). During possession, 'the *lwa* moves into the head of a person and in doing so displaces the individual's "big angel" . . . [that is] the seat of consciousness, emotions and sentiments. . . the personality of the individual' (Morris: 2006: 198, 200). The use of drumming is necessary in providing a common rhythm for all participants, the sound that 'unites' them, depersonalizing them through the collective (Deren 1953: 258), while allowing the archetypes to surface.

The film records the performances of several archetypal Gods surfacing on the anonymous bodies of 'depersonalized' humans. It depicts two types of action: possessions and communication with the *lwa* spirits[1], and ceremonial dances. Of particular importance is the God *Legba*, symbolized by the symbol of a cross-road, a circle with a cross in it, which is drawn on the ground with flour. The cross-road 'is the point of access to the world of The Invisibles, which is the soul of the cosmos' (Deren 1953: 35). A central archetypal God is *Ghede*, the Trickster and Wise Old Man. He arrives uninvited, dressed as a beggar, interrupting the ceremony in honour of *Azaka*, the God of agriculture. With the Trickster's arrival, some of the participants start falling in possession under various spirits, as the phenomenon spreads fast like a virus from one body to the next, forming a 'system of communication' (Lambek 1981: 181–182) between possessed and participants, with the 'priest' *Oungan* acting as the mediator between Gods and humans. Such acts of collective transcendence reveal the existence of a deeper archaic 'collective unconscious', which comes to the conscious surface through '*participation mystique*' (Jung 1969: 255). The dance brings out on the conscious surface archetypes of the anima-image: 'Among primitives, the soul is the magic breath of life (hence the term "anima"), or a flame' (Jung 1968a: 26) – the Flame of Artaud's theatre.

Conclusion: The Oriental as libido

> The primitive "perils of the soul" consist mainly of dangers to consciousness. Fascination, bewitchment, "loss of soul", possession, etc. are obviously phenomena of the dissociation and suppression of consciousness caused by unconscious contents. Even civilized man is not yet entirely free of the darkness of primeval times.
>
> (Jung 1969: 281)

The bourgeois obsession with the Other reveals the collective libido of a Western society fascinated with the exotic. This fascination with the

'Oriental' aimed to 'examine the degree of mental potential from which they have emerged' (Artaud 2001: 54). Deren developed her search towards a 'metaphysical' form of cinema, highlighting the importance of cultural understanding based on the 'equivalent character' and 'parallel function' of art and ritual, as the film becomes 'a cross-cultural counterpoint' analogous to the musical structure of a fugue (see Jackson 2002: 140–144 on the 'visual fugue' project). Her films are personal 'inverted journeys' (Jackson 2002: 191–199) on the margins between fiction and non-fiction, as the comparison of *Ritual* to *Divine Horsemen* reveals an affinity between avant-garde and ethnographic film-making. The famous ethnographer, Margaret Mead, criticized Deren's work as methodologically 'inadmissible' (Jackson 2002: 153) because of historical inaccuracies and over-simplifications, although the quality of the material of her painstaking research was widely recognized. In her defence, Deren argued that she wanted to debark from the illusion of 'the static, "objective" camera style favoured by Margaret Mead as the proper form of visual anthropology' (Nicholls 2001: 19) in order to make the viewers conscious of her experience of possession.

The legacy of the dreamy quality of Deren's film-making, which was influenced by the nightmarish atmosphere of the German expressionist *mise-en scène* of the 1930s, was later developed in popular cinema. For instance, Deren's hypnotic editing rhythm echoes the opening and closing sequences of Coppola's *Apocalypse Now* (1979), and the sequential structure of Scorsese's *Kundun* (1997). Her ironic use of slow-motion, facial close-ups, and frozen frames, in order to break the illusion of reality by stretching time, anticipated Hollywood films such as *American Beauty* (Mendes 1999) and *Donnie Darko* (Kelly 2001), both of which used similar techniques to highlight the institutionalized hypocrisy of college life. On the other hand, the underlying theme of the inverted journey into the abyss of the human soul was negotiated in various *genres*, as in Tarkovsky's sci-fi *Solaris* (USSR 1972) and *Stalker* (USSR 1979), in Petersen's submarine adventure *Das Boot* (West Germany 1981), in Werner Herzog's journeys into the unknown Amazon (*Aguirre* 1972 and *Fitzcarraldo* 1982), and Coppola's adaptation of Joseph Conrad's *Heart of Darkness* [written in 1902] in *Apocalypse Now*, which portrays the initiation of Captain Willard into the 'dark Other' of Colonel Kurtz. Equally, Maya Deren's films demonstrate a collective escapism, as in the initiatory theme of *Ritual*, the liberation of a woman into the wild, which has been revisited in films such as Apted's *Gorillas in the Mist* (1988), the story of Diane Fossey (Sigourney Weaver), who followed her dream to live with gorillas in the jungle, and gradually became 'one of them'.

But ironically, it is the concepts of 'depersonalization' and 'detemporalization' that highlight the 'presence of difference' in Deren's films: 'the visibility of the racial colonial Other is at once a point of identity . . . and at the same time a problem for the attempted closure within discourse' (Bhabha 1994: 81). In *Ritual*, the possessed Rita is conventionally a Trinidadian dancer, while in *Divine Horsemen*, the possessed Haitians' 'depersonalized' state of mind is kept foreign to us, because the film does not acknowledge *who* these dancers are, and *why* are they dancing. Furthermore, in line with the concept of 'detemporalization' during the state of trance, these people are presented without a history, being in a timeless state of mind that differs 'from ours' (Harris 1991: 150–151). In this anonymous context, they become the Shadow of the bourgeois society that is watching them, demonstrating 'an emotional nature, a kind of autonomy, and accordingly an obsessive or, better, possessive quality' (Jung 1968b: 8–11).

> Descriptions of other worlds have introduced imaginary variations within our representation of ourselves . . . traced back to Jean-Jacques Rousseau's fantasy of the "good savage" in denouncing the alienating potential of his society, or to Mead's and Benedict's proposition of cross-cultural comparisons as a "social laboratory" where the cultural relativity of Western notions of normality . . . are tested.
> (Corrin 1998: 81)

Deren's journeys into the unknown reflect upon the collective consciousness of her own social background: the bourgeois desire for the 'Oriental', common to both fictional avant-garde and ethnographic filmmaking: 'It is difficult not to view the current fascination of anthropology for "shifting selves", "embodiment", "subjectivity" as a reflection of the inward narcissist turn to contemporary Western societies' (Corrin 1998: 82). *Ritual in Transfigured Time* and *Divine Horsemen* amplify the exoticism of the Other as dark, invisible, and unknown, echoing both Artaud's 'terror' in his writings on Balinese theatre (2001: 40), and Colonel Kurtz's 'horror' in *Apocalypse Now*. Deren died unexpectedly of a brain haemorrhage a few years after she returned from Haiti, in 1961. She was only 44. Could it be that the Gods had finally caught up with her?

Note

1 The term '*loa*' or '*lwa*' is Congolese, meaning 'god' or 'spirit'. It refers to Gods, spirits of ancestors who once lived in Guinea, and to

historical characters, such as colonial officers of Napoleon. *Lwa* are divided into benevolent personal spirits with protective powers, called *rada*, and the malevolent Shadow spirits called *Petro lwa*, described as 'hot tempered and volatile' (Morris 2006: 195).

References

Artaud, Antonin (1988) *Selected Writings* (Helen Weaver, Trans.; Susan Sontag, Ed.). Berkeley: University of California Press.

—— (2001) *The Theatre and its Double* (Victor Corti, Trans.). London: Calder.

Bhabha, Homi (1994) *The Location of Culture*. London: Routledge.

Conrad, Joseph (1902 [1994]) *Heart of Darkness*. London: Penguin.

Corrin, Ellen (1998) Affects and Symbols in African Spirit Possession Cult. In Michael Lambek and Marilyn Strathern (eds.), *Bodies and Persons: Comparative Perspectives from Africa and Melanesia*. Cambridge: Cambridge University Press (pp. 80–102).

Deren, Maya (1953) *Divine Horsemen: The Living Gods of Haiti*. London: Thames and Hudson.

Durkheim, Emile (1979) The Elementary Forms of the Religious Life. In William A. Lessa and Evon Z. Vogt (eds.), *Reader in Comparative Religion: An Anthropological Approach* (4th edition) (Joseph Ward Swain, Trans.). New York: Harper Collins (pp. 27–35).

Fredericksen, Don (2001) Jung/sign/symbol/film. In Christopher Hauke and Ian Alister (eds.), *Jung and Film: Post-Jungian Takes on the Moving Image*. East Sussex: Brunner-Routledge (pp. 17–55).

Harris, Olivia (1991) Time and Difference in Anthropological Writing. In Lorraine Nencel and Peter Pals (eds.), *Constructing Knowledge, Authority and Critique in Social Science*. London: Sage (pp. 145–161).

Hauke, Christopher and Alister, Ian (2001) *Jung and Film: Post-Jungian Takes on the Moving Image*. East Sussex: Brunner-Routledge.

Innes, Christopher (1981) *Holy Theatre: Ritual and the Avant Garde*. Cambridge: Cambridge University Press.

—— (1993) *Avant-Garde Theatre 1892–1992*. London: Routledge.

Jackson, Renata (2002) *The Modernist Poetics and Experimental Practice of Maya Deren (1917–1961)*. New York: The Edwin Mellen Press.

Jung, Carl Gustav (1967) *The Archetype of Transformation*, CW5 (R.F.C. Hull, Trans.). London: Routledge & Kegan Paul.

—— (1968) *The Archetypes and the Collective Unconscious*, CW9(i) (R.F.C. Hull, Trans.). London: Routledge & Kegan Paul.

—— (1968b) *Aion*, CW9(ii) (R.F.C. Hull, Trans.). London: Routledge and Kegan Paul.

—— (1969) *Psychology and Religion*, CW11 (R.F.C. Hull, Trans.). London: Routledge & Kegan Paul.

Kapferer, Bruce (1983) *A Celebration of Demons: Exorcism and the Aesthetics of Healing in Sri Lanka*. Bloomington: Indiana University Press.

Lambek, Michael (1981) *Human Spirits: A Cultural Account of Trance in Mayotte*. Cambridge: Cambridge University Press.

Levi-Strauss, Claude (1963) The Effectiveness of Symbols. In *Structural Anthropology* (Claire Jakobson and Brook Grundfest Scheepf, Trans.). New York: Basic Books.

Levy-Bruhl, Lucien (1926) *How Natives Think* (Lilian A. Clare, Trans.). London: Allen and Unwin.

Mauss, Marcel (1985) A Category of the Human Mind: The Notion of Person; The Notion of Self. In Michael Carrithers, Steven Collins and Steven Lukes (eds.), *The Category of Person*. Cambridge: Cambridge University Press (pp. 1–25).

Morris, Brian (2006) *Religion and Anthropology*. Cambridge: Cambridge University Press.

Nicholls, Bill (2001) *Maya Deren and the American Avant-Garde*. Berkeley: University of California Press.

Obeyesekere, Gananath (1981) *Medusa's Hair: An Essay on Personal Symbols and Religious Experience*. Chicogo, IL: The University of Chicago Press.

Otto, Rudolf (1958) *The Idea of the Holy* (John W. Harvey, Trans.). Oxford: Oxford University Press.

Paganopoulos, Michelangelo (2010) Jesus Christ and Billy the Kid as Archetypes of the Self in American Cinema. *Journal of Religion and Popular Culture*, 22(1).

Turner, Victor (1967) *The Forest of Symbols: Aspects of Ndembu Ritual*. Ithaca and London: Cornell University Press.

—— (1982) *From Ritual to Theatre: The Human Seriousness of Play*. New York: PAJ.

—— (1987) *The Anthropology of Performance*. New York: PAJ.

Williams, Don (2001) Post-human psychology and *Blade Runner*. In Christopher Hauke and Ian Alister (eds.), *Jung and Film: Post-Jungian Takes on the Moving Image* (pp. 110–129).

Chapter 18

Coppola's *The Conversation*
Typology and a caul to the soul

James Palmer

> Realizing the anima is a critical factor in the development of masculine consciousness, not only because much of the success or failure of men's relationships hinges upon the integration of this otherness, but also because the anima is responsible for a man's connection to his unconscious.
>
> (Loren Pedersen, 1991: 26)

Between his films *The Godfather* (1972) and *The Godfather, Part II* (1974), Francis Coppola directed *The Conversation* (1974). Bracketed by the brilliant *Godfather* films, *The Conversation* was nonetheless nominated by the Academy as best picture of the year only to lose to *Godfather II*. The sustained admiration over the intervening years for *The Conversation* is deserved for many reasons, among them Coppola's script and direction, the superb editing and sound work of Walter Murch, and outstanding performances, especially by Gene Hackman as the West Coast wiretapper Harry Caul. An anonymous and extremely private person, Harry systematically sets about destroying the privacy of others and uses his technology to arrange the world so that he does not have to experience it. Seemingly, *The Conversation* is a thriller with Harry Caul recording a conversation that may involve him in a murder and he spends much of the film trying to decipher his tapes and confront the moral responsibilities arising from his work.

Although Coppola wrote the script in the late 1960s, before the Watergate scandal, the release of the film in March of 1974 had obvious political relevance. Watergate was news, and the Nixon tapes would soon become a national obsession. Harry's competitor in *The Conversation* boasts of recording the conversations of a losing presidential contender. Political dirty tricks were commonplace tactics and abuse of governmental institutions – the FBI, the Department of Justice, the Internal Revenue Service – were rife. Harry Caul's assistant Stan (John Cazale), bored by the conversation he is monitoring, suggests their surveillance job must be at the behest of 'the infernal revenue service.' Given the secret and warrantless wiretapping by the recent Bush administration and the technological advances in the intervening 36 years, a timely examination of Coppola's masterful film may prove both relevant and revelatory. Though this analysis of *The Conversation* will emphasize the personal and psychological rather than the political, a character study of Harry Caul resonates deeply with the current zeitgeist.

Harry Caul is, to quote a Jungian title, a 'modern man in search of a soul' (Jung, 1933). Committed to the rational world and immersed in a technological society that undermines human values and thwarts human needs, Harry embodies moral and psychological challenges to personal wholeness and individuation. Using Jung's typology, one recognizes Harry as an introvert whose reliance on, and obsession with, technology feeds his dominant way of experiencing the world through his senses and his intellect, his thinking function. What remains undeveloped and unacknowledged is Harry's intuition and feeling. In particular, his inability to relate to and evaluate the women in his life, who double as manifestations of his own repressed anima, illuminates much of this puzzling film.

Jungian analyst Loren Pedersen states the case for the importance of the anima archetype:

> We can gain a deeper understanding of a man's behavior in relationships if we include an appreciation of the archetype of the anima, an unconscious factor that shapes the way men feel and act. In the most general way, the anima refers to a man's *unconscious personality*, which Jung considered to be feminine. *Anima* is a Latin word meaning "soul" or "breath."
>
> (Pedersen, 1991: 14)

In many ways Harry typifies the American male. He is independent, competitive, and ingenious in creating his own high-tech wiretapping equipment. He is a highly competent surveillance expert who has maintained a conscientious attitude toward his work, without acknowledging just how he has sacrificed his conscience and his ability to make moral choices. As a pioneer in his field, Harry has made the trek from East to West, starting in New York and ending in San Francisco. Skilled in evading and avoiding himself (and the murderous consequences of his previous surveillance work), he has run out of territory and finds himself at the edge of the continent and ill equipped to understand himself emotionally or psychologically. Harry has been hired to monitor lovers and co-conspirators Ann (Cindy Williams) and Mark (Frederic Forrest) by Ann's suspicious husband, who is also a corporate director (Robert Duvall, uncredited).

Accessing and interpreting the world primarily through his tapes, Harry fears that his own privacy might be invaded and that his work might involve him in murder. An isolated and eccentric man, Harry also fears becoming committed to any personal, intimate relationship. Coppola was well aware of the challenges of making such a character the omnipresent and central figure in this story. In an interview, Coppola outlines the problem:

> It's very tricky to deal with a man who is your main character who you're watching for two hours . . . who doesn't talk to anybody, who lives alone, and who doesn't relate to anybody. I had given myself a very difficult assignment. I gradually tried to deepen him and find ways to get inside of him.
>
> (Rosen, 1974: 44)

Harry uses his intellect to interpret imperfectly what seems to him incontrovertible evidence based on his faith in his technology. In addition, Harry and the viewer struggle to make sense of the images that accompany his listening to the tapes and of his disturbing dream visions, which are manifestations of his increasingly intrusive intuition.

One opportunity for Coppola to explore the psychological complexity of his main character, in part, is through Harry's surname, Caul. How Harry came by this name in the script has a curious and serendipitous history. In a short 1976 review of *The Conversation*, I addressed the meaning and significance of a 'caul' as central not only to Harry's character, but to the visual style and themes of the film (See Palmer, 1976: pp. 26–32; Cowie, 1989, pp. 81–93). In conversation with Michael Ondaatje in 2002, Walter Murch gave a detailed but succinct account of the origin of Harry's name:

> Francis was reading the novel *Steppenwolf* at the time he was writing *The Conversation*, and he transformed *Steppenwolf*'s hero Harry Haller to "Harry Caller". Then he thought, No, that's just too much, too literal – since Harry was a professional eavesdropper . . . and he shortened it to "Harry Call". Then his secretary accidentally typed "Caul". And . . . he thought, this misprint is much better.

"Caul" sounds like "Call," but it gave Francis a visual metaphor for the film of a man who always wears a semi-translucent raincoat, which is a caul-like membrane, and whenever he's threatened or something bad is going to happen, he retreats behind pieces of plastic or rippled glass.

(Ondaatje, 2002: 34)

This fortuitous accident not only enriches the film's texture and its visual motifs, it creates a series of complex allusions that allow us to get 'inside' Harry. (See Hauke, 2005: 114. Hauke uses this same Caller/Call/Caul name permutation in *The Conversation* as one of several examples to describe how unconscious and unintended processes work creatively to enrich and compensate for the over-rational, planned intentions of directors, cinematographers, editors and others collaborating in the film-making practice.)

What are the definitions and properties of a caul that make it such a resonant name for this character? A caul is a 'thin membrane enveloping the foetus, which covers the head of some newly born children: an omen of good fortune with powerful magical properties; it protects sailors from drowning, presumably because it was thought to keep the foetus from drowning in the womb' (Cavendish, 1970, III: 427). The irony of this definition, which stresses 'good fortune' and the magical powers of an amulet, is that it contrasts with Harry's destiny. One is reminded of Jung's belief that what remains unconscious is played out as fate, or as Seneca said, 'Him who is willing the Fates guide, the unwilling they drag' (quoted in Whitmont, 1969/1991: 48). Harry seems fated to become whole in an unwilling and neurotic manner, not consciously. The caul, associated with the birth motif throughout the film, suggests Harry's unformed, naive character; he is, for all of his technological savvy, incomplete and immature – an unborn soul.

Another property of the caul will prove problematic for Harry because the caul can 'confer powers of second sight on their owners' (Cavendish, 1970, II: 427). Harry's repressed intuition erupts in puzzling and disturbing images, such as his vision of the hotel room, the scene of the yet to be committed murder. Though the inferior function is a bridge to the unconscious, it offers Harry no guaranteed insights, no automatic access to his unconscious. Jung insisted that the unconscious is truly unconscious and that the integration of unconscious material into consciousness takes effort. We will struggle toward wholeness, but the question for Jung was always how this struggle might be aided by active imagination or attention to images and dreams, or, on the other hand, resisted by denial or a habitual dependence on one's dominant or superior function. We have little trouble recognizing Harry's struggles, his overly rational resistance to the intuitive, when Marie-Louise von Franz describes the inferior intuition of a person whose superior or dominant function is introverted sensation:

> The disadvantage of this type is that when these tremendous inner phantasies [sic] well up, such a person has great difficulty in assimilating them because of the accuracy and slowness of his conscious function. If such a type is at all willing to take his intuition seriously, he will be inclined to try to put it down very accurately. But how can you do that? Intuition comes like a flash, and if you try to put it down it has gone! So he does not know how to deal with the problem and goes through agonies, because the only way his inferior function can be assimilated is by loosening the hold of the superior [dominant] function.
>
> (von Franz, 1971: 28–29)

No one is solely introverted or extraverted, just as no one whose dominant function is sensation or thinking is without abilities to develop the inferior intuitive or feeling functions. Although there are no pure types, Harry's commitment to his technology ties him to his senses, in particular his hearing, and to his strong auxiliary thinking function. The caul represents Harry's undeveloped, inferior intuition; his failure to evaluate accurately the women in his life points to his weak feeling function and his alienation from the anima, his inner feminine. The caul seemingly protects the introverted Harry, who is so determined to control his environment. Walter Murch accurately describes Harry's translucent raincoat and the dozens of times our view of Harry is obscured by caul-like screens. For instance, Harry wears his raincoat almost constantly, not removing it even when he climbs into bed with Amy (Teri Garr), his inquisitive girlfriend. He also stands behind a plastic sheath that hangs in his warehouse workshop when his wire-tapping competitor, Bernie Moran (Allen Garfield), interrogates Harry about one of his bugging jobs in Chicago, which led to several deaths. Tension and competition between Harry and Bernie are rife, and Bernie functions as Harry's archetypal shadow. A boisterous braggart, con man, and hustler, Bernie represents everything that Harry has repressed; yet they are doubles as professional eavesdroppers. In one of his many acts of denial, Harry can say of the Chicago job that it 'had nothing to do with me. I just turned in the tapes.' While he is behind this sheath,

Harry can deny or evade Bernie by saying, 'Nobody really knows for sure.'

If the caul protects Harry, it also acts to obfuscate and even confuse Harry's vision of himself or his insight into his moral quandaries. He goes to the Jack Tar Hotel to prevent a murder, but ultimately he only succeeds in overhearing it take place in the adjoining room. In yet more variations of the caul, he eventually closes the room's curtains, retreats to a bed, and in a fetal position pulls the bed sheets over his head and falls asleep. Reinforcing the caul/birth motif, Harry awakes to a Flintstones episode blaring on the TV. As Fred rushes Wilma, in labor pains, to the hospital, he is pulled over for speeding. The episode offers an ironic commentary on Harry curled up in the bed; the camera pans to Harry's face as the cop on the TV tells Fred, 'I got to hand it to you, buddy, you sure got intestinal fortitude.'

Harry is especially vulnerable at the surveillance convention, where he wears his name tag but not his raincoat, and Bernie Moran successfully bugs the off-guard Harry with a pen microphone. An advertising sign with the word 'Sentry' looms in the background to provide a silent but ironic commentary on this bugging. Coppola uses the setting of the surveillance conference to enrich our understanding of Harry's strengths and weaknesses. When a salesman is impressed to learn that he is talking to *the* Harry Caul, Harry seems both pleased with his notoriety and aware that he must retain his anonymity. In this encounter with the salesman, Harry is framed between two signs – 'Silent Knight' and 'Spectre' – which accurately describe the personal and professional Harry.

Rich as the caul motif is, it is settings and interior moments such as Harry's saxophone playing, his solitary editing of the tape and his dreams that continue to 'deepen' his character. The taped conversation, repeatedly heard in different contexts, functions not just as an object or prize, sought after by competing characters, but as Harry's imaginal dialogue with himself, his attempt at soul-making (See Watkins, 1986). Jung's view of alchemy is relevant here. Examining early alchemical texts and their arcane symbolism, Jung concluded that the alchemists' quest to turn lead into gold was, psychologically, a search for wholeness and a way to transform consciousness. In alchemical terms, Harry's magnetic tape is *prima materia* and in an act of distilling and refining, he repeatedly attempts to produce a tape free of sonic interference. Harry projects onto his tape (that mix of intricate images and sounds in his head) his own psychic processes, and he seems fixated, caught in the chaos and darkness of the first alchemical stage, called *nigredo*. The practical, task-oriented Harry tries quite literally to transmute his leaden tapes into gold, into the money ($15,000) he eventually receives from the director, but this pay-off is curiously unsatisfactory. At some level, Harry fears this is blood money even as he pockets the cash. This fear is reinforced when Harry asks the unresponsive director, 'What will you do to her?' and the tape playing in the background provides the immediate answer: 'He'd kill us if he got the chance.' Although the film ends with Harry under surveillance and literally cornered in his demolished apartment, I believe a psychological alchemy is present and implicit. In a more optimistic interpretation of the ending than most critics would allow, I argue that Harry's music, emblematic of his encounter with his intuitive and feeling functions, produces a melancholy Harry who finds the gold he needs and seeks. In his concluding commentary on *The Conversation*, Peter Cowie offers a similar view: 'The mood is one of tolerance and devotion. Harry is absolved. Free of the cage enclosing his workshop. Free of the drab encumbrances of his apartment. Free to seek some private peace at the heart of the music' (Cowie, 1989: pp. 92–93; see also Cavalli, 2002, and Marlan, 1997, for additional commentary on the relation of alchemy to psychology).

Harry's 'second sight' or clairvoyance is confounded by his obsession with his technology. Harry seems truly animated only when he fleetingly shows Bernie Moran the bugging devices he has created to capture Ann and Mark's conversation in Union Square. As Harry works on his tapes, he envisions scenes from Union Square; some scenes we surmise are memory, but most we understand to be his mindscreen, his imagined visual recreations of the wandering of Ann and Mark, and his contradictory responses, both guilty and jealous, to their emotional intimacy. It is no accident that during the editing of the tapes Harry's visual imagination frequently focuses on Ann's flirtatious teasing, her powers of observation, and her caressing of Mark. As Jungian analyst Polly Young-Eisendrath points out, 'For male people, anima seems to include both idealized and feared "powers" that are connected to birth, sustenance, beauty, and the life force. Projections of anima onto women may result in men fearing and idealizing women, their bodies and appearances, and their capacities' (Young-Eisendrath, 1992: 153).

A contradictory, repressed man, Harry knows far too little about himself. One key to his character – his actions, his motivations, his inactions – is his complex (in both senses of the word) relation with the women in the film. Because Harry is a surveillance expert, we might expect that his attitude toward women would be that of a voyeur. If he is a voyeur, however, he is an unconventional one. Harry reprimands his assistant, Stan, for taking photographs of two young women applying their lipstick by using the surveillance truck's mirrored one-way window. While Stan enacts the classic voyeur's role inside the truck, encouraging the unsuspecting women to 'give me some tongue, just give me a little tongue,' Harry wants Stan to pay more attention to getting a good recording of the conversation of the couple they are taping. Harry's repressed sexuality is nicely displaced, making his voyeuristic job seem less related to salacious sex than to his high, however amoral, professional standards.

Harry is nothing if not conscientious. This conscientiousness acts as a cover for his inability to take ethical action, working to distance him from the consequences of his work. For instance, he tells Stan, who is curious about the couple's conversation, 'Since when are you here to be entertained . . . I don't care what they're talking about. All I want is a nice, fat recording.' Harry's insistence on giving the surveillance tapes to no one but the director demonstrates that he is not one to betray his profession; his self-betrayal and his betrayal by others, however, are constant themes.

Harry's paranoia and his anima-possessed psyche are explored mainly through five women – Mrs. Evangelista, his landlady; his mother; Ann, the wife of the director and subject of the surveillance plot; Amy, the girlfriend secreted away in a basement apartment; and Meredith (Elizabeth MacRae), the hired seductress who has sex with Harry in order to steal the tapes. Near the end of the film, brief shots of a statue of the Virgin Mary in Harry's apartment complete the anima figures in his life. Two of these women, the landlady and Harry's mother, never appear in the film, and Ann never speaks with Harry, except in his dream. All the women are, of course, people in Harry's past or present life, as well as archetypal aspects of his anima, his contrasexual otherness, and unconscious personality. Ann Ulanov explains the process of confronting our 'otherness' this way:

> Anima or animus forms a bridge, across which the contents of the Self come to address the ego, to put questions to our very existence. These questions seem to issue from the other – personified as an anima or animus figure – who says, in effect: You must deal with me, confront me, respond to me, even if it is to reject me, but here I am and you cannot escape.
>
> (Ulanov, 1992: 25)

The range of women – mother (personal and archetypal), seductress (Meredith), lover/friend (Amy), obsessive ideal and apparent damsel in distress (Ann), and religious figures (Mrs. Evangelista and the Virgin Mary) – typify the spectrum of anima figures many men encounter. The role of each woman is significant as the film centres on Harry's unacknowledged quest to find and save his soul.

Mrs. Evangelista seems to have the most straightforward function of any of the women, for she has violated Harry's apartment, evaded his multiple locks and security system, and invaded his personal space, his fortified solitude, in order to leave a bottle of red wine inside his door as a birthday present. The landlady apparently has read Harry's mail, too, since she knows his exact age (44) from the birthday card from Harry's bank. (It is appropriately ironic that this card is the only other 'personal' birthday greeting Harry receives.) Harry's controlled fury is clear in his phone conversation with Mrs. Evangelista, for the landlady has easily penetrated his elaborate defences. He demands to have the only key to his apartment – he doesn't worry about a fire because he does not 'have anything personal, nothing of value, nothing personal but my keys' – and henceforth will have his mail sent to a PO box. To some degree, we are encouraged to identify with the incensed Harry even though we recognize the irony of what has happened. Despite his elaborate precautions, he has had done to him what he does professionally to others, a situation at the start of the film that foreshadows the darker ending.

The denotations of Mrs. Evangelista's actions are clear enough, but her name and Harry's later use of the wine suggest richer connotations. What is Mrs. Evangelista's mission? Surely her name and the red wine have religious significance, particularly when we learn of Harry's Catholic background. In his otherwise sterile apartment, the one personal touch is the Christmas crèche displayed on an end table. For the isolated and alienated Harry, this bottle of red wine, both birthday gift and violation, might equally signal a breakthrough, as well as a breach in his security system. The wine hints at the need for a rebirth and a call to communion, religious or human. However veiled this reference is to Harry's faith, the film reintroduces the motif when Harry objects to Stan profaning Christ's name. Furthermore, Harry's pathetic attempt at confession, where he admits that his work could be used to hurt people, is immediately followed by his denial of responsibility. For someone so paranoid, so over-identified with his persona and wedded to his job that he has emptied his life of everything personal and pleasurable, the wine might also suggest that his desiccated, one-sided existence could use an infusion of the Dionysian energy that wine can release. Mrs. Evangelista's intrusion is the first of many opportunities for Harry to bridge the ego and the unconscious, to become more whole by acknowledging the other, the alien, the encroaching and complementary anima.

The next time we see the bottle of wine occurs when Harry visits Amy in her cramped basement apartment. This cocoon-like flat is potentially transformational space, in contrast to the sterile, vault-like apartment Harry inhabits. Amy only appears in this one extended sequence, but it reverberates through the rest of the film. (The Amy sequence is frequently cut from the television screenings of *The Conversation* because it does nothing to further the plot, but it is crucial to the film's focused character study of Harry. Also, Amy is an easy character to misread simply as a ditzy blonde speaking 'inane banter' [Cowie, 1989: 87] or 'a sweet, none-too-bright girl,' as Vincent Canby 1974: 127 labels her in his review A Haunting Conversation; still, her incisive questions and insight into Harry's character prove both shrewd and uncanny.) In terms of Jungian typology, Amy is the perfect complement to the introverted, sensate, wire-tapping Harry with his strong auxiliary thinking. Amy, as her name suggests, is not only Harry's friend, but a perceptive character whose intuition and affection offer opportunities for the intimacy, personal growth, and self-revelation that Harry at once longs for but also experiences as threats to his professional and private life.

When he arrives, he hovers on the landing outside Amy's basement, circumspect and hesitant, spying on her (or in some strange way on himself). Then he unlocks her door and soon offers to share the wine in celebration of his birthday. Surprised to learn of Harry's birthday, Amy hopes for some intimacy from her guarded lover. The inquisitive, intuitive Amy is full of questions about Harry's age, his job, even his telephone number. Harry lies about his age (saying he is 42, not 44), about not having a telephone, and about being a freelance musician rather than a surveillance expert. Amy tells Harry that she has observed him spying from the landing in the past and that she even suspects that he listens in on her phone conversations. The scene is resonant with Amy's intuitive instincts. With startling synchronicity, Amy begins to sing the Red, Red Robin song that Ann, Harry's surveillance target, sang earlier in the day.

Though the red wine is opened, Harry remains as closed off as ever. Put off by her questions, Harry prepares to leave, announces that the rent is due, and places the money in a kitchen cupboard. Even though Amy is not a prostitute, this contractual aside shows Harry's attempt to avoid emotional entanglement by keeping a cash nexus as the basis for their relationship. When Harry exits, Amy responds to his rejection of real intimacy by announcing that she no longer intends to wait for him. When he tries to phone her some days later, she has moved. Ironically, the surveillance expert has lost track of her; Harry is stymied and, more important, isolated from the one person who has no desire to exploit him, but has only wanted to know and love him.

Paradoxically, Harry's most intimate relationship, the one that most occupies his psyche, is with Ann. The more physical distance that exists between Harry and the women in the film, the safer it is for him to invest any emotional capital in a relationship. Harry's obsession with both women signifies his flawed but crucial struggle to understand the women in his life and his own internal anima conflicts. In an act of self-betrayal, Harry rejects the direct intimacy he needs by walking away from Amy, while his work on the surveillance tapes creates an increasingly obsessive connection to Ann. He hangs a photo of Ann over his workbench, initiating his ongoing internal dialogue with her.

Once Harry filters out the ambient sound to hear Mark say of Ann's CEO husband, 'He'd *kill* us if he got the chance,' Harry's fears about the use of the tapes and his concern for Ann's safety are joined. Because his previous surveillance jobs have resulted in violence, his moral qualms are fully justified. Crucially, Harry's experience and his assumptions and subjective interpretation have led him to mishear this crucial line, where emphasis is everything. Once Harry realizes he has mistaken the murderers for the potential victims, he later hears the line as 'He'd kill *us* if he got the chance,' an indication that the supposed victims instigated the murder plans. (See Ondaatje [2002: 266] for Walter Murch's explanation and justification for the 'shifting in inflection' in the repeated line, 'He'd kill us if he got a chance.')

Another section of Harry's tape becomes an ongoing refrain as he repeatedly plays the exchange between Ann and Mark concerning a homeless man:

Ann: Oh look. That's terrible.
Mark: He's not hurting anyone.
Ann: Neither are we.
Ann: Oh God! Every time I see one of those old guys I always think the same thing.
Mark: What do you think?
Ann: I always think he was once somebody's baby boy. Really I do. I think he was once somebody's baby boy and he had a mother and a father who loved him and now there he is half-dead on a park bench. And where are his mother or father, all his uncles, now?

Intercut with this soundtrack are shots of Harry in the workshop, the tape equipment, and the photograph of Ann that Harry has taped to his workbench. The exchange has multiple effects on Harry. It misleads him into thinking the couple harmless, even compassionate people. It also initiates a recurring birth motif that relates to the caul and unifies many of the central issues in the film.

Harry's curious, anonymous, isolated relationship with Ann, his mix of guilt over violating her privacy, his almost fatherly protectiveness, and hints of his romantic attraction to her all resonate with her apparent concern for the old man on the bench. Under the guise of professional objectivity, Harry scolds his assistant, Stan, for expressing curiosity about Ann, Mark, and their conversation. Then he speaks a truth more insightful than he knows, an incisive self-assessment that is more personal than professional: 'Listen, if there's one sure fire rule I've learned in this business, it's that I don't know anything about human nature, I don't know anything about curiosity. That's not part of what I do.' Although Harry's curiosity is piqued, and he is drawn emotionally into this job, his failure to understand the people around him is clear. His speech to his assistant could hardly speak more aptly for Harry's weakest functions – intuition and feeling.

Struggle as he might, Harry's misplaced values and flawed assumptions lead to a series of betrayals. The fact that Harry mistrusts Amy and places his trust in two profoundly treacherous women, Ann and Meredith, demonstrates how little he knows of human nature and women. His feeble attempts to play the role of hero and rescuer are thwarted by the deeply deceptive world of *The Conversation*. This modern man in search of salvation, of soul, has no Beatrice, no Virgil to guide him through hell, and the circular tapes entrap and ensnare him in his own technology. As Mark queries Ann on the tape, 'Does it bother you ... walking around in circles?' Harry's futile and misguided attempts to rescue Ann are dangerous and fraught with self-deception. Harry's struggle with his inchoate conscience is an ethical, spiritual, and psychological one. Ann, as a false, deceitful anima figure, cannot act as the bridge to the unconscious and to the integration of the feminine that Harry so desperately needs.

The Conversation is replete with replicas, recordings, and copies. In Union Square, the setting of the brilliant opening scene, a mime artist (Robert Shields) copies the movements of the people he shadows. A model of Union Square appears at the surveillance convention where Harry is followed by Martin Stett (Harrison Ford), the corporate director's assistant. Stan uses a crude blackboard drawing of Union Square to illustrate the challenge of recording the couple wandering in the park.

The tape, the artifact from which the film derives its title, deserves special attention. It is not merely the object of a tug-of-war between Martin Stett and Harry or a commodity stolen by Meredith. Because repetitions of the recording are heard at least eight times in different contexts, the tape itself becomes a kind of recurring character. One can assign it various roles: it functions as a kind of Greek chorus and a commentator, as well as an omniscient narrator and an unreliable narrator; in addition, the tape functions as a plot device, and even as a kind of plot within the plot. The tape most significantly functions as Harry's internal and ongoing imaginal dialogue, something like himself and his electronic voice of conscience. In short, Harry is the creator of this tape in his various roles as director, editor, designer, audience, and interpreter of this conversation.

'You cannot escape,' as Ulanov reminds us about the anima/us figures, and Harry encounters his ubiquitous tape wherever he goes. Amy's Red, Red Robin takes him back to the tape. One expects to hear the multiple tapes as he edits them in his workshop; less predictably, Harry also hears the tapes in his dreams and daytime reveries. As he goes to the corporation to be paid for his surveillance work, the sound of the tape filters through the director's door (which is ironically labeled with the word 'Silence'). The tape is left running as Meredith seduces Harry in his loft workshop and again when Harry counts his money in the director's office. Finally, Harry goes to a hotel to try to prevent any violent confrontation between the couple and the director. Wedged behind the hotel room toilet, Harry uses the spike mic to tap into the sounds of the adjacent hotel room and hears both snatches of an argument and the playing of his tape.

From the beginning, Harry has orchestrated the recording and cleared all interference on the tape. His fingers play with the recording dials that filter the sound; Stan even tells Bernie that the complicated taping of the couple 'was a work of art.' Harry's work closely parallels that of Coppola and Walter Murch, the latter also hired by a 'director' to be sound editor for 'a conversation.' In his book-length interview with Michael Ondaatje, Murch corroborates this identification of Harry Caul with the filmmakers themselves. First, Murch talks about Harry and himself:

> There were many times while making the film that I had a sense of doubling. I'd be working on the film late at night, looking at an image of Harry Caul working on his tape, and there would be four hands, his and mine. Several times I was so tired and disoriented

that Harry Caul would push the button to stop the tape and I would be amazed that the film didn't also stop. Why was it still moving?

(Ondaatje, 2002: 154)

Murch then elaborates on how Harry is also a surrogate for Coppola:

And for Francis, Harry Caul's craft is, of course, very much like film-making. Here's the raw material, and how do you get the best out of that material? *It's an insight into the way such a mind works* [emphasis added]. . . . Also Francis himself has a highly developed technical side. Had his life gone another way, I can easily see him getting even more deeply involved in technology: "Harry Coppola." The story that Harry's rival, Bernie Moran, tells at the party in Harry's loft – how [Bernie] bugged the neighbor's phones when he was twelve? That's actually a story about Francis when he was twelve.

(Ondaatje, 2002: 155)

Although the tape records the conversation between Ann and Mark, it is even more revelatory of Harry and, to quote Murch, 'the way such a mind works.' While it is tempting to analyze every nuanced use of the tape within the film, one extended example of the interaction of the characters, the tape, and Harry's intricate responses will suffice. Harry throws his surveillance colleagues out of his loft after he learns that Bernie has recorded Harry's only really intimate conversation. In his usual ill-judged way, Harry chooses to confide in Meredith, vaguely but hesitantly sharing with her his feelings for the unnamed Amy. That moment of vulnerability produces one of his worst fears. Harry's feelings are taped and exposed, though it is quite apparent that Bernie has no real interest in the content of this recording but wanted to demonstrate his skill and superiority in tricking Harry. In a following scene, Harry listens intently to Ann and Mark's taped conversation, while Meredith cajoles and seduces him into bed. Hardly aware of Meredith's presence, Harry hears Ann repeating the lyrics of the song: 'Wake up. Wake up, you sleepy head.' The lyrics might well refer to the naive Harry, who should wake up to Meredith's manipulations. Harry's most telling response, however, is his interpretation of Ann's state of mind and tone of voice. He says about Ann, more to himself than Meredith, 'She's frightened. She's frightened. This is no ordinary conversation. It makes me feel . . . [long pause] . . . something.' Harry's telling admission points to his feelings of guilt and protection directed to the scheming Ann, as well as his vulnerability and humanity. Though he cannot identify and evaluate what he 'feels,' Harry undergoes a complex confrontation with the anima. Meredith characterizes the tape and Ann's words as 'only a trick ... a job' and tells Harry, 'You're not supposed to feel anything about it. You're just supposed to do it.' Meredith is, of course, right to refer to the tape as a trick, but she is also turning 'a trick,' and her reference to doing a job without feeling is a perfect description of her present intent to seduce Harry and steal the tape. That Meredith can so baldly seduce Harry, denigrate feeling, and announce, even flaunt, her intentions reflects how vulnerable Harry is to the wrong women and how out of touch he is with the archetypal world of the anima, even as he strives to understand Ann and his own tape.

A dream sequence follows immediately as Harry is shown asleep on his bed. His unconscious erupts in words and images that link the caul motif with the first incarnation of a man's anima, his mother. Significantly, the first words in the dream are, 'Listen. My name is Harry Caul.' The scene is a fog-enshrouded park; Harry, wearing his raincoat, follows Ann and tries to warn her. Harry recounts an illness from his childhood that temporarily paralyzed his left arm and leg. He twice invokes his/the mother (personal and archetypal) as he describes the following scene:

> My mother . . . my mother used to lower me into a hot bath as therapy. One time the doorbell rang; she went down to answer it. I started sliding down. I could feel the water starting coming up to my chin, my nose. When I woke up, my body was all greasy from the holy oil she put on my body. I remember being disappointed I survived.

(See Silverman [1988, pp. 87–98] for an alternate, mostly Freudian reading of this dream scene and the film as a whole.)

One hardly needs to elaborate on the caul as a protection against drowning or point to the bad and good dual role of the mother – her abandonment and her subsequent religious ministrations. That the caul also may convey the gift of 'second sight' is crucial because the second part of this dream is a foreshadowing that shows Harry standing outside room 773 at the Jack Tar Hotel ('jack tar' means 'sailor,' and thus fits with certain associations of the caul as protection for sailors against drowning). When Harry enters the room, he envisions the director attacking Ann; he imagines blood-streaked curtains and bathroom walls. Harry's inferior function, his intuition, has supplied these images of the future, so accurate in setting but so wrong in identifying the villains. We will recognize this room later when Harry actually enters the pristine murder scene and flushes the toilet that, like an image of afterbirth, overflows with blood, an image both real and representative of Harry's guilt feelings.

The concluding minutes of *The Conversation* are replete with what we might call enigmatic factors, questions we may want answered, but which have no satisfactory answers. Did Ann and Mark know they were being taped and use that knowledge to set up the murder? Did the murder take place in the hotel room? If so, how was the body removed and the director's death in the car accident plausibly faked? Is the image of the bloody hand on the window that Harry sees from his terrace real and is the overflowing toilet in the hotel real? (Here I would say yes, because I do not see Harry as a psychotic, nor are his misinterpretations signs of madness, of a psychotic breakdown.) Who does Martin Stett really work for, the director or the murderers? Who hired Meredith to steal the tapes? Finally, where is the bug that records the sounds in Harry's apartment? These are teasing questions, but none of them seem central to the film. To focus on unravelling the mystery/murder plot is to shift attention away from this character-driven film and the complex portrait of Harry Caul.

If we knew the answers to these questions, we might have a more satisfactory thriller, but a less complete and engrossing psychological study. Harry may not be an Everyman, but one can sympathize with the tortured soul, victimized by feelings of guilt, hounded by his own past, betrayed by Meredith, and finally misled by the actions of the murderers and a misplaced faith in his own technology. However ineffective his actions are, Harry is no sociopath, no man without a conscience. He is a flawed man forced to live in an ambiguous world. Like Harry, we know little with any certainty. What we do have in *The Conversation* is a brilliant character study of a man whose technology has betrayed him and whose psychological complexes Coppola has explored and exposed.

If there are no clear answers to the enigmatic questions concerning the film's plot or the murder plot, why then is the conclusion of *The Conversation* so haunting and satisfying? Harry does confront the actual murderers as they exit the corporate building and are surrounded by the press shouting such questions as, 'What about your corporate control?' and 'Will your stock now give you controlling interest?' The questions obviously raise doubts about the couple's motives – was this supposedly illicit affair mainly a scheme, a corporate takeover? The editing alternates between Harry's visions and the press scene, both conveying a confused and ominous atmosphere. The sense of threat comes through the eye contact between the major characters – first between Ann and Harry, then Mark and Harry, and finally between Martin Stett and Harry – eye contact that in each case triggers fragments of Harry's vision and new understanding. The soundtrack suddenly reverts to the tape and to Harry's replay of what he imagines happened. It is essential to remember that Harry only heard but did not see any violence, with the possible exception of the unidentified bloody handprint on the glass door that he glimpsed from his terrace. What is shown now on screen is Harry's *imagined* version of the director's murder, ironically accompanied by the tape and Mark's now ominous comment about a Christmas gift for the director who 'doesn't need anything anymore.'

What the viewer at the end of the film sees is a visually scrambled timeline of Harry's version, his revision of the murder he perhaps heard but did not see. Between shots of the dead director covered in clear plastic and laid out on a bed – a reference to the caul, to what has become a birth/death motif, and to the amniotic sac – is Harry's vision of a murderous attack on the director, seen through a gauzy, veil-like curtain, which further emphasizes that this is Harry's imagined perspective. This six-second shot is crucial to understanding Harry's character, his failure to interpret his previous intuitions, his misreading of the couple and of all the women, and the culmination of his worst fears. Ann kneels beside her husband, as Mark, now wearing a plastic rain suit that literally protects him from any blood (and figuratively reminds us of Harry's raincoat/caul), attacks the director from behind, by throwing a clear plastic sheet over him, presumably to immobilize or smother him.

Cauls proliferate in this scene, a scene generated in Harry's mind. These images clearly point to his own sense of guilt, his complicity in this murder. After all, Harry envisions the murder weapon as a caul. Also, as the caul smothers the director, Ann stands up and averts her eyes as she moves away from the violent action. Harry, one surmises, has invested so much in Ann's innocence that he still cannot fully accept her active participation in the murder. Such is not the case with Harry himself, for the very next cut is his memory of the payoff in the director's office. Harry recalls a close-up of a photograph of a smiling Ann and her husband; in front of the photograph is the stack of money Harry was paid for his wiretapping work.

Harry returns to his barren apartment, and the concluding sequence may be described as grim. Harry's saxophone playing is interrupted by two phone calls; the first call Harry answers, but the line is silent. The second call plays a bugged recording of the jazz sounds we just heard in Harry's apartment, and we hear Martin Stett delivering an ominous message: 'We know that you know, Mr. Caul. For your own sake, don't get involved any further. We'll be listening to you.' The phone calls trigger Harry's understandable paranoia and exacerbate his already fragile psychological state, testing the limits of his sanity. Martin Stett's last, perfectly phrased, fearful sentence leads the frantic Harry to tear up his apartment piece by piece in a futile attempt to find the sound transmitting device; he even crushes and rips open his Virgin Mary statuette, only to discover it does not hide the bug. The statuette proves empty in a more significant way, and marks Harry's final and futile confrontation with this last archetypal anima figure.

The last shot is a high-angle back-and-forth surveillance pan of a cornered Harry surrounded by the detritus and chaos of his wrecked world. The end of this film seems marked by entropy and despair. The depiction of a defeated man would be an easy case to make but such a reading seems to overlook signs of hope. Perhaps 'rebirth' is too strong a word to invoke here; nevertheless, there is a curious satisfaction in seeing Harry's impersonal apartment in ruins and in hearing the mournful jazz that Harry, no longer accompanying his jazz records, plays solo, but for the extradiegetic piano. If the mood is melancholy, it is also serene, and, paradoxically, a sense of order seems restored. As Jungian analyst John Van Eenwyk reminds us:

> Jung believed that in the dynamics of the psyche chaos is inevitable. Consequently, he focused a great deal of attention on developing the means to find patterns in that chaos. . . . Perhaps the most important implication of the correspondence between Jung's theories and chaos research is that fantasies about order, that spurious product of reductionism, being the most desirable state-of-being are slowly giving way to the realization that chaos is far healthier than previously imagined. If that proves to be the case, we shall have to revise some of our basic notions about mental health. Like Jung, we may be forced to conclude that, at least with regard to psychological development, chaos is not only unavoidable, but necessary.
> (van Eenwyk, 1997: 13)

Harry has begun his individuation by falling deeper, more authentically and creatively, into his introverted, sensate world. His search for the bugging device moves from obsession and frustration to indifference. From an alchemical perspective, the saxophone Harry holds in his hands is refined gold. His rueful saxophone playing nicely matches the melancholy mood and further suggests that Harry's feeling function, his awareness of values hitherto repressed or marginalized, is acknowledged.

Resigned, but also separated from his professional paranoia and improvising on his saxophone, he has begun to turn his earlier lie to Amy into truth – he has become that expressive freelance musician. One senses that Harry has begun his soul-making journey.

References

Canby, Vincent (1974, April 21) A Haunting Conversation. *New York Times*, pp. 127.
Cavalli, Thom F. (2002) *Alchemical Psychology*. New York: Jeremy P. Tarcher/Putnam.
Cavendish, Richard (ed.) (1970) *Man, Myth, & Magic*, 24 Vols. New York: Marshall Cavendish Corporation.
Cowie, Peter (1989) *Coppola: A Biography*, New York: Charles Scribner's Sons.
Hauke, Christopher (2005) 'What Makes Movies Work: Unconscious Process and the Movie Makers' Craft.' *Spring*, *73* (special issue on Cinema & Psyche).
Jung, C. G. (1933) *Modern Man in Search of a Soul*. New York: Harcourt, Brace & World, Inc.
Marlan, Stanton (ed.) (1997) *Fire in the Stone: The Alchemy of Desire*. Wilmette, IL: Chiron Publications.
Ondaatje, Michael (2002) *The Conversations: Walter Murch and the Art of Editing Film*. New York: Alfred A. Knopf.
Palmer, James W. (1976) *The Conversation*: Coppola's Biography of an Unborn Man. *Film Heritage* (Fall, 1976).
Pederson, Loren E. (1991) *Dark Hearts. The Unconscious Forces That Shape Men's Lives*. Boston & London: Shambhala.
Rosen, Marjorie (1974, July) Francis Ford Coppola Interviewed by Marjorie Rosen. *Film Comment*.
Silverman, Kaja (1988) *The Acoustic Mirror: The Female Voice in Psychoanalysis and Cinema*. Bloomington: Indiana University Press.
Ulanov, Ann Belford (1992) Disguises of the Anima. In Nathan Schwartz-Salant and Murray Stein (eds.), *Gender & Soul in Psychotherapy*. Wilmette, IL: Chiron Publications.
van Eenwyk, John R. (1997) *Archetypes & Strange Attractors: The Chaotic World of Symbols*. Toronto: Inner City Books.
von Franz, Marie-Louise and Hillman, James (1971) *Lectures on Jung's Typology*. Dallas, TX: Spring Publications.
Watkins, Mary (1986) *Invisible Guests: The Development of Imaginal Dialogues*. Hillsdale, NJ: The Analytic Press.
Whitmont, Edward C. (1969/1991) *The Symbolic Quest: Basic Concepts of Analytical Psychology*. Princeton, NJ: Princeton University Press.
Young-Eisendrath, Polly (1992) Gender, Animus, and Related Topics. In Nathan Schwartz-Salant and Murray Stein (eds.), *Gender & Soul in Psychotherapy*, Wilmette, IL: Chiron Publications.

Chapter 19

Navel gazing
Introversion/extraversion and Australian cinema

Terrie Waddell

As a collection of reworked and culturally tweaked myths, the arts allow us to talk to ourselves. It can be argued that audiences engage with creative texts as a form of active imagination. The Australian stories of cinema are an eclectic mixture of the values, repressions and ideals of the country's diverse indigenous, settler and diasporic clusters. In combination, these narratives facilitate what might be thought of as a 'bigger picture', *collective self* sensibility: not a unified or quantifiable identity, but a complex, multi-layered sense of interconnectedness. Still in a state of 'becoming' (adolescent perhaps), Australia is somewhat obsessed with its own internal dialogue, desperately trying to understand its complexity and potential before convincingly looking outward. Enforcing this self-talk, the overarching film and television funding body, Screen Australia, pushes for the global viability of each work it finances while imposing the need for cultural relevance. For these reasons, the Australian film industry seems to thrive on an introverted orientation, where the inner – national stories, cultural themes, and creativity – overrides outer concerns.

In his influential *Australian National Cinema*, Tom O'Regan argues for the hybrid nature of Australian film, 'made of objects, people, stories and problem solving. It is a social fact, a figure of discourse, a site for a range of actions and the domain of a range of problematizations' (1996: 10). When he claims that within this national cinema, 'there is a favouring of political understandings of Australia as a fractured polity over understandings of it as a people united by shared symbols and myths' (ibid.: 22), he appears to be reading 'myth' and 'symbol' a particularly semiotic way. For while I would argue that these concepts, in the Jungian sense, drive all film industries, in terms of national cinema they will always be creatively projected to illuminate any number of cultural, creative and political fractures. The overarching priority, though, is the inner life. We can come to some understanding of this tendency to navel gaze by looking at Jung's influential work on introversion and extraversion: terms now fixed in everyday language, but, I suspect, not entirely understood as having been coined first in the context of analytical psychology. Before looking at more specific examples of introversion in Australian cinema, I will start by concentrating on this intra/extra way of thinking.

Jung's typology

One of the major bellyaches for Jung's critics is the structuralist bent of analytical psychology. While I have argued elsewhere for the postmodern vision within Jung's theories (Waddell, 2006), his ideas on typology appear to play most transparently into notions of the individual as a composite of innate structures guiding her/his personality. This is opposed to the now widely accepted poststructuralist belief that identity is unfixed, fluid and subject to external influences. While the dual functions that Jung argued colour introverted and extraverted attitudes (thinking/feeling and sensation/intuition) have been looked upon with scepticism (largely because of their ambiguity or fuzziness), the introversion/extraversion stand-alone model is a much more attractive and relevant way of decoding behaviour (Arraj, 1986; Beebe, 2006; Loomis, 1982; Metzner & Mahlberg, 1981). Jung described these concepts as binary oppositions in *Psychological Types* (Jung, 1971: 1921), but according to Marie José Dicks-Mireaux, thinking about their real world application as rigid descriptors of personality is a misreading of his intentions: 'Unlike other classifications his concept did not describe individuals as either introvert or extravert, but rather as being in a state of balance between the two poles of a continuum' (Dicks-Mireaux, 1964: 18). John Beebe notes that the terms introversion, where life-energy or libido (in the terminology of analytical psychology) focuses on the 'inner' life, and extraversion, where the focus is on external objects, can be thought of as adjectives rather than nouns. This stress helps us to understand that we have access to both functions and each can influence our behaviour to varying degrees of intensity (Beebe, 2006: 134).

Jung first developed these concepts in his 1913 paper A Contribution to the Study of Psychological Types, presented at the Psychoanalytical Congress in Munich. Of course, thinking in terms of categories as a way of grappling with distinct and easily observable behaviours was not unique to Jung:

> Personality types have been described by many authors: Binet (1900) writes of objective and subjective types, Jung (1921 [1971])

of extravert and introvert, Kretschmer (1925) of cyclothymic and schizothymic, Burt (1937) of sthenic and asthenic, and Pavlov (1941) of inhibitory and excitatory types. Finally there are constitutional types such as the digestive and respiratory cerebal types described by Rostan (1828), the psyknic and leptosomatic types of Kretschmer (1925), and the endomorph and ecomorph types of Sheldon (1940).

(Dicks-Mireaux, 1964: 118)

Hermann Rorschach also published *Psychodiagnostik* in 1921, a text focusing on personality types, introversion/extraversion, and his now famous (and much satirized) inkblot test. According to Florence Brawer and J. Marvin Spiegelman, though, 'That Rorschach disclaimed any similarity with Jung's earlier ideas on the topic seems to have arisen out of pique with Jung's departure from psycho-analytic circles' (1964: 137). In light of this, and seemingly concurrent ways of thinking about the psychological orientations and predispositions mentioned above, the concepts of introvert and extravert, or the *attitudes* as they were called, continue to be associated with Jung.

The attitudes: introversion/extraversion

It is fairly common to stereotype *the* extravert with clichés like the 'life of the party', adept 'social networker', 'attention seeker', or more negatively, 'sycophant'. This overly simplifies and distorts Jung's understanding of the type, for he saw extraversion as an orientation that may be more dominant for some than others and only expressed in certain circumstances. 'The' extravert, then, is more of a fiction than a realistic descriptor of character (Jung, 1971: para. 6). It is more helpful to recognize extraversion as a propensity to give *external* objects prime importance:

> Now, when orientation by the object predominates in a such a way that decisions and actions are determined not by subjective views but by objective conditions, we speak of an extraverted attitude. When this is habitual, we speak of an extraverted type. If a man thinks, feels, acts, and actually lives in a way that is *directly* correlated with the objective conditions and their demands, he is extraverted.
>
> (Jung, 1971: para. 563)

The hitch with this kind of libidinal fascination is that the *inner* world is given less priority and consequently imagination, original thinking and creativity, all products of inward reflection, can remain undeveloped

(Jung, 1971: para. 563). Jung cautions that an over-zealous dependence on the opinions and actions of others can be a self-sacrificing form of rapture: 'This is the extravert's danger: he gets sucked into objects and completely loses himself in them' (Jung, 1971: para. 565). He further found parallels between extraversion and the acute suggestibility and 'exaggerated rapport' of the hysteric (Jung, 1971: para. 566) while also making connections between schizophrenia and introversion (Jung, 1971: para. 860).

If extraversion describes the outward orientation of the libido, then introversion refers to an inward turning of libido. Although Jung maintained that this was his personal orientation (Shamdasani, 2003: 69), there seems to be a more critical and somewhat scathing tone to his writing in *Psychological Types* when he describes introverted behaviour. From this position the object is of less importance than what Jung calls subjective factors: 'By the subjective factor I understand that psychological action or reaction which merges with the effect produced by the object and so gives rise to a new psychic datum' (Jung, 1971: para. 622). Introversion therefore involves a focus not on the object itself, but the feelings and sensations that the object unwittingly generates. These responses may have little to do with the object. Rather than a dependent relationship being forged between object and subject as with extraverted behaviour, there is a separation of the object by the subject that allows for something to be created from a reflection of the engagement – an idea, an image, a feeling, a sense of meaning, etc. Tellingly for this discussion of cinema, Jung exclaimed, 'How extraordinarily strong the subjective factor can be is shown most clearly in art' (Jung, 1971: para. 647).

The experience of engaging with cinema, whether as viewer, critic, or academic, can therefore be seen as an introverted expenditure of energy. Trying to apply the *attitudes* to cultural practices like film production, film industries and funding-body priorities is more problematic. For the purposes of this chapter, it is appropriate to concentrate on introversion and extraversion as overarching concepts without their attached functions, so that we can grapple with the attitude that most dominates Australian cinema. A brief word needs to be said, though, about the value of the *functions* to Jung's formulaic take on typology, for he did not theorize introversion and extraversion in isolation of the functions, but understood them as integral aspects of psychological types.

The functions: Thinking, feeling, sensation, intuition

Jung argued that the attitudes were filtered through four specific, dichotomous human functions, constellated as either dominant or inferior:

thinking and feeling were considered rational, whereas sensation and intuition were thought of as irrational. These modes of consciousness were theorized to work in conjunction with the deployment of the attitudes, and so were split into eight types: introverted thinking (dominant), introverted feeling (inferior); introverted thinking (inferior), introverted feeling (dominant); introverted sensation (dominant); introverted intuition (inferior); introverted sensation (inferior), introverted intuition (dominant), with this replication in extraversion.

It was only after collaborating with his colleague (and lover) Toni Wolff, that Jung added sensation and intuition to his thinking-feeling formula:

> His close association with Toni Wolff made him aware that beyond extraversion-introversion and thinking-feeling, which so far organised the psyche along strictly rational grounds, there was another axis of orientation altogether that his theory would need to take into account, the 'irrational' axis of sensation-intuition. Jung himself seems to have recognised that the difference between his original thinking-feeling axis and Wolff's sensation-intuition axis was that the first pair of functions are deployed in a rational way to interpret experience, whereas the latter merely apprehend what is already given to us by the outer or inner world, and hence do not use any optional process of cognition or evaluation.
>
> (Beebe, 2006: 131)

Katherine Cook Briggs and Isabel Briggs Myers added the dichotomous functions of *perception* and *judgement* to further flesh out their much-debated Myers-Briggs Type Indicator (MBTI) test, first published in 1962. Now modified in five forms, the questionnaire produced by The Myers & Briggs Foundation, mostly for career counselling and business development (www.myersbriggs.org), is a much contested method of measuring personality and workplace adaptability (see Paul 2004). Rather than understanding the attitudes and functions as operating in an oscillating fashion, with dominant and inferior aspects subject to change, the MBTI is much more prescriptive. If administered outside a clinical context, where it is more likely to be skilfully and productively deployed, the test can appear to fix the personality into seemingly inflexible categories.

In understanding how the functions, in conjunction with the attitudes, might apply to cinema, Jung and Beebe have looked toward introverted sensation (dominant) as the type governing the arts. In the following quote, Jung's position is similar to that of mainstream Media Studies audience 'reception' theories introduced by Stuart Hall in the 1970s, where the value and meaning of the text depends on how it is received by the viewer. We might therefore begin to muse on the idea that reception theories pivot on introverted sensation as the predominant mode of textual engagement:

> Actually, he [who expresses introverted sensation] perceives the same things as everybody else, only he does not stop at the purely objective influence, but concerns himself with the subjective perception excited by the objective stimulus.
>
> (Jung, 1971: para. 647)

Beebe stresses Jung's belief that an introverted function gives rise to an archetypal 'idea' (Beebe, 2006: 134). Dependence shifts from the object (foremost in extraversion) to the archetypal idea given breath by the object. This may take the form of 'a profound thought, a value, a metaphorical image, or a model of reality, depending upon whether the introverted function is thinking, feeling, intuition or sensation' (Beebe, 2006: 134). The object thus fuels the imagination and senses so that it is only ever valued as a transitory stimulant. Prime importance is given to that which it stimulates. Beebe, an analyst and film theorist, employs this way of thinking to film, arguing that Alfred Hitchcock's work utilizes introverted sensation so that audiences are able to play with the archetypal potential of his 'seemingly ordinary' screen images (Beebe, 2006: 134).

One might of course argue this point of all film, television, internet or game-related screen material, depending on the depth of the relationship between the text and particular audience members: for some, the ensuing archetypal idea may be significant, for others, negligible. Exploring the functions in depth for their relevance to cinema is probably best reserved for textual analysis or theorizing audience engagement. I am reluctant to align the functions with the *attitudes* in this particular discussion of national cinema. But before an argument can be made for the introverted orientation of Australian film, it is important to clarify the way in which I will be framing and interpreting introversion.

Introversion and Australian film

In talking about the Australian film industry as having an introverted rather than extraverted orientation, there needs to be some clarity in relation to definitions of the 'object'. When Jung talks of energy being directed *to* or *from* the 'object', he is using the inherited terminology of psychoanalysis, where the object can be parts or the whole of an organism, or inorganic matter. When reading national cinema as an introverted industry, the 'object' can be argued to constitute that which is external to the state. In other words, Australian cinema, representative of the national psyche (hybrid and diverse as it is), is more focused on itself than the global community/international audiences, whether or not it inadvertently appeals to that market. Energy is directed internally rather than externally. It is also important to remember analytical psychology's acknowledgement of the vacillation between extraversion and introversion. Australian cinema therefore does not exclusively operate from one pole, but has a degree of movement toward the outer object. One may even argue that both attitudes operate concurrently, as Felicity Collins and Therese Davis intimate in their study of Australian cinema of the 1990s: 'Although there appears to be a clear divide between the global and local film, even the most resolutely parochial Australian films are attuned to trends in international cinema' (Collins & Davis, 2004: 28).

My argument, though, is that the greater deployment of energy remains internal: locked into a series of arguments, images, ideologies, perspectives, and funding requirements that are largely framed within a culturally domestic context. In a Jungian reading, Australian cinema is able to reveal how specific cultural complexes are archetypally projected. While the collective unconscious drives the motifs of myth in all their culturally specific forms, it might be more relevant to frame, in a quite generalized or loose way, Australian film as a collection of stirrings from a kind of personal unconscious. It is as if these gratifying and uncomfortable shadows, born of an elastic, umbilical relationship between this cultural unconscious, the cultural ego, and the global or collective unconscious, are able to nurture a sense of individuation. Australian director George Miller hints at this when he tells us that we 'go to these places [cinemas] and undergo a kind of public dreaming. They are places of meditation' (Malone, 2001: 88). Miller has repeatedly acknowledged the role of the objective psyche in his film-making. He relied on this thinking throughout his *Mad Max* trilogy (1979, 1981, 1985): a series of films based around a futuristic hero/warrior battling violent outlaw gangs and avenging the murder of his wife and child. While the first *Mad Max* (1979) relied on local crew/talent, its success called for the final aspiring blockbuster instalment, *Mad Max: Beyond Thunderdome* (1985), to include the famous US singer Tina Turner as the female lead. Whether intended for local or international consumption, each film explored the collectively resonant dimensions of the hero myth.

One might say that Miller's early artistic energies were not as much directed to the object (a replication of relying on the tried and tested lone warrior to pull a calculated local and overseas market) as the archetypal *idea*, inspired by an intertextual mix of idiosyncratic Australian characters, behaviours and stories. This introverted, archetypal approach implies that his story-making serves a 'larger mono-myth' (Malone, 2001: 86). That is, while Max is a uniquely Australian rendering of the hero developed through an introverted approach to film-making, he is also powerfully resonant for global audiences able to reinterpret the character through any combination of culturally specific hero figures: 'Japan said Max was a Samurai . . . The French picked it up as a western on wheels and Scandinavia saw him as a Viking' (Malone, 2001: 86).

Despite its success overseas, *Mad Max* was both popular and critically well received in Australia. More recent films, however, pitched to a global market with an eye to what I see as the external object (box office, spectacle, dependence on established overseas actors, and even irony at reworking the clichés of cinema), have not been viewed so sympathetically. I'm thinking in particular of the overt and unambiguous extraversion of Baz Luhrmann's Australian box-office hits *Moulin Rouge* (2001) and *Australia* (2008). It is a quality that to some extent has hampered their credibility with Australian commentators and the AFI (Australian Film Institute) award voters (Collins & Davis, 2004: 30). Despite the brutal snubbing of and critical reservations about *Australia*'s plot, structure, historical accuracy, and the inclusion of past injustices against indigenous Australians (the stolen generations in particular), I would also argue that these attacks have something to do with a deep-seated animosity toward brazen extraversion: a kind of showiness directed outward to impress at the expense of cultural sensitivity. What the more vocal critics of *Australia*'s political aspirations (like Germaine Greer, 2008) failed to see was that the film was not intended to be a realistic depiction of colonization, but a pastiche of cinema clichés set against an Australian backdrop for contemporary (global) film-going audiences who might (hopefully) key into its irony and heavy intertextual borrowings.

Introvert/extravert tensions

In a twist to the Australian predilection for inward-looking storytelling, a key driver of the Australian Post New Wave movement of the 1990s (see Collins & Davis, 2004, for an excellent analysis of this decade), Australian artists who have successfully ventured abroad, directing their attention toward *the other*, are (in the most generalized sense) celebrated for their verve, courage, and talent: for example, the directors George Miller, Fred Schepisi, Jane Campion, and the actors Nicole Kidman, Hugh Jackman, Russel Crowe, Cate Blanchett and Geoffrey Rush. After artists have garnered enough box-office clout to carry an internationally pitched film, they are reclaimed as leads for the local product. The push to employ foreign actors as a draw for audiences and investors is avoided, and a sense of 'purity' is maintained.

Even intrinsically Australian films that have been popular overseas, launched the international careers of performers and directors, or have been responsible for significant American awards such as Oscars or Golden Globes, are more often than not disproportionately held up as examples of local success stories – (*Mad Max* (Miller, 1979, 1981, 1985); *Crocodile Dundee* (Faiman, 1986); *The Piano* (Campion, 1993); *The Adventures of Priscilla Queen of the Desert* (Elliot, 1994); *Muriel's Wedding* (Hogan, 1994); *Shine* (Hicks, 1996). When looking at the domestic attitude to these instances of extraverted endeavour, Australians seem most proud of their compatriots only after they have been positively received by *the other*: behaviour/energy directed outward, dependent on the approval of the object, as a means of validation. At the Melbourne launch of the Screen Worlds: The Story of Film, Television and Digital Culture exhibition (September, 2009), guest speaker Cate Blanchett expressed a little nostalgia for her old Melbourne stamping ground. Victorian Premier John Brumby jokingly offered her her own postcode if she agreed to move back. In watching this outpouring of admiration, and despite Blanchett's artistic integrity, I wondered if Brumby would have been as openly admiring had she never left Australia (say moved to another state) to pursue her career.

As if to compensate for this tendency to seek validation through external approval, the 'tall poppy syndrome' still pulses away under the Australian veneer of global savvy. According to N. T. Feather's research, the name of this kind of vitriol began with the Roman elder Tarquinius. In lopping off the flowering heads of his largest garden poppies, he was able to teach his son, Sextus Tarquinius, that to maintain or achieve power one must divest oneself of all competition, or at least cut them down to size (Feather, 1994: 2). Today, this kind of undermining kicks in when there is a perception that certain individuals are given unwarranted adulation. The media and general public can turn savagely critical in an attempt to expose the excessive/shallow nature of such praise and/ or self-promotion. This is far from the American cultural practice of disproportionate praise for celebrity. The tall poppy syndrome may very well be a defensive reaction to extraversion: a way of cutting 'our own' back down to size and maintaining an inward-looking focus. I would argue, though, that because Australian popular culture is so consumed with American media, this need to ground the overinflated has largely given way to a more uncritical worship of fame (as opposed to talent).

The push for introversion

In the 1970s and 1980s, Australian films claimed 70 per cent of all Australian box-office returns. In 2009 it was 6.5 per cent (a rise from the last decade's 4.4 average). National debates on Australian radio and television place this squarely on the shoulders of a dominant introverted push by funding bodies for 'cultural worthiness' (Quinn, 2009: 22). Collins and Davis argue that the 1990s Post New Wave film period 'signifies the return of unreconciled national issues, at the very moment when a cinema of national identity seems most redundant' (Collins & Davis, 2004: 26). They find this extraordinary because of the country's history of (introverted) media and film regulation aimed at protecting the industry and preserving national identity against an ever-increasing stream of imports, coupled with (extravert oriented) government policies designed to propel the industry competitively outward into the international playing field (Collins & Davis, 2004: 26). I will discuss how these policies operate today within the film-funding schemes offered by Screen Australia and federal tax breaks, but for the moment I want to look back.

In the mid 1980s I had a miniscule role in Fred Schepisi's *Evil Angels* (a.k.a. *A Cry in the Dark*, 1988), a Cinema Verity, Evil Angels Films and Cannon International co-production. In terms of Australian presences on screen, it seemed that practically every young actor cutting their teeth in the industry, every recognizable working performer, and every film/television legend was marshalled to the call of re-enacting one of Australia's most notorious trials by media – Lindy Chamberlain's case of infanticide. While most of my tiny film snippets fell to the cutting room floor, I had solid, lucrative employment for four months in a country that produces more acting graduates than will ever make a living from their training. Shot in Victoria's Broadmeadows Film Studios (now demolished), Alice Springs, Ayers Rock (Uluru) and Darwin, the film grossed ADU $2,416,000 and US$6,908,797 at the box office and employed an Australian cast of 350 actors and nearly 4,000 extras (Beard, 2001; Screen Australia, 2009c, 2009d). Although the 10BA film tax concessions of 1980–88 (offset at between 150 and 120 per cent) most probably benefitted the production, Schepisi battled the actors' union – then Actors Equity (AE), 1982–93 – which required all actors to be Australian unless a suitable national could not be found (ATUA, 2002). The financial drawing power of Meryl Streep (as Lindy Chamberlain) was a noteworthy exception to the rule of the day. Here's what AE's 1985–88 Defense of Employment Policy on Imported Artists stipulated:

> Imported artists will not be considered for projects based on Australia's national cultural heritage or those based on historical fact unless the character as written in the case of literature, or in fact in the case of history, is of ethnic background which cannot be cast within Australia (following a casting exercise).
> (MEAA, 2009: 5)

After renegotiation in 1988 the policy was retitled Guidelines on the Entry of Overseas Artists for Film and Television, and the following amendment was added:

> Producers will avoid casting overseas actors in roles as traditional Australian characters. Because of difficulties of definition, each case will be considered on its merits. In extraordinary circumstances such as the casting of Meryl Streep as Lindy Chamberlain in *Evil Angels*, an overseas actor may be considered in what is agreed to be a traditional Australian role.
> (MEAA, 2009: 5)

While the film was an apology of sorts to the Chamberlains for the parochial public and press behaviour during Lindy's murder trial, incarceration and eventual exoneration (1982–86), *Evil Angels* looked toward an international audience. One might say it had an extraverted attitude – focused on the outer international object/market and the rewards it offered. Yet the employment of more Australians on one shoot than ever before, the protectionist push of the union, and the (some might say) cultural redemption of *Evil Angels*, allow us to look back on the production as an intrinsically inward-looking piece of film-making.

While the film doesn't adequately encapsulate cinema of the period, and was exceptional for its push into the American market, it is a recognizable example (for international readers of this chapter) of the restraints placed on Australian film-makers in order that they comply with an imposed 'culturally pure'/introverted focus. While we have moved on from an almost xenophobic fear of overseas actors/'talent' in an attempt to attract box-office pull and guarantee financial backing (MEAA, 2009: 5–6), the current national funding body, Screen Australia, seems to have still clung, until very recently, to a protectionist ethos (see www.screenaustralia.gov.au, a 2008 amalgamation of the previous film development and production subsidy bodies – Film Finance Corporation, Film Australia Limited, and The Australian Film Commission).

Holding tight to cultural significance

While an official co-production with another country automatically meets the 'significant Australian content' test according to Screen Australia's funding and tax break guidelines (introduced in 2007), under current legislation film-makers can only apply for a producer tax offset of 40 per cent (administered by Screen Australia as a rebate against expenditure) if their production meets certain benchmarks. The criteria for eligibility involve the following:

> A project must have cultural benefits for Australia to attract such a high level of Australian Government support. Therefore, Screen Australia must be satisfied that the project has 'significant Australian content' for it to qualify for the Offset. In considering this issue, Screen Australia must have regard to the following:
>
> - the subject matter
> - the place where the film or program was made
> - the nationalities and places of residence of the people who took part in making it
> - the details of production expenditure incurred, and
> - any other matters that Screen Australia considers to be relevant.
>
> (Screen Australia, 2009a)

These stipulations seem fairly wide-ranging and somewhat ambiguous. The last stipulation is possibly the most controversial, lending Screen Australia a considerable amount of control and discretion over what it deems to be culturally relevant. Protectionist regulations were a particular bone of contention for George Miller in the planning of his upcoming (seemingly on-again, off-again) *Justice League: Mortal* (dated for release, 2011). In an interview on the Australian ABC political/current affairs flagship *The 7.30 Report* in June 2009, Miller argued his case with journalist Rebecca Baillie:

Miller: I've got that dilemma now, you know. Do I work overseas or do I stay here?
Baillie: The director has all but decided to take his $200 million blockbuster, *Justice League: Mortal*, offshore and thousands of jobs with it. Even though George Miller could have used a largely Australian cast and crew, because the idea originated in Hollywood, there are concerns it's not Australian enough to qualify for a generous 40 per cent tax break.
Miller: It was suggested that I was somehow the stooge of the American studio, that I didn't have enough creative control.
(Baillie, 2008)

Brian Rosen, Chief Executive of the former Film Finance Corporation in 2008 (responsible for the departments of investment, business affairs, policy and public relations, recoupment, and finance/administration), argued in defence of his decision to quash Miller's bid: 'This is tax-payer's money and if the money is just paid across and goes offshore and doesn't have any long-term benefit to Australia then you have to question why you give them such a strong incentive' (Baillie, 2008). Current debates in the Australian media regarding the lack of growth in Australian film pinpoint this introverted push of cultural/protectionist worthiness as the key factor limiting the Australian film industry. Local audiences account for box-office takings of a billion each year, yet only 65 million of that sum is spent viewing Australian films in comparison to American audiences, for instance, who watch 97 per cent of their own product (Quinn, 2009: 22). While there have been notable high-grossing exceptions – (*Australia* (Luhrmann, 2008); *Samson and Delilah* (Thornton, 2009); *Mao's Last Dancer* (Beresford, 2009) – it has been argued in mainstream radio talk-back and the print media that over the last decade Australians have not been terribly receptive to their own films, regarding them as depressing, navel gazing, and overly eager to appear culturally appropriate.

Ruth Harley beat Rosen to the post of Screen Australia's Chief Executive. As former Chief Executive of the New Zealand Film Commission, she comes from a background of broader thinking in relation to film funding. It is thought that she'll inject new life into the flagging Australian film industry with her determination to support big-budget, mainstream-targeted projects and encourage the growth of box-office-rich genre films that have contributed to the success of the American market (Quinn, 2009: 22; Strickland, 2009: 19). It is therefore likely that the following decade will usher in a much more extraverted/outward-looking approach to national film-making at the expense of smaller, more culturally introverted/inward-looking projects. This proposed funding trajectory is already causing concern within film circles (Strickland, 2009: 19), but as Lisa French and Mark Poole argue in their historical study of the Australian Film Institute:

> Film-making is a global industry and many Australians have taken up offers from Hollywood and elsewhere. Ideas of "the national" are becoming increasingly more redundant as the Australian industry becomes ever more globally integrated and it becomes clearer that the industry will have to find a place in the world markets in order to maintain any place at all – particularly given our relatively small population and the frequently poor performances of our films at home.
>
> (French & Poole, 2009: 16)

The AFI's annual awards, however, have in the past been conspicuous in their snubbing of more globally focused productions. Miller's *Happy Feet* (a 2006 Australia-US co-production) received a special Global Achievement Award in 2007 – a somewhat 'benevolent' (almost patronizing) concession, first introduced in 2001 to recognize the achievements of outward/extraverted Australians working abroad. Collins and Davis argue in relation to Luhrmann's *Moulin Rouge* that minor 'craft awards for special effects damned the film with faint praise' (Collins & Davis, 2004: 30). The critical failure, but box-office success, of his follow-up pastiche *Australia* seemed to ensure that the film was largely overlooked in more significant categories at the 2009 AFI Awards, winning in the four lesser areas of Highest Grossing Film (ADU $29,844,258 and US$120 million worldwide), Best Production Design, Best Visual Effects, and Best Costume Design (Screen Australia, 2009b). Regardless of the artistic merits or demerits of *Australia*, it can be argued that the critical vitriol was in part fed by a deep-seated sense of tall-poppy-cringe at Luhrmann's entrepreneurial, exhibitionist and rampantly extraverted showmanship and self-promotion. This brief extract from a critique by Peter Conrad is telling:

> I said that the film is our shared failure because it betrays a lack of confidence in our autonomy, an incomprehension of our uniqueness, a stooped deference to the larger, louder, richer worlds far away whose attention we seek. That ingratiation is coupled, in a way that is inimitably Australian, with a touchy, aggressive xenophobia.
>
> (Conrad, 2009)

Conclusion

This argument, that the contemporary Australian film industry and its associated funding arms display a marked sense of introversion, is of course a much more complex situation than I have presented here. As an Australian, I might dare to generalize that 'our' introversion has been nurtured by a government funding history rooted in the need to develop an Australian film culture that is capable of generating employment, screen literacy and educational support, while also providing a forum for our own storytelling. To insist on cultural relevance and survive in the global community is a tough balancing act. But one might also argue, along the lines of the adage that the personal is political, that culturally relevant issues are also global issues driven by common themes, ideologies, oppressions and archetypal energies.

It is therefore no surprise that the Australian box-office success and critically acclaimed *Samson and Delilah* (Thornton, 2009) won Best Film at the Dublin film festival as well as the prestigious Camera D'Or at Cannes for best first feature film. This unsentimental narrative of two indigenous adolescents from the outer reaches of Alice Springs (Northern Territory), who confront love, racism, oppression and poverty, is a universal story. In arguing that the Australian film industry could be more outward-looking, extraverted and globally aware in its support systems, it is critical to consider that culturally sensitive/introspective films will inevitably cross cultural boundaries if they're able to tap bigger-picture archetypal thinking *and* are adequately marketed.

While those in the grip of introversion stew on ideas and acknowledge outer objects principally to create (new ideas, products, texts, etc.), they also/therefore facilitate cultural dialogue and extraverted engagement. What is then called for is balance of both positions. Introversion and extraversion are not exclusive poles but, as Jung argued, oscillate and borrow from each other. What good is a motivating idea or a creative take on one's culture that can speak to other cultures if denied its outer-world expression? *Samson and Delilah* is therefore a striking example of introversion facilitated by extraversion – culturally specific with global resonance. The stories of Australian film are not unique. Still . . . 'our' navel gazing has served us well in the past. It has fed our sense of lack, fear, tall poppy syndrome, adolescence, skewed uniqueness, shadow, film industry, and, of course, creativity. Unfortunately, Australian box-office sales tell us that this simply is not enough any more.

References

Arraj, J. (1986) Jung's Forgotten Bridge. *Journal of Analytical Psychology*, *31*, 173–180.

ATUA (2002) *Australian Trade Union Archives*, University of Melbourne. Retrieved from: www.atua.org.au/biogs/ALE0030b.htm

Baillie, R. (2008, June 11) Screen Australia hopes to revitalise Australian film industry. *The 7.30 Report*. Sydney, Australia: ABC television.

Beard, V. (2001) Evil Angels/A Cry in the Dark. Retrieved from: wwwmcc.murdoch.edu.au/ReadingRoom/film/dbase/2000/EvilAngels.html

Beebe, J. (2006) Psychological Types. In: Renos K. Papadopoulos (ed.), *The Handbook of Jungian Psychology: Theory Practice and Applications*. London and New York: Routledge (pp. 130–52).

Binet, A. (1900) Attention et adaptation. *L'année psychologique*, *6*(248), 404–13.

Brawer, F. B. & Spiegelman, J. M (1964) Rorschach and Jung: A study of introversion-extraversion. *The Journal of Analytical Psychology*, *9*(2), 137–49.

Burt, C. (1937) The analysis of temperament. British Journal of Medical Psychology, *17*, 1959–88.

Collins, F. and Davis, T. (2004) *Australian Cinema After Mabo*. Cambridge, Port Melbourne: Cambridge University Press.

Conrad, P. (2009, February) Gone with the Wind. *The Monthly*, *42*. Retrieved from: www.themonthly.com.au/monthly-essays-peter-conrad-gone-wind-australian-fiasco-1410

Dicks-Mireaux, M. J. (1964) Extraversion-Introversion in Experimental Psychology: Examples of Experimental Evidence and Their Theoretical Implications. *Journal of Analytical Psychology*, *9*(2), 17–128.

Feather, T. (1994) Attitudes Toward High Achievers and Reactions to their Fall: Theory and Research Concerning Tall Poppies. *Advances in Experimental Social Psychology*, *26*, 1–73.

French, L. and Poole, M. (2009) *Shining a Light: 50 Years of the Australian Film Institute*. Melbourne: Australian Teachers of Media (ATOM).

Greer, G. (2008, December 16) Once upon a time in a land, far, far away. *The Guardian*. Retrieved from: www.guardian.co.uk/film/2008/dec/16/baz-luhrmann-australia

Jung, C. G. (1971) *Psychological Types, Collected Works Vol. 6*. London: Routledge & Kegan Paul.

Kretschmer, E. (1925) *Physique and Character*. London: Kegan Paul; New York: Harcort Brace.

Loomis, M. (1982) A New Perspective for Jung's Typology: The Singer-Loomis inventory of personality. *Journal of Analytical Psychology*, *27*, 59–69.

Malone, P. (2001) *Myth and Meaning: Australian Film Directors in Their Own Words*. NSW: Currency Press.

MEAA (2009) Submission by Media, Entertainment & Arts Alliance to department of Environment, Water, Heritage and the Arts regarding guidelines on the entry into Australia of foreign actors for the purpose of employment in film and television productions. DEWHA Entry Guidelines for Foreign Actors. Retrieved from: www.alliance.org.au/resources/2009_submissions

Metzner, R. and Mahlberg, A. (1981) Towards a Reformulation of the Typology of Functions. *Journal of Analytical Psychology*, 26, 33–47.

O'Regan, T. (1996) *Australian National Cinema*. London and New York: Routledge.

Paul, A. M. (2004) *The Cult of Personality: How Personality Tests are Leading us to Miseducate our Children, Mismanage our Companies and Misunderstand Ourselves*. New York: Free Press.

Pavlov, I. P. (1941) *Conditioned Reflexes and Psychiatry*. London: Lawrence & Wishart.

Quinn, K. (2009, November 29) Last Chance to See. *The Sunday Age*, pp. 22.

Rorschach, H. (1964, original 1921) *Psychodiagnostik* (6th edition). Berne: H. Huber.

Rostan, L. (1828) *Cours Elémentaire D'hygiène*. Paris: Bechet.

Screen Australia (2009a) Producer offset: Guidance on significant Australian content (SAC). Retrieved from: www.screenaustralia.gov.au/producer_offset/eligibility.asp

Screen Australia (2009b) Australian films at the local box office in 2008. Retrieved from: www.screenaustralia.gov.au/news_and_events/2009/mr_090115_boxoffice.asp

Screen Australia (2009c) Top five Australian feature films each year, and gross Australian box-office earnt that year, 1988–2008. Retrieved from: www.screenaustralia.gov.au/gtp/mrboxausttop5.html

Screen Australia (2009d) Australian films earning more than US$100,000 gross at the US box office, 1981–2008. Retrieved from: www.screenaustralia.gov.au/gtp/mrboxus.html

Shamdasani, S. (2003) *Jung and the Making of Modern Psychology: The Dream of Science*. Cambridge: Cambridge University Press.

Sheldon, W. H. (1940) *The Varieties of Human Physique*. New York: Harper.

Strickland, K. (2009, Nov 12) Film Body Comments Cause Scene. *The Australian Financial Review*, pp. 19.

Waddell, T. (2006) *Mis/takes: Archetype, Myth and Identity in Screen Fiction*. London and New York: Routledge.

Chapter 20

The Wizard of Oz
A vision of development in the American political psyche

John Beebe[1]

The Wizard of Oz, the 1939 MGM colour musical starring Judy Garland, Bert Lahr, and Ray Bolger, has been reissued so often that its presence within the American psyche has the quality of a recurrent dream. As nearly everyone knows, it is about a little farm girl, Dorothy, who, in what may or may not be a dream, is blown with her little dog Toto from Kansas by cyclone to the fairyland of Oz. With the help of a Scarecrow, a Tin Man, and a Cowardly Lion whom she meets along the Yellow Brick Road that leads to Oz's capital, she must persuade the country's ruling Wizard to develop a way for her to return home. In the course of these adventures, Dorothy kills two Wicked Witches and secures the invaluable protection of a Good Witch, who in the end turns out to be the mentor who guides her safely home.

This sentimental mythology is made to work because of the sure vaudevillian touch with which the transcendental meanings are delivered – as if Ralph Waldo Emerson were being pantomimed by a troupe led by Ed Wynn, right up to the end, when the players gather for a curtain call. After years of simply enjoying its magic, I have thought to reflect on the film in these pages because it seems to address the American psyche, and particularly its politics, directly. As the title of this chapter suggests, I think this movie about a journey across incommensurable realms offers a vision for bridging other opposites of the kind that divide the American nation in its present crisis of value.

An analysis of the film by Salman Rushdie (1992) indicates the highest estimation this seeming child's entertainment has achieved in its sixty years of repeated re-release. In the fall of 1998, a restored, colour and sound corrected digital print won new respect not only for the high achievement of the film's various components – script, acting, cinematography, special effects, music, dance, costumes, and sets – but for their integration into a meaningful whole. As Rushdie notes, this integrity is all the more remarkable because 'it's extremely difficult to say who the artist is' (Rushdie 1992: 13). *The Wizard of Oz* had a producer and associate producer with strongly creative personalities, four successive directors, at least two sublime stars and, by the filming's bumpy end, three charismatic supporting actors, as well as an exceptional team of expert scriptwriters and a remarkable lyricist and composer to shape the meaning of its story (see also Harmetz 1998). A newspaperman and early specialist in marketing techniques, L. Frank Baum, had first told the story at the turn of the century to his own children (Traxel 1998: 140, 300–3). He developed it into a best-selling children's book that quickly became the basis for a stage musical – the first of the major reconfigurings by other than the original author's hands (Gardner and Nye 1994: 26). Yet we will not be misled if we linger awhile with the problem of Baum's original intention in creating this profitable property.

Baum himself said in his April 1900 preface to the first Chicago edition of *The Wonderful Wizard of Oz* that it 'was written solely to pleasure children of today' and that it 'aspires to being a modernized fairy tale, in which the wonderment and joy are retained and the heartaches and nightmares are left out' (Hearn 1983: 2). But it seems clear that he also took the occasion to playfully limn the political reality of his turn-of-the-century America. As Henry M. Littlefield first suggested in the similarly turbulent year of 1968, the cyclone that Baum envisages as hitting Kansas was likely to have been his allegory for the Populist movement. By the time Baum began to compose *The Wizard of Oz*, this movement had swept the entire Midwest into its vortex and had propelled the 'silver-tongued orator,' Nebraska Senator William Jennings Bryan, into his crusading 1896 run for the Presidency against the Eastern financiers' favourite (and eventual winner), William McKinley. The animus Bryan, a democrat, held against the Republican Establishment 'monometallists,' who wanted America's paper currency to be backed up only by gold bullion, was enunciated by his famous 'Cross of Gold' speech at the Chicago Democratic Party Convention ('You shall not crucify mankind upon a Cross of Gold'). His aim was to protect the farmers who preferred a loose, even inflationary monetary policy, since they had frequent need of credit. The Populist solution that he had appropriated for his party was to continue to use silver as well as gold to back the currency, a strategy that also appealed to silver mining interests in the West. Bryan won the nomination, and L. Frank Baum participated in his torchlit parades. Bryan's rhetoric must have moved Baum to imagine, in his American fairy tale, the Republican approach to economics as a mythical Yellow Brick Road leading America toward an illusory

Emerald City of centralized affluence, where McKinley would be presiding as humbug Wizard (Littlefield, in Hearn 1983: 221–233).[2]

Of the passionate, yet stubbornly abstruse twenty-five-year political debate over Free Silver versus the Gold Standard, historians Samuel Eliot Morison and Henry Steele Commager made a classic assessment:

> We can see now that the issue was both deeper and less dangerous than contemporaries realized. It was deeper because it involved a struggle for the ultimate control of government and of economy between the business interests of the East and the agrarian interests of the South and the West – a struggle in which gold and silver were mere symbols. It was less dangerous because, in all probability, none of the calamities so freely prophesied would have followed the adoption of either the gold or the silver standard at any time during these years. When the gold standard was finally adopted in 1900, the event made not a ripple on the placid seas of our economic life. When the gold standard was abandoned by Great Britain and the United States, a full generation later, the event led to no untoward results. Historical parallels and analogies are always dangerous, but we are safe in saying that in light of the experience of the 1930s much of the high-flown discussion of the 1890s was fantastic.
> (Morison and Commager 1950: 249)

Today, with the tools of Jungian psychology, we might better recognize why the idea of a Gold Standard elicited such an angry response from the political unconscious at the end of the nineteenth century. As an image symbolic of the metal that in alchemy was the earthly counterpart of the sun (Sol), an exclusive privileging of gold suggested the predominance of solar masculine values within the ruling establishment. In the grip of religious fervour unaccounted for by his economic argument, Bryan was urging his party to balance the Gold Standard with that of Silver, a metal which we know from Jung's alchemical researches to be the terrestrial representative of Luna and thus a symbol of the Feminine Principle. Already, through the charismatic leadership of the 'silver-tongued orator,' the Democratic Party's twentieth-century matriarchal stance, with its Eros toward the economically less fortunate, was taking shape in opposition to the more traditionally patriarchal Republican position emphasizing self-reliance.[3] But although such an interpretation of Bryan's movement was fully compatible with the preeminence that Baum gives to the feminine in the narrative structure of the Oz books as a whole,[4] its full implications would not have been conscious for Baum at the time. The often whimsical Baum probably turned his fancy to the politics of his day as part of a more general strategy to amuse children by exposing the pretensions of their elders, but this move gave his intuition its chance to explore the American political psyche in a way that continues to fascinate. Littlefield, who has shrewdly deciphered the allegorical level of the text, believes that the Scarecrow, with his anxiety over his intelligence, originally reflected the lack of intellectual self-confidence of many Midwesterners in Baum's time, when they were still reeling from the accusation recently levelled against them by William Allen White in an 1896 article, *What's the Matter with Kansas*? White, asserting that Kansas's farmers were ignorant, irrational and generally muddle-headed (Hearn 1983: 227), had suggested they should be worried about their thinking. The Cowardly Lion, according to Littlefield, is Bryan himself, with his mighty oratorical roar, his underlying chronic insecurity, and his ultimate courage in taking on the East Coast establishment. The rusted Tin Man's unwilling immobility represents the fate of the unemployed workers in the East after the depression of 1893. The pair of Wicked Witches might refer to the threats posed, on the one hand, by the environment (i.e. drought, the traditional witch 'of the West' that can only be 'put out' by water) and, on the other hand, by the market (traditionally under the negative control 'of the East'). These adversaries, Baum's allegory argues, can be defeated by the energy provided by the Populist cyclone if only farmers can learn to think for themselves, mobilize their potential allies among the politically rusty East Coast workforce, and muster their courage in standing up to the hypocrisy of central government. Otherwise, the soul of traditional agrarian America must remain, like Dorothy, lost and unable to find its way home.

Although this first detailed political reading of the tale has much to recommend it, we cannot reduce the meanings of this perennially popular story to these topical references of the time of its creation or even to the probable intentions of its creator, L. Frank Baum. Rather, Littlefield's exposure of the election-year subtext serves us best if it enables us to grasp that *The Wizard of Oz*, like so many works that have captured the American imagination, derives a good deal of its energy from a primary concern for the political health of the nation.

In the case of *The Wonderful Wizard of Oz*, this concern survives in the later constructions that have been placed on the tale. When the story was made into a film forty years after Baum first wrote it out, for instance, the allegory's point of reference seemed to have shifted to Midwestern anxiety over America's turn to internationalism on the eve of the Second

World War. Its 1938 script certainly trumpets the message so often sounded by the isolationists at that time: 'There's no place like home.' In the 1970s, with the advent of women's liberation and the feminist and gay rethinking of the constrictions of traditional gender roles for men and women, the film began (in Jungian terms) to signal a triumph of matriarchal values over the threatening patriarchal anima (Witch) and the pompous patriarchal animus (Wizard). A liberated gay man, for instance, might describe himself as a 'friend of Dorothy' and locate his own individuation story in hers (Hopcke 1989). Today, two decades after winning the Cold War against Soviet Russia, Americans watch *The Wizard of Oz* knowing that their young nation's fate, inevitable as Dorothy's in the face of the cyclone, has too long been to be swept onto the international stage in the uncomfortably prominent role of peacekeeper, the destroyer of all world wickedness. From that last perspective, the film can now seem to my compatriots like a warning dream coming from some prescience in the American psyche of 1939, urging us to stiffen our integrity lest we lose our national centre in the inflation of becoming the world's leading power, one indeed 'not in Kansas anymore.'

The Wizard of Oz, however, is more than a warning, for it resolves the tensions it creates. The anxiety is beautifully brought to life by Judy Garland, who is an image less of Baum's little Dorothy, as captured by W. W. Denslow's original drawings, than of a growing, insecure nation on the verge of its debut as a mature world power. But the film moves its heroine, and our sense of ourselves as a nation, toward the mature integrity we feel at the end when Dorothy, in a closing set piece suggestive of wholeness, is back from the dream and nightmare of Oz, and finds herself safe in her own bed, surrounded by seven of the Kansas characters. This final scene is like the coda of a human symphony, making explicit an eightfold structure of consciousness in the relation of these characters to each other and to Dorothy. With this tableau as a key to the structure of the film, it is possible to trace how Dorothy's individuation proceeds through her links to the other characters.

The interaction of eight characters is one way to visualize the differentiation of consciousness in an individuating psyche.[5] Within such a polyphonic arrangement, the distinct consciousnesses represented by the characters have, like so many voices in a democracy, a potential for harmony, but one that will be either undermined or achieved by the particular political process which the film records. I call that process *political* because it involves alliances, contending parties, and struggles for audience and power, all revealed by the way the characters in a film play out their psychological roles – their different consciousnesses – in relation to each other. In a film with particular resonance like *The Wizard of Oz*, these roles can be specifically metaphoric of the political developments taking place in the American psyche at the moment of the film's construction.

A natural starting point in elucidating this political structure within *The Wizard of Oz* is with Dorothy herself. In terms of the film's idiosyncratic politics of American consciousness, the little girl's standpoint is privileged. She emblematizes a form of what nowadays is called 'emotional intelligence' (Goleman 1995). As played by Judy Garland, who is ever poised to react to the feelings of the other characters (including her little dog Toto) and make them her concern, this standpoint is what C. G. Jung has called *extraverted feeling*.[6] It is in relation to this apparent strength of her character that we can understand her special relationship to the Scarecrow, the first of the fantastic companions she picks up on the Yellow Brick Road. The Scarecrow, who famously starts their acquaintance by singing and dancing Harburg and Arlen's *If I Only Had a Brain*, is a marvellous depiction of the insecurities captured by Jung's phrase, 'inferior introverted thinking.' According to Jung's theory of psychological types – that is, types of psychological consciousness, or what present-day cognitive psychologists call 'intelligences' (Gardner 1983; Thompson 1985) – *introverted thinking* is at the opposite end of a rational axis from extraverted feeling.

There is also a power differential in these arrangements. If extraverted feeling is the superior, dominant function, introverted thinking will regard itself as inferior. And indeed, the Scarecrow has an inferiority complex and gives image, with his comical physical incoordination, to the inherent unreliability of any 'inferior function.' The character's movements are not entirely under his conscious control due to the flimsy quality of his embodiment as a cloth man stuffed with straw. But his connection with Dorothy gives him a 'spine' to replace the beanpole she helps him down from. We can visualize the two characters together as the backbone of the movie itself. Their relationship is central to the integrity of the film. Figure 20.1 illustrates what I mean.

In parenthesis, I have defined each character in Jungian terms according to the typical form of consciousness which that character displays throughout the film. The *position* of the characters in relation to the other is also important if we want to understand the consciousness politics of the film. In relation to the Scarecrow on the spine or axis of integrity of the film, Dorothy is in the superior position. We have already suggested as much by saying that throughout the film her kind of

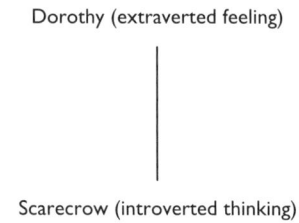

Figure 20.1 The relationship between Dorothy and the Scarecrow

intelligence is privileged. Although Dorothy describes herself as 'the Small and the Meek' when introducing herself to the Wizard (who with characteristic puffery has described himself as 'Oz, the Great and Terrible'), there is little doubt that she trusts her feeling responses more than does any other character. In the end, it is just an uncensored spontaneous reaction that allows her to accomplish the heroic deed of melting the witch by throwing a bucket of water over her. Dorothy is related to as a superior person, not only by the Munchkins whose Mayor and officials greet her as a visiting dignitary, indeed their 'national heroine,' but also by all the other characters. She is thus a perfect image of Jung's 'superior function' of consciousness, a political designation that I have elsewhere described as the locus of the hero archetype in any psyche (see Harris 1996). Similarly, the Scarecrow – a marginally adapted even if magical figure with whom most people would not want to be seen in public – is a good personification of the way the animus (in relation to a woman's more comfortably dominant superior function) is forced to carry the 'inferior function' role.[7] We could therefore draw our diagram again with new labels that emphasize the political relationship of archetypes in this arrangement of consciousness (Figure 20.2).

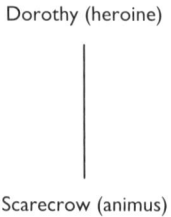

Figure 20.2 The political relationship between Dorothy and the Scarecrow (1)

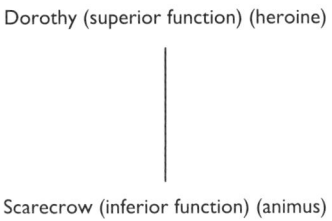

Figure 20.3 The political relationship between Dorothy and the Scarecrow (2)

Putting the two types of construction – hierarchical status and archetype – together, the political diagram of these relationships would resemble Figure 20.3.

When we start to introduce the other characters around this 'spine' that defines the politics of consciousness within *The Wizard of Oz*, we can also identify an axis of 'auxiliary' functions that set out to assist Dorothy in mature and less mature ways. This much more 'irrational' axis is defined by Glinda the Good and the Cowardly Lion. Glinda represents a very motherly, and I would say introverted, intuition, which 'knows' the right magic to protect Dorothy but largely keeps her knowledge of its workings to herself, until the time seems right to share it. The Yellow Brick Road that she asks Dorothy to follow is itself an image of intuition, which Jung notes is frequently symbolized in fantasy by the color yellow (Jung 1959: 335, 379). On the other hand, the Cowardly Lion, in his physical size, his bullying swagger, and his need to impose his body on others ('Put 'em up, put 'em up!' he demands, as he thrusts forth his clenched fists and swings his tail) is defined in terms of *extraverted sensation*. This type of consciousness, according to Jung, can be a formidable intelligence, too, the inverse of *introverted intuition* in its immediate attention to present realities, but here it is in a primitive level of development. In contrast to Glinda's implied parental position within the story as Great Mother, he has the status of the Great Baby, whom the other characters must chide or reassure. He oscillates between boastful omnipotence ('I'll be King of the Forest') and cowering terror ('Why'd you have to do that?' he blubbers, when Dorothy slaps him across the nose for growling at Toto). Indeed, part of the comedy of the Lion, as played by Bert Lahr, is that his intuition is so inferior that, for all his fearfulness, he never seems to anticipate the real danger he invites by the physical (extraverted sensation) abandon with which he wades into each new situation. It is not so much that he lacks courage as that his courage is of the *puer aeternus* type. Bert Lahr's Lion displays an inflated sense of what he can pull off that is easily punctured by reality, at which point he falls into despair over his own cowardice. The *puer aeternus*, like the Great Mother, is an archetype that Jungian psychology has reintroduced to Western culture. The Latin (from Ovid) means eternal, or perpetual, boy. This certainly seems to define the Cowardly Lion. And so we can draw an auxiliary character axis for these two opposed consciousnesses that bring their strength to Dorothy (Figure 20.4).

Locating these characters now around Dorothy and the Scarecrow, we get a basic quaternity of figures that defines the particular pattern of consciousness which emanates from the story itself (Figure 20.5).

Glinda (Great Mother)   Cowardly Lion (*puer aeternus*)
(introverted intuition)  (extraverted sensation)

Figure 20.4 An auxiliary character axis.

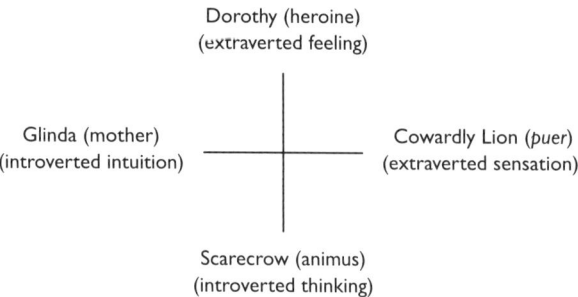

Figure 20.5 The pattern of consciousness emanating from the story

If, however, we replace the particular character names and the archetypal roles they occupy in the story by names for the consciousnesses they represent and add a political designation to suggest their relative *power* within the story, our diagram would resemble Figure 20.6.

Figure 20.6, as *aficionados* of Jungian type theory will recognize, defines the consciousness of the extraverted feeling type with auxiliary introverted intuition, or what the Myers-Briggs Type Indicator (a standard

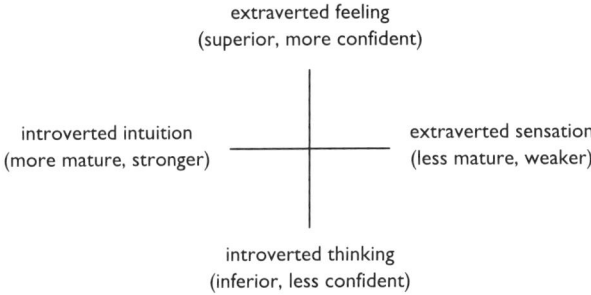

Figure 20.6 Consciousnesses and their political designations

test of the pattern of consciousness preferences in individuals) scores as ENFJ. A recent description of ENFJ in the type literature follows:

> On the great highway of life, ENFJs are car poolers, making sure that everyone has a ride, wears a seat belt, and gets where they're going, safe and sound. . . . They have a psychological turn of mind, an interest in the journeys people take and how they're negotiated.
> (Thomson 1998: 357)

This description sounds like the sensibility of *The Wizard of Oz* taken as a whole. The consciousness of the characters and their relative positions combine to give the film itself a definite consciousness – that is, a certain set of concerns which define it not only as a psychological, but also a political space. By establishing the positions of the characters in relation to each other in terms of the way they feel about themselves, how the other characters relate to them, and the degree of emotional development they display, we can understand the consciousness politics of the film.

Movies, of course, do not depend only on functions of consciousness to get their effects. They also, notoriously, depict forms of unconsciousness that challenge the more conscious characters with life's threats, dangers, and complications, as well as their own defences against moving forward. Unconsciousness itself is a political force in *The Wizard of Oz*, as we see in the remarkable scene where the enchanted poppies put the flesh-and-blood characters to sleep and threaten to stop this particular 'road movie' in its tracks. And of course the entire film (unlike Baum's novel) is cast as a dream experienced by Dorothy in a coma, after a blow on the head by a window loosened in the cyclone. That the unconscious presents itself to Dorothy and her conscious helpers in the form of various personalities who represent a system of threats and defences suggests that the film expresses a reaction to trauma itself. As Donald Kalsched has demonstrated, such shadow figures play a major role in the psyche's response to being traumatized, and they are both ambivalent sources of further complication as well as unexpected sources of help from within. What Kalsched (1996: 62) has written about therapeutic work is also true for our struggle to make sense of the psyche in art and politics:

> We encounter here a supreme irony in our work with the psyche. The selfsame powers that seem so set on undermining our . . . efforts – so ostensibly devoted to death, dismemberment, and annihilation of consciousness – are the very reservoir from which new life, fuller integration, and true enlightenment derive.

From the standpoint of Baum's allegory, the trauma from which Dorothy is seeking to recover is the split in the American political psyche itself, its historic, tragic tension between populist and plutocratic interests. It is from this 'basic fault' in the American political psyche that the characters in the Oz story first drew life, and their tensions survive the later retellings of the tale.

We will now examine figures in both the novel and the film that are truly shadowy, in that neither their potential for good nor for evil is entirely clear, even when it seems to be. Rather, they participate in the murky ambivalence of the unconscious itself, as something not just to be overcome but to be faced and learned from. The most obvious of these characters is the Wizard. When he is unmasked at last by Toto, who pulls aside the curtain, revealing the humbug, as the Scarecrow correctly names him, Dorothy is moved to offer one of her spontaneous, forceful feeling evaluations: 'Oh, you're a very bad man!' The Wizard replies, 'Oh no, my dear, I – I'm a very good man. I'm just a very bad wizard' (Langley *et al.* 1994: 62). Yet the same man, who with callous opportunism sent Dorothy and her friends to bring back the broomstick of the Wicked Witch of the West (a politically 'smart' move, since the Witch had already sky-written with that broom her command to him to 'surrender Dorothy'), proceeds to use his rhetoric to show them how best to think about themselves. In other words, he serves initially to undermine the confidence of the ultimately prevailing characters, but ends up supporting it. He is an image of the power of the unconscious to be used in both cruel and kind ways. Such ambivalence is characteristic of a psychological intelligence used demonically, and the Wizard as described by Baum in the novel resembles a demon in the way he assumes different shapes. To Dorothy he appears as a great Head, to the Scarecrow, a lovely Lady, and to her other, more sensitive companion, the Tin Man as a 'most terrible Beast.' (This last demonic avatar reminds us that the remarkable ability of a demonic figure to be 'cruel and kind at the same time' was perhaps first remarked upon, as Joseph Henderson has noted [Jung *et al.* 1964: 138], by Beauty's father in the quintessentially psychological fairy tale *Beauty and the Beast*.)

In the film, however, it is the Scarecrow who is in the best position to stand up to the Wizard's impressive iconography and rhetoric by saying, 'You humbug,' a choice of words Frank Morgan's *extraverted thinking* Wizard for once does not correct and subvert ('Yes, that's exactly so, I'm a humbug'[8]). This is a crucial moment in the politics of the film when the integrity of the Scarecrow's incisive introverted thinking succeeds in standing up to the obfuscations of the Wizard's demonic extraverted thinking. This confrontation near the end of the film is reminiscent of the moment before the cyclone trip to Oz when Dorothy rebukes Almira Gulch (who is trying to have the biting and cat-chasing Toto destroyed) by exclaiming, 'You wicked old witch!' In that earlier confrontation, our extraverted feeling heroine stands up to a strongly opposing will symbolized by another feeling standpoint, the antagonistic *introverted feeling*[9] of Miss Gulch, who is so concerned with protecting her own interests that she doesn't care enough about the feelings of others.

Like Dorothy, we are being intitiated into the politics of confrontation, where consciousnesses encounter opposing attitudes, with respect to introversion and extraversion, in the form of figures they experience as shadowy. The characters that give the film its spine of integrity can be diagrammed in relation to their antagonists, naming the psychological types associated with each character. We should understand that even a figure of the unconscious can exhibit a characteristic type, implying that there is intelligence in the unconscious, although it is typically used in an unconscious and frequently unethical way, hence the description of such functions of potential but problematic consciousness as 'in shadow' (Figure 20.7). In this scheme, we can see that Dorothy's heroic extraverted feeling is opposed by the introverted feeling of Almira Gulch, and that the Scarecrow's righteous indignation, expressing an animus demand for a higher standard of integrity, is directed against the pompous obfuscations of the Wizard.

The connection of the extraverted feeling Dorothy to the introverted thinking Scarecrow is an axis of integrity created by their love for each

314 Image, type and archetype

Figure 20.7 Dorothy and the Scarecrow in relation to their antagonists

other. By contrast, the introverted feeling Almira Gulch and, at least initially, the Wizard, are mere deployers of power, tyrants in their respective realms. We need to look more closely at these characters who define a shadow axis that poses a political threat to the integrity of Dorothy and the Scarecrow.

Although played by the same actress, Almira Gulch does *not* correspond in every psychological detail to the Witch she becomes in Dorothy's 'dream'. Margaret Hamilton's performance is in fact a dual role no less extraordinary than the twin sisters played a few years later by Bette Davis in *A Stolen Life* (Bemhardt, 1946) and Olivia de Havilland in *The Dark Mirror* (Siodmak, 1946), films which make explicit this Hollywood convention. The challenge to an actress playing two sharply contrasting characters in the same picture is traditionally posed in classic American film by one character being (in the language of psychological type) extraverted and irrational, and the other introverted and rational. The political preference within the traditional American psyche for women who are introverted and rational, usually introverted feeling, can readily be noticed here. In terms of traditional American values, this has the psychological implication of asking women to take up the position of anima figures, supporting and granting the legitimation of their approval to the heroic extraverted thinking of its ruling men.

In the world of *The Wizard of Oz*, everything is topsy-turvy. The extraverted thinking 'ruling man' is the humbug Wizard in Oz, and the introverted feeling Almira Gulch owns 'half the county' in Kansas, in which Aunt Em's farm is located. Far from being represented as an anima figure supporting the integrity of the power structure, she is presented as an opposing personality threatening the rule of care in governing human relationships. Yet even though her 'better' character is already shadowy, Margaret Hamilton runs true to the dual role genre in which her performance falls, in being asked to play an even more wicked character who is extraverted and irrational. Her magnificently menacing Witch, who is constantly threatening Dorothy with what she is *going* to do to her, is a marvellous example of the shadowy (negatively witchy) use of the psychological consciousness which Jung calls *extraverted intuition*, the function which concerns itself, in any situation, with future possibilities. She discloses this promise of bad things to come not just with specific frightening suggestions but with the anticipatory delight of her evil cackle.

And, unlike Hamilton's Almira Gulch, her Witch finds her typological opposite in the film not in Dorothy, but Glinda. Glinda the Good Witch (who almost never discloses her designs) and the Wicked Witch of the West (who always does), take opposite attitudes toward the irrational intuitive power (the ability to perceive and conjure by way of the unconscious) that is traditionally the province of any witch. Again in the language of Jung's typology of character, Glinda the Good's attitude is that of the introverted intuitive, and the Wicked Witch of the West's attitude is that of the extraverted intuitive. The Wicked Witch's winged monkeys rather perfectly embody an intuition used to terrify others with its unexpected ability to get to them, just as the Witch is always inserting herself into Dorothy's private spaces and thoughts – for instance, in the crystal ball sequence in the Witch's castle when she elicits and then mocks Dorothy's anxieties about Aunt Em. This is the opposite of Glinda's reassuringly introverted self-contained, bubble-enclosed, intuition used to solace and focus Dorothy without intruding on the girl's autonomy.

We find a similar pair of opposed attitudes in the two animal characters in the film, who together occupy the other pole – sensation – of the irrational axis. Toto and the Cowardly Lion are opposed from the moment the Cowardly Lion makes his first appearance. When the Lion growls and threatens Dorothy, the Scarecrow, and the Tin Man, Toto barks. The Lion goes after Toto, but Dorothy slaps the larger beast, reducing him, as we have seen, to a sort of whimpering baby. Toto's role here is to facilitate in the exposing of the reality behind the bluster. That is precisely what the little dog again does when the Wizard of Oz tries to put off keeping his promise to reward Dorothy, the Scarecrow, the Tin Man, and the Lion after they succeed in bringing him the broomstick of the Wicked Witch of the West. This time it is the Wizard who roars, 'Do not arouse the wrath of the Great and Powerful Oz.' At this point, Toto runs to the background of the big screening room on which Oz's propaganda image surmounts the throne and pulls aside a curtain hanging to one side. That is when the human Wizard is finally revealed, talking into a microphone.

Toto, who is normally rather still and never charismatic, is really the character to expose what Rushdie calls the Great Humbug. Rushdie confesses that he 'cannot stand' Toto, finding even the purposive bit with the curtain 'an irritating piece of mischief-making' (Rushdie 1992: 17–18). Toto, who works behind the scenes, is personally unprepossessing, does not usually call attention to himself, and makes few wasted movements, is a marvellous image of *introverted sensation*, a consciousness close to intelligent animal sense which concerns itself with identifying what is real. In the final scene of *The Wizard of Oz*, when Aunt Em's rational solution to Dorothy's account of the journey to Oz is to tell the girl, 'We dream lots of silly things,' Dorothy cries exasperatedly to the Kansans assembled around her bed, 'Doesn't anyone believe me?' and Toto jumps up beside her, as if to say he can vouch for the reality of her experience. Introverted sensation, as Jung (1921) was the first to emphasize, is an irrational function, which can appreciate the reality of the psyche even against rational considerations, because it trusts the evidence of its own senses.

But Toto is also a trickster, who consistently moves the plot forward by creating some kind of mischief that breaks with an established order of things (biting Almira Gulch, growling at the Lion, jumping out of the hot-air balloon just as the Wizard is about to take Dorothy back to America). The effect is usually to subvert an inflated use of power and force Dorothy, out of her feeling for Toto, to take a stronger position in defence of caring generally. In other words, Toto galvanizes Dorothy's instinctive courage, the very quality which the Cowardly Lion lacks. The puerile Lion therefore reflects something immature in Dorothy's character that Toto is helping her to grow beyond.

By adding the shadow functions carried by the (Wicked) Witch and trickster, we can now more fully illustrate the interplay of consciousnesses that gives energy to the auxiliary axis between intuition and sensation, which drives the irrational plot of the film, forcing Dorothy through their cross-fire to develop her integrity as a character (Figure 20.8).

The Witch's role in bringing out Dorothy's courage is obvious; that portion of the tale is a nineteenth-century hero story, with an obvious

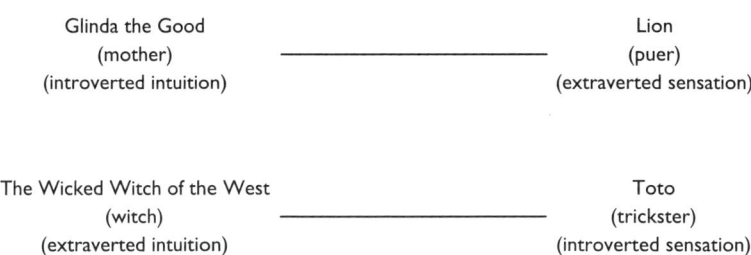

Figure 20.8 The interplay of auxiliary consciousnesses

nod to Dumas. Dorothy becomes, perhaps, d'Artagnan (although she has to split this role with Toto), and the Lion, the Scarecrow, and Tin Man become the Three Musketeers. This is the side of political effectiveness that is celebrated by successful revolutions, holy wars, and being on the 'right' side in elections. It leaves out the deeper part of the shadow to catalyze political individuation, a development that can only take place when the shadow is included and appreciated as part of one's own political consciousness, rather than simply defeated or repressed as belonging to an Other who is 'wrong.' Heroic victories generally result in inflating the winner's standpoint beyond its true value. Here it really is up to the trickster to take the story of one's political development beyond simply 'putting out the Witch.' Anyone studying what Samuels has called 'the political development of the person' (Samuels 1993: 53–61) should take heed of the way Toto forces even the victorious Dorothy to rethink her own values.

Nowhere in the film is Toto's shadowy role in forcing Dorothy to think and feel for herself made more evident than in the final scene of the Technicolor (Oz) portion of the film, when, as a consequence of Toto jumping out of the balloon basket, Dorothy is forced to turn to Glinda for help getting back home. When Glinda in her introverted way finally discloses to Dorothy the secret of the ruby slippers by leading Dorothy to articulate what she has learned in Oz about her 'heart's desire,' Dorothy is able to say with full heart, 'There's no place like home.' This is introverted feeling at last from the extraverted feeling heroine, and it is this expression of it that directs the slippers to grant her wish.

The deep red of the slippers would alone have justified the decision of the producers at MGM to film *The Wizard of Oz* in colour, for the hue imparts a value, and a psychological meaning, that Baum's allegorical Silver Shoes could not convey. The 'power' in the slippers is not just the force of the feminine principle, but the power of conscious introverted feeling to deepen and ground love. This explains the role of two important characters in the film whom I have left until now to discuss: Aunt Em and the Tin Man. They are linked in Dorothy's fantasy by her shared concern for their hearts. In the Tin Man's case, the problem with his heart is simply his feeling that he lacks one, a problem that Dorothy takes on as if it were her own. In Aunt Em's case, real heart trouble is at issue. Or so Dorothy believes, for in the first crystal ball vision, related to Dorothy while she is still in Kansas by Professor Marvel shortly after she runs away with Toto to escape Miss Gulch, the fortune teller has seen Aunt Em putting her hand on her heart and falling onto a bed. Both Aunt Em and the Tin Man induce Dorothy to begin to reflect on the problem that lies within her own feeling, a deficiency that is masked by the abundant empathy she shows for all the other characters and the appreciation they bestow on her for it. Dorothy's feeling, despite its privileged, even valorized, status in the film, is somehow too unthinkingly, and too one-sidedly, extraverted.

It was not just Almira Gulch who was annoyed by Dorothy in Kansas. Aunt Em, that kindly, reserved keeper of order on the farm, whose caring for everyone is always held in reserve, is driven to ask Dorothy early in the film to 'just help us out today and find yourself where you won't get into any trouble!' That place, of course, is 'Over the Rainbow' – in Oz, where Dorothy is put magically in touch with the deeper value of harmony with her surroundings that Aunt Em is trying to convey to her.

One of the neatest psychological touches in the film is how the quietly, kind Aunt Em and the noisily mean Almira Gulch are, on the inside, so similar. Both are concerned with property, and proper order, and both, I think, exhibit the same Jungian type in their brief but memorable onscreen appearances. Miss Gulch, recognizing that others may not understand where she is coming from, butresses her introverted feeling with an extraverted thinking animus (personified by the Sheriff, whose order to have Toto seized she brandishes). The less defensive Aunt Em shows the vulnerability of their type more openly when she says, 'Almira Gulch . . . just because you own half the county doesn't mean you have the power to run the rest of us! For twenty-three years I've been dying to tell you what I thought of you . . . and now . . . well – being a Christian woman – I can't say it!' Interestingly, Miss Gulch can't find the words to respond to Aunt Em, either. The inability to articulate emotion that is nonetheless strongly felt is a particular hallmark of introverted feeling. But both women, with their apparently different, nicer and nastier styles of doing so, are united in wanting to oppose Dorothy's heedless extraverted feeling wilfulness with strong feeling wills of their own coming from another direction.

> Introverted feeling, as Jung was the first to get us to see, is a valuation function which works at the archetypal (not the personal) level, taking the deepest possible sounding of a situation. It not only enables but compels us to feel the rightness and wrongness of images, arrogating from its very closeness to the archetypal a bench of judgment that grants it the power to decide what is appropriate and what is not.
> (Beebe 1992: 135)

This theme is carried forward in the Oz section of the film, when Dorothy happily starts to pick apples off an inviting-looking tree. The tree (an introverted feeling type) turns out to have other feelings than the extraverted generosity Dorothy instinctively expects. It asks, 'How would you like to have someone come along and pick something off of you?' At this point in the film, Dorothy is no match for such an attitude; she simply fails to understand it. The feeling value concealed in this standpoint is conveyed by the deep red of the apples on the tree, which 'rhymes' visually with the ruby slippers. The overtones of the Garden of Eden in the forbidden apples suggest a Knowledge of which Dorothy is psychologically innocent. And this, of course, is the political issue at the heart of the film: the tension between extraverted feeling and introverted feeling. The value of introverted feeling is unavailable to extraverted feeling because of the latter's blindness toward it. The tree is thus a marvellous symbol of the consciousness (and political problem) that I have already identified as the opposing personality challenging the heroine. It actually starts to throw its apples at Dorothy when manipulated to do so by the clever Scarecrow, who sees a way to get Dorothy her snack. But this comedic interlude, which culminates in Dorothy happily scrambling to pick up the apples, turns suddenly serious when her hand (that is, her extraverted feeling) presses into the hard, still foot of the Tin Man. The figure is rusty and immobile, and even after she oils him, so that he can talk, he quickly opposes her cheerful assurance that he's 'perfect now' with a sarcastic retort: 'Oh, bang on my chest if you think I'm perfect.' Then the Tin Man explains that his chest is hollow because he hasn't got a heart.

In the ensuing song sequence, part of which is a duet, Jack Haley's Tin Man seems almost effeminately competitive with Garland's Dorothy. Like Almira Gulch, Aunt Em, and the Grouchy Apple Tree, the Tin Man embodies a feeling attitude that is opposed to Dorothy's. His appearance on the scene creates within the vaudeville show business leitmotiv of the film a political complication between the actors (upstaging) that was absent from Garland's previous duet with Bolger. From his sentimentality, moreover, it is obvious that the Tin Man doesn't exactly lack a heart; what he lacks (as the Wizard shrewdly figures out) is a testimonial, that is, an extraverted attestation of his feeling (which the Wizard gives him in the form of a heart-shaped watch). That the Tin Man is, moreover, all armour suggests that his introverted feeling is somehow rigid. By now, the audience will already have noted that stiffening up is one of Dorothy's most characteristic defences, conveyed perfectly by Judy Garland's self-referential double takes. The narcissistic side of this defence does in a way lack 'heart,' because it cuts the character off from appreciating the introverted feeling of others. For all Dorothy's vaunted empathy, where is her feeling for Miss Gulch's concern over cat and garden, and for Aunt Em's desire for order on the farm?

One can trace a whole chain of figures and images representing the opposing personality type which Dorothy is gradually coming to terms with in the film   from Almira Gulch and Aunt Em, through the Grouchy Apple Tree and the Tin Man, and on to the Witch's Cossack-like guard. The series is punctuated by, and culminates in, the most mysterious of all these images of introverted feeling: the ruby slippers.

These slippers, which once belonged to the 'sister' of the Wicked Witch of the West, that is, to the Wicked Witch of the East, are, I think, meant to represent the concealed introverted feeling standpoint of Almira Gulch, which, in a more appealing presentation, is that of Aunt Em as well. In running away from both of these women, and then being swept up by the cyclone – the objectified force of her own instinctive repudiation of their standpoint – Dorothy has in effect 'killed' introverted feeling and has to accept the psychological consequences. Herein lies a complication in the assertion of power that Jung understood better than any other psychologist, one that very few contemporary politicians are subtle enough to grasp. Jung tells us that when someone succeeds in killing, that is overcoming, the *mana* of another person (Jung defines this Polynesian word for charisma as the 'bewitching quality of a person'), the conqueror then automatically [acquires] that mana (Jung 1966: 227–228). This, Jung tells us, is in accord 'with the primitive belief that when a man kills the mana-person he assimilates the mana into his own body' (ibid.). Our extraverted feeling heroine must therefore accept the mana of what she has defeated, which is the introverted feeling standpoint not just of Almira Gulch but of Aunt Em as well. That is why the ruby slippers, carrying the power she has arrogated, appear on her own feet and seem almost to be attached to them, so that the Wicked Witch of the West realizes that she will have to kill her to get them back. Dorothy does not learn how to use the slippers' power, however, until the end of the film.

Again, we can illustrate these stations in Dorothy's political development, which gradually transform her character from someone who is merely a partisan of her own standpoint to someone who is truly able to appreciate the value of a standpoint that is completely opposed to her own (Figure 20.9).

It is an appreciation for the introverted side of feeling that Glinda the Good is able at last to bring out in Dorothy when she gets her to articulate the value that the film calls 'There's no place like home.' This is the part of the script which many dismiss as sentimental or cynical, including Rushdie (1992), who calls it 'a conservative little homily,' and Zipes, who says it 'is all a lie' since the point of Baum's Oz stories is that 'home cannot be found in America' (Zipes 1998: ix). What Zipes calls this 'Home Sweet Home' ending can easily seem to lock onto the isolationist Republican discourse of the America Firsters who were opposing Franklin Roosevelt's increasing interest in the problems of Europe at the time the film was made. Indeed, its introverted feeling was not at all a popular message by the time the film was released. Several re-releases were needed before the film made a profit, and only a series of annual television showings secured its status as a classic. America, after 1939, moved on to its manifest destiny to make the world safe for democracy, and extraverted feeling values were to predominate – that is,

Extraverted feeling	(stance toward)	*Introverted feeling*
Dorothy	initially opposed to	Aunt Em
	kills	Wicked Witch of the East
	doesn't understand	Ruby Slippers
	is attacked by	Grouchy Apple Tree
	oils and helps to heal	Tin Man
	wins over	Winkie Guard
	learns to use	Ruby Slippers
	finally appreciates	Aunt Em

Figure 20.9 Stations in Dorothy's political development

the values associated with selling and promoting 'the American way of life.'

We watch the film today in an age that has almost forgotten what introverted feeling is (could Gary Cooper be a star today?), and the return home to Aunt Em seems anticlimactic to many. At best the movie seems to record a return to traditional values which many sophisticated people are unwilling to make. Yet if one lets the magic of Judy Garland's performance work on one's American political sensitivities, one can see how extraordinary it can be for a liberal extraverted feeling to make a gesture toward the other, more conservative, feeling standpoint. (Just as conservative introverted feeling in American politics perennially dismisses extraverted feeling empathy as 'bleeding heart liberalism,' so liberal extraverted feeling routinely discounts introverted feeling's emphasis on individual responsibility as cold and judgmental.) It is much more common, in American films, for a cold, introverted feeling to warm up and make a concession to extraverted feeling. Garland's Dorothy, realizing as her own the power implied by the ruby slippers, really reaches out to Aunt Em, and we want to embrace her for it. On the part of the character, this is a step beyond maintaining the consistency of her own attitude, and also beyond the way she sharpened her integrity in Oz with the support of her magical helpers. Her final gesture, without disavowing her Oz experiences, is a stunning acknowledgment of a value beyond the heroic. Her political development and, indeed, achievement in the film is finally not about justifying her own standpoint, but about finding common ground for the continuity of value.

Dorothy's ability, back in Kansas, to move herself into the territory originally pre-empted by Almira Gulch is paralleled by the Scarecrow's ascendance to the rulership of Oz when the Wizard abdicates in his favour. Together, Dorothy and the Scarecrow seem to represent a new, more conscious order with the integrity to supplant the patriarchal anima (Miss Gulch) and animus (the Wizard), who simply disappear from the story, like the totalitarian Wicked Witch of the West who melts away. This is of course the wishful level of Baum's fairy tale, carried forward by the film. The Scarecrow, with his newly legitimized introverted thinking, promises to be a truly loving philosopher king, but this is in Oz, and ironic, because empathic introverted thinking has rarely prevailed in American politics. Even more rarely does the extraverted thinking that dominates America's discourse yield the power it wields by having control of the nation's image of itself. That power is satirized here in the portrait of the media-manipulating Wizard, Oz (he even bears the same name as the country he rules). This Wizard, however, is at best a well-intentioned purveyor of persona, at worst a propagandist, and his gracious surrender of power is exactly what we don't observe in this aspect of the American political character.

And just as ironic, in its distance beyond what we usually see, is the development of Dorothy's feeling. In an America whose dominant consciousness is extraverted thinking, extraverted feeling is in fact the function least likely to individuate. It is the one most likely to remain ambivalently in shadow, and thus to operate through rigid polarities of gratuitous charm and simplistic condemnation of what it does not understand. (John Travolta's character Vincent Vega in *Pulp Fiction* [Tarantino, 1994] is, today, a far more usual presentation of this side of the American character than Judy Garland's unusual Dorothy.) And what is America's feeling, finally, but political feeling? People in other countries often complain about America's lack of grace in world affairs, its failure to stand by the values that once defined it. These are lapses of introverted feeling. Yet for many of us who live in America, what concerns us most about our political life is that extraverted feeling is so often put on the defensive (Gormley 2010).

Ever since Ronald Reagan's presidency, extraverted feeling in America has been summoned as if it might heal us, but in an increasingly cynical culture, and often with disastrous consequences for the political health of the nation. The contempt Americans so often and so publicly display toward each other became the major theme of the country's films in the 1990s, some of the best of which explore the possibility of extraverted feeling's eventual redemption. For instance, in *Groundhog Day* (Ramis, 1993), a sourly citified Bill Murray discovers that he won't be able to escape the extraverted feeling demands of small-town life in which he is repetitively forced to attend to the feelings of others; indeed he grows into them. In *As Good As It Gets* (Brooks, 1998), Jack Nicholson plays an even more cynical, characterologically wounded man whose sarcastic extraverted feeling is led to reinvent itself to earn the love of the introverted feeling waitress played by Helen Hunt. The happy endings these films managed to eke out for their challenged extraverted feeling protagonists in the 1990s are still poignant when seen today, but they also seem a bit naive. In America today, there is little evidence of what they promised. Recently, apart from the movie screen, dramatized antagonisms are shared on radio and television news. America, not so evolved from the shrill debates over metals that divided Bryan and McKinley, continues to engage in a vitriolic argument over the passage of essentially moderate health insurance reform, a controversy in which an introverted feeling insistence on privacy and self-reliance has repeatedly undercut any satisfaction that might be felt

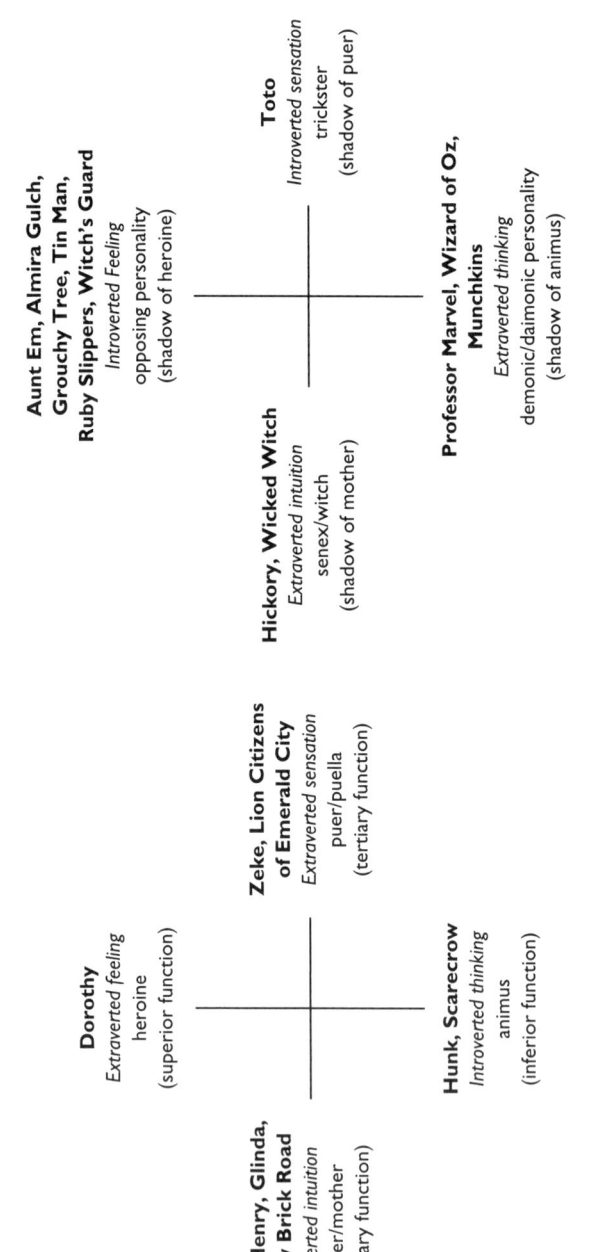

Figure 20.10 Archetypal complexes carrying the eight functions of consciousness as seen in *The Wizard of Oz* © John Beebe, MD, 2002

around having joined together to insure our mutual health. Within such a climate, Dorothy's Oz-born readiness to join arms with an assortment of opposed and like-minded companions to create an at-home feeling for all seems more than ever a foreign sentiment.

Notes

1 Reprinted, with permission, from Thomas Singer (ed.) (2000) *The Vision Thing*. London and New York: Routledge and revised by the author.
2 See also Hearn (1973: 69) for a critique of these ideas, including the suggestion that, since the grandiloquent Wizard is originally from Omaha, Bryan may really have served as the inspiration for the character.
3 James Hillman, in his magisterial essay on the alchemical, archetypal meanings of silver (Hillman 1980, 1981), has noted that 'the total collapse of the values of silver came during the heyday of western materialism, between 1870 and 1930, a debasement of silver that cannot be accounted for wholly in terms of new mines and mining methods' (1980: 36). This was a time during which fact became divorced from value in many other areas of life. See especially Hillman, 1980: 35–37.
4 As the novelist Alison Lurie, an expert on subversively adult elements in children's literature, has argued (Lurie 2000), this may have also reflected the status in his life of his mother-in-law, the American feminist Matilda Joslyn Gage (1826–1898), who had seved as president of the National Woman Suffrage Association from 1875 to 1876.
5 For a discussion of my work on the differentiation of consciousness, see Harris, 1996: Chapters 4 and 5 and Beebe 2004). In *The Wizard of Oz*, eight individual functions of consciousness are depicted: extraverted feeling (Dorothy), introverted feeling (Aunt Em, Almira Gulch, the Tin Man, the ruby slippers, the grouchy Apple Tree, the Witch's Guard), extraverted thinking (Professor Marvel, the Munchkins, the Wizard of Oz), introverted thinking (Hunk, the Scarecrow), extraverted intuition (Hickory, the Wicked Witch of the West, the Winged Monkeys), introverted intuition (Uncle Henry, Glinda, the Yellow Brick Road), extraverted sensation (Zeke, the Cowardly Lion, the Citizens of the Emerald City), and introverted sensation (Toto). Note that two of the actors (Margaret Hamilton and Jack Haley) exchange psychological type when they move between the Kansas and the Oz sections of the film. Although particular characters are left behind in Oz, in the last scene the final *consciousnesses* come together in a final tableau. The archetypal complexes, i.e. subpersonalities, that I think structure this particular arrangement of functions and attitudes are shown in Figure 20.10, where the relationship of the types to each other in *The Wizard of Oz* is illustrated.
6 'The extraverted feeling function concerns itself with other people's emotions – especially those that lie on or near the surface and are easy to sympathize with. Placing a value on people's feelings, extraverted feeling relates to them with discrimination, empathy, and tact ... In its shadow aspect, extraverted feeling tends to discriminate against feelings that are less easy to identify with, and therefore less socially acceptable.' (Beebe 1992: 135).

7 Ann Ulanov has interpreted Dorothy's story 'as a paradigm of a young girl's series of encounters with the animus function and with her ego's integration of the contents that the animus brings to it' (Ulanov 1971: 277–285). The animus, in Jungian psychology, refers to the support the unconscious gives to a woman's authority and is usually symbolized by contrasexual, i.e. male, figures. (The corresponding supportive and tutelary figure in the male unconscious is the anima.) From this standpoint, the Tin Man, the Cowardly Lion, the Wizard, and even Toto would be animus figures for Dorothy. I prefer, however, to reserve the term 'animus' for the figure most closely associated with the inferior function, who, when brought into relationship with the standpoint of the superior function, creates a plumb line of sufficient depth to allow the ego access to the ground of being (Jung's deep Self). This ego-Self axis associated with the animus is symbolized, in *The Wizard of Oz*, by the beanpole from which the Scarecrow attempts to give Dorothy directions when she has lost her way. Their ensuing contact succeeds in replacing this rigid, archetypal delineation of his potential to guide and ground her with a living, human relationship that suggests the integrity Dorothy achieves through her connection with this 'other.' She later confesses that he is [the] one she thinks she'll 'miss most of all' when she leaves the transformative Land of Oz.

8 The dialogue quoted from *The Wizard of Oz* is as given in the movie script published on the fifty-fifth anniversary of the film's release (Langley *et al.* 1994).

9 'The introverted feeling function concerns itself with the values expressed in the archetypal aspects of situations, often relating to the actual situation by measuring it against an ideal. When the actual is found wanting, introverted feeling can become intensely disappointed. Although it often finds it hard to articulate its judgments, or simply prefers to keep them to itself, introverted feeling also tends to ignore social limits regarding the communication of critical responses, to the point of appearing to depreciate others. It may withhold positive feelings as insincere and fail to offer healing gestures to smooth over difficult situations. In its shadow aspect, introverted feeling becomes rageful, anxious, and sullen. It may withdraw all support for attitudes it has decided are simply wrong, even at the risk of rupturing relationship and agreed-upon standards of fellow-feeling' (Beebe 1992: 135).

References

Beebe, J. (1992) Identifying the American Shadow: Typological Reflections on the Los Angeles Riots. *Psychological Perspectives*, 27, 135–139.

Beebe, J. (2004) Understanding Consciousness Through the Theory of Psychological Types. In J. Cambray and L. Carter (eds.), *Analytical Psychology: Contemporary Perspectives in Jungian Analysis*. Hove: Brunner-Routledge (pp. 83–115).

Gardner, H. (1983) *Frames of Mind: The Theory of Multiple Intelligences*. New York: Basic Books.

Gardner, M. and Nye, R. B. (1994) *The Wizard of Oz and Who He Was*. East Lansing: Michigan State University Press.

Goleman, D. (1995) *Emotional Intelligence*. New York: Bantam.
Gormley, K. (2010) *The Death of American Virtue: Clinton vs Starr*. New York: Crown Press.
Harmetz, A. (1998) *The Making of The Wizard of Oz*. New York: Hyperion.
Harris, A. S. (1996) *Living with Paradox; An Introduction to Jungian Psychology*. Pacific Grove, CA: Brooks/Cole Publishing Co.
Hearn, M. P. (ed.) (1973) *The Annotated Wizard of Oz*. New York: Clarkson N. Potter.
—— (1983) *The Wizard of Oz by L. Frank Baum*. New York: Schocken Books.
Hillman, J. (1980) Silver and the White Earth (Part One). *Spring*: 21–48.
—— (1981) Silver and the White Earth (Part Two). *Spring*: 21–66.
Hopcke, R. (1989) Dorothy and Her Friends: Symbols of Gay Male Individuation in the Wizard of Oz. *Quadrant*, *22*(2), 65–77.
Jung, C. G. (1921) *Psychological Types*. Princeton, NJ: Princeton University Press.
Jung, C. G. (1959) *The Archetypes and the Collective Unconscious*. Princeton, NJ: Princeton University Press.
—— (1966) *Two Essays on Analytical Psychology* (2nd edn). Princeton, NJ: Princeton University Press.
Jung, C. G., von Franz, M., Henderson, J., Jacobi, J. and Jaffé, A. (1964) *Man and His Symbols*. Garden City, NJ: Doubleday & Company, Inc.
Kalsched, D. (1996) *The Inner World of Trauma: Archetypal Defenses of the Personal Spirit*. London and New York: Routledge.
Langley, N., Ryerson, F. and Woolf, E. A. (1994) *The Wizard of Oz*. Monterey Park, CA: The Movie Script Library, O.S.P. Publishing, Inc.
Lurie, A. (2000) The Oddness of Oz. *The New York Review of Books*, 47/20: 16–24.
Morison, S. E. and Commager, H. S. (1950) *The Growth of the American Republic*, Volume Two. New York: Oxford University Press.
Rushdie, S. (1992) *The Wizard of Oz*. London: British Film Institute.
Samuels, A. (1993) *The Political Psyche*. London and New York: Routledge.
Thompson, K. (1985) Cognitive and Analytical Psychology (Review of Howard Gardner's *Frames of Mind*). *The San Francisco Jung Institute Library Journal*, *5*(4), 40–64.
Thomson, L. (1998) *Personality Type: An Owner's Manual*. Boston, MA and London: Shambhala.
Traxel, D. (1998) *1898: The Birth of the American Century*. New York: Knopf.
Ulanov, A. B. (1971) *The Feminine in Jungian Psychology and in Christian Theology*. Evanston: Northwestern University Press.
Zipes, J. (ed.) (1998) Introduction. In L. F. Baum, *The Wonderful Wizard of Oz*. New York: Penguin.

Glossary

Active imagination A way of lowering the normal threshhold of consciousness so that a state similar to dreaming is achieved but one in which conscious ego-control is still present. As dream-type images come, the individual is able to engage more consciously with them and create a dialogue with them. These images also have a life of their own and unfold according to their own logic. Psychologically this creates a new situation as previously unconscious mental contents become more available to ego-consciousness.

Alchemy Jung viewed the methods and symbols of the alchemists as revealing not so much chemical experimentation but psychological exploration similar to – and therefore a precursor of – Jung's own method of analytical psychology. The alchemists projected their internal processes onto the materials and the experiments they were engaged in and thus when working on their *materia* they were in fact working on their inner conscious–unconscious processes. In a similar way, Jung believed that analyst and patient were mutually involved in a transformative relationship with 'the other' and that from such a joining together in the work – or *coniunctio* – transformation of the personality is able to occur. (As writers in the present volume often suggest, an analogy to this 'alchemical' process is the relationship between the viewer and the numinous image on the cinema screen – which may involve a projection of an as yet unknown internal figure with whom a mutative relationship can be developed.)

Amplification Association provides a way of developing meaning from spontaneous imagery and dream motifs by allowing linked images and meaningful associations to the original stimulus to be found. By contrast, amplification does not require the individual to travel away from the image in a chain of links but instead to go further into the image in detail and thus make it fuller, richer and more detailed. It is rather like turning up the volume on a stereo so that the full impact and dynamic range of the music (or image) actually present is available through such an amplification.

Anima and *animus* The internal psychological feminine principle held by a man and the corresponding masculine principle at work in a woman's psyche. Both are psychic images arising from an inherent archetypal structure common to all human beings. As the fundamental forms which underlie the 'feminine' aspects of man and the 'masculine' aspects of woman, they are seen as opposites.

Archetype Archetypes are the unconscious structuring principles of the psyche which make our experience, perception and behaviour distinctly human – although the expression of this may vary widely between cultures and across history. Archetypes are the parts of the psyche which are inherited, instinctual patterns which may be realised in the individual personality. The archetype is a psychosomatic concept, linking body and psyche, instinct and image. Jung did not regard psychology and imagery as correlates or reflections of biological drives as if the latter were primary, and so his assertion that images evoke the aim of the instincts implies that they are linked in a non-hierarchical way.

Complex While the contents of the collective unconscious are the archetypes, complexes are the contents of the personal unconscious in Jung's psychology. A complex is a collection of images, ideas and behaviours which have a common emotional tone; it derives its force ultimately from a corresponding archetype. Complexes contribute to behavioural patterns and are marked by their powerful emotional tone. As Jung said, you do not have complexes but complexes have you! Jung opposed 'monolithic' ideas of personality, proposing that we have many selves or sub-personalities and that it is the complexes which constitute these minor personalities within us and which may, under certain circumstances, behave like independent beings and undermine the best intentions of our ego.

Ego Jung saw the ego as the centre of consciousness, concerned with such matters as maintenance of personality, perception, cognition and mediation between conscious and unconscious. However, he also emphasised that the ego was far from the whole – or the most important part of – the personality and was in fact influenced by what he called the Self (often with a small 's'); thus it is important that the ego–self axis or relationship – which parallels the conscious–unconscious relationship – is fostered and attended to.

Imaginal world Analogous to the results and aims of active imagination, the *mundus imaginalis* is a state of psychological perception that is neither wholly rational or sense dependent nor wholly lost in the ego-less realm of dream imagery, but is a state midway between the two. From this state arises insights not normally available to consciousness.

Individuation While fostering individuation is the aim of analytical psychology treatment, Jung believed that there was an impetus towards individuation in every living thing. It refers to the tendency for an organism to continue to become itself, to fulfil its own unique potential to become wholly itself. Jung was at pains to emphasise that for humans this would not mean a self-centred individualism but, on the contrary, by becoming oneself one was able to be more deeply in touch with the collective and thus with the experience of other people.

Myth Jung believed that the preconditions for the formation of myths must be present within the structure of the psyche itself, and that they are experienced by human beings rather than invented. Mythic tales and motifs illustrate what happens in the primitive areas of the mind when an archetype has free rein and there is little conscious intervention on the part of man.

Numinous A word first coined by Rudolf Otto in the anthropology of religious experience and used by Jung to describe powerful emotional or spiritual experiences encountered either in dreams or in waking consciousness. Although the power of the experience is archetypal, mysterious and enigmatic, an individual message is conveyed which remains deeply impressive. (Our contention is that some film imagery can have this effect.)

Self 'The self' is Jung's term for the whole personality, including the ego which is the aspect of personality of which we are consciously aware. The self (spelt with a small 's' in the *Collected Works* to distinguish it from the eastern idea of Atman or the great Self) is so vast we cannot expect to know all of it during our lifetimes, but the task of individuation is to go as far as we can towards this. The self is also an archetypal image of man's fullest potential and the unity of the personality as a whole. The self has another shade of meaning as the unifying principle – the self archetype – within the human psyche, where it occupies the central position of authority in relation to psychological life and, therefore, the destiny of the individual.

Shadow The part of the personality that one does not identify with or wishes to disown; it usually refers to negative aspects, but may also include positive aspects that – due to family or social beliefs – have remained rejected and unavailable to the individual. It is an archetype whose powerful affects – obsessional, possessive, autonomous – are capable of startling and overwhelming the well-ordered ego, and it often takes the form of a projection onto others. It is one of the aspects of the unconscious that is encountered early on in a Jungian analysis.

Symbol For Jung, if an expression stands for a known thing, even if this expression is commonly called 'symbolic', it is not a symbol but a sign. If an expression stands for an unknown something, which, therefore, by definition cannot be expressed or represented more clearly in any way, then such an expression is a symbol. For Jung, the semiotic refers to representations of known things, while the symbolic refers to representations of the unknown. He understood a symbol as an intuitive idea that cannot yet be formulated in any other or better way.

Syzygy A term applied to any pair of opposites when spoken of as a pair, whether in conjunction or opposition, and most frequently used in relation to the linkage of the masculine and the feminine principles expressed as anima and animus.

Temenos A term borrowed by the alchemists to refer to the womb-like container which was used to combine matter in a closed space and to which heat may be applied. In psychotherapy, the rules or boundaries of the therapist–client relationship provide containment or a frame within which the healing may occur. Similarly, watching films acts as a temenos or frame which makes transformative effects possible.

Note: For a fuller and more comprehensive collection of definitions we suggest you refer to Andrew Samuels, Bani Shorter and Fred Plaut (1986) *A Critical Dictionary of Jungian Analysis*. London: Routledge.

Index

abandonment 77, 84–5, 212
active imagination 28, 30, 110, 285; cinephilia 178; definition of 328; personal films 100; symbols 160
active subject 190
Adler, Alfred 88
The Adventures of Priscilla Queen of the Desert (Elliot, 1994) 293
agency 189, 191, 195, 202
aggression 230
Aguirre (Herzog, 1972) 262
alchemy: American politics 304; *The Conversation* 271–2; definition of 328; personal films 100
Alice in Wonderland (Burton, 2010) 207, 209, 212, 214, 215–16
alienation 175, 179, 258
Alister, Ian 254–5, 258
Almodóvar, Pedro 44
American Beauty (Mendes, 1999) 262
amplification 28, 121, 194; definition of 328–9; Jungian film criticism 39–41; personal films 100; 'psychological life' 105; transpersonal 123; *The Twilight Saga* 197
analytical psychology: archetypal imagery 100–1; images 21–2, 26–33; individuation 8; Jung's formulation of 110; structuralism 286; *see also* Jungian analysis
anger 214
anima: confronting one's otherness 273; *The Conversation* 267, 270, 273–6, 277, 280, 283; definition of 329; idealised and feared powers 272; *The Piano* 237; possession rituals 261; projection of 78; traditional American values 314; Venus 246; *The Wizard of Oz* 306, 322; *see also* soul
anima mundi 92, 93, 95
animation 100
animus: confronting one's otherness 273; definition of 329; hero fantasies 85; inferior function 326n7; projection of 76; *The Twilight Saga* 199; *The Wizard of Oz* 306, 308, 318, 322, 324, 326n7
annihilation, fear of 59
anthropology 259, 262, 263
anti-individuation 45–6
Aphrodite 155, 160, 246
Apocalypse Now (Coppola, 1979) 262, 263
Apperson, Virginia 11
archetypal imagery 100–1, 104, 106, 187–8, 196; diachronic reading 202; *The Twilight Saga* 197; unconscious activation 121–2
archetypal literalism 102
archetypes: anti-individuation 45–6; collective unconscious 187; common experiences 123; definition of 329; director's role 199; Eco on 163, 167, 169–70; envy 31, 32; identity 191; possession rituals 261; *puer aeternus* 310; self 157; symbolic art 121; transformation of the libido 258

Arehart-Treichel, Joan 244
Ares 246, 247
Arrington, L. 201
art 18–19; corruption of consciousness 102–3; symbolic 121
art cinema 100
Artaud, Antoine 253–4, 261, 262, 263
As Good As It Gets (Brooks, 1998) 323
association experiments 21–2
At Land (Deren, 1944) 254
attitudes 287–8
audiences 174, 176, 178, 253
Austen, Jane 151–2, 153, 157, 158
Austin, Sue 64
Australia 10, 285, 290–9
Australia (Luhrmann, 2008) 292, 297
auteur theory 199
authorship 175–6
Avatar (Cameron, 2009) 177–8

baby boomer generation 243–4, 250
Bacall, Lauren 68, 84
Baillie, Rebecca 296–7
Balasz, Bela 165
the banal 5, 109, 110–11, 117
Barker, C. 190, 191, 193, 195, 202
Barry Lynden (Kubrick, 1975) 79
Barthes, Roland 6, 132, 137, 165, 174, 175, 176
Bassil-Morozow, Helena 8, 11, 12, 206–24
Batman (Burton, 1989) 207, 209, 211, 212, 215, 218, 219–20, 221
Batman Returns (Burton, 1989) 209, 211, 212, 215, 216, 223
Baum, L. Frank 303, 304–5, 312
Bayley, H. 57
beauty 53–4
Beebe, John 10–11, 286, 289–90, 302–27
Being Human (tv show) 200
Belson, Jordan 103
Benedict, Ruth 263
Benjamin, J. 53
Benjamin, Walter 106, 182
Bergman, Ingrid 168
Bhabha, H. 263
Big Fish (Burton, 2003) 211–12, 213, 214–15

Binet, A. 286
birth 68
Birth (Glazer, 2004) 4, 66–91
Bitton, D. 201
Blade Runner (Scott, 1982) 49, 140, 220
Blanchett, Cate 293
Blue Velvet (Lynch, 1986) 120
body: *Breaking the Waves* 47; gender and 149, 151; rediscovery of the 39; suffering 250, 251
Bogart, Humphrey 168
Boon, Marcus 104
Bordo, Susan 219
boredom 174–5
Bowlby, John 214
Bradley, A. 185
Bram Stoker's Dracula (Coppola, 1992) 198
Brawer, Florence 287
Breaking Dawn (Condon, 2011) 186
Breaking the Waves (Von Trier, 1996) 3, 35–48
Briggs, Katherine Cook 289
Bright, Cameron 4, 69, 70
Brolin, Josh 93
Brontë, Emily 152
Brook, Peter 253
Brooker, Will 168, 173
Brumby, John 293
Bryan, William Jennings 303, 304, 325n2
Buffy the Vampire Slayer (tv show) 200
Burt, C. 287
Burton, Tim 8, 206–24
Bushman, R. L. 201
Butler, J. 53, 63

The Cabinet of Dr. Caligari (Wiene, 1920) 221
Campbell, Joseph 150, 154
Campion, Jane 293
Canby, Vincent 275
capitalism 221, 222
Cartier-Bresson, Henri 17, 18–19, 20, 22, 29, 33
Casablanca (Curtiz, 1942) 163, 167, 168–9, 192

Casino (Scorsese, 1995) 111
Catwoman 215, 216
Cavendish, Richard 269
chaos 247, 283
Charlie and the Chocolate Factory (Burton, 2005) 209, 212, 214, 216, 218, 221–2, 223
Child archetype 4, 69, 72–3, 76, 117
Christiani, Rita 255–9
Christianity 92, 117, 157, 213
cinéma vérité 22
cinephilia 7, 163–84
Cirlot, J. E. 247
cities 220–1
Clark, Giles 56, 58
Clooney, George 3, 50
Close Encounters of the Third Kind (Spielberg, 1977) 178, 179–82
Clover, C. 192
Cobb, Noel 59
Coen brothers 4–5, 92
Coleman, Warren 54, 58–60, 61
collective consciousness 246, 251, 255, 263
collective symbols 195
collective unconscious 29, 32, 121, 186–7; cultural unconscious 188; images 40; individuation 44–5; myth 291; rituals 255, 261; *The Twilight Saga* 197; *The Wrestler* 243, 244
Collingwood, R. G. 102–3
Collins, Felicity 291, 294, 298
Commager, Henry Steele 304
community 209
complexes 77, 188; cultural 188–9, 191, 192, 193, 195, 202; definition of 329
coniunctio 4, 71–2, 78, 82, 87, 158, 328
Conrad, Joseph 262
Conrad, Peter 298
consciousness: blurring of division with unconsciousness 136; corruption of 102–3; discourse theory 185; dissociation of 259, 261; drive to enhance and specialise 72; expansion of 53, 57; individuation 45; psyche 29;

Solaris 63; *The Wizard of Oz* 306–11, 313, 316–17, 319, 325n5
containment 331
The Conversation (Coppola, 1974) 10, 266–84
Coppola, Francis Ford 10, 111, 262, 266–7, 268, 271, 278–9
Corbin, H. 60, 61
Corpse Bride (Burton, 2005) 208, 215
Corrin, Ellen 259, 263
countertransference 133, 141–2
Coupland, N. 190
couple relationships 45–6, 75, 77
Cowie, Peter 272
Crocodile Dundee (Faiman, 1986) 293
Crowe, Russel 293
A Cry in the Dark (Schepisi, 1988) 294–5
cult films 167, 174
cultural complex 188–9, 191, 192, 193, 195, 202
Cultural Symbols 170
cultural theory 179, 189
culture 186, 189, 192–3; collective unconscious 187, 188; cultural unconscious 188–9; discourse theory 190; Western culture's projection of shadow onto native peoples 233
Cumbow, Robert 71, 78–9, 90n3
Curtiz, Michael 168–9

Daguerre, Louis 138
Dancemaker (Diamond, 1998) 22–3, 24
Dark City (Proyas, 1998) 5–6, 49, 119, 120, 123–6, 128–9
The Dark Mirror (Siodmak, 1946) 314
Das Boot (Petersen, 1981) 262
Davis, Bette 314
Davis, Therese 291, 294, 298
Daybreakers (Spierig and Spierig, 2009) 200
De Havilland, Olivia 314
De Palma, Brian 111
De Vito, Danny 211
death 68, 72, 114

Index

decisive images 17, 18; documentary cinematography 23–6, 33; Jungian analysis 26, 27, 30, 31–2, 33; photography 20–1
defences 45
The Departed (Scorsese, 2006) 111
depersonalization 258–9, 261, 263
Depp, Johnny 207
depression 244
depth metaphor 145–6
depth psychology 92, 135
Deren, Maya 1, 9, 106, 253–65
Derrida, Jacques 180
Desplat, Alexandre 67, 73, 89
Devouring Mother archetype 85
Dicks-Mireaux, Marie José 286–7
diegesis 138–9, 141
dioramas 138
direct cinema 22
directors 199
discourse theory 7–8, 185–6, 189, 190–6, 197, 200–2
distraction 106
Divine Horsemen: The Living Gods of Haiti (Deren, 1985) 255, 259–61, 263
documentary cinematography 17–18, 22–6, 28, 30, 32, 33, 40, 100
Dogma 95 manifesto 35
dominant function *see* superior function
Donnie Darko (Kelly, 2001) 262
Dougherty, Mary 8, 227–42
Dovalis, Joanna 4, 12, 66–91
Dr. Mabuse, der Spieler (Lang, 1922) 221
Dracula (Fisher, 1958) 198
Dracula (Browing, 1931) 198
dreams 129, 134–5, 136; *The Conversation* 280; decisive images 30, 31–2; films as 42
Drew, Robert 22
Drews, A. 195
Dreyer, Carl 69–70
Dreyfuss, Richard 181
drugs 103–4
Durkheim, Emile 209, 255
DVDs 180

Earth Mother Goddess 158, 159, 247
Eclipse (Slade, 2010) 186, 202
Eco, Umberto 163, 167, 168–71, 172, 174, 176, 192
Ed Wood (Burton, 1994) 209
Edinger, Edward 71–2
editing: *Breaking the Waves* 35–6; *The Conversation* 281; Deren's films 254, 262; documentary cinematography 26; *Solaris* 56
Edward Scissorhands (Burton, 1990) 207, 211, 213, 214, 215, 216–18, 219, 223
ego 39, 41; animus 326n7; anti-individuation 45; definition of 329; guided by the unconscious 53, 81; individuation 44–5; myths 160; positive-integral 213–14; symbols 105; urge to power 88; *The Wrestler* 244; *see also* self
ego complex 29, 229, 230
Eigen, Michael 58, 63
8½ (Fellini, 1963) 120
Eliot, T. S. 217
emotions 40, 124; cinephilia 165, 166; collective 193; images and 27
energy: images 30, 31; *The Piano* 237; 'third image' 177; *see also* libido
Enlightenment 208–9, 211, 219
envy 23, 31, 32
Ericka, Miss 260
Eros 57, 103, 154, 155, 158, 160, 246, 304
evil 117
Evil Angels (Schepisi, 1988) 294–5
experience, importance of 27
extraversion: American values 321–2, 323; Australian cinema 292, 293, 295, 298, 299; extraverted feeling function 325n6; Jung's typology 286–90; *The Piano* 232; *The Wizard of Oz* 307–8, 309–11, 313–15, 317, 319, 321–2, 324
Eyes Wide Shut (Kubrick, 1999) 67, 90n8

factories 218–19, 221–2
Falconetti, Maria 69–70

fandom 168, 171, 173, 177–8
fantasies: experience of 27; hero 85; the imaginary 58–9; integration of the psyche 90
fantasy-images 135–6
fascism 179, 182
fate 269
father-son dynamic 211–14, 223
fear 59, 115
Feather, N. T. 293
feeling 286, 288–9, 290; *The Conversation* 267, 270; transcendent function 246; *The Wizard of Oz* 307–8, 310–11, 314, 319, 320, 321–2, 324
Fellini, Federico 120
feminine gaze 7, 151, 161
femininity: Burton's films 213, 215–16; the dark feminine in *The Wrestler* 244, 245–6, 247, 249, 250; Eros and Psyche myth 154, 155; feminine values in novels 151; intuition 82; male gaze 148; patriarchal myth 154; Persephone myth 154, 155–8, 160–1; *The Twilight Saga* 200; *see also* anima
feminism 149, 200
Ferris Bueller's Day Off (Hughes, 1986) 194
film studies 5, 99–108; cinephilia 163–4, 165–6; *see also* Jungian film criticism
'first image' 132, 137–9, 142
Fisher King *see* the king
Fitzcarraldo (Herzog, 1982) 262
Ford, Harrison 140, 171, 172, 277
Ford, John 172
Forrest Gump (Zemeckis, 1994) 172
Fossey, Diane 262
Foucault, Michel 190–1, 192, 193
Frank, Robert 22
Frankenweenie (Burton, 1984) 211, 218
Frederickson, Don 2, 5, 11–12, 99–108, 120–1, 126, 150, 160, 169
French, Lisa 298
Freud, Sigmund 88, 120–1, 122, 124–6, 149

Freudian psychoanalysis 5–6, 119–26, 128, 148, 191, 195
Friedberg, Anne 172
functions 288–90; *see also* inferior function; superior function

Gage, Matilda Joslyn 325n4
Galasinski, D. 190, 191, 193, 195, 202
gangster films 111–12
Garbo, Greta 165
Garland, Judy 302, 306, 307, 320, 322
Garr, Teri 181
gaze 7, 148, 151, 157, 161
gender 148–9, 151, 192; *see also* femininity; masculinity
Genette, Gerard 180
German expressionism 206, 209, 221, 262
Gibbs, J. 164
Gibran, K. 58
Glazer, Jonathan 4, 66, 68, 71
God 122, 211, 213, 219, 223, 257
The Godfather (Coppola, 1972) 111, 266
The Godfather, Part II (Coppola, 1974) 266
Goethe, Johann Wolfgang von 17, 19
Gold Standard 303–4
Golem (Wegener, 1915) 221
Goodfellas (Scorsese, 1990) 111
Gorillas in the Mist (Apted, 1988) 262
Gotham City 220
Gothicism 206, 208, 221
Grant, Cary 165
Greer, Germaine 292
grief 68, 88
Grof, Stanislav 104
Grotowski, Jerzy 253
Groundhog Day (Ramis, 1993) 323

Hackman, Gene 10, 266
Hall, S. 191, 193, 290
Hamilton, Margaret 314, 315
Han Solo 171–3
hands 216–18
Happy Feet (Miller, 2006) 298
Harley, Ruth 297
Harris, Charlaine 200
Hasidism 213

Hasin, Deborah 244
Haslam, J. 192
Hauke, Christopher 2, 4, 6, 9, 11–12, 92–5, 109–18, 129–30, 166, 169, 254–5, 258
Heche, Anne 69
Hell 109, 110, 113, 114, 118
Henderson, J. 188, 313
Henreid, Paul 168
hero myth 150, 151, 154, 291
Herzog, Werner 262
Hewison, David 3, 11, 35–48
Hillman, James 92–3, 95, 102–3, 105–6, 129, 212–13, 216–17, 250, 325n3
Hitchcock, Alfred 105, 290
Hobson, R. 64
Hockley, Luke 2, 6–7, 11–12, 129–30, 132–47, 166, 178–9
holding environment 27
Hollywood 103, 151, 172, 185, 195, 200–1
homosexuality 126
Hopkins, Gerard Manley 122
Hughes, Darren 67, 85
Hunt, Helen 323
Hunter, Holly 8, 227, 229
Hurwitz, Tom 1, 3, 17–34
Huston, Danny 68

id 79
idealisation 75, 272
identity: discourse theory 191; gender 149
ideology 172
images 3, 17–34, 133–6, 187–8; act of interpretation 132, 137, 139–40; active imagination 328; amplification 328–9; *Dark City* 123–4; denotative and connotative aspects 136–7; documentary cinematography 22–6; Freudian approach 122–3; Jungian analysis 26–33; Jungian film criticism 39–41; photography 18–22; screen image 132, 137–9; symbolic 59, 62, 160; transcendent function 53; *see also* archetypal imagery; 'third image'

imaginal world 330
the imaginary 58–60, 61
imagination 58, 59–60, 61
imago, maternal 82–3
improvisation: documentary cinematography 25, 26; Jungian analysis 28, 30
incest 42, 78, 82
incompleteness 215, 218
individualism 111, 170, 208, 211
individual/society relationship 206–7, 209, 211, 222–3
individuation 2, 8, 49, 53, 207–8; *Breaking the Waves* 3, 44–7; Child archetype 73; completion of 71; *The Conversation* 283; *Dark City* 119; definition of 330; inhibition of 75; Jung's crisis of 110; Persephone myth 157; *The Piano* 240; possession 259; rebirth 259; return to the community 32–3; *Ritual in Transfigured Time* 259; role of intuition 82; *Sense and Sensibility* 161; *Solaris* 3–4; struggle with the Shadow 109; 'third image' 130; *The Wizard of Oz* 306
infancy 85
inferior function 288–9; animus 326n7; *The Conversation* 269, 270, 280; shadow as 232; *The Wizard of Oz* 307, 308, 309, 324
intentionality, authorial 180
intersubjectivity 53
intertextuality 168, 169, 194, 202
introversion: Australian cinema 10, 285, 290–9; *The Conversation* 267, 270; introverted feeling function 326n9; Jung's typology 286–90; libido 258; *The Piano* 232; *The Wizard of Oz* 307–8, 310–11, 313–19, 320–2, 324
intuition 286, 288–9, 290; *Birth* 82; *The Conversation* 267, 269, 270, 280; *The Wizard of Oz* 309, 310–11, 315, 317, 324
Ionesco, Eugène 253
Izod, John 4, 6, 11–12, 40–1, 66–91, 128–31, 135, 165, 169, 177–8

Jackman, Hugh 293
Jackson, Renata 260, 262
Jacobi, J. 188, 191, 194, 195, 208
Jacobs, Michael 5–6, 119–27, 128
Jäger, S. 192, 194
Jameson, Fredric 172
Janowitz, Hans 221
Jaworski, A. 190
Jenkins, Henry 176–7
JFK (Stone, 1991) 172
Jones, Tommy Lee 93
jouissance 174
Joyce, James 159
Jung, Carl Gustav: abandonment motif 212; alchemy 271, 328; archetypes 187; chaos 283; Child archetype 73; on cinema 39, 112–13; collective life 186; complexes 188, 329; consciousness 72; de-souling of the world 94; dialectical therapeutic relationship 52; disappointment 249; dream material 129; Earth Mother Goddess 159; ego 329; on evil 117; experience 27; fascism 182; fate 269; gender 149; group identification 210–11; images 17, 20, 21–2, 30, 32–3, 132, 133–6, 187, 329; 'Immersion in the Bath' 78; individuation 45, 207–8, 330; inner voice 257; introversion/extraversion 286–90, 307; the king 9, 244, 245, 246, 247; literature and psychology 105; love 238; mana 320–1; need for independence 85; neurosis 88, 231; the 'object' 290–1; persona 243; personal interactions 235; possession 259; psyche 246, 257; *Red Book* 5, 109–10, 112–14, 115, 117–18; reductive analytical programmes of Freud and Adler 88; ritual 255; self archetype 157; self-knowledge 103; shadow 56, 229, 230; *sol niger* 250–1; the soul 261; symbolic art 121; symbols 99, 101, 104, 120, 141, 144, 160, 193, 331; synthesis 251; technology 178; tombstone inscription 5; transcendent function 28–9, 241; transformation of the libido 258; the unconscious 30, 88–9, 136, 149–50, 186–7, 269; unjustly injured man 86; *unus mundus* 89; water 257
Jung Forum 1–2
Jungian analysis 186–9; discourse theory and 185–6, 193–6; experience of self 53; images 17, 21–2, 26–33; shadow 56–7; *see also* analytical psychology
Jungian film criticism 5, 39–41, 99–108; cinephilia 177–8; comparison with Freudian approaches 119–26, 129; discourse theory and 7–8, 185–6, 196, 202; meaning of films 166; 'third image' 129–30; *The Twilight Saga* 197–9, 201
Justice League: Mortal (Miller, 2011) 296–7

Kalsched, Donald 218, 312
Kapferer, Bruce 259
Kaplan, Abraham 103, 105
Keathley, Christian 163, 164, 175
Keaton, Michael 207
Keitel, Harvey 8, 229
Kidman, Nicole 4, 66, 69–70, 71, 73, 90n8, 293
Kimbles, S. 186, 189, 192, 193
the king 9, 244, 245–6, 247, 249
Kleinian psychoanalysis 41, 119
Klenck, Margaret 1, 3, 17–34
Knox, J. 52
Kracauer, S. 174–5
Kretschmer, E. 287
Kubrick, Stanley 4, 67, 79
Kundun (Scorsese, 1997) 262

Lacan, Jacques 149
Lacanian psychoanalysis 119, 120, 141, 174, 191, 195
Lamb, Wally 90n7
landscape 93–4, 152
Lang, Fritz 221
Lange, Dorthea 19, 21
Le Guin, Ursula K. 150, 158

Leacock, Richard 22
Lee, Ang 7, 148, 151, 152
Lee, Christopher 198
Lem, Stanislav 49
Lennihan, Lydia 8–9, 243–52
Let The Right One In (Alfredson, 2008) 115–17, 200
Levinas, Emmanuel 63
Levi-Strauss, C. 259
Levy-Bruhl, Lucien 255
libido 26, 177, 258; collective 261; images 30; introversion/extraversion 288
lighting 68–9
liminality 100, 258
literalism 102
Littlefield, Henry M. 303, 305
London 220
Lone Gunman figure 170, 171, 172, 173
loss 53, 57–8; anger as response to 214; integration of 52, 64; *Solaris* 54, 59, 60–1, 63
love 52, 53, 58; *Birth* 74–5, 77–8, 82, 89; *Breaking the Waves* 43; capacity to 64; *The Piano* 237, 238; *Solaris* 62
Lowery, David 66
Lucas, George 168, 172, 173
Lugosi, Bela 198
Luhrmann, Baz 292, 298
Lurie, Alison 325n4

Mad Max (Miller, 1979) 291–2, 293
Mad Max: Beyond Thunderdome (Miller, 1985) 291
Maier, F. 192, 194
male gaze 148, 161
mana 320–1
Manguel, Alberto 2
Mao's Last Dancer (Beresford, 2009) 297
Marker, Chris 22
marriage 71–2, 75, 77, 79, 258
Mars Attacks (Burton, 1996) 209, 211
Marxism 119, 121
masculinity: *Breaking the Waves* 42, 43, 47; changing modes of 172; hero myth 154; male gaze 148,
161; patriarchy 149; *The Twilight Saga* 200; *The Wrestler* 246; *see also* animus
masks 257, 258
materialism 153
The Matrix (Wachowski Brothers, 1999) 192
Mauss, Marcel 257
Mayer, Carl 221
Maysles, Albert and David 22
McCarthy, Cormac 93
McDowell, Alex 222
McIntyre, Patience and Prudence 87–8
McKinley, William 303–4
Mead, Margaret 262, 263
meaning 132–3, 136–7; cinephilia 164, 171, 176; co-creation of 174; discourse theory 190; fantasy-images 135–6; 'first image' 137, 138, 139; Jungian film criticism 166; personal and social context 186; 'second image' 139–40; 'third image' 139, 141, 142–3, 145
'mechanical body' paradigm 219
Meshes of the Afternoon (Deren, 1943) 254
metonymy 215
Metropolis (Lang, 1927) 220, 221
Meyer, M. 190, 195, 198
Meyer, Stephenie 196, 201
Miller, Catriona 7–8, 185–205
Miller, George 291–2, 293, 296–7
mimesis 138
mirror phase 141
'misreading' of films 133
Mitchell, Stephen 74
modernity: alienation 179; Burton's films 206, 208, 210, 219, 220, 222; German expressionism 221; sufferings of 94
modes of film 104–5, 107
Mormonism 201
Morris, Brian 260, 261
Morrison, Samuel Eliot 304
Moses 17–18, 24–5
mothers 82–3, 85, 213, 214, 280
Moulin Rouge (Luhrmann, 2001) 292, 298

mourning: *Birth* 68; Butler on 53; grieving distinction 88; *Solaris* 58, 59, 64
Mulvey, Laura 7, 148, 161
Murch, Walter 266, 270, 276, 278–9
Muriel's Wedding (Hogan, 1994) 293
Murnau, Friedrich 221
Murray, Bill 323
Myers, Isabel Briggs 289
Myers-Briggs Type Indicator (MBTI) 289, 310–11
myth: Australian cinema 285; collective unconscious 291; definition of 330; gender-related 151; hero 150, 151, 154, 291; intertextual archetypicality 183; novels 158; parental wounds 212–13; symbolic images 160; symbol-world of mythology 182

narcissism: *Birth* 85; moving beyond 64; personal films 100; *Solaris* 49, 53, 54, 55, 56, 63
Naremore, James 165
Natural Born Killers (Stone, 1999) 103–4
Natural Symbols 170
nature 92–3, 95, 151, 154, 158
Neill, Sam 8, 229
Neumann, Erich 82, 84, 213
neurosis 88, 103, 124, 125, 231
New Moon (Weitz, 2009) 186, 197
New York 220
Nicholson, Jack 211, 323
The Nightmare Before Christmas (Burton, 1993) 215, 216, 218
nightmares 93
Nin, Anaïs 255–6, 258
Nixon (Stone, 1995) 172
No Country for Old Men (Coen brothers, 2008) 4–5, 92–5
North, Julia 152–3
North by Northwest (Hitchcock, 1959) 165
Nosferatu (Murnau, 1922) 221
novels 150–1, 158, 159
numinosity 89, 160, 255, 330

O'Connor, Flannery 104
Oedipus complex 72, 149
Oldman, Gary 198
Omnibus television program 22
omnipotence 54, 58
Ondaatje, Michael 268–9, 278–9
O'Regan, Tom 285
the 'Oriental' 259–60, 261–2, 263
Orphée (Cocteau, 1950) 11–12
otherness 52, 57, 63, 263, 273
Otto, Rudolf 330

Paganopoulos, Michelangelo 9, 253–65
Palmer, James 10, 11, 266–84
Pan 93, 95
'panoramic perception' 175
Paquin, Anna 8, 227, 229
paranoia 125, 126
parental wounds 212–13
parenting 84–5
participation mystique 210, 261
The Passion of Joan of Arc (Dreyer, 1928) 69–70
The Passion of the Christ (Gibson, 2004) 243
patriarchy 149–50, 151, 154
Pattinson, Robert 200
Pavlov, I. P. 287
Pedersen, Loren 266, 267
Pee Wee's Big Adventure (Burton, 1985) 207, 218, 219
Pennebaker, D. A. 22
Perrill, Sue 151, 152
Persephone 154, 155–8, 160–1
persona 243, 244, 257
personal films 100
personality: *Breaking the Waves* 3, 44, 46–7; Child archetype 73; complexes 329; expansion of 57; film as 41; introversion/extraversion 286–90; Myers-Briggs Type Indicator 289, 310–11; shadow aspects of 229, 230, 232; total 39; *see also* self
perversion 38, 43–4
phallic symbols 126
phallus 148–9
phenomenology 189

photography: decisive image 17, 18–22, 24, 29; meanings 132; punctum 174
The Piano (Campion, 1993) 8, 227–42, 293
Picasso, Pablo 134
Pierson, Michele 174
Pinocchio (Luske and Sharpsteen, 1940) 181
Pinter, Harold 253
Planet of the Apes (Burton, 2001) 209
poetry 150
Polidori, John 198
politics, American 10–11, 303–5, 306–7, 312, 321, 322–5
Poole, Mark 298
popular film 107, 109–10; archetypal imagery 104, 106; archetypical characters 167; distraction 106; drug use 103–4; focus on 100–1; gangster films 111–12; symbolic register 105; vampire films 111, 114–17, 196–202
Populist movement 303, 305, 312
positive-integral ego 213–14
possession 259, 260–1
postmodernism 200, 202
power 52, 54, 55–7, 88
Pratt, Annis 198
pre-digestion 103, 105
'primitivism' 253
projection 56–7, 76, 78, 82
protectionism 294, 295, 296, 297
Proyas, Alex 128
psyche 33, 39, 179, 246; blocking of the 257; images 29–30, 31; integration of the 90, 92; myth 330; split in the 32; 'third image' 129; transcendent function 241; *unus mundus* 89; *see also* ego; self
Psyche myth 154, 155, 158, 160, 161
psychoanalysis: Freudian 5–6, 119–26, 128, 148, 191, 195; intersubjectivity 53; Kleinian 41, 119; Lacanian 119, 120, 141, 174, 191, 195
'psychological life' 105–6
psychological mode 105
puer aeternus 310

Pulp Fiction (Tarantino, 1994) 323
punctum 174, 175, 176
Punter, David 208
Pye, D. 164

Raiders of the Lost Ark (Spielberg, 1981) 169
Reagan, Ronald 323
realism 138
reason 124
rebirth: *Birth* 4, 66–7, 68, 72, 79, 82, 83, 89–90; *The Conversation* 283; *Dark City* 124; individuation 259; *Ritual in Transfigured Time* 257
reception theories 290
recollective experiences 178
redemption: *Breaking the Waves* 38, 42–3, 46; definition of 57; *Solaris* 62
referents 132
rejection 38, 214
relatedness 25–6, 82
renewal 244, 247
repression: *Birth* 77, 85–6, 88, 90; Freudian theory 125; shadow aspects of the personality 229, 232; unlived capacities and desires 235
Reubens, Paul 207
revisionism 172
Rigaud, Odette 260
Rilke, Rainer Maria 53–4
rites of passage 116, 254
ritual 9, 253–4, 255, 257, 258–9, 260–1
Ritual in Transfigured Time (Deren, 1946) 254, 255–9, 262, 263
Roeg, Nicholas 105
Romantics 198, 208
Rorschach, Hermann 287
Rosen, Brian 297
Rostan, L. 287
Rouche, Jean 22
Rourke, Mickey 9, 243
Rousseau, Jean-Jacques 263
Rowland, Susan 7, 11, 148–62
Roy, Deep 222
Rush, Geoffrey 293
Rushdie, Salman 302–3, 316, 321

Ryan, Jane 5–6, 119, 120, 123, 124, 126, 128, 130

the sacred 37
sadomasochism 46, 120
Salman, Sherry 26–7
salt 245–6, 249, 251
Samson and Delilah (Thornton, 2009) 297, 299
Samuels, Andrew 100–1, 120, 123, 145–6, 188, 194, 317
Savides, Harry 68–9
Scarface (De Palma, 1983) 111
Schepisi, Fred 293, 294–5
Schreber, Daniel 124–6, 128–9
scopophilia 148, 174
Scorsese, Martin 111, 262
Screen Australia 10, 285, 294, 296, 297
The Searchers (Ford, 1956) 172
'second image' 132, 137, 139–40, 142
The Secret Passion (Huston, 1962) 120
self: *Breaking the Waves* 43; definition of 330; ego relationship 39, 81, 244, 329; encounter with the 33; exile from 57; images 40; individuation 44–5; Jungian film criticism 40–1; killing of egocentric self 58; relational 53; self archetype 157, 330; *Solaris* 54–5; *see also* ego; personality
self-emergence 57, 61
self-harm 218
self-knowledge 33, 103
self-regulation 39
self-sacrifice 258
semiotics 132, 137, 139, 169
Seneca 269
senex 103, 324
sensation 286, 288–9, 290; *The Conversation* 270; *The Wizard of Oz* 309–11, 315–16, 317, 324
Sense and Sensibility (Lee, 1995) 7, 148–62
sexism 213
sexuality 148–9, 151; *The Conversation* 273; *The Piano* 236, 237; *Sense and Sensibility* 154, 156; vampire films 115

Seymour, Cara 73
shadow 56–7, 109; *Birth* 77; collective 251; definition of 330–1; encounter with the 237; gangster films 111; Han Solo 173; *The Piano* 8, 229–35, 237, 238–9, 240, 241; revealed in marriage 75; vampires 198, 199; Western culture's projection of shadow onto native peoples 233; *The Wizard of Oz* 312, 314–15, 316, 317, 324; *The Wrestler* 246
shamanistic rituals 259
Sheldon, W. H. 287
Shine (Hicks, 1996) 293
The Shining (Kubrick, 1980) 67
Shone, Tom 171
signifier/signified 132, 137
signs 104, 120, 139, 141, 170, 193, 331
Singer, T. 186, 189, 192, 193
Singh, Greg 7, 11, 12, 163–84
Slater, G. 194
Sleepy Hollow (Burton, 1999) 209, 213, 214, 216
Smith, Huston 107
Soderbergh, Steven 49, 56, 62, 63–4
sol niger (black sun) 250–1
Solaris (Tarkovsky, 1972) 49, 262
Solaris (Soderbergh, 2002) 3–4, 49–65
soul 89, 92–5, 250, 257, 261; *see also* anima
soundtracks 67, 70, 73, 80, 87–8, 89
Spiegelman, J. Marvin 287
Spielberg, Steven 172, 179
Stalker (Tarkovsky, 1979) 49, 262
Star Wars (Lucas, 1977) 7, 99, 167–8, 171–3
Stein, Murray 100, 105
Stevens, A. 237
Stewart, Kristen 200
A Stolen Life (Bernhardt, 1946) 314
Stone, Oliver 103–4
Stormare, Peter 69
storytelling 25
Streep, Meryl 295
structuralism 286
studium 175

subcultures 176–7
subjectivity 149, 188, 202
the sublime 152
suffering 94, 240, 250, 251
superior (dominant) function 288–9, 326n7; *The Conversation* 270; *The Wizard of Oz* 307, 308, 309, 324
Sweeney Todd: The Demon Barber of Fleet Street (Burton, 2007) 207, 209, 216–17, 218, 219–20, 223
symbolism: *Blade Runner* 140; Deren's films 254; Eco on 170, 171; Goethe on 17, 19; mythology 182; *Ritual in Transfigured Time* 255, 257, 258; *The Twilight Saga* 197
symbols 193–5; active imagination 30; Australian cinema 285; Cultural and Natural 170; decisive images 26–7, 32; definition of 331; de-godding of nature 92; forward-looking 89; imaginal symbolic capacity 58, 59, 61, 62; infinite meanings 176; Jung on 99, 101, 104, 120, 141, 144, 160, 193; modes of film 104–5; phallic 126; psychological third 145–6; shamanistic rituals 259; transcendent function 29
synecdoche 215
syzygy 117, 128, 331

'tall poppy syndrome' 293–4, 298, 299
Tarkovsky, Andrei 49, 262
Taxi Driver (Scorsese, 1976) 111
Taylor, Paul 22–3
technology 176–7, 178, 179, 182; *The Conversation* 267, 270, 272, 279, 281; documentary film 22
television 200
temenos 9, 254, 331
The Terminator (Cameron, 1984) 143–4
texts 134, 135, 136
theatre 253–4
therapeutic relationship 52, 141–2
thinking 286, 288–9, 290; *The Conversation* 267, 270; *The Wizard of Oz* 307–8, 310–11, 314, 324

third, therapeutic 142
'third image' 6, 129–30, 132–3, 137, 139, 141–6, 166, 170, 177
Thomas, Dylan 62
Thomson, L. 311
Tomei, Marisa 243
'total theatre' 253–4
transcendent function 28–9, 53, 250; *The Piano* 241; symbols 104; *The Wrestler* 246
transference 133, 141–2
transformation 32, 53, 250, 255, 257, 258, 259
the transpersonal 122, 123
trauma: *Breaking the Waves* 46, 47; childhood sources of 88; *Dark City* 123; early relational 77; *Solaris* 60; *The Wizard of Oz* 312
Travolta, John 323
trickster: *Breaking the Waves* 43; *Divine Horsemen* 261; Waddell's work 11; *The Wizard of Oz* 316, 317, 324
True Blood (tv show) 200
Turner, Victor 210, 258
Twilight (Hardwicke, 2008) 115, 186, 200
The Twilight Saga 8, 186, 196–202
2001: A Space Odyssey (Kubrick, 1968) 49, 68, 130

Ulanov, Ann 273, 278, 326n7
the unconscious 5, 74, 88–9, 186–7; active 30; cinema's engagement with 254; cultural 188–9; *Dark City* 124; dreams 134–5, 136; ego guided by 53, 81; film's connection with 195; Freud/Jung contrast 120–1; integrated with consciousness 259, 269; patriarchy 150; *The Piano* 238–9, 240; repression 88; symbols 160; transcendent function 28, 241; unknowable nature of 149; *The Wizard of Oz* 311–12, 313
underworld 155–8, 160–1, 247
unus mundus 89
uroboric incest 82

values: American 314, 321–2; feminine 151; *Star Wars* 172
Vampire Diaries (tv show) 200
vampire films 111, 114–17, 196–202
Van Eenwyk, John 283
vertical structure 106
Vertigo (Hitchcock, 1952) 105
Vincent (Burton, 1984) 207, 213, 218
violence 111, 112
visionary mode 105
Vogler, Christopher 150
Volver (Almodóvar, 2006) 44
von Franz, M.-L. 229, 230, 270
von Trier, Lars 35, 36–7, 44, 47

Waddell, Terrie 10, 11, 40, 187, 285–301
Wagner, Richard 4, 70, 71, 73, 78–9
Walkabout (Roeg, 1971) 105
Wasikowska, Mia 207
Wasko, Janet 171–2
water 245, 247, 257
Watergate scandal 266
Watson, Emily 36
Wegener, Paul 221

West, R. 233
Westbrook, Frank 256–7
Western culture 233
Wetherall, M. 190
White, William Allen 305
Wiene, Robert 221
Wild Strawberries (Bergman, 1957) 120
Williams, Don 255
Winnicott, D. W. 27
Winogrand, Gary 22
The Wizard of Oz (Fleming, 1939) 10–11, 302–27
Wodak, R. 190, 195
Wolff, Toni 289
women *see* femininity
The Wonderful Wizard of Oz (Baum, 1900) 303, 304–5
world-soul 92
The Wrestler (Aronofsky, 2009) 9, 243–52

Young-Eisendrath, Polly 272

Zanardo, Andre 3–4, 49–65
Zipes, Jack 321